3-24-04

√√
4/04

Pillsbury Bake-Off®

Pillsbury
BEST
OF THE
Bake-Off®
Cookbook

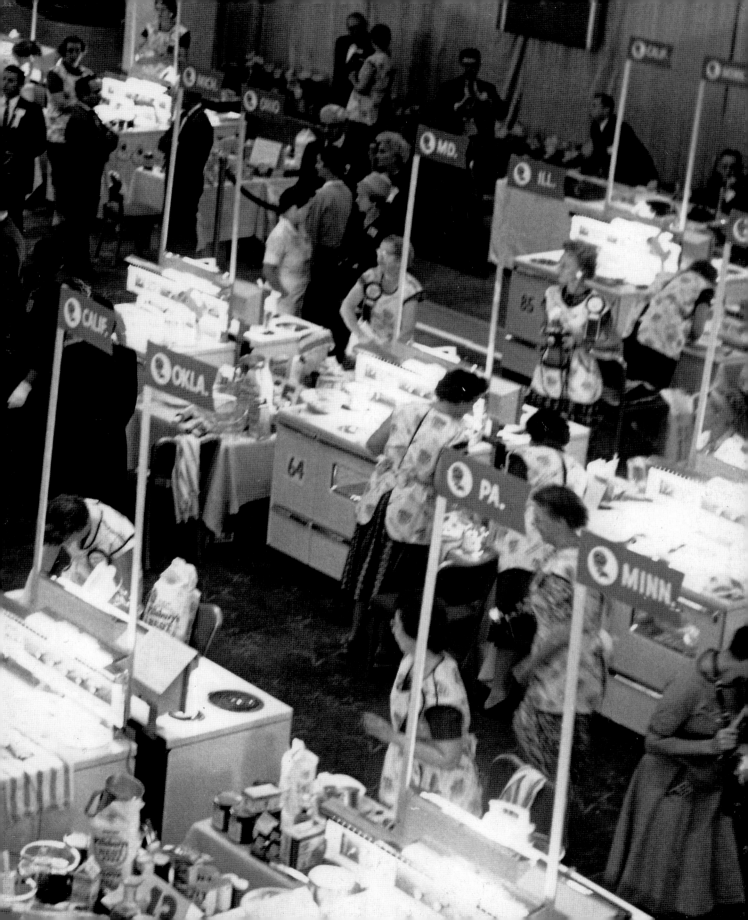

Pillsbury
BEST
OF THE
Bake-Off®
Cookbook

Recipes from
America's Favorite
Cooking Contest

New Edition
with a Quick & Easy Main Meals Chapter!

By The Pillsbury Editors

Clarkson Potter/Publishers

New York

Home of the Pillsbury Bake-Off®

*Our recipes have been
tested in the Pillsbury Kitchens
and meet our standards of easy
preparation, reliability and great taste.*

For more great recipes, visit pillsbury.com

FRONT COVER PHOTOGRAPH: PARMESAN CHICKEN WITH PASTA RAGS, PAGE 346
BACK COVER PHOTOGRAPH: CHICKEN FLORENTINE PANINI, PAGE 352
FRONTIS PHOTOGRAPH: ORANGE-CUMIN CHICKEN AND VEGETABLES, PAGE 65

Copyright © 1996, 2001, 2004 by General Mills, Inc.
Minneapolis, Minnesota

Published by Clarkson Potter/Publishers, New York, New York.
Member of the Crown Publishing Group,
a division of Random House, Inc.
www.randomhouse.com

The trademarks referred to herein are trademarks of
The Pillsbury Company or its affiliates.

Bundt is a registered trademark of Northland
Aluminum Products, Inc.
HERSHEY®'S KISSES® milk chocolates and the Conical
Configuration are registered trademarks of The
Hershey Foods Corporation.

CLARKSON N. POTTER is a trademark and POTTER and
colophon are registered trademarks of Random House, Inc.

Originally published in different form by Clarkson Potter/Publishers,
a division of Random House, Inc., in 1996 and 2001.

Printed in Japan

Design by Barbara Balch

Library of Congress Cataloging-in-Publication Data
is available upon request.

ISBN 1-4000-5133-9

10 9 8 7 6 5 4 3 2 1

REVISED AND UPDATED EDITION

CREDITS
GENERAL MILLS, INC.
Director, Book and Online Publishing: Kim Walter
Manager and Editor, Book Publishing: Lois Tlusty
Recipe Development and Testing: Pillsbury Kitchens
Photography: General Mills Photo Studios
    and Image Center

CLARKSON POTTER/PUBLISHERS
THE CROWN PUBLISHING GROUP
President: Jenny Frost
Senior Vice President/Publisher: Lauren Shakely
Editor: Rosemary Ngo
Editorial Assistant: Jennifer Defilippi
Vice President/Managing Editor: Amy Boorstein
Associate Managing Editor: Mark McCauslin
Senior Production Editor: Sibylle Kazeroid
Senior Production Manager: Joan Denman
Director of Publicity: Leigh Ann Ambrosi

Contents

Introduction

With its emphasis on quick and easy meal ideals for families, the 2002 Bake-Off® Contest, held at the Portofino Bay Hotel in Orlando, Florida, remained true to its 53-year heritage of reflecting changes in consumer lifestyles, ingredients and tastes. The flavorful dishes entered in the 40th Bake-Off® Contest are easy to prepare and require relatively little time in the kitchen—not surprising when you consider that more than half of the 100 finalists work full- or part-time outside the home. All too familiar with busy days spent juggling jobs and families, these talented cooks were more than up to the task of creating fuss-free recipes that are as delicious as they are fast. The quick and easy theme carried over to entering the contest as well. Aspiring cooks should log on to bakeoff.com to check out Bake-Off® Contest rules

Eleanor Pillsbury awarded Mari Petrelli the Grand Prize for her Golden Gate Snack Bread at the 17th Bake-Off® Contest in 1966.

and submit their entries via the Internet, a far cry from previous contests, when everything was done through the mail.

Imagine that first contest. The year was 1949. President Harry Truman had a plan to lead the world to peace and prosperity. Soldiers had returned from the war in the Pacific and Europe. Women moved from their wartime jobs to full-time homemaking. Wartime sugar rationing had finally ended, and home cooks were baking up a storm: cookies, cakes, pies and brownies. There was a spirit of celebration in the air—and why not? The nation had made a transition from a period of terrible adversity to a time of prosperity. At Pillsbury, President Philip Pillsbury felt like celebrating, too; he wanted to recognize the achievements of those unsung heroes of the dining room and cookie jar—home cooks.

What was missing from the life of devoted, industrious home cooks? Public recognition, glamour and rewards for their culinary talents. Where was the most glamorous place in the country? The ballroom of the Waldorf-Astoria Hotel in New York City. So, what if 100 of the best home cooks were gathered together, treated like royalty and rewarded for their efforts? Wouldn't that bring excitement and respect to kitchens from the shores of Florida to the mountains of Alaska? A competition was announced, an avalanche of entries arrived and what was to become Pillsbury's Bake-Off® Contest was born.

Those first years of the Bake-Off® Contest were amazing. Contestants from all over the country and from every walk of life were showered with luxury to convey the message that the quiet work they did daily—the cooking, the baking, the serving, the planning, the attention to detail—was appreciated and esteemed. Many contestants had never been on a train or stayed in a hotel before. And they certainly had never met the likes of former first lady and nationally syndicated columnist Eleanor Roosevelt, or television and radio personality Art Linkletter. These celebrities were at the first event, then known as the Grand National Recipe and Baking Contest. Contestants were served breakfast in bed, treated to a luncheon that included pheasant under glass, and pampered with the kind of admiring attention formerly reserved for captains of industry and film stars. In retrospect, those first Bake-Off® Contests could be read as a sign of the changes that would transform American society over the next fifty years. Women would soon begin to extend their activities outside the home again, to pursue professional achievements and professional status. Is it any wonder that the Smithsonian Institution recently accepted Pillsbury contest memorabilia into their permanent collection?

In fact, the recipes popularized through the Bake-Off® Contest have become a part of our culture. No collection of the favorite recipes of the century would be complete without a nod to Peanut Blossoms, cookies made with a chocolate kiss baked in a peanut-butter thumbprint. For that timeless cookie, thank Freda Smith, who invented them for Bake-Off® Contest 9, in 1957. French Silk Chocolate Pie has become such an American icon it can be found from the humblest diners to the fanciest restaurants— Betty Cooper worked up the recipe for Bake-Off® Contest 3, in 1951. And the Tunnel of Fudge Cake? Millions of these cakes have been served since Ella Rita Helfrich invented it for Bake-Off® Contest 17, in 1966.

Classic recipes such as these have permeated the culture so thoroughly that many families think of them as family heirlooms. People who have picked up a recipe for a particularly good herbed bread made with cottage cheese over the years don't know it's Leona Schnuelle's Dilly Casserole Bread, the Grand Prize winner from Bake-Off® Contest 12, in 1960—they only know it's delicious.

To celebrate these recipes and their impact on the way that Americans eat, Pillsbury has created the Bake-Off® Contest Hall of Fame. Hall of Fame recipes include the most popular and time-tested dishes and desserts from the first fifty years of the contest, chosen by both Pillsbury's home economists and consumers.

Who's in the Hall of Fame?

- Madella Bathke, for her Zesty Italian Crescent Casserole from Bake-Off® Contest 28, in 1978

- Julie (Konecne) Bengtson, for her Chocolate Praline Layer Cake from Bake-Off® Contest 33, in 1988

- Betty Cooper, for her French Silk Chocolate Pie, from Bake-Off® Contest 3, in 1951

- Ronna Sue Farley, for her Ham and Cheese Crescent Snacks, from Bake-Off® Contest 26, in 1975

- Lois Ann Groves, for her Crescent Caramel Swirl, from Bake-Off® Contest 27, in 1976

- Ella Rita Helfrich, for her Tunnel of Fudge Cake, from Bake-Off® Contest 17 in 1966

- Barbara Van Itallie, for her Broccoli Cauliflower Tetrazzini, from Bake-Off® Contest 33, in 1988

- Millicent (Caplan) Nathan, for her Italian Zucchini Crescent Pie, from Bake-Off® Contest 29, in 1980

- Peter Russell, for his Poppin' Fresh Barbecups, from Bake-Off® Contest 19, in 1968

- Leona Schnuelle, for her Dilly Casserole Bread, from Bake-Off® Contest 12, in 1960

- Gertrude Schweitzerhof, for her Salted Peanut Chews, from Bake-Off® Contest 29, in 1980

- Freda Smith, for her Peanut Blossoms, from Bake-Off® Contest 9, in 1957

- Edna (Holmgren) Walker, for her Magic Marshmallow Crescent Puffs, from Bake-Off® Contest 20, in 1969

- Penelope Weiss, for her Black & White Brownies, from Bake-Off® Contest 35, in 1992

Is getting into this Hall of Fame a realistic dream for home cooks? Yes. The Bake-Off® is an abso-

Category winners Debbie Freeman (right) and Pamela Kenney (left) congratulate Grand Prize Winner Mary Ann Tyndal at the 36th Bake-Off® Contest.

lutely upright, thorough and principled contest. Every precaution is taken to ensure that
entries are original. To keep the competition
fair for home cooks, food professionals and, of
course, Pillsbury employees are barred from
participating.

Of course, the first step on the road to the
Hall of Fame is to become a contestant in the
Bake-Off® Contest. If you're a home cook with
a good recipe, fill out an entry form—they are
available online, in packages of Pillsbury products,

through the mail, in special Pillsbury displays in
grocery stores, in Pillsbury publications such as
Classic Cookbooks and at special Pillsbury promo-
tional events hosted by past finalists. Keys to a top-
notch entry are:

1. Follow the contest rules, paying attention to
deadlines and making sure the recipe is original.

2. Be specific when listing ingredients, mea-

**Chairman Emeritus Philip Pillsbury leads contestants in
the "Grand March" at the 31st Bake-Off® Contest
in 1984.**

surements, pan sizes, cooking temperatures and preparation method.

After that, chances for a winning entry can be increased by thinking about a recipe's popular appeal: that is, would family cooks nationwide be able to reproduce your results? A dish's creativity, attractiveness and reasonable preparation time will also increase chances of success.

The entries go directly to an independent judging agency, which screens all the recipes, first eliminating those recipes that fail to follow the rules. The next step: removing all identifying information, such as names or addresses, from the selected recipes, and coding them so that the screening will be completely anonymous. The coded recipes are then forwarded to Pillsbury for kitchen testing.

A staff of Bake-Off® home economists carefully reads through the recipes, selecting those that are the most interesting and creative without requiring unusual equipment or ingredients. Those recipes then get a workout in the famous Pillsbury test kitchens. Each recipe is prepared and evaluated by a panel of home economists for taste, appearance, creativity, ease of preparation, general appeal and appropriate use of Pillsbury products. Recipes approved by the panel continue through the evaluation process to a team of researchers that examines each recipe for originality. Recipes are compared to a computer database and a large library of food publications, to make sure that the recipe isn't too similar to one that has been previously published. The recipe must feature several significant changes from a published recipe to be considered original. Testing continues until the 100 top recipes shine through.

The delightful task of notifying finalists comes next. Finalists are often overwhelmed by the news,

some crying tears of joy. Many finalists have been entering recipes for years. One woman had entered every year from 1949 through 1988, until she finally won. The news of their success is thrilling for everyone. Next, forms and releases are completed, and travel arrangements are made. Some Bake-Off® details are taken care of long before cooks even consider sending in their entries. For example, the site of the Bake-Off® Contest is chosen years in advance, since so few hotels are able to accommodate this huge event. Pillsbury also arranges for the ranges, refrigerators and other technical needs months before entries arrive. A team of Pillsbury employees begins to compile grocery, equipment and utensil lists for each finalist, checking and double-checking to make sure everything is accounted for. A few days before the contest, the giant list of groceries is purchased, the 100 Bake-Off® kitchens are set up and excitement builds to a feverish pitch.

What's the typical weekend of a Bake-Off® finalist like? On the Saturday before the awards announcement, finalists arrive from all over the country and are greeted by Bake-Off® representatives at the airport. Finalists check into the hotel, begin to meet their fellow contestants and are treated to a gala dinner. The next morning, after a luxurious breakfast, contestants go through the Bake-Off® orientation, where they find out what will happen on contest day and get a chance to see the ballroom where the competition will take place. The rest of the day is given over to sightseeing and a celebratory dinner and entertainment. The friendships formed at the Bake-Off® Contest are often lifelong. Former contestants often write to Pillsbury with news of their Bake-Off® friends' whereabouts, and some "round-robin" letters involving Bake-Off® winners have been going for several decades. The big day then arrives and many contestants wake up to butterflies in their stomach because so much depends on the next few hours' work.

After an early breakfast, the contestants line up four-abreast and march into a ballroom full of kitchens, cameras, media people and Bake-Off® staffers to the strains of "When the Saints Go Marching In." The contestants have from 8 A.M. to 2 P.M. to prepare their recipe twice: once for the judges and once to be photographed. Sweet and savory aromas fill the ballroom as reporters, television crews and celebrities mingle with the Bake-Off® contestants. Contestants share samples, mug for cameras and put the finishing touches on the dishes that are brought to the sequestered judges. The rest of the day is spent unwinding, topped off with a festive dinner that allows contestants to revel in the day's excitement. The next morning brings the moment all have been waiting for—the awards ceremony.

The Bake-Off® Contest has been going strong for more than fifty years. All agree it is because of one thing—integrity. The scrupulousness of the judging process and the original idea behind the contest—promoting wholesome family meals— have combined to create an American institution of utmost integrity.

Much has changed in the Bake-Off® Contest over the years: For example, the only ingredient required for early Bake-Off® recipes was at least one-half cup of flour. Today there are many qualifying products; soups, salads and entrees are welcome additions to the Bake-Off® table. New companies to the Pillsbury family, such as Green Giant, have prompted the introduction of products like frozen vegetables to the list of eligible ingredients. Many things, however, have remained the same, including the rigor of the selection and judging process, the impressiveness of the contestants and their recipes and the joy that surrounds each Bake-Off® Contest. That's why the Bake-Off® event has always produced a true cross-section of Americans, along with a personal glimpse of the food they cook.

Bake-Off® recipes are special because they are a reflection of how Americans are living and eating. These are not recipes created by a master chef, or the thoughts of a single company, but are the accumulated wisdom and experience of hundreds of thousands of cooks. The Bake-Off® recipes are a testament to how, what and sometimes even why Americans cook.

Pillsbury: Best of the Bake-Off® Cookbook is a comprehensive collection of the most popular Bake-Off® recipes, including all of the Grand Prize– winning recipes from every contest. Most of the recipes will look familiar to Bake-Off® Contest followers, although many have been updated to conform to currently available products or to eliminate any food-safety concerns that the original recipes might have raised. These pages hold the benefit of all these cooks' experiences and accumulated cooking wisdom: their practical time-saving tips, their heirloom recipes, their innovative or improvised ideas, their diversity of background and taste and, above all, their prize-winning recipes.

Measuring Equipment and Equivalent Measures and Weights

Equivalent Measures and Weights

Dash	= $^1/_{16}$ teaspoon or half of $^1/_8$ teaspoon
3 teaspoons	= 1 tablespoon
2 tablespoons	= $^1/_8$ cup or 1 fluid ounce
4 tablespoons	= $^1/_4$ cup
$5^1/_3$ tablespoons	= $^1/_3$ cup
8 tablespoons	= $^1/_2$ cup
12 tablespoons	= $^3/_4$ cup
16 tablespoons	= 1 cup
1 cup	= 8 fluid ounces
2 cups	= 1 pint or 16 fluid ounces
4 cups	= 2 pints or 1 quart or 32 fluid ounces
4 quarts	= 1 gallon
8 quarts	= 1 peck
4 pecks	= 1 bushel
16 ounces	= 1 pound
1 ounce	= 28.35 grams
1 liter	= 1.06 quarts

Measuring Equipment

- *Liquid Measures.* Liquid measuring cups tend to be glass, come in 1-, 2- and 4-cup sizes and have graded measurements indicated on the surface. To measure liquids, place the cup on a level surface and fill, reading the measuring mark at eye level.

- *Dry Measures.* Dry measuring cups come in nested sets that can include $^1/_4$-cup, $^1/_3$-cup, $^1/_2$-cup and 1-cup measures. They are meant to be filled to the top and leveled off with a knife.

- *Shortening and Brown Sugar.* To measure shortening and brown sugar, firmly press into a dry measuring cup and level off with a spatula or knife.

- *Dry Ingredients.* To measure flour, sugar or other dry ingredients, lightly spoon the ingredient into the measuring cup and then level it off with the straight edge of a spatula or knife. Flour does not need additional sifting.

- *Spices.* Never measure ingredients over your mixing bowl; a slip when measuring a spice or salt can ruin an entire recipe.
- *Sticky Syrups.* Before measuring a syrupy ingredient like molasses or corn syrup, lightly coat your measuring utensil with oil to help release every drop of the sticky sweetener.

High-Altitude Baking

If you'll be doing your baking at an altitude of 3,500 feet or more, you may have to make adjustments in some recipes because of the lower air pressure, which causes water to have a lower boiling point, making liquids evaporate more quickly. All of the recipes in this book were tested at high altitudes; any necessary changes are listed below the recipe. Generally, at high altitudes:

- Cakes take longer to bake, owing to a lower internal temperature caused by lower air pressure.
- Sugar levels become extremely important because too much sugar can weaken the structure of the cake at high altitudes.
- The leavening agent in a baked good (yeast, baking powder or baking soda) reacts more actively in high altitudes, giving a greater number of and larger gas bubbles that expand faster and collapse more easily. This causes breads and cakes to fall.
- Liquids evaporate faster at high altitudes, so carefully watch foods such as cooked frostings and candies, which will become harder more rapidly.
- Use the largest pan specified for best results.
- Yeast breads require a shorter rising time, and should rise only until doubled in size to prevent them from collapsing during baking.

Emergency Substitutions

Although best results are achieved using the ingredients called for in recipes, emergency substitutions can sometimes be made. Recipe results may vary slightly.

Baking

Ingredient	Substitute
1 teaspoon baking powder	$1/4$ teaspoon baking soda plus $1/2$ teaspoon cream of tartar
1 pkg. active dry yeast	1 tablespoon dry or 1 cake compressed yeast, crumbled
1 cup honey	$1^{1}/4$ cups sugar plus $1/4$ cup liquid
1 cup cake flour	1 cup sifted all-purpose flour minus 2 tablespoons
All-purpose flour	An equal amount of whole wheat flour can be substituted in some breads, cookies and bars. Texture will be coarser.
$1/4$ cup dry bread crumbs	$1/4$ cup cracker crumbs or 1 slice bread, cubed, or $2/3$ cup quick-cooking oats

Chocolate

Ingredient	Substitute
1 oz. (1 square) unsweetened chocolate	3 tablespoons cocoa plus 1 tablespoon shortening or margarine
1 oz. (1 square) semi-sweet chocolate	1 square unsweetened chocolate plus 1 tablespoon sugar
$1/2$ cup semi-sweet chocolate pieces for melting	3 oz. (3 squares) semi-sweet chocolate

Dairy Products

Ingredient	Substitute
1 cup whole milk	$^1/_2$ cup evaporated milk plus $^1/_2$ cup water, or 1 cup reconstituted nonfat dry or skim milk plus 2 teaspoons butter or oil
1 cup buttermilk or or sour milk	1 tablespoon cider vinegar or lemon juice plus enough milk to equal 1 cup; allow to stand 5 minutes
1 cup dairy sour cream	1 cup plain yogurt, or 1 cup evaporated milk plus 1 tablespoon vinegar, or 1 cup cottage cheese mixed in blender with 2 tablespoons milk and 1 tablespoon lemon juice
1 cup half-and-half	$^7/_8$ cup milk plus 3 tablespoons margarine or butter, or 1 cup evaporated milk
1 cup plain yogurt	1 cup sour milk or 1 cup buttermilk
Eggs	For 1 egg, substitute either 2 egg yolks (for custards and puddings) or 2 egg yolks plus 1 tablespoon water (for cookies and bars). Liquid products sold as egg substitutes can be substituted for whole eggs; note equivalent information on package

Herbs, Spices, Seasonings and Flavors

Ingredient	Substitute
1 tablespoon snipped fresh herbs	1 teaspoon same herb, dried, or $^1/_4$ teaspoon powdered or ground
1 teaspoon dry mustard	2 teaspoons prepared mustard
1 teaspoon poultry seasoning	$^1/_4$ teaspoon thyme plus $^3/_4$ teaspoon sage
1 teaspoon pumpkin pie spice	$^1/_2$ teaspoon cinnamon, $^1/_2$ teaspoon ginger, $^1/_8$ teaspoon ground allspice, $^1/_8$ teaspoon nutmeg
1 clove garlic	$^1/_8$ to $^1/_4$ teaspoon instant minced or pressed minced garlic, or $^1/_8$ teaspoon garlic powder
1 medium onion	2 tablespoons instant chopped or minced onion or onion flakes, or $1^1/_2$ teaspoons onion powder
1 medium lemon	2 to 3 tablespoons juice (fresh or bottled)
1 medium orange	$^1/_4$ to $^1/_3$ cup orange juice (fresh or reconstituted frozen)
White wine	Equal amount apple juice or cider
1 cup chicken or beef broth	1 teaspoon instant bouillon or bouillon cube plus 1 cup hot water

Thickeners

Ingredient	Substitute
1 tablespoon cornstarch	2 tablespoons flour, or 1⅓ tablespoons quick-cooking tapioca
1 tablespoon flour	½ tablespoon cornstarch, or 2 teaspoons quick-cooking tapioca, or 2 egg yolks
1 tablespoon tapioca	1½ tablespoons all-purpose flour

Vegetables

Ingredient	Substitute
1 cup canned tomatoes	1⅓ cups cut-up fresh tomatoes, simmered 10 minutes
1 cup tomato sauce	8-oz. can stewed tomatoes, blended in blender or 1 cup tomato puree seasoned or ¾ cup tomato paste plus ¼ cup water
1 cup tomato juice	½ cup tomato sauce plus ½ cup water
½ cup ketchup or chili sauce	½ cup tomato sauce plus 2 tablespoons sugar and 1 tablespoon vinegar
½ lb. fresh mushrooms	4-oz. can mushrooms
Legumes	With the exception of lentils, dried beans can be used interchangeably to suit personal preference.

How to Use Our Nutrition Information

The key to healthy eating is a varied diet including many fruits, vegetables and grains. The detailed nutrition information at the end of each Bake-Off® recipe can help you estimate the contribution of specific recipes in your overall menu plan. At the end of each recipe, we list the calories per serving as well as the amount of protein, carbohydrate, fat and sodium. If you are following a medically prescribed diet, consult your physician or registered dietitian about this nutrition information.

How to Calculate Nutrition Information

To determine a serving size for calculating nutrients for a recipe, we base our analysis on a single unit (for example, 1 cookie) or a specific amount (1 cup).

Other considerations for calculating nutrition information are:

- The first ingredient mentioned when the recipe gives options—for example, if "butter or margarine" is listed, butter would be calculated
- The larger amount of an ingredient when there's a range
- Garnishing or "if desired" ingredients when included in the ingredient list
- The estimated amount of marinade or frying oil absorbed during preparation

Tailoring Your Daily Diet

The following chart outlines some average daily nutritional needs for moderately active adults. Since your sex, age, size and activity level all affect dietary considerations, your requirements may deviate from those shown here.

What You Need Daily	Women Age: 25–50	Women Over 50	Men 25–50
Calories	2200	1900	2900
Total Fat	73g or less	63	97
Saturated Fat	24g or less	21	32
Cholesterol	300mg or less	300	300
Sodium	2400mg	2400	2400
Calcium	800mg	800	800
Iron	15mg	10	10

(Note: Although individual needs vary, a 2000-calorie diet is used as the reference diet on packaging because it approximates average daily requirements and provides a round number for easier calculating.)

Alice Reese receives the Grand Prize award from host Art Linkletter at the 13th Bake-Off® Contest in 1961.

Pan Substitutions

Changing pan sizes alters baking times and may alter final results. This chart will help you make practical size substitutions if necessary.

Recipe Calls For	Substitute
8×4-inch loaf pan	Two 5½×3¼-inch loaf pans
9×5-inch loaf pan	Two 7½×3¾-inch loaf pans or three 5½×3½-inch loaf pans
One 9-inch round cake pan	One 8-inch square pan

Recipe Calls For	Substitute
Two 9-inch round pans	Three 8-inch round cake cake pans
12-cup Bundt pan	One 10-inch tube pan or two 9×5-inch loaf pans
13×9-inch pan	Two 9-inch round cake pans or two 8-inch round cake pans or two 8-inch square pans

Freezer Storage

Most foods freeze well, although there are some that change unpleasantly in texture, flavor or appearance. Don't freeze salad greens, bananas, custard, mayonnaise, sour cream, mayonnaise and sour cream dressings, lunch meats, fried meats, hard-cooked egg whites and boiled frostings.

For best quality, use freezer wraps and containers designed specifically for maintaining the freshness, texture and color of frozen foods. Freezer paper, foil and heavy-duty plastic bags and plastic wraps will protect foods against cold air deterioration.

The Elements of Successful Cooking and Baking

- Read through the entire recipe before you start, taking note of what ingredients and equipment you will need, and how much preparation and cooking time is necessary.
- Use the best ingredients for the best results. Fresh ingredients will help ensure that your final product is a success.
- Clean equipment and work surfaces as you go, to reduce clutter and final cleanup.

- Preheat your oven for 15 minutes before baking.
- Invest in an oven thermometer to monitor the accuracy of your oven's temperature.
- Carefully space pans in the oven, placing single pans in the center rack. When using more than one pan, make sure that there are 2 inches of space around each pan in every direction.

Pie Baking
- Use dark metal, dull-finish aluminum or glass pie pans, since shiny pie pans can cause a pie to have a soggy bottom. When using glass pans, reduce the oven temperature by 25 degrees, as the pan will tend to hold heat.
- Don't stretch pie crusts as you place them in the pan. Stretching will cause the crust to shrink during baking.
- Brushing the top of a pie crust with 1 beaten egg white or cold milk will give it a light sheen; brushing the crust with 1 egg yolk mixed with 1 tablespoon water or whipping cream will make a glossy, golden dark brown crust. A mixture of 2 tablespoons water and 1 tablespoon granulated sugar will produce a crisp, sweet crust. Plain water will produce a crisp crust, too.
- Don't brush glaze on the crimped edges of a pie crust until the last 10 minutes of baking, or the edges might get too dark.

Tips for Using Common Ingredients

Eggs
Eggs provide structure and volume and bind ingredients together.

- Use *large* eggs in recipes unless another size is specified. (Jumbo eggs weigh 30 ounces per dozen, large eggs weigh 24 ounces per dozen, and small eggs weigh 18 ounces per dozen, so differences in size are substantial and could significantly affect the outcome of a recipe.)

- Refrigerate eggs whenever they're not in use. At room temperature, eggs lose as much quality in a day as they would in a week in the refrigerator.

- Store eggs away from strong-smelling foods like cut onions or fish. Eggs can absorb odors through their shells.

- When adding eggs to a batter, always break the eggs into a small bowl first to prevent shells or spoiled eggs from ruining your recipe.

Butter, Margarine and Shortening

Fats like butter, margarine, shortening, oils and lard tenderize prepared foods, provide flavor, help bind ingredients together and produce browning in baked goods.

- Butter yields: 1 pound = 4 sticks = 2 cups. 1 stick = $1/2$ cup = 8 tablespoons.

- One cup butter = 1 cup margarine = $7/8$ cup vegetable oil = $7/8$ cup lard or vegetable shortening.

- Butter is interchangeable with stick margarine in most recipes.

- Whipped butter contains between 30 and 45 percent air, and so should be measured by weight. Eight ounces of whipped butter equals 1 cup.

- Set cold butter over, not in, a bowl of hot water to soften it for baking.

- Margarine is made from oils, such as corn or soybean, combined with air. For best results, use margarine, not a reduced-fat oil spread, for baking.

- Vegetable oils are low in saturated fats, don't contain cholesterol and are pressed from a vari-

ety of seeds and kernels, such as corn, canola, sunflower, safflower and soybean. They are referred to here as "oil" and can be used interchangeably in our recipes.

- Solid vegetable shortening is made from vegetable oils that have been processed with air. We call it "shortening."

- Low- or nonfat spreads don't have the essential fats needed for baking, so avoid using them in baked goods. They tend to produce more cake-like products that will not brown, will dry out quickly and may stick to pans.

Flavorings

Add flavorings, extracts and liqueurs to other ingredients at room temperature.

Flour

The recipes in this book have been tested with bleached all-purpose flour; unbleached all-purpose flour also may be used.

- The best way to measure flour is to lightly spoon the flour into your measuring cup and level it off.

- To prevent spoilage, store flour in an airtight container at less than 75° F. Flour can be stored in the freezer for up to one year, but it should be brought to room temperature before using in batters.

Fruit

- Choose fresh fruit that is ripe, with a tight, smooth skin that is free of blemishes. Wash all fresh fruit before use.

- Good baking apples include Cortland, Crispin, Criterion, Empire, Fuji, Granny Smith, Gravenstein, Jona-gold, Jonathan, Lady, Macoun, McIntosh, Newtown Pippin, Northern

Spy, Stayman, Rome Beauty, Stayman Winesap, and York Imperial.

- Apple yields: 1 pound fresh = 2 large, 3 medium or 4 small apples = $2^{1}/_{2}$ to 3 cups chopped or sliced apples.

- To revive apples for baking that are past their prime, chop them coarsely, cover with apple juice and refrigerate for 30 minutes.

Milk

- Use only the freshest milk and dairy products.

- For baking, 1 cup of skim milk plus 2 tablespoons of melted unsalted butter can be substituted for 1 cup of whole milk.

Nuts

- Yields: 4 ounces of chopped nuts generally equal 1 cup of chopped nuts.

- When buying shelled packaged nuts, check for freshness by squeezing the nuts through the plastic package. If the nuts bend or feel cakey, they are no longer fresh.

- Store nuts in an airtight, dark container in a cool, dry place, or freeze them for up to eight months.

Spices, Herbs and Seeds

- Store dried herbs, spices and seeds in airtight containers in a cool, dark, dry spot. Seasonings lose flavor in hot, bright conditions, such as over a stove or on a tabletop spice rack. Dried herbs and spices should be replaced annually.

- Store fresh herbs in the refrigerator, their stems submerged in a glass of water.

- Equivalents: 1 tablespoon of fresh herbs is equivalent to 1 teaspoon of crushed dried herbs or $^{1}/_{4}$ teaspoon of ground herbs.

George and Sally Pillsbury lead the parade of 100 finalists into the competition area at the 35th Pillsbury Bake-Off® Cooking and Baking Contest in Orlando, Florida.

Chapter 1

Soups, Sandwiches and Snacks

It's now popular to think of the United States not so much as a melting pot but as a giant tossed salad, since its components—the people, their cultures—tend to retain much of their original character, blending with, yet complementing one another. Nowhere is this more apparent in American cooking than in the recipes for light meals and snacks.

The influences of Western Europe are well represented here, from the French taste of Garlic Chicken Provençal Soup to the many Italian-derived recipes such as Italian Spinach Torta and Sicilian Mushroom Flatbread to Greek flavors in dishes such as Mushroom Phyllo Tarts. Asian-influenced recipes include Sweet 'n Sour Chicken Wraps, while Indian flavors are present in Crescent Samosa Sandwiches. Mexican and Southwestern U.S. flavors are very popular, visible in dishes from chimichangas to Puffy Chiles Rellenos, reflecting the profound impact these zesty flavors have had on the way Americans eat. Other regional American cuisines are also well represented, from Black-eyed Peas and Pork Gumbo from the South to Great Northern Bean Stew, which speaks of New England. And of course, there is the broad category of food that might be called "comfort food" because the recipes are so thoroughly American and taste wonderfully familiar—Tuna Cheese Flips and Savory Salmon-Filled Crescents are perfect examples, appealing to both adults and children. As American lifestyles become busier and busier, no food is better for a satisfying meal-on-the-go than a hearty sandwich. Soups, sandwiches and snacks have become a flexible part of the American diet, enjoyed morning, noon and night, and they are being adapted in an endless variety of ways.

Top to bottom: **Crescent Chick-Be-Quicks, page 39, Italian Pasta Sausage Soup, page 32**

Black-Eyed Peas and Pork Gumbo

Bernice Wilkinson *Lake Kiowa, Texas*
Bake-Off® Contest 35, 1992

The thickening in this soup starts with a roux—a mixture of flour and fat that's cooked to a golden brown.

GUMBO
$^1/_3$ **cup oil**
$^1/_3$ **cup all-purpose flour**
1 to 2 tablespoons oil
1$^1/_2$ cups sliced fresh okra*
1 cup chopped onions
$^3/_4$ **cup chopped celery**
3 garlic cloves, minced
4 cups water
2 cups chopped tomatoes or 14.5-oz. can whole tomatoes, drained, cut up
$^1/_3$ **cup chopped fresh parsley**
1$^1/_2$ teaspoons salt
$^1/_2$ **teaspoon dried thyme leaves**
$^1/_4$ **teaspoon ground red pepper (cayenne)**
$^1/_4$ **teaspoon pepper**
2 bay leaves
$^3/_4$ **lb. smoked pork chops, well trimmed, boned and cubed, or $^1/_2$ lb. cubed cooked ham**
1 (15-oz.) can black-eyed peas, undrained

TOPPINGS
2 cups hot cooked rice
$^1/_4$ **cup chopped fresh parsley**
$^1/_4$ **cup chopped green onions, if desired**

Heat $^1/_3$ cup oil in small saucepan or skillet over medium-low heat until hot. Using wire whisk, stir in flour. Cook 5 to 7 minutes or until golden brown, stirring constantly. Set aside.

Heat 1 to 2 tablespoons oil in 3-quart heavy saucepan or 4-quart Dutch oven over medium heat until hot. Add okra, onions, celery and garlic; cook 8 to 10 minutes or until vegetables are tender, stirring occasionally. Stir in flour mixture until well blended. Add water, tomatoes, $^1/_3$ cup parsley, salt, thyme, ground red pepper, pepper and bay leaves. Bring to a boil. Reduce heat; simmer 20 minutes.

Add cubed pork; cook an additional 15 to 20 minutes or until pork is tender and no longer pink. Stir in black-eyed peas; cook until thoroughly heated. Remove bay leaves. Ladle gumbo into 8 individual soup bowls; top each with $^1/_4$ cup rice. Sprinkle servings with $^1/_4$ cup parsley and green onions.

Yield: 8 servings

*Tip: Frozen okra can be substituted for fresh okra; add with tomatoes.

Nutrition Per Serving: Calories 300; Protein 12g; Carbohydrate 29g; Fat 15g; Sodium 540mg

Creamy Chicken Vegetable Chowder

Mary Lou Cook *Fallbrook, California*
Bake-Off® Contest 34, 1990 Prize Winner

This creamy soup is ready in just minutes and is served with Mexican-flavored crescent rolls.

CHOWDER
1$^1/_2$ cups milk or half-and-half
1 cup chicken broth
1 (10$^3/_4$-oz.) can condensed cream of potato soup
1 (10$^3/_4$-oz.) can condensed cream of chicken soup
2 cups cubed cooked chicken or turkey
$^1/_3$ **cup chopped green onions**
1 (11-oz.) can vacuum-packed whole kernel corn with red and green peppers, drained
1 (4.5-oz.) jar sliced mushrooms, undrained
1 (4.5-oz.) can chopped green chiles, drained
6 oz. (1$^1/_2$ cups) shredded Cheddar cheese

CRESCENTS
1 (8-oz.) can refrigerated crescent dinner rolls
$^1/_4$ **cup crushed nacho-flavored tortilla chips**

Heat oven to 375°F. In 4-quart saucepan or Dutch oven, combine milk, broth, potato soup and chicken soup; blend well. Add remaining chowder ingredients except cheese; mix well. Cook over medium heat 5 to 8 minutes or until thoroughly heated, stirring occasionally. Remove from heat. Add cheese; stir until melted.

While chowder is heating, bake rolls. Shape dough as directed on package. Press top of each roll in crushed chips. Place on ungreased cookie sheet. Bake at 375°F. for 11 to 13 minutes or until golden brown. Serve chowder with crescents.

Yield: 6 servings

Nutrition Per Serving: Calories 520; Protein 30g; Carbohydrate 40g; Fat 27g; Sodium 1730mg

Sherried Mushroom Bisque

Dorothy Crow *Ocean City, Maryland*
Bake-Off® Contest 38, 1998 Prize Winner

Here's a bisque so creamy and satisfying that it's a quick, hot meal in itself. Add some toasty garlic bread for dipping and you're set.

2 to 4 tablespoons butter or margarine
1/2 cup finely chopped onion
2 (4.5-oz.) jars sliced mushrooms, drained
1/2 cup cream sherry or chicken broth
3 cups chicken broth
1 (4.5- to 5.5-oz.) container garlic and herb soft spreadable cheese
2 cups half-and-half or milk
1 cup mashed potato flakes
1/8 teaspoon salt
1/8 teaspoon pepper
Chopped fresh chives, if desired
Garlic croutons, if desired

Melt butter in large saucepan over medium-high heat. Add onion; cook and stir 3 to 5 minutes or until tender. Increase heat to high. Add mushrooms and sherry; cook and stir 3 to 5 minutes or until liquid is reduced by half. Stir in broth; bring to a boil. Add cheese, half-and-half, potato flakes, salt and pepper; cook and stir just until cheese is melted and mixture is thoroughly heated, reducing heat if necessary. DO NOT BOIL.

Garnish each serving with chives or croutons.

Yield: 6 (1-cup) servings

Nutrition Per Serving: Calories 370; Protein 10g; Carbohydrate 21g; Fat 27g; Sodium 1010mg

Harvest-Fresh Spinach Soup

Olga Jason *New Bedford, Massachusetts*
Bake-Off® Contest 33, 1988

After entering every Bake-Off® Contest from 1949 to 1988, this contestant became a finalist at last with this delicately flavored, easy cream soup. It can be served hot or cold.

1/4 cup margarine or butter
1/4 cup chopped onion
1/4 cup all-purpose flour
1 teaspoon salt, if desired
1/2 teaspoon dry mustard
1/4 teaspoon nutmeg
1 (10 1/2-oz.) can condensed chicken broth
1/2 cup shredded carrot
1 (9-oz.) pkg. frozen spinach in a pouch
2 1/2 cups milk

Melt margarine in 2-quart saucepan over medium heat. Add onion; cook and stir until tender. Reduce heat to low. Stir in flour, salt, dry mustard and nutmeg; cook and stir until mixture is smooth and bubbly. Gradually stir in broth. Bring to a boil, stirring constantly. Add carrot and spinach. Reduce heat to medium; simmer 10 minutes or until carrot is tender and spinach is thawed, stirring occasionally.*

In blender container or food processor bowl with metal blade, puree spinach mixture until smooth. Return mixture to saucepan; stir in milk. Cook over low heat until thoroughly heated, stirring frequently.

Yield: 5 (1-cup) servings

Microwave Directions: In 8-cup microwave-safe measuring cup or large bowl, combine margarine and onion. Microwave on HIGH for 45 to 60 seconds or until onion is tender. Stir in flour, salt, dry mustard and nutmeg; gradually stir in broth. Microwave on HIGH for 4 to 5 minutes or until mixture comes to a boil, stirring once halfway through cooking. Add carrot and spinach. Microwave on HIGH for 8 to 9 minutes or until carrot is tender and spinach is thawed, stirring twice during cooking.*

In blender container or food processor bowl with metal blade, puree spinach mixture until smooth. Return mixture to measuring cup; stir in milk. Microwave on HIGH for 4 to 6 minutes or until thoroughly heated, stirring twice during cooking.

*Tip: To serve soup cold, at this point cool spinach mixture to lukewarm; puree in blender container or food processor bowl with metal blade until smooth. Stir in milk. Cover; refrigerate until thoroughly chilled. Garnish each serving with lemon slice, if desired.

Nutrition Per Serving: Calories 210; Protein 9g; Carbohydrate 15g; Fat 12g; Sodium 1010mg

Corn and Pumpkin Soup with Jalapeño Pesto

Marilou Robinson *Portland, Oregon*
Bake-Off® Contest 35, 1992

Although most people have tasted pumpkin only in pies and other baked goods, pumpkin also makes great savory dishes, such as this tasty soup.

JALAPEÑO PESTO
1 cup fresh cilantro
1 cup fresh parsley
1/2 cup pine nuts, lightly toasted*
1/2 cup grated Parmesan cheese
5 garlic cloves, minced
4 jalapeño peppers, cut up
1 teaspoon lime juice
1/2 teaspoon grated lime peel
3/4 cup olive oil

SOUP
4 (14 1/2-oz.) cans ready-to-serve chicken broth
2 (11-oz.) cans vacuum-packed whole kernel corn, drained
1/4 cup finely chopped onion
2 tablespoons finely chopped jalapeño pepper
1 (16-oz.) can pumpkin

1 cup half-and-half
1/2 teaspoon salt
1/4 teaspoon pepper
11 (8 or 6-inch) corn tortillas or 8-inch flour tortillas, warmed

In food processor bowl with metal blade or blender container, combine cilantro, parsley, pine nuts, cheese and garlic. Process 10 to 15 seconds to chop mixture. Add 4 cut-up jalapeño peppers, lime juice and lime peel; process 5 to 10 seconds to blend. With machine running, add oil through feed tube or opening in blender lid in slow, steady stream just until well blended. Set aside.

In large saucepan, combine broth, corn, onion and 2 tablespoons jalapeño pepper. Bring to a boil. Reduce heat; cover and simmer 20 to 25 minutes or until onion and jalapeño pepper are tender. Stir in pumpkin; blend well. Cover; simmer 5 to 10 minutes or until thoroughly heated. Add half-and-half, salt and pepper; cook and stir until thoroughly heated. DO NOT BOIL.

To serve, line 11 soup bowls with warmed tortillas; ladle hot soup into tortilla-lined bowls. Spoon scant 2 tablespoons pesto onto each serving.

Yield: 11 (1-cup) servings

Marilou Robinson: Corn and Pumpkin Soup with Jalapeño Pesto

You don't need a big, daring family to be a recipe-inventing success, as Marilou Robinson proves. "My biggest encouragement is my husband Bud—he is not an adventurous eater, preferring meat and potatoes, but will run all over the city to find a particular ingredient. He loves to invite people over to try my new recipes, even though he may not participate!" When guests aren't around to sample Marilou's latest creations, she uses her in-house taster. "Our German Shepherd, Tatoosh, is a great help in working out recipes—there are very few things she won't eat. And if she walks off, I know there is a problem!"

*Tip: To toast pine nuts, spread on cookie sheet; bake at 350° F. for 3 to 6 minutes or until light golden brown, stirring occasionally.

Nutrition Per Serving: Calories 370; Protein 11g; Carbohydrate 32g; Fat 23g; Sodium 840mg

Corn and Pumpkin Soup with Jalapeño Pesto

Garlic Chicken Provençal Soup

Mildred Wittan *Boca Raton, Florida*
Bake-Off® Contest 36, 1994

Provençal refers to cooking based on the flavors popular in Provence, a region in southern France.

SOUP

2 tablespoons butter or margarine
¹/₂ cup chopped onion
¹/₄ cup butter or margarine
4 boneless, skinless chicken breast halves
2 (16-oz.) cans Italian plum tomatoes or whole tomatoes, undrained, cut into pieces
1 cup dry white wine or water
1 (16-oz.) pkg. frozen pasta, broccoli, corn and carrots in a garlic-seasoned sauce

GARNISHES, IF DESIRED

¹/₄ cup grated Parmesan cheese
¹/₄ cup chopped fresh parsley

Melt 2 tablespoons butter in Dutch oven over medium-high heat. Add onion; cook and stir 3 to 5 minutes or until softened. Remove from pan; set aside.

In same Dutch oven, melt ¹/₄ cup butter; add chicken and cook 8 to 10 minutes or until golden brown, turning once. Add tomatoes, wine and reserved onion. Bring to a boil. Reduce heat; simmer uncovered 10 to 15 minutes or until chicken is no longer pink. Stir in frozen vegetables with pasta. Bring to a boil. Reduce heat; simmer 3 to 5 minutes or until vegetables are crisp-tender.

To serve, place 1 chicken breast half in each of 4 large shallow soup bowls; ladle hot soup over chicken. Garnish with Parmesan cheese and parsley.

Yield: 4 servings

Nutrition Per Serving: Calories 570; Protein 36g; Carbohydrate 34g; Fat 29g; Sodium 1120mg

Creole Gumbo

Elaine Thornton *Long Beach, Mississippi*
Bake-Off® Contest 6, 1954

Tomatoes, crab meat and okra team up for a winning flavor combination in this marvelous gumbo from the 1950s. It has been updated to use refrigerated flaky biscuit dough for the crouton toppers, speeding up the preparation time.

GUMBO

³/₄ cup chopped celery
¹/₃ cup chopped green bell pepper
¹/₃ cup chopped onion
2 garlic cloves, minced
3 tablespoons olive oil
¹/₄ cup all-purpose flour
3 cups water
1 (16-oz.) can whole tomatoes, undrained, cut up
1 tablespoon chopped fresh parsley
1 teaspoon salt
¹/₈ teaspoon pepper
1 cup diced canned, frozen or fresh okra
1 (6-oz.) can crab meat, drained

CROUTONS

1 (12-oz.) can refrigerated flaky biscuits
1 tablespoon margarine or butter, melted
2 tablespoons grated Parmesan cheese
Paprika

In large saucepan, cook celery, bell pepper, onion and garlic in oil 5 minutes. Blend in flour; cook over medium heat about 10 minutes or until mixture browns, stirring constantly. Gradually add water and tomatoes, stirring constantly. Stir in remaining gumbo ingredients. Bring to a boil. Reduce heat; cover and simmer 1 hour.

Heat oven to 400°F. Separate dough into 10 biscuits; cut each into 4 pieces. Place on ungreased cookie sheet. Brush with margarine; sprinkle with Parmesan cheese and paprika. Bake at 400°F. for 6 to 9 minutes or until golden brown. Remove from cookie sheet immediately; cool on wire racks. Pour gumbo into individual serving bowls; top each serving with croutons.

Yield: 4 (1¹/₄-cup) servings

Nutrition Per Serving: Calories 500; Protein 16g; Carbohydrate 51g; Fat 26g; Sodium 2080mg

Garlic Chicken Provençal Soup

Great Northern Bean Stew

Ellen Anders *Big Bend, Wisconsin*
Bake-Off® Contest 35, 1992 Prize Winner

This richly flavored sausage and vegetable stew is just the thing to warm you up on a chilly evening. Using canned beans, it's ready to serve in under 30 minutes.

1 lb. bulk pork sausage
1 cup coarsely chopped onions
1 cup thinly sliced carrots
2 cups chopped cabbage
1 tablespoon brown sugar
1 (28-oz.) can whole tomatoes, undrained, cut up
1 (15.5-oz.) can great northern beans, drained
1/2 teaspoon paprika
1/2 teaspoon dried thyme leaves
1/4 to 1/2 teaspoon salt
1/2 teaspoon pepper
1 tablespoon vinegar
1/4 teaspoon hot pepper sauce
1/3 cup chopped fresh parsley or 1 tablespoon dried parsley flakes

In large saucepan or 4-quart Dutch oven, brown sausage and onions; drain. Stir in all remaining ingredients; bring to a boil. Reduce heat; cover and simmer 15 minutes.

Yield: 6 (1-cup) servings

Nutrition Per Serving: Calories 200; Protein 11g; Carbohydrate 20g; Fat 10g; Sodium 840mg

Italian Spinach Dumpling Stew

Joan Schweger *Elburn, Illinois*
Bake-Off® Contest 34, 1990 Prize Winner

Fluffy and tender spinach-cheese dumplings top this hearty stove-top stew.

1 lb. ground beef
2 tablespoons oil, if desired
1 (32-oz.) jar spaghetti sauce
1 (4.5-oz.) jar sliced mushrooms
2 tablespoons purchased creamy garlic or creamy Italian salad dressing
1/4 cup water

DUMPLINGS
1 cup all-purpose flour
2 teaspoons baking powder
1/4 teaspoon salt
1 cup frozen cut leaf spinach (from 1-lb. pkg.), thawed, squeezed to drain
1/2 cup grated Romano or Parmesan cheese
2 tablespoons oil
1 egg
1/4 to 1/3 cup milk

In large skillet, brown ground beef in oil until thoroughly cooked; drain. Add spaghetti sauce, mushrooms, salad dressing and water; mix well. Bring to a boil. Reduce heat; simmer while preparing dumplings, stirring occasionally.

In medium bowl, combine flour, baking powder and salt; blend well. In small bowl, combine spinach, cheese, 2 tablespoons oil, egg and 1/4 cup milk; mix well. Add to dry ingredients; stir until dry ingredients are just moistened, adding more milk if necessary to form a soft dough. Drop dough by rounded tablespoonfuls onto hot stew mixture. Cover tightly. Simmer 12 to 15 minutes or until dumplings are fluffy and no longer doughy on bottom.

Yield: 6 servings

High Altitude—Above 3,500 feet: Prepare as directed above. Simmer dumplings 17 to 22 minutes.

Nutrition Per Serving: Calories 560; Protein 23g; Carbohydrate 44g; Fat 32g; Sodium 1205mg

Italian Pasta Sausage Soup

Julie Winter *Grosse Pointe Woods, Michigan*
Bake-Off® Contest 34, 1990

In Italy, soup is often served as the main course for a light supper. Garlic-seasoned vegetables and pasta make this soup quick to prepare for an easy meal.

1 lb. hot or sweet Italian sausage links
1 (28-oz.) can whole tomatoes, undrained, cut up
1 (14 1/2-oz.) can ready-to-serve chicken broth
1 (8-oz.) can tomato sauce
1 teaspoon dried basil leaves
1 teaspoon dried oregano leaves
1 (16-oz.) pkg. frozen pasta, broccoli, corn and carrots in a garlic-seasoned sauce
Grated fresh Parmesan cheese

Place sausage links in large saucepan or 5-quart Dutch oven. Add water to a depth of about 1/2 inch. Bring to a boil. Reduce heat; cover and simmer 10 minutes or until sausage is partially cooked. Drain.

Slice sausage into ½-inch slices; return to saucepan. Add tomatoes, broth, tomato sauce, basil and oregano; blend well. Bring to a boil. Reduce heat; cover and simmer 20 minutes, stirring occasionally. Stir in frozen vegetables with pasta. Cover; bring to a boil. Reduce heat; simmer 3 to 5 minutes or until vegetables are crisp-tender. Sprinkle with Parmesan cheese.

Yield: 6 (1½-cup) servings

Nutrition Per Serving: Calories 310; Protein 17g; Carbohydrate 23g; Fat 17g; Sodium 1600mg

Nancy Hindenach: Mexican Vegetable Soup

How can you stack the deck to end up with a child who's a master chef? Several Bake-Off® contestants reported stories similar to the one Nancy Hindenach shared. "On Christmas, when I was nine years old, Santa brought me a baking kit full of little boxes of cake mixes, frostings and little pans to bake them in. I had so much fun making cakes for my family that I asked for the kit for my next two Christmases." Years later, Nancy's family is still reaping the benefit of those tasty gifts.

Vegetable Bean Soup Mexicana

Nancy Flesch *Kent, Ohio*
Bake-Off® Contest 36, 1994 Prize Winner

This high-fiber, vegetable-rich soup is easy enough for every day, special enough for parties.

2 tablespoons olive oil or vegetable oil
1 cup thinly sliced zucchini
½ cup chopped green onions
½ cup chopped red or green bell pepper
2 (14½-oz.) cans ready-to-serve chicken broth or chicken broth with ⅓ less sodium
1 (15-oz.) can spicy chili beans, undrained
1 (15-oz.) can garbanzo beans, or 15.5-oz. can dark red kidney beans, drained
1 (14½-oz.) can stewed tomatoes, undrained
2 tablespoons chopped fresh cilantro or 2 teaspoons dried cilantro leaves
2 teaspoons cumin
¼ to ½ teaspoon ground red pepper (cayenne)
1½ cups fresh baby carrots
1 (9-oz.) pkg. frozen shoepeg white corn in a pouch

Heat oil in large saucepan or Dutch oven over medium-high heat. Add zucchini, green onions and bell pepper; cook and stir 3 to 4 minutes or until crisp-tender. Add remaining ingredients except carrots and corn; mix well. Bring to a boil.

Add carrots and corn; return to a boil. Reduce heat to low; cover and simmer 10 to 12 minutes or until vegetables are tender, stirring occasionally.

Yield: 7 (1½-cup) servings

Nutrition Per Serving: Calories 230; Protein 10g; Carbohydrate 31g; Fat 7g; Sodium 890mg

Mexican Vegetable Soup

Nancy Hindenach *Dearborn Heights, Michigan*
Bake-Off® Contest 33, 1988 Prize Winner

Mixed vegetables add variety to this quick chili-like soup. It's topped off with corn chips and Cheddar cheese.

1 lb. ground beef
1 (1.25-oz.) pkg. taco seasoning mix
1 (46-oz.) can (6 cups) tomato juice
1 (12-oz.) can tomato paste
1 (1-lb.) pkg. frozen mixed vegetables
1 (15-oz.) can chili hot beans
2 cups crushed corn chips
8 oz. (2 cups) shredded Cheddar cheese

In 5-quart Dutch oven, brown ground beef until thoroughly cooked; drain. Add all remaining ingredients except chips and cheese; mix well. Bring just to a boil. Reduce heat; simmer uncovered 20 to 25 minutes or until vegetables are tender, stirring occasionally. Top each serving with chips and cheese.

Yield: 11 (1-cup) servings

Nutrition Per Serving: Calories 340; Protein 18g; Carbohydrate 29g; Fat 17g; Sodium 1180mg

White Chili with Salsa Verde

Reta Smith *Libertyville, Illinois*
Bake-Off® Contest 35, 1992 Prize Winner

Tomatillos, sometimes called Mexican green tomatoes, are frequently available fresh in produce departments, but canned tomatillos are usually available only in large supermarkets.

SALSA VERDE
2 cups coarsely chopped fresh tomatillos or 2 (11-oz.) cans tomatillos, chopped, well drained*
¹/₂ cup chopped onion
¹/₂ cup chopped fresh cilantro or parsley
1 pickled jalapeño pepper (from 10-oz. jar), chopped
1 garlic clove, minced
¹/₂ teaspoon lemon pepper seasoning
¹/₂ teaspoon dried oregano leaves

¹/₂ teaspoon adobo seasoning or garlic powder**
2 to 3 tablespoons lime juice

CHILI
2¹/₂ cups water
1 teaspoon lemon pepper seasoning
1 teaspoon cumin seed
4 chicken breast halves (about 1¹/₂ lb.), skin removed

Top to bottom: **White Chili with Salsa Verde, Black-Eyed Peas and Pork Gumbo, page 26**

Olive oil nonstick cooking spray
   or 1 teaspoon olive oil
1 garlic clove, minced
1 cup chopped onions
2 (9-oz.) pkg. frozen shoepeg
   white corn in a pouch, thawed
2 (4.5-oz.) cans chopped green
   chiles, undrained
1 teaspoon cumin
2 to 3 tablespoons lime juice
2 (15-oz.) cans great northern
   beans, undrained
2/3 cup crushed tortilla chips
1¹/₂ oz. (²/₃ cup) shredded
   reduced-fat Monterey Jack
   cheese

Combine all salsa ingredients in medium bowl; mix well. Refrigerate 30 minutes to blend flavors.

Meanwhile, in large saucepan, combine water, 1 teaspoon lemon pepper seasoning and cumin seed; bring to a boil. Add chicken breast halves. Reduce heat to low; cover and simmer 20 to 28 minutes or until chicken is fork-tender and juices run clear. Remove chicken from bones; cut into 1-inch pieces. Return chicken to saucepan.

Spray medium skillet with nonstick cooking spray; heat over medium heat. Add garlic clove; cook and stir 1 minute. Remove from skillet; add to chicken mixture. Add 1 cup onions to skillet; cook and stir until tender. Add cooked onions, corn, chiles, cumin and 2 to 3 tablespoons lime juice to chicken mixture. Bring to a boil. Add beans; cook until thoroughly heated.

To serve, place about 1 tablespoon each of tortilla chips and cheese in 8 individual soup bowls; ladle hot soup over cheese. Serve with salsa.

Yield: 8 (1-cup) servings

Reta Smith: White Chili with Salsa Verde

Necessity is often the mother of invention. "After my husband received his doctorate in 1960," says Reta Smith, "we moved to a very small community in northwest Missouri and lived on a farm. He began a very busy large-animal veterinary practice. We raised three children and also had a cow and calf operation. Our home was run like a restaurant and small hotel, since our area was very remote. I went to a grocery warehouse every three months to do our shopping. . . . With this in mind, my cooking was very creative, and as the time grew closer to my next three-month trip, became even more so." But with results like White Chili with Salsa Verde, no one would complain!

*Tip: If fresh or canned tomatillos are not available, 2 cups coarsely chopped green tomatoes can be substituted.

**Adobo is a specialty seasoning available in Hispanic grocery stores.

Nutrition Per Serving: Calories 290; Protein 24g; Carbohydrate 39g; Fat 7g; Sodium 1010mg

Zesty Chicken Vegetable Bisque

Taylor Arnold *Kemah, Texas*
Bake-Off® Contest 33, 1988

This spicy chicken and vegetable one-dish meal is like Brunswick stew. Large pieces of boneless chicken, a variety of vegetables and a well-seasoned broth are spooned over rice in individual serving bowls.

3 whole chicken breasts,
   skinned, boned and
   halved
3 tablespoons margarine or
   butter
1 cup sliced onions
3 garlic cloves, minced
2 tablespoons all-purpose
   flour
2 (14¹/₂-oz.) cans ready-to-
   serve chicken broth
1 (16-oz.) can whole tomatoes,
   undrained, cut up
1 tablespoon chopped fresh
   parsley
1 teaspoon dried thyme
   leaves
¹/₂ to 1¹/₂ teaspoons salt
1 teaspoon hot pepper sauce
2 bay leaves
2 cups chopped green bell
   peppers
1 cup frozen corn (from
   1-lb. pkg.)
1 cup frozen sweet peas (from
   1-lb. pkg.)
1 (4.5-oz.) jar sliced
   mushrooms, undrained
3 cups hot cooked rice

Brown chicken breasts in margarine in large, deep skillet over medium heat. Remove chicken breasts from skillet. Add onions and garlic; cook over medium heat until onions are tender, about 3 minutes. Remove from heat. Stir in flour. Add broth, tomatoes, parsley, thyme, salt, hot pepper sauce and bay leaves; blend well. Add browned chicken breasts; cook over low heat 30 minutes, stirring occasionally. Add bell peppers; cook an additional 10 minutes. Add corn, peas and mushrooms; cook an additional 10 to 15 minutes or until chicken is tender. Remove bay leaves before serving.

To serve, place ¹/₂ cup rice in each of six individual serving bowls. Top with chicken breast half and generous 1 cup of bisque.

Yield: 6 servings

Nutrition Per Serving: Calories 420; Protein 34g; Carbohydrate 45g; Fat 10g; Sodium 1370mg

Caribbean Chili

Caribbean Chili

Ralph Berger *Jamestown, North Carolina*
Bake-Off® Contest 37, 1996

This tropical twist to an all-time favorite just might awaken the chili lover in everyone. Green chiles add zip to ham sweetened with brown sugar and orange marmalade. It's topped by a surprisingly tasty combo of banana and fresh cilantro.

CHILI
2 cups diced cooked ham
1 tablespoon brown sugar
$1/2$ to 1 teaspoon allspice
$1/4$ cup orange marmalade
2 tablespoons fresh lemon juice
2 (15-oz.) cans black beans, drained, rinsed
1 (14.5- to 16-oz.) can whole tomatoes, undrained, cut up
1 (4.5-oz.) can chopped green chiles

TOPPING
1 banana
1 teaspoon fresh lemon juice, if desired
1 tablespoon chopped fresh cilantro

In large saucepan or Dutch oven, combine all chili ingredients. Cook over medium-high heat for 10 to 12 minutes or until chili is thoroughly heated and flavors are blended, stirring occasionally.

Slice banana into small bowl. Add lemon juice; toss to coat. Top each serving of chili with banana slices and cilantro.

Yield: 4 (1¼-cup) servings

Nutrition Per Serving: Calories 390; Protein 26g; Carbohydrate 60g; Fat 5g; Sodium 1750mg

Spicy Meatball Soup

Debra Freeman *Jefferson, Maryland*
Bake-Off® Contest 36, 1994 Prize Winner

Cilantro, cumin and salsa flavor this spicy Mexican soup. Serve it with flour tortillas.

MEATBALLS
1 lb. extra-lean ground beef
1 (11-oz.) can vacuum-packed whole kernel corn, drained
$1/3$ cup hot picante salsa
$1/2$ cup thinly sliced green onions with tops
2 tablespoons chopped fresh cilantro
$1/2$ to 1 teaspoon salt
1 teaspoon cumin
1 teaspoon finely chopped garlic
1 egg white

SOUP
1 (28-oz.) can whole tomatoes, undrained, cut up
1 (15.5-oz.) can dark or light red kidney beans, drained
1 cup beef broth
$2/3$ cup hot picante salsa
2 tablespoons chopped fresh cilantro
1 cup chopped green bell pepper
1 teaspoon cumin
1 teaspoon chili powder
$1/2$ teaspoon finely chopped garlic

TOPPINGS, IF DESIRED
$1/4$ cup chopped fresh cilantro
$1/4$ cup chopped green onions with tops
$1/4$ cup dairy sour cream

In large bowl, combine ground beef, $1/2$ cup of the corn and remaining meatball ingredients; mix well. Shape into 1-inch balls; place on cookie sheet. Refrigerate 30 minutes or until set.

In 5-quart Dutch oven or stockpot, combine remaining corn and all soup ingredients. Bring to a boil over high heat. Reduce heat to low; carefully add uncooked meatballs. Simmer uncovered 45 to 60 minutes or until flavors blend and meatballs are no longer pink in the center. Garnish individual servings with toppings.

Yield: 6 (1½-cup) servings

Nutrition Per Serving: Calories 330; Protein 24g; Carbohydrate 31g; Fat 12g; Sodium 1510mg

Southwest Tortellini Chowder

Loanne Chiu *Fort Worth, Texas*
Bake-Off® Contest 37, 1996 Prize Winner

Psychologist Loanne Chiu has lived in Indonesia and Germany and has studied the foods of all the regions in China. After exposure to so many different cuisines, it's not surprising that her spicy main dish is a fusion of flavors from the American Southwest and Italy.

3 (10¹/₂-oz.) cans condensed chicken broth
1¹/₂ cups mild chunky-style salsa or picante
¹/₂ teaspoon grated orange peel
2 (9-oz.) pkg. refrigerated meat-filled or cheese-filled tortellini*
2 cups frozen cut broccoli (from 1-lb. pkg.)
1 cup frozen corn (from 1-lb. pkg.)
¹/₂ cup coarsely chopped red bell pepper
1 (5-oz.) can evaporated milk

Dash salt
¹/₄ cup chopped fresh cilantro

In Dutch oven or large saucepan, combine broth, salsa and orange peel. Bring to a boil. Reduce heat to low; simmer 3 minutes.

Stir in tortellini and vegetables; cook over medium heat for 6 to 8 minutes or until tortellini and vegetables are tender.

Southwest Tortellini Chowder

Stir in milk and salt; cook 1 to 2 minutes or just until thoroughly heated, stirring occasionally. DO NOT BOIL. Top each serving of chowder with cilantro. Serve immediately.

Yield: 6 (1¹/₂-cup) servings

*Tip: One 16-oz. pkg. frozen tortellini can be substituted for refrigerated tortellini. Add frozen tortellini to simmered broth mixture; cook 4 minutes. Add vegetables; cook an additional 6 to 8 minutes or until tortellini and vegetables are tender.

Nutrition Per Serving: Calories 400; Protein 20g; Carbohydrate 52g; Fat 12g; Sodium 1750mg

Cheese-Steak Crescent Braid

Cindy Joy *Alameda, California*
Bake-Off® Contest 33, 1988

This attractive sandwich braid has the flavors of the popular Philadelphia cheese-steak sandwich.

4 portions frozen, thinly sliced sandwich steaks, cut crosswise into ¹/₂-inch strips
2 tablespoons margarine or butter
¹/₂ cup chopped onion
1 large green bell pepper, cut into strips (1¹/₂ cups)
Salt and pepper to taste
2 (8-oz.) cans refrigerated crescent dinner rolls
4 oz. (1 cup) shredded mozzarella cheese
1 egg, beaten, if desired

Heat oven to 350° F. In large skillet over medium-high heat, cook and stir steak strips in margarine until no longer pink; remove from skillet. Add onion and bell pepper; cook until crisp-tender, about 5 minutes. Add cooked steak; season with salt and pepper.

Unroll 1 can dough into 2 long rectangles. Place on ungreased cookie sheet with long sides overlapping ¹/₂ inch; firmly press edges and perforations to seal. Press or roll out to form 13×7-inch rectangle. Spoon heaping cupful of meat mixture in 2-inch strip lengthwise down center of dough to within ¹/₄ inch of each end. Sprinkle ¹/₂ cup of the cheese over meat mixture. Make cuts 1 inch apart on longest sides of rectangle just to edge of filling. To give braided appearance, fold strips of dough at an angle halfway across filling, alternating from side to side. Fold ends of braid under to seal.

On second ungreased cookie sheet, repeat using remaining can of dough, meat mixture and cheese. Brush braids with beaten egg. Bake at 350° F. for 16 to 22 minutes or until golden brown. Cool slightly; remove from cookie sheet. Cool 5 minutes before serving.

Yield: 6 servings

Nutrition Per Serving: Calories 440; Protein 22g; Carbohydrate 32g; Fat 25g; Sodium 960mg

Crescent Chick-Be-Quicks

Rosemarie Berger *Jamestown, North Carolina*
Bake-Off® Contest 33, 1988 Prize Winner

To create this hot chicken snack, fresh chicken pieces coated with french-fried onions are baked in tiny crescent dough triangles. Serve them with sweet-and-sour sauce for dipping.

³/₄ cup crushed canned french-fried onions
1 tablespoon all-purpose flour
¹/₄ teaspoon seasoned salt
1 (8-oz.) can refrigerated crescent dinner rolls
1 whole chicken breast, skinned, boned and cut into 16 pieces (¹/₂ lb.)
1 egg, beaten
Sesame or poppy seed

Heat oven to 375° F. Lightly grease cookie sheet. In small bowl, combine french-fried onions, flour and salt; blend well. Set aside. Separate dough into 8 triangles. Cut each in half lengthwise to make 16 long triangles. Dip chicken pieces in beaten egg; coat with onion mixture. Place 1 coated piece on wide end of each triangle; roll to opposite point. Place point side down on greased cookie sheet. Brush tops with remaining beaten egg; sprinkle with sesame seed. Bake at 375° F. for 12 to 15 minutes or until golden brown. Serve warm or cold.

Yield: 16 servings

Nutrition Per Serving: Calories 100; Protein 5g; Carbohydrate 7g; Fat 5g; Sodium 160mg

Crescent Cristo Sandwich Loaf

Lori Ann Rizzo *College Station, Texas*
Bake-Off® Contest 36, 1994

Ham, turkey and Muenster cheese are layered with flaky crescent dough in this delicious honey-glazed sandwich loaf.

LOAF
2 (8-oz.) cans refrigerated crescent dinner rolls
2 tablespoons margarine or butter, melted
2 tablespoons honey
6 oz. thinly sliced smoked cooked turkey breast
6 oz. medium-sliced Muenster cheese
6 oz. thinly sliced cooked ham
1/3 to 1/2 cup red raspberry preserves

TOPPING
2 tablespoons honey
1 tablespoon sesame seed

Heat oven to 375° F. Separate dough into 4 long rectangles. Place rectangles crosswise on 1 large or 2 small ungreased cookie sheets (rectangles should not touch); firmly press perforations to seal. In small bowl, combine margarine and 2 tablespoons honey; mix well. Brush over dough.

Bake at 375° F. for 8 to 12 minutes or until light golden brown; cool 15 minutes.

Grease 15×10×1-inch baking pan. Carefully place 1 crust on pan. Top evenly with turkey. Place second crust over turkey; top with cheese and ham. Place third crust over ham; spread evenly with preserves. Top with fourth crust; brush top with 2 tablespoons honey. Sprinkle honey with sesame seed.

Bake at 375° F. for 10 to 15 minutes or until crust is deep golden brown and loaf is hot. Let stand 5 minutes. Cut into 8 slices.

Yield: 8 servings

Nutrition Per Serving: Calories 440; Protein 17g; Carbohydrate 45g; Fat 23g; Sodium 1220mg

Crescent Samosa Sandwiches

Elisabeth Crawford *San Francisco, California*
Bake-Off® Contest 36, 1994 Prize Winner

Samosas are fried triangular pastries filled with vegetables or meat. This version is prepared quickly and easily with crescent rolls.

FILLING
1 tablespoon oil
1/2 cup finely chopped onion
2 garlic cloves, minced
1/4 lb. lean ground beef
1 cup diced cooked potato
1/2 cup diced cooked carrot
1/2 cup frozen sweet peas (from 1-lb. pkg.), thawed
5 teaspoons soy sauce
1 teaspoon curry powder
1/2 teaspoon cumin
1/4 teaspoon coriander
1/4 teaspoon ginger
1/4 teaspoon turmeric
Dash crushed red pepper flakes

CRESCENTS
2 (8-oz.) cans refrigerated crescent dinner rolls

HONEY DIPPING SAUCE
1/3 cup honey
1 tablespoon lime juice
1 tablespoon soy sauce
1/4 teaspoon crushed red pepper flakes
2 garlic cloves, minced

Heat oven to 375° F. Heat oil in large skillet over medium heat. Add onion and 2 minced garlic cloves; cook and stir about 5 minutes or until onion is tender. Remove from skillet. Add ground beef; cook and stir 3 to 5 minutes or until browned. Drain. Stir in onion mixture and remaining filling ingredients. Season to taste with salt, if desired.

Separate 1 can of dough into 4 rectangles; firmly press perforations to seal. (Keep remaining can refrigerated until ready to use.) Cut rectangles in half crosswise to form 8 squares. Spoon 1 heaping tablespoon of filling in center of each square. Fold 1 corner of dough over filling to form a triangular packet; firmly press edges to seal. Repeat with remaining can of dough and filling. Place on ungreased cookie sheets. If desired, sprinkle triangles with cumin.

Bake on middle oven racks at 375° F. for 10 to 15 minutes or until golden brown, switching positions of sheets halfway through baking. Meanwhile, in small bowl combine all sauce ingredients; mix well. Serve warm sandwiches with dipping sauce.

Yield: 16 servings; 1/2 cup sauce

Nutrition Per Serving: Calories 160; Protein 4g; Carbohydrate 21g; Fat 8g; Sodium 410mg

Crescent Cristo Sandwich Loaf

Crescent Three-Cheese Calzone

Irene McEwen *Phoenix, Arizona*
Bake-Off® Contest 32, 1986

Serve these hand-held pizzas with a mixed green salad for a satisfying meal.

2 eggs
1 (15-oz.) container
   (1³/₄ cups) ricotta cheese
2 oz. (¹/₂ cup) shredded
   mozzarella cheese
¹/₄ cup grated Parmesan
   cheese
¹/₂ teaspoon salt, if desired
¹/₂ teaspoon dried basil leaves
¹/₂ teaspoon dried oregano
   leaves
¹/₄ teaspoon pepper
1 garlic clove, minced, or
   ¹/₈ teaspoon instant minced
   garlic
2 (8-oz.) cans refrigerated
   crescent dinner rolls

SAUCE
2 (8-oz.) cans tomato sauce
   with mushrooms*
2 to 4 tablespoons red wine, if
   desired
¹/₄ teaspoon dried basil leaves
¹/₄ teaspoon dried oregano
   leaves

Heat oven to 375° F. In large bowl, beat eggs slightly. Add cheeses, salt, ¹/₂ teaspoon basil, ¹/₂ teaspoon oregano, pepper and garlic; blend well. Separate dough into 8 rectangles; firmly press perforations to seal. Press or roll out each to 7×5-inch rectangle. Spoon scant ¹/₃ cup cheese mixture onto half of each rectangle to within 1 inch of edges. Fold dough in half over filling; firmly pinch edges to seal. Place on ungreased cookie sheet. With sharp knife, cut 3 slits in top of each filled rectangle. Bake at 375° F. for 14 to 17 minutes or until deep golden brown.

In small saucepan, combine all sauce ingredients; bring to a boil. Reduce heat; simmer uncovered 15 minutes to blend flavors. Spoon over each serving.

Yield: 8 servings

*Tips: One (8-oz.) can tomato sauce and 1 (2.5-oz.) jar sliced mushrooms, drained, can be substituted for the tomato sauce with mushrooms.

To reheat, wrap loosely in foil; heat at 375° F. for 15 to 20 minutes or until warm.

Nutrition Per Serving: Calories 350; Protein 15g; Carbohydrate 30g; Fat 19g; Sodium 1030mg

Chicken and Cheese Crescent Chimichangas

Marlene Zebleckis *Salinas, California*
Bake-Off® Contest 33, 1988

Chimichangas are made with a flour tortilla that's wrapped around a seasoned filling and fried until crisp. In this recipe, chimichangas are made easier when light, flaky crescents replace the tortilla and they are baked in the oven.

¹/₂ cup chopped onion
2 garlic cloves, minced
3 tablespoons oil
2¹/₂ cups shredded cooked
   chicken
2 (8-oz.) cans refrigerated
   crescent dinner rolls
¹/₂ cup picante salsa
8 oz. (2 cups) shredded
   Cheddar cheese
Dairy sour cream
Salsa

Heat oven to 350° F. Grease large cookie sheet. In large skillet, cook onion and garlic in oil until onion is tender. Add chicken; cook over low heat until thoroughly heated, stirring occasionally. Remove from heat.

Separate dough into 8 rectangles; firmly press perforations to seal. Spread about 2 teaspoons of the salsa on each rectangle to within ¹/₂ inch of edges. Stir 1 cup of the cheese into chicken mixture. Spoon heaping ¹/₃ cup chicken mixture onto half of each rectangle. Starting at shortest side topped with chicken, roll up; pinch ends to seal. Place seam side down on greased cookie sheet.

Bake at 350° F. for 16 to 21 minutes or until golden brown. Remove from oven; top each with about 2 tablespoons of the remaining cheese. Bake an additional 1 to 2 minutes or until cheese is melted. Serve with sour cream and additional salsa.

Yield: 8 servings

Nutrition Per Serving: Calories 490; Protein 24g; Carbohydrate 26g; Fat 32g; Sodium 920mg

Crescent Oriental Egg Rolls

Judith Wilson Merritt *Phoenix, New York*
Bake-Off® Contest 32, 1986

What a great, easy way to make homemade egg rolls!

PLUM SAUCE
1 (4.75-oz.) jar strained plums
 with tapioca baby food*
3 tablespoons brown sugar
2 tablespoons vinegar
1/4 teaspoon instant minced
 onion
1/8 teaspoon garlic powder
1/8 teaspoon ginger

EGG ROLLS
1 cup finely shredded cabbage
1/2 cup shredded carrots
1/2 cup finely chopped celery
1 tablespoon oil
1/2 lb. ground beef
1 teaspoon sugar
1/4 teaspoon garlic powder
Dash pepper
2 to 3 tablespoons peanut
 butter
2 to 4 teaspoons soy sauce
2 (8-oz.) cans refrigerated
 crescent dinner rolls**
1 egg, slightly beaten
1 tablespoon sesame seed

Heat oven to 375°F. In small saucepan, combine all sauce ingredients; mix well. Bring to a boil, stirring constantly. Remove from heat; cool.

Grease large cookie sheet. In large skillet, cook cabbage, carrots and celery in oil until crisp-tender, stirring constantly. Remove vegetables from skillet; set aside. In same skillet, brown ground beef; drain.

Stir in sugar, 1/4 teaspoon garlic powder, pepper, peanut butter and soy sauce; cook until peanut butter is melted, stirring frequently. Remove from heat; stir in cooked vegetables.

Separate 1 can dough into 4 rectangles; firmly press perforations to seal. Press or roll out each to 6×4-inch rectangle. Cut each rectangle crosswise into three 4×2-inch pieces. Spoon 1 tablespoon filling on half of each small rectangle to within 1/4 inch of edges. Fold dough in half over filling; pinch edges to seal. Roll slightly to form 3-inch egg roll shape.

Place on greased cookie sheet. Repeat with remaining can of dough. Brush beaten egg over rolls; sprinkle with sesame seed. Bake at 375°F. for 12 to 16 minutes or until golden brown. Serve warm with plum sauce.

Yield: 24 servings

*Tips: One-half cup canned plums can be substituted for baby food. Drain and pit plums; puree in food processor.

**For best results, keep dough refrigerated until ready to use.

To make ahead, prepare up to the point of baking, cover and refrigerate up to 2 hours; bake as directed above.

To reheat, wrap loosely in foil; heat at 375°F. for 15 to 18 minutes or until warm.

Nutrition Per Serving: Calories 120; Protein 4g; Carbohydrate 11g; Fat 7g; Sodium 240mg

Don't Mind Her, She's a Cook

Pillsbury makes every effort to be sure contestants feel at home, and most do—but some take the cake!

• One Hawaiian contestant danced the hula for photographers as her cake baked.

• A mother brought her newborn infant to the Bake-Off® Contest and set the baby basket right next to her range while she cooked.

• A finalist from Washington State was extremely suspicious about the quality of eggs in New York City—so she brought her own, on the train, across the entire country.

• One year a woman sat beside her stove, quietly reading, as flashbulbs popped, TV crews roamed, reporters questioned, and all the hubbub of the Bake-Off® Contest roiled around her. Asked how she could be so tranquil in all the tumult, she smiled and replied that this was nothing compared to cooking with her five small children around her ankles.

Broccoli Ham and Swiss Rolls

Angela Schlueter *Orange, California*
Bake-Off® Contest 33, 1988

These filled kaiser rolls are a meal in a roll! Serve them for a light meal or brunch.

2 tablespoons margarine or butter
2 tablespoons all-purpose flour
¹⁄₂ cup milk
1 (9-oz.) pkg. frozen cut broccoli in a pouch, thawed, drained
¹⁄₄ cup dairy sour cream
1 teaspoon lemon juice
¹⁄₄ teaspoon hot pepper sauce
4 (4-inch) kaiser rolls, unsliced
4 thin slices cooked ham
4 slices tomato, ¹⁄₄ inch thick
4 thin slices Swiss cheese

Melt margarine in medium saucepan over low heat. Stir in flour; cook and stir until mixture is smooth and bubbly. Gradually stir in milk. Cook over medium heat until mixture thickens and boils, stirring constantly. Add broccoli, sour cream, lemon juice and hot pepper sauce. Cook until thoroughly heated, stirring occasionally.

Heat broiler. Using sharp knife, remove ¹⁄₂-inch slice from top of each roll; set aside. Remove bread from inside of rolls, leaving about ¹⁄₂-inch shell. Spoon about ¹⁄₃ cup hot broccoli mixture into each roll. Place on ungreased cookie sheet or broiler pan. Top each with 1 slice ham, 1 slice tomato and 1 slice cheese. Broil 4 to 6 inches from heat 1 to 2 min-utes or until cheese is melted. Place top of roll on each sandwich.

Yield: 4 servings

Nutrition Per Serving: Calories 410; Protein 20g; Carbohydrate 40g; Fat 20g; Sodium 660mg

Chicken Salad Focaccia Sandwiches

Westy Gabany *Olney, Maryland*
Bake-Off® Contest 38, 1998 Prize Winner

A classic Italian flatbread, focaccia has become an American favorite. Now you can bake your own gourmet treat with this winning fast focaccia wrapped around a delicious herb-style chicken salad.

FOCACCIA
1 (10-oz.) can refrigerated pizza crust
2 to 3 tablespoons olive oil
2 garlic cloves, minced
¹⁄₂ to 1¹⁄₂ teaspoons coarse salt
1¹⁄₂ teaspoons dried rosemary leaves

SALAD
1 (10-oz.) can chunk chicken in water, drained, or 1¹⁄₃ cups chopped cooked chicken
¹⁄₂ cup chopped celery
¹⁄₂ cup mayonnaise
2 green onions, chopped
1 teaspoon dried tarragon leaves
¹⁄₂ teaspoon prepared mustard
Dash garlic powder
Dash onion powder

Heat oven to 350°F. Lightly spray cookie sheet with nonstick cooking spray. Unroll dough onto sprayed cookie sheet to form 12×10-inch rectangle. Starting with short end, fold dough in half; press lightly.

In small bowl, combine oil and minced garlic; mix well. Spread over dough. Sprinkle with salt and rosemary. Bake at 350°F. for 20 to 25 minutes or until edges are golden brown.

Meanwhile, in medium bowl, combine all salad ingredients; mix well. Refrigerate 15 minutes.

To serve, cut warm focaccia into 4 pieces. Split each piece to form 2 layers. Spoon and spread salad on bottom halves of focaccia pieces; cover with top halves to form sandwiches.

Yield: 4 sandwiches

Nutrition Per Serving: Calories 570; Protein 25g; Carbohydrate 36g; Fat 36g; Sodium 1600mg

Biscuit Mini Focaccia

Linda J. Greeson *Spring Valley, California*
Bake-Off® Contest 37, 1996 Prize Winner

A quick version of herb-topped Italian flat bread, this is the creation of Linda Greeson, who began cooking inventively when she was first married and on a tight budget.

¹/₂ **cup fresh basil leaves**
¹/₄ **cup fresh thyme sprigs**

2 **garlic cloves, chopped**
¹/₄ **teaspoon salt, if desired**
Dash pepper
¹/₄ **cup olive oil or vegetable oil**
1 **(12-oz.) can refrigerated**
   flaky biscuits
¹/₄ **cup pine nuts**
¹/₃ **cup grated Parmesan**
   cheese

Heat oven to 400° F. In blender container or food processor bowl with metal blade, combine basil, thyme, garlic, salt, pepper and oil. Cover; blend until finely chopped, scraping down sides of container, if necessary.

Separate dough into 10 biscuits. On ungreased cookie sheets, press or roll each biscuit to a 3-inch circle. Make several indentations with fingers in tops of biscuits. Spread about 1 teaspoon basil mixture evenly over each biscuit. Sprinkle each biscuit evenly with 1 teaspoon pine nuts; press gently. Sprinkle with cheese.

Bake at 400° F. for 10 to 12 minutes or until biscuits are golden brown. Serve warm.

Yield: 10 servings

Nutrition Per Serving: Calories 180; Protein 4g; Carbohydrate 15g; Fat 12g; Sodium 470mg

Biscuit Mini Focaccia

WAYNE HU

The bond between grandparents and grandchildren is a special one—of teaching, of sharing, of growing and of hope. Grandparents touch their grandchildren's hearts and influence their lives through many channels—stories, photos, proverbs, traditions and food—by passing on their wisdom to the young.

Wayne Hu perfects his recipes for his grandchildren. "My grandson loves Chinese food. My daughter doesn't live far from me, and once or twice a week they come over to eat with us. He walks in, and he smells Chinese Black Bean sauce, which is very fragrant. 'Boy,' he says, 'that smells good! Papa, are you making Black Bean sauce?' My pepper-tomato steak with black bean sauce has become his top choice." One of Wayne's little granddaughters likes to stand on a chair beside him. "Sometimes I let her drop the Chinese noodles in the water, but I have to watch her

carefully so she doesn't get too close to the stove. She also loves to wash the rice in water," following an ancient Chinese method. Today, everyone in Wayne's family clamors for his Bake-Off® winning Chinese Roast Pork Buns, which are a traditional Asian version of a hot sandwich.

Wayne worked hard to be able to enjoy the delights of grandfatherhood. He fled China on the last boat out of Shanghai before World War II consumed the Pacific, and he made his way to Michigan, where he attended the University of Michigan, pursuing graduate studies in engineering, and then established himself as a structural engineer. Wayne taught himself to cook, starting in college, when he realized "if you want good Chinese food, you have to learn how to cook it. I am proud to say I have perfected my Peking Duck."

Chinese Roast Pork Buns

Wayne Hu *West Bloomfield, Michigan*
Bake-Off® Contest 36, 1994 Prize Winner

Biscuit dough is wrapped around a barbecue filling to make a Chinese treat known in China as bau buns.

ROAST PORK
¼ cup firmly packed brown sugar
¼ cup ketchup
2 tablespoons soy sauce

2 tablespoons hoisin sauce
1 tablespoon dry sherry
1 garlic clove, minced
1½ lb. pork steaks (½ inch thick)

SAUCE
1 tablespoon cornstarch
1 tablespoon dry sherry
1 tablespoon peanut oil or vegetable oil
½ cup chopped onion
½ cup chopped water chestnuts
1 tablespoon soy sauce
1 tablespoon hoisin sauce
½ cup chicken broth

PASTRY
1 (1 lb. 0.3-oz.) can large refrigerated buttermilk biscuits

GLAZE
1 teaspoon sugar
1 teaspoon water
1 egg white

Heat oven to 375° F. Line broiler pan with foil. In blender container or food processor bowl with metal blade, combine all roast pork ingredients except pork; blend until smooth.* Generously brush both sides of the pork steaks,

reserving remaining basting sauce. Place pork steaks on foil-lined broiler pan.

Bake at 375°F. for 30 minutes. Remove pork from oven. Brush both sides of steaks with remaining basting sauce. Bake an additional 10 to 20 minutes or until no longer pink in the center. Remove from oven; cool (leave the oven on). Remove meat from bone; finely chop. Set aside.

In small bowl, combine cornstarch and 1 tablespoon sherry;

Chinese Roast Pork Buns

blend well. Heat oil in wok or large skillet over high heat. Add onion and water chestnuts; cook and stir 2 to 3 minutes or until onion begins to brown. Add 1 tablespoon soy sauce and 1 tablespoon hoisin sauce; stir to coat. Add broth. Stir in cornstarch mixture; cook and stir until mixture begins to thicken. Remove from heat; stir in pork.**

Separate dough into 8 biscuits. On lightly floured surface, press or roll each biscuit into 5-inch circle. Place about ⅓ cup pork mixture in center of each biscuit. Gathering up edges, twist and pinch to seal. Place seam side down on ungreased

cookie sheet. In small bowl, beat glaze ingredients until well blended; brush over buns.

Bake at 375°F. for 14 to 18 minutes or until golden brown.

Yield: 8 servings

*Tips: Mixture also can be blended in small bowl with wire whisk.

**At this point, pork mixture can be covered and refrigerated. Heat until warm before making sandwiches.

Nutrition Per Serving: Calories 360; Protein 16g; Carbohydrate 36g; Fat 17g; Sodium 1130mg

Ham and Swiss Crescent Braid

Lorraine Maggio *Manlius, New York*
Bake-Off® Contest 39, 2000 Prize Winner

Versatile, classic ingredients are wrapped in a flaky crust to create a fabulously filling dish for a special brunch, elegant lunch or family dinner.

¾ lb. cooked ham, chopped (2¼ cups)
1 cup frozen broccoli florets, thawed
4 oz. (1 cup) shredded Swiss cheese
1 (4.5-oz.) jar sliced mushrooms, drained
½ cup mayonnaise or salad dressing
1 tablespoon honey mustard
2 (8-oz.) cans refrigerated crescent dinner rolls
1 egg white, beaten
2 tablespoons slivered almonds

Heat oven to 375° F. Spray cookie sheet with nonstick cooking spray. In large bowl, combine ham, broccoli, cheese, mushrooms, mayonnaise and mustard; mix well.

Unroll both cans of dough. Place dough with long sides together on sprayed cookie sheet, forming 15×12-inch rectangle. Press edges and perforations to seal.

Spoon and spread ham mixture in 6-inch strip lengthwise down center of dough. With scissors or sharp knife, make cuts 1½ inches apart on long sides of dough to within ½ inch of filling. Twisting each strip once, alternately cross strips over filling. Tuck short ends under; press to seal. Brush dough with beaten egg white; sprinkle with almonds.

Bake at 375° F. for 28 to 33 minutes or until deep golden brown. Cool 5 minutes. Cut into crosswise slices.

Yield: 8 servings

Nutrition Per Serving: Calories 440; Protein 18g; Carbohydrate 26g; Fat 29g; Sodium 1230mg

Puffy Chiles Rellenos

Helen Novak *Fontana, California*
Bake-Off® Contest 29, 1980 Prize Winner

A Mexican specialty, chiles rellenos are stuffed peppers covered with crisp batter. This version is easily made with refrigerated biscuits.

2 (4-oz.) cans whole green chiles
8 oz. Monterey Jack or Cheddar cheese
1 (12-oz.) can refrigerated flaky biscuits

TOPPING
3 eggs, separated
¼ teaspoon salt
1 (8-oz.) jar taco sauce

Heat oven to 375° F. Grease cookie sheet. Cut chiles lengthwise to make 10 pieces. Remove seeds and ribs; rinse and drain. Cut cheese into ten 3×½×½-inch pieces. Wrap each piece of cheese with piece of chile. Separate dough into 10 biscuits. Press or roll out each to 4-inch circle. Place 1 chile-wrapped cheese piece onto each circle; fold dough over to cover completely. Firmly pinch edges to seal. Form each into finger-shaped roll; place seam side up on greased cookie sheet.*

Bake at 375° F. for 10 to 12 minutes or until light golden brown. Meanwhile, prepare topping. In small bowl, beat egg whites until stiff peaks form. In second small bowl, beat egg yolks and salt. Gently fold egg yolk mixture into beaten egg whites until just blended. Spoon mounds of egg mixture over each partially baked roll, covering each completely. Bake an additional 12 to 15 minutes or until golden brown. In small saucepan, heat taco sauce. Spoon hot taco sauce over chile rellenos.

Yield: 10 servings

*Tip: To make ahead, chiles rellenos can be prepared to this point. Cover and refrigerate up to 2 hours. Continue as directed above.

Nutrition Per Serving: Calories 230; Protein 10g; Carbohydrate 17g; Fat 13g; Sodium 980mg

Poppin' Fresh® Barbecups

Peter Russell *Shawnee-Mission, Kansas Bake-Off® Contest 19, 1968 Prize Winner*

This Junior prize-winning recipe was created by a twelve-year-old boy. He and his sister prepared this great-tasting simple-to-do recipe for dinner on the nights his mom and dad worked late. Pillsbury has promoted many versions of the recipe since its creation.

1 lb. ground beef
1/2 cup barbecue sauce
1 tablespoon instant minced onion or 1/4 cup chopped onion
1 to 2 tablespoons brown sugar
1 (12-oz.) can refrigerated flaky biscuits
2 oz. (1/2 cup) shredded Cheddar or American cheese

Heat oven to 400°F. Grease 10 muffin cups. Brown ground beef in large skillet until thoroughly cooked; drain. Stir in barbecue sauce, onion and brown sugar. Cook 1 minute to blend flavors, stirring constantly.

Separate dough into 10 biscuits. Place 1 biscuit in each greased muffin cup; firmly press in bottom and up sides, forming 1/4-inch rim. Spoon about 1/4 cup meat mixture into each biscuit-lined cup. Sprinkle each with cheese.

Bake at 400°F. for 10 to 12 minutes or until edges of biscuits are golden brown. Cool 1 minute; remove from pan.

Yield: 10 servings

Tip: To make ahead, prepare as directed above. Cover; refrigerate for up to 2 hours. Bake as directed above.

Nutrition Per Serving: Calories 240; Protein 11g; Carbohydrate 19g; Fat 13g; Sodium 520mg

Spicy Meat Pies with Yogurt Sauce

Julie Winter *Grosse Pointe Park, Michigan Bake-Off® Contest 36, 1994 Prize Winner*

Lemon, mint and oregano provide a Lebanese flavor to these sandwiches.

SAUCE
1 cup plain yogurt
1/2 teaspoon dried mint leaves
1/4 teaspoon salt

FILLING
1/2 lb. ground lamb or beef
1/2 cup chopped onion
1/4 cup shredded carrot
2 tablespoons pine nuts or slivered almonds
2 tablespoons chopped fresh parsley or 2 teaspoons dried parsley flakes
1/2 teaspoon dried mint leaves
1/4 teaspoon dried oregano leaves
1/4 teaspoon salt
1/8 teaspoon pepper
1 teaspoon grated lemon peel
1 tablespoon lemon juice
1 garlic clove, minced

BISCUITS
1 (1 lb. 0.3-oz.) can large refrigerated buttermilk biscuits
1 teaspoon sesame or poppy seed

In small bowl, combine all sauce ingredients. Let stand 15 minutes.

Heat oven to 375°F. In large skillet over medium heat, cook lamb and onion until meat is no longer pink and onion is tender, stirring occasionally; drain. Add remaining filling ingredients; cook and stir for 1 minute. Remove from heat.

Separate dough into 8 biscuits. Press or roll each biscuit into 5-inch circle. Place scant 1/4 cup filling in center of each biscuit. Fold dough over filling to form half circle. Press edges together; seal with fork. Place on ungreased cookie sheet. Sprinkle tops with sesame seed or poppy seed; lightly press into biscuits.

Bake at 375°F. for 13 to 15 minutes or until golden brown. Immediately remove from cookie sheet. Serve hot meat pies with sauce.

Yield: 8 servings; 1 cup sauce

Nutrition Per Serving: Calories 280; Protein 11g; Carbohydrate 28g; Fat 14g; Sodium 770mg

Tex-Mex Biscuit Sandwiches

Elaine Schultz *Miami, Florida*
Bake-Off® Contest 33, 1988

Mexican recipes dominated the ethnic recipe category in the 1988 contest, so it took an exceptionally good one like this to be chosen as a finalist. The barbecued beef filling gives true south-of-the-border flavor to the big baked sandwiches.

2¹/₂ oz. deli roast beef, chopped (¹/₂ cup)
¹/₄ cup taco sauce
¹/₄ cup barbecue sauce
¹/₄ cup sliced green onions
¹/₄ cup sliced ripe olives, drained
2 oz. (¹/₂ cup) shredded Cheddar cheese
1 (12-oz.) can refrigerated flaky biscuits
2 tablespoons cornmeal
¹/₂ cup dairy sour cream
10 pimiento slices
10 ripe olive slices

Heat oven to 350°F. In medium bowl, combine roast beef, taco sauce, barbecue sauce, green onions, ¹/₄ cup olives and cheese; set aside.

Separate dough into 10 biscuits. Dip both sides of each biscuit in cornmeal. Press or roll out each to 5-inch circle. Place 5 circles on ungreased cookie sheet. Spoon about ¹/₄ cup of roast beef mixture onto center of each circle. Brush edges lightly with water. Place remaining 5 biscuit circles over roast beef mixture. Press edges with fork to seal. Using back of table-spoon, make indentation in center of each sandwich. Sprinkle sandwiches with remaining cornmeal.

Bake at 350°F. for 14 to 22 minutes or until golden brown. Remove from oven; gently repeat indentation if necessary. Fill each with heaping tablespoonful of sour cream. Garnish each with 2 pimiento slices and 2 ripe olive slices.

Yield: 5 servings

Nutrition Per Serving: Calories 380; Protein 13g; Carbohydrate 35g; Fat 21g; Sodium 1070mg

Karen Durrett: Chicken and Black Bean Tostizzas

I grew up in a large family—seven children—in a small town in Indiana," Karen Durrett says. "It was great. My mother was the traditional homemaker, and my greatest memories growing up all relate to food. There was always a pot of something on the stove. My mom expressed love through food." The beauty of American cooking is that a small-town Indiana girl can combine elements of Italian, Mexican and Midwestern cuisines to create a spectacular result that is pure American: Chicken and Black Bean Tostizzas.

Chicken and Black Bean Tostizzas

Chicken and Black Bean Tostizzas

Karen Durrett *Portland, Oregon*
Bake-Off® Contest 36, 1994

Flavored like a tostada, shaped like a pizza!

PIZZA
1 (1 lb. 1.3-oz.) can large refrigerated flaky biscuits
¹/₂ cup thick and chunky salsa
1 cup diced cooked chicken
1 cup canned black beans (from 15-oz. can), drained
¹/₄ cup chopped fresh cilantro
¹/₄ teaspoon cumin
2 green onions, chopped
¹/₂ cup green or red bell pepper strips (1 inch long)
6 oz. (1¹/₂ cups) shredded Cheddar cheese

GARNISH, IF DESIRED
¹/₂ cup dairy sour cream
¹/₂ cup guacamole

Heat oven to 350°F. Separate dough into 8 biscuits. On ungreased cookie sheets, press or roll each biscuit into 5¹/₂-inch circle. In medium bowl, combine salsa, chicken, black beans, cilantro and cumin; mix well. Spread evenly over biscuits to within ¹/₄ inch of edges. Top evenly with green onions, bell pepper strips and cheese.

Bake at 350°F. for 20 to 24 minutes or until biscuits are golden brown and cheese is melted. To serve, garnish with sour cream and guacamole.

Yield: 8 servings

Nutrition Per Serving: Calories 400; Protein 17g; Carbohydrate 32g; Fat 23g; Sodium 1010mg

Ham and Cheese Biscuit Pockets

Carol J. Gross *Fort Morgan, Colorado*
Bake-Off® Contest 31, 1984 Prize Winner

In this recipe, flaky biscuits and ham, Swiss cheese and crunchy apple filling bake together to form a pocket sandwich.

1 cup cubed cooked ham
4 oz. (1 cup) shredded Swiss cheese
¹/₂ cup finely chopped peeled apple
1 (12-oz.) can refrigerated flaky biscuits
1 egg, slightly beaten
1 teaspoon water
Alfalfa sprouts, if desired
Chopped tomato, if desired

Heat oven to 375°F. Lightly grease large cookie sheet. In small bowl, combine ham, cheese and apple; mix gently. Separate dough into 10 biscuits. On greased cookie sheet, press or roll out 5 biscuits to 4-inch circles.

Place about ¹/₂ cup ham mixture onto center of each circle. Press or roll out remaining 5 biscuits to 5-inch circles. Place each over filling. Press edges with fork to seal. Combine egg and water; brush over filled biscuits.

Bake at 375°F. for 13 to 18 minutes or until golden brown. Cut each in half to form pocket sandwiches. To serve, garnish with alfalfa sprouts and tomato. Serve warm.

Yield: 5 servings

Nutrition Per Serving: Calories 370; Protein 17g; Carbohydrate 33g; Fat 19g; Sodium 1160mg

Reuben-in-the-Round Crescents

Irene Dunn *Cuyahoga Falls, Ohio*
Bake-Off® Contest 27, 1976

Here's a new twist on the popular Reuben sandwich. Traditional filling ingredients are baked in a pizza pan between layers of flaky crescent roll dough, then cut into servings.

2 (8-oz.) cans refrigerated crescent dinner rolls
1 (8-oz.) pkg. thinly sliced pastrami or corned beef
1 (6-oz.) pkg. (4 slices) Swiss or mozzarella cheese
1 (8-oz.) can (1 cup) sauerkraut, drained
¹/₂ teaspoon caraway seed
¹/₂ teaspoon sesame seed

Heat oven to 400°F. Separate 1 can of dough into 4 rectangles. Place in ungreased 12-inch pizza pan or 13×9-inch pan; press over bottom and ¹/₂ inch up sides to form crust. Seal perforations. Arrange pastrami, cheese and sauerkraut in layers over dough. Sprinkle with caraway seed. Separate second can of dough into 8 triangles. Arrange triangles spoke-fashion over filling, with points toward center. Do not seal outer edges of triangles to bottom crust. Sprinkle with sesame seed.

Bake at 400°F. for 15 to 25 minutes or until golden brown. Serve immediately.

Yield: 8 servings

Tips: To make ahead, prepare, cover and refrigerate up to 2 hours; bake as directed above.

To reheat, cover loosely with foil; heat at 375°F. for 15 to 18 minutes or until warm.

Nutrition Per Serving: Calories 380; Protein 15g; Carbohydrate 24g; Fat 25g; Sodium 1000mg

Sweet 'n Sour Chicken Wraps

Carol Winder *Murray, Utah*
Bake-Off® Contest 35, 1992 Prize Winner

You'll like the subtle honey-and-soy–flavored filling in these quick and easy sandwiches. Serve them at your next luncheon or shower.

1 cup chopped cooked chicken
2 tablespoons chopped green onions, including tops
1 tablespoon canned crushed pineapple, well drained
2 tablespoons honey
1 tablespoon soy sauce
2 teaspoons prepared mustard
1 (8-oz.) can refrigerated crescent dinner rolls
1 egg, beaten
2 teaspoons sesame seed, toasted*
Green onions, if desired

Heat oven to 375°F. In small bowl, combine chicken, 2 tablespoons green onions and pineapple; mix well. In another small bowl, combine honey, soy sauce and mustard; blend well. Pour over chicken mixture; stir to coat.

Separate dough into 4 rectangles; firmly press perforations to seal. Cut each rectangle in half crosswise. Spoon 1 rounded tablespoon chicken filling onto center of each square. To make each wrap, pull 4 corners of dough to center of filling; twist ends and pinch seams to seal. Brush wraps with egg; sprinkle with sesame seed. Place on ungreased cookie sheet.

Bake at 375°F. for 10 to 15 minutes or until deep golden brown. Arrange on serving platter; garnish with whole green onions.

Yield: 8 servings

*Tip: To toast sesame seed, spread in baking pan; bake at 350°F. for 6 to 8 minutes or until light golden brown, stirring occasionally. Or, place seeds in a skillet; stir over medium heat for 8 to 10 minutes or until light golden brown.

Nutrition Per Serving: Calories 170; Protein 8g; Carbohydrate 16g; Fat 8g; Sodium 400mg

Changing the Tools of the Trade

The face of contemporary cooking is always changing, and the Bake-Off® has been an active force in spurring some of those changes.

- In 1954, Open Sesame Pie featured an innovative sesame seed crust. Sesame seed was then a regional specialty of a small area of the South, but after this Bake-Off® prize-winning recipe was announced, there was instant national demand for the little nutty-tasting seed. Because of that recipe, sesame seed became a regularly stocked item in most grocery stores.

- In 1968, the Grand Prize-winning Buttercream Pound Cake featured another then-exotic seed: poppy seed, used in a filling that swirled throughout the lemon cake. After the recipe was published, poppy seed and lemon cake became a classic combination, like apples and cinnamon.

- In 1966, the terrifically popular Tunnel of Fudge Cake was introduced, using what was then the little-known Bundt cake pan. Pillsbury received more than 200,000 requests from home cooks for help in locating the ring-shaped, fluted pan, and ever since then Bundt cakes have shown up on cake trays nationwide.

Savory Crescent Chicken Squares

Doris Castle *River Forest, Illinois*
Bake-Off® Contest 25, 1974 Grand Prize Winner

This quick and easy warm chicken sandwich is perfect to serve for brunch, lunch or supper.

1 (3-oz.) pkg. cream cheese, softened
1 tablespoon margarine or butter, softened
2 cups cubed cooked chicken*
1 tablespoon chopped chives or onion
¹/₄ teaspoon salt
¹/₈ teaspoon pepper

2 tablespoons milk
1 tablespoon chopped pimiento, if desired
1 (8-oz.) can refrigerated crescent dinner rolls
1 tablespoon margarine or butter, melted
³/₄ cup seasoned croutons, crushed

Heat oven to 350°F. In medium bowl, beat cream cheese and 1 tablespoon softened margarine until smooth. Add chicken, chives, salt, pepper, milk and pimiento; mix well.

Separate crescent dough into 4 rectangles. Firmly press perforations to seal. Spoon ¹/₂ cup of chicken mixture onto center of each

rectangle. Pull 4 corners of dough to center of chicken mixture; twist firmly. Pinch edges to seal. Place on ungreased cookie sheet. Brush tops of sandwiches with 1 tablespoon melted margarine; sprinkle with crushed croutons.

Bake at 350°F. for 25 to 30 minutes or until golden brown.

Yield: 4 servings

*Tip: Two 5-oz. cans chunk chicken, drained and flaked, can be substituted for cubed cooked chicken.

Nutrition Per Serving: Calories 500; Protein 27g; Carbohydrate 28g; Fat 31g; Sodium 890mg

Rosemary Chicken and Brie en Croute

Mary Lou Cook *Fallbrook, California*
Bake-Off® Contest 36, 1994

En croute is the French term for a food wrapped and baked in pastry. Crescent rolls make it easy.

1 (8-oz.) can refrigerated
    crescent dinner rolls
2 tablespoons finely chopped
    green onions
6 oz. Brie cheese, rind
    removed, cubed
1½ cups chopped cooked
    chicken breast
1 egg, beaten
1 teaspoon crushed dried
    rosemary leaves
1 tablespoon grated Parmesan
    cheese

GARNISH, IF DESIRED
1 medium tomato, cut into
    8 wedges
4 green onions

Heat oven to 350° F. Separate dough into 4 rectangles; firmly press perforations to seal. Spoon ¼ of chopped green onions onto center of each rectangle; top with ¼ of cheese cubes. Top each with ¼ of chicken, pressing into cheese. Fold short ends over chicken, overlapping slightly. Fold open ends over about ½ inch to form rectangle. Press all edges to seal. Place seam side down on ungreased 15×10×1-inch baking pan or cookie sheet. Cut three 1-inch slashes on top of each roll to form steam vents. Brush with egg; sprinkle with rosemary and Parmesan cheese.

Bake at 350° F. for 21 to 26 minutes or until golden brown. Garnish each sandwich with 2 tomato wedges and 1 green onion. Let stand 5 minutes before serving.

Yield: 4 servings

Tip: For easy cleanup, line baking pan with foil.

Nutrition Per Serving: Calories 450; Protein 30g; Carbohydrate 25g; Fat 25g; Sodium 790mg

Spinach and Cheese Bruschetta

John Kelly *Warrenville, Illinois*
Bake-Off® Contest 35, 1992

Bruschetta is a traditional garlic bread made with olive oil, garlic, salt and pepper, then served warm. You'll like this updated version that features spinach, tomatoes, cheese and fresh basil.

1 (1-lb.) loaf French or Italian
    bread
3 tablespoons olive oil
1 medium onion, chopped
2 garlic cloves, minced
1 (9-oz.) pkg. frozen spinach in
    a pouch, thawed, squeezed to
    drain
1 tablespoon grated Parmesan
    cheese
1 teaspoon dried Italian
    seasoning
½ teaspoon fennel seed,
    crushed
1 large tomato, seeded,
    chopped
6 oz. (1½ cups) shredded
    mozzarella cheese
¼ cup chopped fresh basil or
    1 tablespoon dried basil
    leaves
Sliced red chile peppers, if
    desired
Fresh Italian parsley or
    tarragon, if desired

Heat oven to 400° F. Line cookie sheet with foil. Cut bread in half lengthwise. Place cut side up on foil-lined cookie sheet. Heat oil in medium skillet over medium-high heat until hot. Add onion and garlic; cook and stir until tender, 4 to 5 minutes. Add spinach; heat 1 minute or until spinach is warm. Remove from heat; stir in Parmesan cheese, Italian seasoning and fennel seed; mix well. Spread spinach mixture evenly over bread halves. Sprinkle with tomato, mozzarella cheese and basil.

Bake at 400° F. for 7 to 10 minutes or until cheese is melted and edges of bread are golden brown. To serve, cut into slices. Garnish with pepper slices and parsley.

Yield: 8 servings

Nutrition Per Serving: Calories 290; Protein 13g; Carbohydrate 37g; Fat 11g; Sodium 610mg

Rosemary Chicken and Brie
en Croute

Italian Spinach Torta

Larry Elder *Charlotte, North Carolina*
Bake-Off® Contest 33, 1988

Torta is an Italian term for cake or pie. In this recipe, the torta is an impressive appetizer pie. Serve thin wedges as the first course at a dinner party.

1 (15-oz.) pkg. refrigerated pie crusts
1 teaspoon all-purpose flour

FILLING
1 (9-oz.) pkg. frozen spinach in a pouch, thawed, squeezed to drain
1 cup ricotta cheese
¹/₂ cup grated Parmesan cheese
¹/₄ to ¹/₂ teaspoon garlic salt
¹/₄ teaspoon pepper
1 egg, separated
1 teaspoon water

Heat oven to 400° F. Place oven rack at lowest position. Prepare pie crust according to package directions for *two-crust pie* using 10-inch tart pan with removable bottom or 9-inch pie pan. Place 1 prepared pie crust in pan; press in bottom and up sides of pan. Trim edges if necessary.

In medium bowl, combine spinach, ricotta cheese, Parmesan cheese, garlic salt, pepper and egg yolk; blend well. Spread evenly in pie crust-lined pan.

To make lattice top, cut remaining crust into ³/₄-inch-wide strips. Arrange strips in lattice design over spinach mixture. Trim and seal edges. In small bowl, combine egg white and water; beat well. Gently brush over lattice. Bake at 400° F. on lowest oven rack for 45 to 50 minutes or until dark golden brown.* Cool 10 minutes; remove sides of pan. Serve warm.

Yield: 12 servings

*****Tip:** Cover torta with foil during last 5 to 10 minutes of baking if necessary to prevent excessive browning.

Nutrition Per Serving: Calories 220; Protein 6g; Carbohydrate 18g; Fat 14g; Sodium 480mg

Sicilian Mushroom Flatbread

Patricia Schroedl *Jefferson, Wisconsin*
Bake-Off® Contest 36, 1994 Prize Winner

Sun-dried tomatoes are sweet and intensely flavored. They add a rich flavor to this focaccia-type bread that's great to serve as an appetizer or with a robust soup.

2 teaspoons olive oil or vegetable oil
¹/₃ cup finely chopped onion
2 tablespoons finely chopped oil-packed sun-dried tomatoes
1 tablespoon finely chopped fresh oregano or 1 teaspoon dried oregano leaves

2 to 3 teaspoons finely chopped fresh rosemary or 1 teaspoon dried rosemary leaves
1 teaspoon finely chopped garlic
1 (4.5-oz.) jar sliced mushrooms, drained
1 (10-oz.) can refrigerated pizza crust
¹/₄ cup grated Parmesan cheese

Heat oven to 425° F. Grease 15×10×1-inch baking pan or large cookie sheet. Heat oil in small skillet over medium heat. Add onion, tomatoes, oregano, rosemary and garlic; cook and stir 4 minutes or until onion is tender. Stir in mushrooms. Remove from heat.

Unroll dough and place in greased pan; starting at center, press out with hands to 12×9-inch rectangle. Spread onion mixture evenly over dough. Sprinkle with cheese.

Bake at 425° F. for 12 to 14 minutes or until edges of crust are golden brown. Cut into 16 rectangles.

Yield: 8 servings; 16 appetizers

Nutrition Per Serving: Calories 120; Protein 5g; Carbohydrate 18g; Fat 3g; Sodium 300mg

Italian Biscuit Flatbread

Edith L. Shulman *Grapevine, Texas*
Bake-Off® Contest 32, 1986 Prize Winner

This is an easy-to-make version of the Italian hearth bread, focaccia.

^{1}/$_3$ **cup mayonnaise or salad dressing**
^{1}/$_3$ **cup grated Parmesan cheese**
^{1}/$_4$ **teaspoon dried basil leaves**
^{1}/$_4$ **teaspoon dried oregano leaves**
3 green onions, sliced
1 garlic clove, minced or ^{1}/$_8$ teaspoon garlic powder
1 (12-oz.) can refrigerated flaky biscuits

Heat oven to 400° F. In small bowl, combine mayonnaise and Parmesan cheese; stir in basil, oregano, green onions and garlic. Separate dough into 10 biscuits. On ungreased cookie sheets, press or roll out each biscuit to 4-inch circle. Spread about 1 tablespoon cheese mixture over each circle to within ^{1}/$_4$ inch of edge. Bake at 400° F. for 10 to 13 minutes or until golden brown. Serve warm.

Yield: 10 servings

Nutrition Per Serving: Calories 180; Protein 4g; Carbohydrate 15g; Fat 11g; Sodium 460mg

Tuna Cheese Flips

Marilyn Belschner *Amherst, Nebraska*
Bake-Off® Contest 27, 1976

This creamy tuna sandwich with a crunchy potato chip coating was added to the list of America's favorites in 1976, our bicentennial year.

2 (6-oz.) cans tuna, drained, flaked
^{1}/$_8$ **teaspoon lemon pepper seasoning**
^{1}/$_3$ **cup sliced ripe or green olives, drained**
^{1}/$_3$ **cup mayonnaise or salad dressing**
2 oz. (^{1}/$_2$ cup) shredded Monterey Jack or Cheddar cheese
1 (12-oz.) can refrigerated flaky biscuits
1 egg, beaten or 2 tablespoons milk
1 cup crushed potato chips

Heat oven to 375° F. In small bowl, combine tuna, lemon pepper seasoning, olives, mayonnaise and cheese. Separate dough into 10 biscuits. Press or roll out each to 5-inch circle. Spoon about ^{1}/$_4$ cup tuna mixture onto center of each circle. Fold dough in half over filling; press edges with fork to seal. Brush both sides of each sandwich with egg; press both sides in chips. Place on ungreased cookie sheet. With sharp knife, make two or three ^{1}/$_2$-inch slits in top of each sandwich. Bake at 375° F. for 18 to 24 minutes or until deep golden brown.

Yield: 10 servings

Tip: To reheat, wrap loosely in foil; heat at 350° F. for 10 to 15 minutes or until warm.

Nutrition Per Serving: Calories 260; Protein 12g; Carbohydrate 18g; Fat 15g; Sodium 620mg

Marilyn Belschner: Tuna Cheese Flips

Many Bake-Off® Contest finalists agree that the feelings that come out of preparing and sharing a meal are as significant as the ingredients that go into it: "I feel meal time is a very important together time for the family," Marilyn Belschner says. "A time when family members can communicate with each other under pleasant circumstances, while enjoying food that will nourish their bodies. Of all the ills that threaten mankind today, few can penetrate a happy family at a well-appointed table."

Mushroom Phyllo Tarts

Melissa Daston *Laurel, Maryland*
Bake-Off® Contest 33, 1988

Tender, flaky phyllo dough is placed in muffin cups, filled with a well-seasoned cream cheese mixture and topped with whole mushrooms to create this appetizer. They are easy to make and impressive to serve.

³/4 **cup dairy sour cream**
1 **(3-oz.) pkg. cream cheese,
    softened**
¹/4 **cup dry bread crumbs**
1 **tablespoon dried dill weed**
¹/2 **teaspoon salt**
1 **to 2 tablespoons lemon juice**
1 **(4.5-oz.) jar sliced
    mushrooms, drained**
1 **garlic clove, minced**
¹/2 **cup butter or margarine**
8 **(18×14-inch) frozen phyllo
    (filo) pastry sheets, thawed**
1 **(4.5-oz.) jar whole
    mushrooms, drained**

Heat oven to 350° F. In small bowl, combine sour cream, cream cheese, bread crumbs, dill weed, salt and lemon juice; blend well. Stir in sliced mushrooms. Set aside.

To make garlic butter, in small skillet over low heat, cook garlic in butter until tender, stirring constantly. Coat 16 muffin cups with garlic butter. Set aside.

Brush large cookie sheet with garlic butter. Unroll phyllo sheets; cover with plastic wrap or towel. Brush 1 phyllo sheet lightly with garlic butter; place on buttered cookie sheet. Brush second phyllo sheet lightly with garlic butter; place on top of first buttered sheet. Repeat with remaining phyllo sheets. With sharp knife, cut through all layers of phyllo sheets to make 16 rectangles. Lightly press each rectangle into garlic-buttered muffin cup.

Spoon heaping tablespoon of sour cream mixture into each cup. Top each with whole mushroom, pushing stem into filling. Drizzle with remaining garlic butter. Bake at 350° F. for 18 to 20 minutes or until light golden brown.

Yield: 16 servings

Tip: To make ahead, prepare, cover and refrigerate up to 4 hours before baking; bake as directed above.

Nutrition Per Serving: Calories 120; Protein 2g; Carbohydrate 5g; Fat 10g; Sodium 250mg

Tomato-Topped Onion Bread Wedges

Sandra Bangham *Rockville, Maryland*
Bake-Off® Contest 36, 1994

Serve with soup or cut into small wedges for an appetizer.

SALAD
1 **tablespoon olive oil or
    vegetable oil**
2 **large tomatoes, chopped**
1 **red bell pepper, chopped**
1 **tablespoon chopped fresh
    parsley**
1 **tablespoon tarragon vinegar**
¹/2 **teaspoon dried basil leaves**
¹/2 **teaspoon dried oregano
    leaves**
¹/8 **teaspoon pepper**

BREAD
¹/3 **cup olive oil or vegetable
    oil**
¹/3 **cup chopped onion**
1 **garlic clove, minced**
1 **(10-oz.) can refrigerated
    pizza crust**
¹/4 **cup grated Parmesan
    cheese**

Heat oven to 400° F. Heat 1 tablespoon oil in large skillet over medium-low heat until hot. Add tomatoes and bell pepper; cook 10 to 15 minutes or until most of the liquid has evaporated, stirring occasionally. Remove from heat; stir in remaining salad ingredients. Cool. Set aside.

Heat ¹/3 cup oil in large skillet over medium heat until hot. Add onion and garlic; cook and stir until onion is tender. Drain, reserving oil; set onion mixture aside. Grease 9-inch round cake pan with 1 tablespoon of reserved oil. Unroll dough; press or roll into 10-inch circle. Place dough in oiled pan; gently press dough to cover bottom and ¹/2 inch up sides of pan. Using tip of knife, poke holes in dough every 2 inches. Pour remaining reserved oil over dough, spreading evenly. Sprinkle with reserved onion mixture and Parmesan cheese.

Bake at 400° F. for 18 to 20 minutes or until golden brown and center is slightly puffed. Cool slightly; remove from pan. Place on serving plate; top warm bread with salad.

Yield: 6 servings

Nutrition Per Serving: Calories 280; Protein 7g; Carbohydrate 27g; Fat 17g; Sodium 320mg

Top to bottom: **Tomato-Topped Onion Bread Wedges, Spinach Pierogi Pizza, page 98**

Savory Salmon-Filled Crescents

Carol DuVall *New York, New York*
Bake-Off® Contest 26, 1975

In this recipe, a savory salmon salad is enclosed and baked in flaky pastry for a quick luncheon or main-meal sandwich.

1 (16-oz.) can salmon or
    2 (6-oz.) cans tuna, drained,
    flaked
1¹/₂ cups seasoned croutons
¹/₂ cup chopped onion
2 tablespoons chopped fresh
    parsley or 2 teaspoons dried
    parsley flakes
1 teaspoon dried dill weed
¹/₂ teaspoon garlic salt
¹/₄ teaspoon pepper
¹/₂ cup mayonnaise or salad
    dressing
¹/₂ cup dairy sour cream
4 eggs, hard-cooked, coarsely
    chopped
2 (8-oz.) cans refrigerated
    crescent dinner rolls
1 to 2 tablespoons margarine
    or butter, melted
Chopped fresh parsley, if
    desired

Heat oven to 350° F. In medium bowl, combine salmon, croutons, onion, 2 tablespoons parsley, dill weed, garlic salt, pepper, mayonnaise, sour cream and eggs; toss lightly. Separate dough into 8 rectangles; firmly press on perforations to seal. Spoon about ¹/₂ cup salmon mixture onto center of each rectangle. Pull 4 corners of dough to center of salmon mixture; twist firmly.

Pinch edges to seal. Place on ungreased cookie sheets. Brush each with margarine; sprinkle with parsley. Bake at 350° F. for 18 to 28 minutes or until golden brown. Serve immediately.

Yield: 8 servings

Tip: To reheat, wrap loosely in foil; heat at 350° F. for 15 to 20 minutes or until warm.

Nutrition Per Serving: Calories 500; Protein 19g; Carbohydrate 25g; Fat 36g; Sodium 770mg

Ham and Cheese Crescent Snacks

Ronna Sue Farley *Rockville, Maryland*
Bake-Off® Contest 26, 1975

Take a whack at snack attacks with this ham and cheese treat. On-hand ingredients are ready to bake into an effortless appetizer that you can make whenever the urge strikes.

1 (8-oz.) can refrigerated
    crescent dinner rolls
2 tablespoons margarine or
    butter, softened
1 teaspoon prepared mustard
1 cup cubed cooked ham
¹/₃ cup chopped onion
¹/₃ cup chopped green bell
    pepper
4 oz. (1 cup) shredded
    Cheddar or American cheese

Heat oven to 375° F. Unroll dough onto ungreased cookie sheet. Press or roll dough into a 13×9-inch rectangle, sealing perforations. Pinch edges to form rim.

In small bowl, combine margarine and mustard; mix well. Spread mixture over crust. Sprinkle ham, onion, bell pepper and cheese over mixture.*

Bake at 375° F. for 18 to 25 minutes or until edges are golden brown. Cut into pieces; serve warm. Store in refrigerator.

Yield: 24 snacks

*****Tip:** At this point, recipe can be covered with plastic wrap and refrigerated for up to 2 hours. Bake as directed above.

Nutrition Per Serving: Calories 70; Protein 3g; Carbohydrate 4g; Fat 5g; Sodium 200mg

Tex-Mex Appetizer Tart

Richard McHargue *Richmond, Kentucky*
Bake-Off® Contest 38, 1998 Prize Winner

Here's a new twist for serving popular Tex-Mex flavors. Serve it with a fruit salad for lunch, as a tasty afternoon snack for the kids or an hors d'oeuvre that dinner guests will love.

CRUST
1 refrigerated pie crust (from 15-oz. pkg.)

FILLING
6 oz. (1½ cups) shredded colby-Monterey Jack cheese blend
½ cup roasted red bell peppers (from 7.25-oz. jar), drained, chopped
½ cup mayonnaise
1 (4.5-oz.) can chopped green chiles

TOPPING
¼ cup chopped fresh cilantro or parsley

Heat oven to 375°F. Bring pie crust to room temperature as directed on package. Unfold crust; place on ungreased cookie sheet. Press out fold lines.

In medium bowl, combine all filling ingredients; mix well. Spread over crust to within 1 inch of edges. Fold crust edges over filling to form 1-inch border; flute.

Bake at 375°F. for 25 to 35 minutes or until crust is golden brown. Sprinkle with cilantro. Let stand 10 minutes before serving. Cut into wedges. Serve warm.

Yield: 16 servings

Nutrition Per Serving: Calories 150; Protein 3g; Carbohydrate 8g; Fat 12g; Sodium 180mg

Pesto Crescent Twists with Feta Spread

Judy Wood *Vestavia Hills, Alabama*
Bake-Off® Contest 39, 2000 Prize Winner

For a quick appetizer, plunge these pesto-filled crescent strips into this delightfully creamy spread. Save any extra spread for topping baked potatoes, tossing with pasta, or for serving as a thick sauce with chicken.

TWISTS
2 (8-oz.) cans refrigerated crescent dinner rolls
½ cup purchased pesto
2 tablespoons finely chopped walnuts

SPREAD
¼ cup dairy sour cream
4 oz. (1 cup) crumbled feta cheese
1 (3-oz.) pkg. cream cheese, softened
2 teaspoons olive oil
1 teaspoon purchased pesto

Heat oven to 375°F. Grease cookie sheets. Unroll 1 can of dough onto cutting board or sheet of waxed paper. Firmly press perforations to seal. Press or roll to form 13×7-inch rectangle. In small bowl, combine ½ cup pesto and walnuts; mix well. Spread mixture over dough.

Unroll remaining can of dough. Firmly press perforations to seal. Press or roll to form 13×7-inch rectangle. Carefully place dough rectangle over pesto and walnut filling. Cut filled dough in half crosswise to make two 7×6½-inch pieces. Cut each half into 8 strips. Twist each strip tightly; place on greased cookie sheets.

Bake at 375°F. for 14 to 19 minutes or until golden brown.

Meanwhile, in medium bowl, combine sour cream, feta cheese and cream cheese; mix until well blended. Place in small serving bowl. In another small bowl, combine oil and 1 teaspoon pesto. Drizzle over cheese mixture. With tip of knife, stir to marble. Serve warm twists with spread. Store any remaining spread in refrigerator.

Yield: 16 appetizers

Nutrition Per Serving: Calories 200; Protein 4g; Carbohydrate 12g; Fat 15g; Sodium 370mg

Chapter 2

Main Dishes

How can I cook a fabulous meal without spending my entire day in front of the stove? Decades of reading America's favorite recipes have led us to believe that this is the question cooks ask themselves most as they approach their kitchens. Meals, of course, are about hospitality and care, but American cooks have long realized that their guests—whether they're family or special visitors—would prefer to dine with a relaxed host serving a good meal than with an exhausted host serving a fancy one.

California Casserole was the first main dish to capture a Grand Prize, at the eighth Bake-Off® Contest in 1956, and is a good example of how the question of cooking quickly and spectacularly is solved. Margaret Hatheway took an Austrian dish and made the sauces easy by starting with a base of canned cream of chicken soup. It's the kind of dish that seems like it would take half a day's labor—but doesn't. The 1959 contest's Crab Meat Salad Pie was a typical country-club-type dish that Evelyn Robinson adapted for home cooks, another example of impressive fare that can be put together without denting a busy schedule. More recent recipes, like 1994's Italian- and French-influenced Spicy Broccoli Aïoli Pizza, reflect today's interest in international flavors. Every Bake-Off® Contest dish, however, expands on the most significant of perennial yet contemporary cooking trends: convenience.

Orange-Cumin Chicken and Vegetables, page 65

Biscuit-Topped Italian Casserole

Robert Wick *Altamonte Springs, Florida*
Bake-Off® Contest 33, 1988

Robert Wick was a high school junior when he competed in the 1988 contest with this family-favorite meat pie. By arranging the meat mixture, cheese and vegetables in layers and topping the casserole with an overlapping layer of split biscuits, he added eye appeal to the tasty medley.

1 lb. ground beef
1/2 cup chopped onion
1 tablespoon oil, if desired
3/4 cup water
1/2 teaspoon salt, if desired
1/4 teaspoon pepper
1 (8-oz.) can tomato sauce
1 (6-oz.) can tomato paste
8 oz. (2 cups) shredded
  mozzarella cheese
1 1/2 cups frozen mixed
  vegetables (from 1-lb. pkg.),
  thawed
2 (12-oz.) cans refrigerated
  flaky biscuits
1 tablespoon margarine or
  butter, melted
1/2 teaspoon dried oregano
  leaves, crushed

Heat oven to 375° F. Grease 13×9-inch (3-quart) baking dish. In large skillet, brown ground beef and onion in oil until beef is thoroughly cooked; drain. Stir in water, salt, pepper, tomato sauce and tomato paste; simmer 15 minutes, stirring occasionally. Place half of *hot* meat mixture in greased baking dish; sprinkle with 2/3 cup of the cheese.

Spoon mixed vegetables evenly over cheese; sprinkle an additional 2/3 cup cheese over vegetables. Spoon remaining *hot* meat mixture evenly over cheese and vegetables; sprinkle with remaining 2/3 cup cheese.

Separate dough into 20 biscuits. Separate each biscuit into 3 layers. Arrange layers over hot meat mixture, overlapping, in 3 rows of 20 layers each. Gently brush biscuits with margarine; sprinkle with oregano. Bake at 375° F. for 22 to 27 minutes or until biscuit topping is golden brown.

Yield: 10 servings

Nutrition Per Serving: Calories 420; Protein 19g; Carbohydrate 36g; Fat 22g; Sodium 1240mg

Del Tinsley: Cajun Red Beans and Rice

Jazz great Louis Armstrong signed his letters "Red beans and ricely yours," because the dish was so close to his heart. Red beans and rice is a dish that, if you grew up on it, is fiercely adored comfort food. Del Tinsley has long known the value of simple recipes in a busy kitchen. "From the time I started walking," she says, "I followed Nana (my grandmother) around the kitchen like a little puppy dog. I never thought I couldn't cook, I just imitated her." From underfoot Del learned how to make dinner, with love.

Cajun Red Beans and Rice

Del Tinsley *Nashville, Tennessee*
Bake-Off® Contest 35, 1992

Red beans and rice is a traditional Southern favorite made with a spicy, heavily smoked sausage of French origin, called andouille.

3/4 lb. finely chopped hickory-
  smoked andouille sausage,
  skinned, or cooked hot
  Italian sausage
1 cup chopped onions
2 (15.5-oz.) cans red beans,
  drained
1 (8-oz.) can tomato sauce
1/2 cup diced green bell pepper
1/2 cup diced yellow bell
  pepper
2 garlic cloves, minced
1 teaspoon dried oregano
  leaves
1 teaspoon dried thyme leaves
1 tablespoon dry sherry, if
  desired
6 cups hot cooked rice
1/3 cup sliced green onions
Hot pepper sauce

In large skillet, brown sausage and onions over medium-high heat for 3 minutes, stirring frequently; drain. Stir in beans, tomato sauce, bell peppers, garlic, oregano and thyme. Reduce heat to low; simmer 15 minutes, stirring occasionally. Stir in sherry. Serve over rice; garnish with green onions. Serve with hot pepper sauce.

Yield: 6 servings

Nutrition Per Serving: Calories 470; Protein 18g; Carbohydrate 85g; Fat 8g; Sodium 730mg

Orange-Cumin Chicken and Vegetables

Arnold Shulman *Sedona, Arizona*
Bake-Off® Contest 39, 2000

Cumin, used as a component of curry and chili powder, adds zip to this dish.

2 cups uncooked instant white rice, if desired
2 cups water, if desired
1 teaspoon coriander
¼ teaspoon salt
¼ teaspoon coarsely ground black pepper
4 (4- to 6-oz.) boneless, skinless chicken breast halves
¼ cup salsa
1 teaspoon cornstarch
½ teaspoon cumin
1 tablespoon oil
1 red bell pepper, cut into thin strips
1 (9-oz.) pkg. frozen sugar snap peas in a pouch
¾ cup orange juice

Cook rice in water as directed on package. Cover to keep warm. Meanwhile, in small bowl, combine coriander, salt and pepper; mix well. Rub mixture on all sides of chicken breast halves. Discard any remaining seasoning mixture. In another small bowl, combine salsa, cornstarch and cumin; mix well.

Heat oil in large skillet over medium-high heat until hot. Add chicken; cook 2 minutes on each side or until browned. Add bell pepper and sugar snap peas; cook and stir 4 minutes. Reduce heat to medium-low. Add 2 tablespoons of the orange juice; cover and cook 6 minutes or until chicken is fork-tender and juices run clear, and vegetables are crisp-tender. Remove chicken from skillet; cover to keep warm.

Add salsa mixture and remaining orange juice to skillet; mix well. Bring to a boil. Cook until slightly thickened, stirring occasionally. Cut chicken crosswise into ½-inch slices. Arrange chicken on individual plates. Spoon vegetable mixture over chicken. Serve with rice.

Yield: 4 servings

Nutrition Per Serving: Calories 420; Protein 33g; Carbohydrate 55g; Fat 7g; Sodium 380mg

Spicy Broccoli Aïoli Pizza

Gilda Lester *Chadds Ford, Pennsylvania*
Bake-Off® Contest 36, 1994 Prize Winner

Gilda Lester made a garlicky herbed vinaigrette interpretation of the traditional garlic mayonnaise sauce to drizzle over her broccoli and cheese pizza.

CRUST
2 tablespoons cornmeal
1 (10-oz.) can refrigerated pizza crust

TOPPING
¼ cup olive oil or vegetable oil
3 to 4 garlic cloves, chopped
2 tablespoons chopped shallots or onion
1 tablespoon balsamic vinegar or red wine vinegar
⅓ cup grated Romano or Parmesan cheese
½ teaspoon dried basil leaves
½ teaspoon dried thyme leaves
½ teaspoon dried oregano leaves
¼ teaspoon crushed red pepper flakes
6 oz. sliced Havarti or Monterey Jack cheese
1 (1-lb.) pkg. frozen cut broccoli, thawed, well drained
1 (7-oz.) jar roasted red peppers, drained, sliced into 2×¼-inch strips
½ cup grated Parmesan or Romano cheese

Gilda Lester: Spicy Broccoli Aïoli Pizza

Earlier this century the traditional woman's work really was never done. Each week required a full day of baking, of washing and of ironing. Few would return to those days, but it did leave space for quiet family interaction that many feel is unfortunately missing from modern life. "My grandmother had a hearth oven, which she used to bake bread for the week," Gilda Lester recalls. "I helped her, and she always saved a small piece of dough for a pizza for me. I wouldn't give up those days with my grandmother for anything. I helped start the fire, then when the embers had smoldered for just the right amount of time, we cleared the oven for the loaves of bread. Most of my recipes are in my head. They are things that my grandmother, and then my mother, passed on to me."

Heat oven to 425° F. Lightly grease 12-inch pizza pan or 13×9-inch pan; sprinkle with cornmeal. Unroll dough; press in bottom and up sides of greased pan to form a rim. Bake at 425° F. for 5 to 8 minutes or until light golden brown.

In food processor bowl with metal blade or blender container, combine oil, garlic, shallots, vinegar, Romano cheese, basil, thyme, oregano and red pepper flakes. Process until smooth; set aside. Arrange Havarti cheese over partially baked crust. Place broccoli evenly over cheese. Dollop oil mixture evenly over top. Arrange pepper strips over broccoli; sprinkle with Parmesan cheese.

Bake at 425° F. for 17 to 22 minutes or until edges of crust are deep golden brown. Serve immediately.

Yield: 8 servings

Nutrition Per Serving: Calories 310; Protein 14g; Carbohydrate 24g; Fat 19g; Sodium 470mg

California Casserole

Margaret Hatheway *Santa Barbara, California Bake-Off® Contest 8, 1956 Grand Prize Winner*

Although this recipe has a long list of ingredients, it's really quite easy to make. It's a Tyrolean specialty that's been passed down through a family.

CASEROLE
1/3 **cup all-purpose flour**
1 **teaspoon paprika**
2 **lb. boneless veal or pork, cut into 1-inch pieces**
1/4 **cup oil**
1/2 **teaspoon salt**
1/8 **teaspoon pepper**

1 **cup water**
1 **(10 3/4-oz.) can condensed cream of chicken soup**
1 1/2 **cups water**
1 **(16-oz.) jar (1 1/2 cups) small onions, drained**

DUMPLINGS
2 **cups all-purpose flour**
4 **teaspoons baking powder**
1 **tablespoon poppy seed, if desired**
1 **teaspoon instant minced onion**
1 **teaspoon celery seed**
1 **teaspoon poultry seasoning**
1/4 **teaspoon salt**
1/4 **cup oil**
3/4 **to 1 cup milk**
2 **tablespoons margarine or butter, melted**
1/2 **cup dry bread crumbs**

SAUCE
1 **(10 3/4-oz.) can condensed cream of chicken soup**
1 **cup dairy sour cream**
1/4 **cup milk**

In small bowl or plastic bag, combine 1/3 cup flour and paprika; shake well. Add veal; coat well with flour mixture. In large skillet, heat 1/4 cup oil over medium-high heat. Add veal; cook until browned. Add 1/2 teaspoon salt, pepper and 1 cup water. Bring to a boil. Reduce heat; simmer uncovered 30 minutes or until veal is tender. Transfer veal mixture to ungreased 13×9-inch (3-quart) baking dish or 3-quart casserole.

In same skillet, combine 1 can cream of chicken soup and 1 1/2 cups water; bring to a boil, stirring constantly. Pour over veal mixture in baking dish. Add onions; mix well.

Heat oven to 425° F. In large bowl, combine 2 cups flour, baking powder, poppy seed, minced onion,

Margaret Hatheway: California Casserole

Part of Margaret Hatheway's prize in the eighth Bake-Off® was a Cook's Tour of Europe, with stops in Rome, Paris and London. She learned how to make steak and kidney pie in England, crepes in France and pasta in Italy. In return Margaret taught all the chefs she met how to make her prize-winning California Casserole. They inquired about the casseroles of the remaining forty-seven states, but Margaret replied that that was the work of future generations.

celery seed, poultry seasoning and 1/4 teaspoon salt; mix well. Add 1/4 cup oil and enough milk so that, when stirred, dry ingredients are just moistened.

In small bowl, combine margarine and bread crumbs. Drop rounded tablespoons of dough into crumb mixture; roll to coat well. Arrange dumplings over warm veal mixture. Bake at 425° F. for 20 to 25 minutes or until dumplings are deep golden brown.

Meanwhile, in medium saucepan, combine all sauce ingredients. Bring just to a boil. Reduce heat; simmer 2 to 3 minutes or until thoroughly heated, stirring frequently. Serve sauce with casserole and dumplings.

Yield: 10 servings

Nutrition Per Serving: Calories 510; Protein 20g; Carbohydrate 42g; Fat 29g; Sodium 1050mg

California Casserole

Bean and Sausage Bake

Marjorie Fortier *West Redding, Connecticut*
Bake-Off® Contest 35, 1992

This is a pleasing combination of beans, corn and sausage in a slightly sweet sauce.

³/4 **lb. bulk hot Italian sausage**
¹/2 **cup coarsely chopped onion**
¹/2 **cup coarsely chopped green bell pepper**
¹/2 **cup coarsely chopped red bell pepper**
1 **tablespoon finely minced garlic cloves**
³/4 **cup ketchup**
3 **teaspoons chili powder**
2 **teaspoons dried cilantro leaves, crushed, or**
  1 **tablespoon chopped fresh cilantro**
³/4 **teaspoon cumin**
1 **(16-oz.) can baked beans**
1 **(15-oz.) can black beans, drained, rinsed**
1 **(15-oz.) can garbanzo beans, drained**
1 **(11-oz.) can vacuum-packed whole kernel corn, drained**

TOPPINGS
4 **to 8 oz. (1 to 2 cups) shredded Monterey Jack cheese**
1 **to 1¹/2 cups dairy sour cream**
Crushed red pepper flakes, if desired

Top to bottom: **Bean and Sausage Bake, Cajun Red Beans and Rice, page 64**

Heat oven to 375° F. In large skillet, brown sausage with onion, bell peppers and garlic over medium-high heat until sausage is cooked and vegetables are crisp-tender; drain. Stir in ketchup, chili powder, cilantro and cumin; mix well. In 13×9-inch (3-quart) baking dish, combine baked beans, black beans, garbanzo beans and corn; mix well. Spoon sausage mixture over beans. DO NOT STIR.

Bake at 375° F. for 25 to 30 minutes or until bubbly and thoroughly heated. Remove from oven; stir well. Serve with cheese, sour cream and crushed red pepper flakes.

Yield: 8 (1-cup) servings

Nutrition Per Serving: Calories 470; Protein 22g; Carbohydrate 46g; Fat 25g; Sodium 1080mg

Chicken Broccoli Stroganoff

Patricia Kiewiet *La Grange, Illinois*
Bake-Off® Contest 33, 1988

Chicken and broccoli in a light cream sauce results in a new version of a popular family main dish. Make it in minutes in your microwave.

2 **cups frozen cut broccoli (from 1-lb. pkg.)**
1 **tablespoon margarine or butter**
¹/4 **cup chopped onion**
3 **tablespoons all-purpose flour**
1 **(10¹/2-oz.) can condensed chicken broth**
2 **cups cubed cooked chicken***

1 **(2.5-oz.) jar sliced mushrooms, drained**
1 **(8-oz.) container (1 cup) dairy sour cream**
Hot cooked noodles
Chopped fresh parsley

Microwave Directions: Cook broccoli in microwave according to package directions until crisp-tender. Drain; set aside. In 2-quart microwave-safe casserole, microwave margarine on HIGH for 20 seconds or until melted. Add onion; toss to coat. Cover with microwave-safe plastic wrap. Microwave on HIGH for 2 minutes or until crisp-tender. Add flour; blend well. Using wire whisk, stir broth into onion mixture; blend well. Microwave on HIGH for 4 to 6 minutes or until mixture thickens and bubbles, stirring once halfway through cooking.** Add chicken, cooked broccoli, mushrooms and sour cream; blend well. Microwave on HIGH for 3 to 5 minutes or until mixture is thoroughly heated and bubbles around edges, stirring once halfway through cooking. Serve over noodles; garnish with parsley.

Yield: 6 servings

*Tips: Cooked turkey or ham can be substituted for chicken.

**For compact microwave ovens under 600 watts, microwave broth-onion mixture on HIGH for 7 to 8 minutes or until mixture thickens and bubbles, stirring once halfway through cooking. Continue as directed above.

Nutrition Per Serving: Calories 490; Protein 26g; Carbohydrate 58g; Fat 17g; Sodium 445mg

Peppers Olé

Susan Kakuk *Plymouth, Minnesota*
Bake-Off® Contest 36, 1994

Raising a bumper crop of green peppers in her Minnesota garden inspired Susan Kakuk to create this south-of-the-border meatless filling for her family. The flavorful stuffed peppers can be baked in a conventional oven or microwaved.

Top to bottom: **Mexican Fiesta Biscuit Bake, page 118, Peppers Olé**

PEPPERS
4 large green bell peppers, halved, seeded
2 tablespoons water

FILLING
2 cups cooked rice
4 oz. (1 cup) shredded sharp Cheddar cheese
1/2 cup dairy sour cream
1 (15-oz.) can spicy chili beans, undrained
1 (11-oz.) can vacuum-packed whole kernel corn with red and green peppers, drained

GARNISH
1/2 cup picante salsa
8 tortilla chips
Fresh cilantro, if desired

Microwave Directions: Place peppers and water in ungreased 13×9-inch (3-quart) microwave-safe dish or divide peppers and water between two 8-inch (1½-quart) microwave-safe dishes. Cover with microwave-safe plastic wrap; microwave on HIGH for 2 minutes. Drain.

In medium bowl, combine all filling ingredients. Spoon heaping 1/2 cup of filling into each pepper half. Cover; microwave 13×9-inch dish on HIGH for 15 to 16 minutes or until peppers are tender. (Microwave each 8-inch dish for 6 to 8 minutes.) Top each pepper with 1 tablespoon of salsa, a tortilla chip and cilantro.

Conventional Directions: Heat oven to 350° F. In medium bowl, combine all filling ingredients. Spoon heaping ¹/₂ cup of filling into each pepper half. Place filled peppers in ungreased 13×9-inch (3-quart) baking dish or pan. Omit water. Cover with foil; bake at 350° F. for 50 to 60 minutes or until peppers are tender. Garnish as directed above.

Yield: 8 servings

Nutrition Per Serving: Calories 270; Protein 10g; Carbohydrate 37g; Fat 10g; Sodium 570mg

Quick-Topped Vegetable Chicken Casserole

Bernice Malinowski *Custer, Wisconsin*
Bake-Off® Contest 31, 1984 Prize Winner

As Americans began to eat less red meat in the 1980s, many excellent chicken recipes became Bake-Off® winners. The new twist for this old-fashioned chicken and vegetable pie is the spoon-on crust made with pancake mix.

CASSEROLE
1 (10³/₄-oz.) can condensed cream of chicken soup
1 (3-oz.) pkg. cream cheese, softened

¹/₂ cup milk
¹/₂ cup chopped celery
¹/₂ cup chopped onion
¹/₄ cup grated Parmesan cheese
¹/₄ cup chopped green bell pepper
¹/₄ cup shredded carrot
2 to 3 cups cubed cooked chicken
1 (9-oz.) pkg. frozen cut broccoli in a pouch, cooked, drained

TOPPING
1 cup complete or buttermilk pancake mix
¹/₄ cup slivered almonds
4 oz. (1 cup) shredded Cheddar cheese
¹/₄ cup milk
1 tablespoon oil
1 egg, slightly beaten

Heat oven to 375° F. In large saucepan, combine soup, cream cheese, ¹/₂ cup milk, celery, onion, Parmesan cheese, bell pepper and carrot. Cook over medium heat until mixture is hot and cream cheese is melted, stirring frequently. Stir in chicken and broccoli. Pour into ungreased 2-quart casserole or 12×8-inch (2-quart) baking dish.

In medium bowl, combine all topping ingredients; blend well. Spoon tablespoonfuls of topping over hot chicken mixture.

Bake at 375° F. for 20 to 30 minutes or until topping is golden brown and chicken mixture bubbles around edges.

Yield: 6 servings

High Altitude—Above 3,500 feet: No change.

Nutrition Per Serving: Calories 510; Protein 35g; Carbohydrate 29g; Fat 28g; Sodium 1140mg

Biscuit Stuffin' Atop Chops

Marion Ohl *Clyde, Ohio*
Bake-Off® Contest 22, 1971

Contestants in 1971 got the bonus of the trip to Hawaii when Honolulu was selected as the Bake-Off® site. The innovative idea of turning refrigerated biscuits into a golden-brown stuffing to dress up baked pork chops won the trip for this contestant.

6 (¹/₂-inch-thick) pork chops
1 tablespoon oil
1 (10 ³/₄-oz.) can condensed cream of chicken soup
1 cup chopped celery
1 cup chopped onions
¹/₄ teaspoon pepper
¹/₈ teaspoon poultry seasoning or sage
1 egg
1 (7.5-oz.) can refrigerated biscuits

Heat oven to 350° F. In large skillet, brown pork chops in oil. Place in ungreased 13×9-inch pan. In medium bowl, combine soup, celery, onions, pepper, poultry seasoning and egg; mix well. Separate dough into 10 biscuits; cut each into 8 pieces. Stir biscuit pieces into soup mixture; spoon over pork chops. Bake at 350° F. for 45 to 55 minutes or until biscuit pieces are golden brown.

Yield: 6 servings

Nutrition Per Serving: Calories 340; Protein 24g; Carbohydrate 23g; Fat 17g; Sodium 770mg

Zesty Italian Crescent Casserole

Madella Bathke *Wells, Minnesota*
Bake-Off® Contest 28, 1978

A casserole with Italian flair that bakes into a hearty pot pie. Your family will give this one an enthusiastic response.

1 lb. lean ground beef
¼ cup chopped onion
1 cup spaghetti sauce
6 oz. (1½ cups) shredded mozzarella or Monterey Jack cheese
½ cup dairy sour cream
1 (8-oz.) can refrigerated crescent dinner rolls
⅓ cup grated Parmesan cheese
2 tablespoons margarine or butter, melted

Heat oven to 375°F. In large skillet, brown ground beef and onion until beef is thoroughly cooked. Drain. Stir in spaghetti sauce; heat thoroughly.

In medium bowl, stir together mozzarella cheese and sour cream.

Pour hot meat mixture into ungreased 12×8-inch (2-quart) baking dish or 9½- or 10-inch deep dish pie pan. Spoon cheese mixture over meat mixture.

Unroll dough over cheese mixture.* In small bowl, combine Parmesan cheese and margarine; spread evenly over dough.

Bake at 375°F. for 18 to 25 minutes or until deep golden brown.

Yield: 6 servings

*Tip: If using pie pan, separate dough into 8 triangles. Arrange points toward center over cheese mixture, crimping outside edges if necessary.

Nutrition Per Serving: Calories 490; Protein 27g; Carbohydrate 21g; Fat 33g; Sodium 780mg

Creamy Spinach and Tortellini

Jeanine Alfano *Montauk, New York*
Bake-Off® Contest 34, 1990 Prize Winner

Garlic and basil provide the seasoning, while spinach and tomato add the color to this light-sauced tortellini main dish.

1 lb. uncooked fresh or frozen cheese tortellini
2 tablespoons olive oil or vegetable oil
½ cup chopped onion
3 garlic cloves, minced
1 (9-oz.) pkg. frozen spinach in a pouch, thawed
1 cup cubed, seeded tomato
¼ cup chopped fresh basil or 1½ teaspoons dried basil leaves
½ teaspoon salt
½ teaspoon pepper
1 cup whipping cream
¼ cup grated Parmesan or Romano cheese

Cook tortellini to desired doneness as directed on package. Drain; keep warm.

Meanwhile, heat oil in large skillet over medium heat until hot. Add onion and garlic; cook until tender and lightly browned, about 4 minutes. Add spinach, tomato, basil, salt and pepper; cook 5 minutes, stirring occasionally. Stir in whipping cream and Parmesan cheese; cook until mixture just comes to a boil. Reduce heat to low; stir in cooked tortellini. Cook an additional 4 to 5 minutes or until thoroughly heated. Serve with additional Parmesan cheese, if desired.

Yield: 4 servings

Nutrition Per Serving: Calories 670; Protein 25g; Carbohydrate 62g; Fat 37g; Sodium 1080mg

Creamy Spinach and Tortellini

Easy Seafood Dinner

Nancy Signorelli *Miami, Florida*
Bake-Off® Contest 33, 1988

In this recipe, a creamy seafood-vegetable sauce is served over tender crescent pinwheels for a quick dinner idea.

1 (8-oz.) can refrigerated crescent dinner rolls
1 (4¼-oz.) can tiny shrimp, drained, reserving liquid
1 lb. frozen cod or haddock, thawed, cut into ½-inch cubes
4 green onions, sliced
⅓ cup all-purpose flour
1 cup milk
1 tablespoon dried parsley flakes
½ to 1 teaspoon garlic powder
1 cup dairy sour cream
3 tablespoons dry sherry, if desired
1½ cups frozen sweet peas (from 1-lb. pkg.), thawed, drained
1 (8-oz.) can sliced water chestnuts, drained
1 (2.5-oz.) jar sliced mushrooms, drained

Heat oven to 350° F. Remove dough from can in rolled sections; do not unroll. Cut each section into 6 slices. Place on ungreased cookie sheet; slightly flatten each slice. Bake at 350° F. for 13 to 16 minutes or until golden brown. Set aside.

In large skillet, combine reserved shrimp liquid, cod and green onions. Bring to a boil. Reduce heat; cover and simmer

Celebrities

Glamour is a key word at the Bake-Off® festivities, and celebrities have played a starring role. The United States' first ladies Eleanor Roosevelt, Bess Truman, Mamie Eisenhower and Pat Nixon mingled with the first ladies of home kitchens. The Duke and Duchess of Windsor shared time with finalists who were working on their own crowning achievements. Abigail "Dear Abby" Van Buren had no advice for the accomplished cooks of 1961—but she could have recommended that they hold on to their pictures with actor Ronald Reagan, because they'd really be something for the neighbors to marvel over twenty years down the road.

3 to 5 minutes or until fish flakes easily with fork. Remove from heat; do not drain.

In medium saucepan using wire whisk, stir flour into milk. Cook over medium heat about 2 minutes or until mixture thickens and boils, stirring constantly. Stir in parsley flakes, garlic powder, sour cream and sherry. Add shrimp, peas, water chestnuts and mushrooms; mix well. Gently blend sour cream mixture into fish mixture in skillet.* Heat over low heat about 5 minutes, stirring occasionally. To serve, place 2 baked crescent pinwheels on plate; spoon about 1 cup of fish mixture over pinwheels.

Yield: 6 servings

*Tip: To make ahead, fish mixture can be prepared to this point. Cover and refrigerate. Just before serving, prepare crescent pinwheels as directed. Heat seafood mixture, covered, over low heat, stirring occasionally. Serve as directed above.

Nutrition Per Serving: Calories 420; Protein 26g; Carbohydrate 37g; Fat 18g; Sodium 500mg

West African Chicken and Groundnut Stew

Joyce Bowman *Raleigh, North Carolina*
Bake-Off® Contest 36, 1994 Prize Winner

On the western coast of Africa, the peanut is referred to as a groundnut. The combination of chicken and peanut butter sauce is popular in the Ivory Coast.

2 whole boneless, skinless chicken breasts, cut into ½-inch pieces
1 tablespoon peanut oil or vegetable oil
1 medium onion, chopped
1 garlic clove, minced
1 (28-oz.) can whole tomatoes, undrained, cut up
1 (15.5-oz.) can great northern beans, undrained
1 (11-oz.) can vacuum-packed whole kernel corn, drained
1 sweet potato, peeled, chopped

³/₄ cup water
¹/₄ cup peanut butter
1 tablespoon tomato paste
1 teaspoon salt
1 teaspoon chili powder
¹/₂ teaspoon ginger
¹/₂ teaspoon ground red
    pepper (cayenne)
3 cups hot cooked rice

In 4-quart Dutch oven over medium-high heat, cook chicken in oil until chicken is lightly browned and no longer pink, stirring frequently. Add onion and garlic; cook and stir 3 to 4 minutes or until onion is tender. Add remaining ingredients except rice; mix well. Bring to a boil. Reduce heat to medium-low; cover and cook 30 minutes or until sweet potato is tender, stirring occasionally. If stew becomes too thick, add additional water. Serve stew over hot rice.

Yield: 8 (1¹/₂-cup) servings

Nutrition Per Serving: Calories 370; Protein 22g; Carbohydrate 52g; Fat 8g; Sodium 730mg

West African Chicken and Groundnut Stew

Smoky Southwestern Shepherd's Pie

Kristina Vanni *Libertyville, Illinois*
Bake-Off® Contest 39, 2000

You don't have to live in the Southwest to round up this flavorful enchilada-style shepherd's pie.

1½ lb. lean ground beef round
½ cup chopped onion
2 cups water
3 tablespoons margarine or butter
½ teaspoon salt
¾ cup milk
2 cups mashed potato flakes
1 (4.5-oz.) can chopped green chiles
4 oz. (1 cup) shredded Mexican cheese blend
1 (10-oz.) can enchilada sauce
1 to 2 canned chipotle chiles in adobo sauce (from 11-oz. can), drained, seeded and chopped
½ teaspoon cumin
½ teaspoon dried oregano leaves
1 (11-oz.) can vacuum-packed whole kernel corn with red and green peppers, drained
⅛ teaspoon paprika
⅓ cup sliced green onions
1 small tomato, cut into 6 wedges

Heat oven to 400° F. In large skillet, brown ground beef round with onion over medium-high heat for 8 to 10 minutes or until beef is thoroughly cooked, stirring frequently.

Meanwhile, in medium saucepan, combine water, margarine and salt. Bring to a boil. Remove from heat. Stir in milk and potato flakes. Cover; let stand 5 minutes. Stir in green chiles and ½ cup of the cheese.

Drain beef mixture. Add enchilada sauce, chipotle chiles, cumin and oregano; mix well. Bring to a boil. Remove from heat. Spread beef mixture in ungreased shallow 2-quart casserole. Top with corn. Spread potatoes evenly over corn. Sprinkle with remaining ½ cup cheese.

Bake at 400° F. for 13 to 17 minutes or until cheese is melted and filling is bubbly. Sprinkle with paprika and green onions. Arrange tomato wedges in center of casserole. Let stand 5 minutes before serving.

Yield: 6 servings

Nutrition Per Serving: Calories 530; Protein 29g; Carbohydrate 37g; Fat 29g; Sodium 930mg

Salsa Couscous Chicken

Ellie Mathews *Seattle, Washington*
Bake-Off® Contest 38, 1998 Grand Prize Winner

Currants and cinnamon lend a spicy-sweet flavor to this swinging salsa-style chicken dish. It is served with couscous, a Mediterranean favorite that is becoming increasingly popular in North America.

1 tablespoon olive oil or vegetable oil
¼ cup coarsely chopped almonds
2 garlic cloves, minced
8 chicken thighs, skin removed
1 cup salsa
¼ cup water
2 tablespoons dried currants or raisins
1 tablespoon honey
¾ teaspoon cumin
½ teaspoon cinnamon
3 cups hot cooked couscous or rice

Heat oil in large skillet over medium-high heat until hot. Add almonds; cook 1 to 2 minutes or until golden brown. Remove almonds from skillet with slotted spoon; set aside.

Add garlic to skillet; cook and stir 30 seconds. Add chicken; cook 4 to 5 minutes or until browned, turning once.

In medium bowl, combine salsa and all remaining ingredients except couscous; mix well. Add to chicken; mix well. Reduce heat to medium; cover and cook 20 minutes or until chicken is fork-tender and juices run clear, stirring occasionally. Stir in almonds. Serve chicken mixture with couscous.

Yield: 4 servings

Nutrition Per Serving: Calories 490; Protein 34g; Carbohydrate 46g; Fat 19g; Sodium 560mg

Smoky Southwestern Shepherd's Pie

Crafty Crescent Lasagna

Betty Taylor *Dallas, Texas*
Bake-Off® Contest 19, 1968 Prize Winner

In this recipe, a crescent dough crust is stuffed with a well-seasoned meat and cheese filling. It's a creative way to get to a great-tasting lasagna.

MEAT FILLING
1/2 lb. pork sausage
1/2 lb. ground beef
3/4 cup chopped onion
1 tablespoon dried parsley flakes
1/2 teaspoon dried basil leaves
1/2 teaspoon dried oregano leaves
1 small garlic clove, minced
Dash pepper
1 (6-oz.) can tomato paste

CHEESE FILLING
1/4 cup grated Parmesan cheese
1 cup creamed cottage cheese
1 egg

CRUST
2 (8-oz.) cans refrigerated crescent dinner rolls
2 (7×4-inch) slices mozzarella cheese
1 tablespoon milk
1 tablespoon sesame seed

Heat oven to 375°F. In large skillet, brown sausage and ground beef; drain. Stir in remaining meat filling ingredients; simmer uncovered 5 minutes, stirring occasionally.

In small bowl, combine all cheese filling ingredients; blend well. Unroll dough into 4 long rectangles. Place on ungreased cookie sheet with long sides overlapping 1/2 inch; firmly press edges and perforations to seal. Press or roll out to form 15×13-inch rectangle. Spoon half of meat filling mixture in 6-inch strip lengthwise down center of dough to within 1 inch of each end. Spoon cheese filling mixture over meat mixture; top with remaining meat mixture. Arrange mozzarella cheese slices over meat mixture. Fold shortest sides of dough 1 inch over filling. Fold long sides of dough tightly over filling, overlapping edges in center 1/4 inch; firmly pinch center seam and ends to seal. Brush with milk; sprinkle with sesame seed. Bake at 375°F. for 23 to 27 minutes or until deep golden brown.

Yield: 8 servings

Tip: To reheat, wrap loosely in foil; heat at 375°F. for 18 to 20 minutes or until warm.

Nutrition Per Serving: Calories 430; Protein 22g; Carbohydrate 30g; Fat 25g; Sodium 1070mg

Broccoli Brunch Braid

Diane Tucker *Blackfoot, Idaho*
Bake-Off® Contest 33, 1988

Follow the easy recipe directions to make the handsome braided crust for this elegant light main dish. The filling is a rich-flavored combination of broccoli, mushrooms and cheeses, combined with a small amount of spicy sausage.

1/2 lb. ground pork sausage
2 cups frozen cut broccoli (from 1-lb. pkg.)
1 egg, beaten
1 tablespoon all-purpose flour
1/4 teaspoon baking powder
1/2 cup ricotta cheese
4 oz. (1 cup) shredded Cheddar cheese
1 (4.5-oz.) jar sliced mushrooms, drained
1 (8-oz.) can refrigerated crescent dinner rolls
1 egg white, beaten
1/4 teaspoon caraway seed

In medium skillet, brown sausage. Drain well; set aside. Cook broccoli as directed on package. Drain; set aside.

Heat oven to 325°F. In large bowl, combine 1 beaten egg, flour and baking powder; beat well. Stir in ricotta cheese, Cheddar cheese, mushrooms, cooked sausage and broccoli. Unroll dough into 2 long rectangles. Place on large ungreased cookie sheet with long sides overlapping 1/2 inch; firmly press edges and perforations to seal. Press or roll out to form 14×10-inch rectangle. Spoon sausage mixture in 3 1/2-inch strip lengthwise down center of dough to within 1/4 inch of each end. Form sausage mixture into mounded shape. Make cuts 1 inch apart on longest sides of rectangle just to edge of filling. To give braided appearance, fold strips of dough at an angle halfway across filling, alternating from side to side with edges of strips slightly overlapping. Brush with beaten egg white; sprinkle with caraway seed.

Bake at 325°F. for 25 to 35 minutes or until deep golden brown. Cool 5 minutes; remove from cookie sheet. Cut into slices.

Yield: 8 servings

Nutrition Per Serving: Calories 260; Protein 12g; Carbohydrate 15g; Fat 16g; Sodium 660mg

Chicken Prosciutto with Mushroom Sauce

Frances Kovar *Staten Island, New York*
Bake-Off® Contest 33, 1988 Prize Winner

Prosciutto, or Italian thin-sliced smoked ham, is tucked under tender pieces of chicken in this outstanding main dish. The special flavor of the ham and mushroom-wine sauce makes this dish perfect for entertaining.

3 whole chicken breasts, skinned, boned, halved
5 tablespoons margarine or butter
$1/4$ cup chopped onion
$1/4$ cup all-purpose flour
2 tablespoons Dijon mustard
1 cup chicken broth
1 cup half-and-half
$1/4$ cup dry white wine or water
3 (4.5-oz.) jars sliced mushrooms, drained
4 oz. (1 cup) shredded Swiss cheese
1 (1-lb.) pkg. frozen cut broccoli
6 slices prosciutto or thin-sliced cooked ham
Paprika

Place 1 chicken breast half between 2 pieces of plastic wrap. Pound chicken with meat mallet or rolling pin until about $1/4$ inch thick; remove wrap. Repeat with remaining chicken breasts.

Heat oven to 400°F. In large skillet over medium heat, melt 2 tablespoons of the margarine. Cook chicken in margarine until lightly browned on both sides, about 5 minutes. Remove chicken. In same skillet, melt remaining 3 tablespoons margarine; add onion. Cook until onion is tender, about 2 minutes, stirring frequently. Remove from heat; stir in flour and mustard. Gradually stir in broth, half-and-half and wine. Cook over low heat until mixture thickens and boils, stirring constantly. Add mushrooms and $1/2$ cup of the cheese; stir until cheese is melted. Arrange broccoli in bottom of ungreased 13×9-inch (3-quart) baking dish. Spoon half (2 cups) of sauce over broccoli. Over sauce down center of dish, alternate ham slices and chicken breasts slightly overlapping; tuck ends of ham slices under chicken. Pour remaining sauce over chicken.

Bake at 400°F. for 20 to 30 minutes or until chicken is tender and no longer pink. Remove from oven; sprinkle with remaining $1/2$ cup cheese and paprika. Return to oven. Bake an additional 2 minutes or until cheese is melted.

Yield: 6 servings

Nutrition Per Serving: Calories 460; Protein 42g; Carbohydrate 13g; Fat 25g; Sodium 1040mg

Thai Curry Chicken and Vegetables

Manika Misra *North Miami Beach, Florida*
Bake-Off® Contest 35, 1992 Prize Winner

Manika Misra adds her own blend of spices to commercial curry powder to give this chicken curry a more authentic flavor. Look for coconut milk with other canned milk products and for five-spice powder in the spice section of large supermarkets or in Asian grocery stores.

2 tablespoons oil
1 teaspoon five-spice powder
$1/2$ to $1^1/2$ teaspoons salt
$1/2$ teaspoon monosodium glutamate (MSG), if desired
$1/2$ teaspoon garlic powder
$1/2$ teaspoon ginger
$1/2$ teaspoon pepper
$1/2$ teaspoon ground red pepper (cayenne)
1 tablespoon soy sauce
$1^1/2$ lb. chicken breasts, skinned, boned, cut into 1-inch pieces
1 cup chicken broth
3 teaspoons curry powder
2 tablespoons rice vinegar or vinegar
1 (14-oz.) can coconut milk (not cream of coconut)
1 (1-lb.) pkg. frozen broccoli, carrots and water chestnuts
5 cups hot cooked rice

Heat oil in large skillet or wok over medium-high heat until hot. Stir in five spice powder, salt, monosodium glutamate, garlic powder, ginger, pepper, ground red pepper and soy sauce; blend well. Add chicken; cook and stir 5 to 8 minutes or until coated with seasonings, lightly browned and no longer pink. Add broth, curry powder, vinegar and coconut milk; stir. Bring to a boil. Reduce heat; simmer uncovered 20 to 25 minutes, stirring occasionally.

Add vegetables to skillet; bring to a boil. Cook 3 to 5 minutes or until vegetables are crisp-tender. Serve over rice.

Yield: 10 (1-cup) servings

Nutrition Per Serving: Calories 340; Protein 20g; Carbohydrate 34g; Fat 14g; Sodium 570mg

Chick-n-Broccoli Pot Pies

Linda L. Wood *Indianapolis, Indiana*
Bake-Off® Contest 28, 1978 Grand Prize Winner

By substituting a reduced-sodium soup, we've lowered the sodium but not the flavor in this prize-winning main dish.

1 (12-oz.) can refrigerated flaky biscuits
²/₃ cup shredded Cheddar or American cheese
²/₃ cup crisp rice cereal
1 (9-oz.) pkg. frozen cut broccoli, thawed
1 cup cubed cooked chicken or turkey
1 (10³/₄-oz.) can reduced-sodium condensed cream of chicken or mushroom soup
¹/₃ cup slivered or sliced almonds

Heat oven to 375°F. Separate dough into 10 biscuits. Place 1 biscuit in each of 10 ungreased muffin cups; firmly press in bottom and up sides, forming ¹/₂-inch rim over edge of muffin cup. Spoon about 1 tablespoon each of cheese and cereal into each biscuit-lined cup. Press mixture into bottom of each cup.

Top to bottom: Savory Crescent Chicken Squares, page 53, Chick-n-Broccoli Pot Pies

Linda Wood: Chick-n-Broccoli Pot Pies

Parents have been trying to improve their children's eating habits since the dawn of time. Linda Wood came up with her prize-winning Chick-n-Broccoli Pot Pies to interest her son in eating broccoli from their garden. Of course, Linda's own father had something to say about it. "My father said the reason I won was that I finally remembered to put all the ingredients into the recipe. When I was younger and still living at home I made so many mistakes. . . . I shaped up when I got married." Now Linda is an ace cook, her son eats his broccoli and progress reigns supreme.

Cut large pieces of broccoli in half. In large bowl, combine broccoli, chicken and soup; mix well. Spoon about 1/3 cup of chicken mixture over cereal. Cups will be full. Sprinkle with almonds.

Bake at 375° F. for 20 to 25 minutes or until edges of biscuits are deep golden brown.

Yield: 10 servings

Tips: To make ahead, prepare, cover and refrigerate up to 2 hours; bake as directed above.

To reheat, wrap loosely in foil; heat at 375° F. for 18 to 20 minutes.

Nutrition Per Serving: Calories 220; Protein 10g; Carbohydrate 20g; Fat 11g; Sodium 600mg

Wild Rice and Ham Country Tart

Robert Holt *Mendota Heights, Minnesota*
Bake-Off® Contest 34, 1990 Prize Winner

This recipe was developed by the contestant when he was looking for a way to use wild rice in a dish that also included other favorite ingredients. We think you'll agree that it's a winner!

1 refrigerated pie crust
(from 15-oz. pkg.)

FILLING
1 cup cubed cooked ham
1/2 cup cooked wild rice, drained
1/3 cup finely chopped red bell pepper
1/4 cup thinly sliced green onion tops
1 (4.5-oz.) jar sliced mushrooms, well drained

CUSTARD
3 eggs
1 cup dairy sour cream
1 tablespoon country-style Dijon mustard
1/2 teaspoon salt
1/8 teaspoon pepper

TOPPING
8 oz. (2 cups) shredded Swiss cheese
11 pecan halves

Heat oven to 425° F. Prepare pie crust according to package directions for *one-crust baked shell* using 10-inch tart pan with removable bottom or 9-inch pie pan. Place prepared crust in pan; press in bottom and up sides of pan. Trim edges if necessary. Do not prick crust. Bake at 425° F. for 10 to 12 minutes or until crust is very light golden brown. Remove from oven. Reduce heat to 400° F.*

In medium bowl, combine all filling ingredients; set aside. In small bowl, beat eggs until blended. Add sour cream, mustard, salt and pepper; blend well.

Sprinkle 1 cup of the cheese over bottom of baked shell. Spread filling mixture over cheese. Pour custard mixture over filling; sprinkle with remaining 1 cup cheese. Arrange pecan halves on top.

Bake at 400° F. for 30 to 35 minutes or until knife inserted in center comes out clean. Let stand 10 minutes before serving.

Yield: 8 servings

Nutrition Per Serving: Calories 400; Protein 18g; Carbohydrate 26g; Fat 25g; Sodium 650mg

Bacon Quiche Biscuit Cups

Doris Geist *Bethlehem, Pennsylvania*
Bake-Off® Contest 34, 1990

Enjoy this bacon and eggs breakfast combination at home or on the go.

1 (8-oz.) pkg. cream cheese, softened
2 tablespoons milk
2 eggs
2 oz. (1/2 cup) shredded Swiss cheese
2 tablespoons chopped green onions
1 (12-oz.) can refrigerated flaky biscuits
5 slices bacon, crisply cooked, finely crumbled

Heat oven to 375°F. Grease 10 muffin cups. In small bowl, beat cream cheese, milk and eggs on low speed until smooth. Stir in Swiss cheese and green onions; set aside.

Separate dough into 10 biscuits. Place 1 biscuit in each greased muffin cup; firmly press in bottom and up sides, forming 1/4-inch rim. Place half of bacon in bottom of dough-lined muffin cups. Spoon about 2 tablespoons of cheese mixture over bacon in cups.

Bake at 375°F. for 21 to 26 minutes or until filling is set and edges of biscuits are golden brown. Sprinkle each with remaining bacon; lightly press into filling. Remove from pan.

Yield: 10 servings

Nutrition Per Serving: Calories 240; Protein 8g; Carbohydrate 15g; Fat 16g; Sodium 500mg

Dotted Swiss and Spinach Quiche

Ellen Burr *Truro, Massachusetts*
Bake-Off® Contest 34, 1990

A generous sprinkling of toasted sesame seed provides the dots on this attractive two-layer quiche.

CRUST
1 refrigerated pie crust (from 15-oz. pkg.)
2 teaspoons honey mustard or sweet hot mustard
1 teaspoon half-and-half or milk
1 tablespoon sesame seed

FILLING
1 tablespoon margarine or butter
1/4 cup chopped green onions
1 cup frozen cut leaf spinach (from 1-lb. pkg.), thawed, well drained
1/2 cup finely chopped prosciutto ham
1/2 teaspoon dried thyme leaves
1/4 cup all-purpose flour
1/8 teaspoon white pepper or pepper
1/8 teaspoon mace or nutmeg
1 cup whipping cream
3 eggs
4 oz. (1 cup) shredded Swiss cheese
2 tablespoons sesame seed, toasted*

Prepare pie crust according to package directions for *one-crust filled pie* using 9-inch pie pan. Brush mustard over bottom of crust. Brush edge of crust with half-and-half. Press 1 tablespoon sesame seed onto crust edge. Place oven rack at lowest position. Heat oven to 400°F.

Melt margarine in medium skillet over medium heat. Add green onions; cook until crisp-tender, stirring frequently. Stir in spinach, ham and thyme. Reduce heat; simmer until spinach is thoroughly heated. Remove from heat. Spread spinach mixture over mustard in bottom of crust.

In small bowl using wire whisk, combine flour, white pepper, mace, whipping cream and eggs until well blended. Pour egg mixture over spinach layer. Sprinkle with cheese and 2 tablespoons toasted sesame seed.

Bake at 400°F. on lowest oven rack for 35 to 40 minutes or until knife inserted in center comes out clean and edges of crust are deep golden brown. Cover edge of pie crust with strips of foil after 15 to 20 minutes of baking to prevent excessive browning. Let stand 5 minutes before serving.

Yield: 8 servings

*Tip: To toast sesame seed, spread on baking pan; bake at 400°F. for 3 to 5 minutes or until light golden brown.

Nutrition Per Serving: Calories 380; Protein 12g; Carbohydrate 19g; Fat 28g; Sodium 340mg

Ellen Burr: Dotted Swiss and Spinach Quiche

So much of American cooking has international roots, but a sense of what the cooking of indigenous Americans was like can be gleaned from Cape Cod resident Ellen Burr's harvest. "I love to gather wild edibles: bolete mushrooms, dandelion greens, sassafras leaves (to dry for filé powder for gumbo). I pick lots of berries—blueberries, strawberries, shad berries, raspberries, blackberries, gooseberries, cranberries, elderberries, rosehips, rum cherries, and English blueberries—for desserts, for freezing, for preserves, and for jellies. I also dig clams, gather oysters and mussels, go crabbing and fish for trout and perch." Although Ellen has devoted so much of her keen attention to native foods, she also turns to foods with an international heritage for inspiration, and comes up with hits like her Dotted Swiss and Spinach Quiche.

Top to bottom: **Dotted Swiss and Spinach Quiche, Wild Rice and Ham Country Tart, page 81**

NINA REYES

When Nina Reyes came to the United States from Cuba to attend school in Pennsylvania, she knew right away that she had found her true homeland. When she returned to Cuba to marry, Nina decided, "I will never give up until I return to the United States and this time it will be for good. Because this is the country of my heart."

Nina and her husband did return to the United States and raised their family in Miami. She entered numerous recipes in cooking contests. "Every time I entered, my son would say 'Mom, don't you ever give up?' and I said 'I'll keep on trying, and we shall see who laughs last.' Many times I lay awake at night, mixing up things in my dreams. If I can't go to sleep—I cook in my mind. Sometimes I get up and write the idea down, so I don't forget."

One night Nina's dreams turned to what has been called Cuba's national dish, Picadillo. Picadillo is a special dish, almost like barbecue, or chili, in that every cook prides herself on her own version, with many variations. Some cooks use beef, eggs, wine, peppers, raisins or almonds; others wrap their picadillo with a yeast bread instead of a pastry crust.

"I used to use so many people for guinea pigs," recalls Nina about testing her Bake-Off® Contest recipes, "and everybody feels differently. This time I thought, 'I'm not going to ask anyone how they like it. I'm just going to make it and send it in.'" Nina says she quit making her picadillo for years "because my crusts were nothing to brag about," but when she discovered refrigerated pie crusts she started making it again. Now Nina's Chicken Picadillo Pie is on its way to becoming an American classic. "That makes me so happy," says Nina.

Chicken Picadillo Pie

Nina Reyes *Miami, Florida*
Bake-Off® Contest 32, 1986

Subtle, spicy flavors characterize a Cuban classic.

CRUST
1 (15-oz.) pkg. refrigerated pie crusts

Chicken Picadillo Pie

FILLING
3 tablespoons margarine or butter
1 tablespoon cornstarch
$1/8$ teaspoon ginger
Dash pepper
1 tablespoon prepared mustard
1 tablespoon soy sauce, if desired
1 tablespoon Worcestershire sauce
1 cup orange juice

2 tablespoons margarine or butter

2 large whole chicken breasts, skinned, boned, cut into bite-sized pieces
1 cup finely chopped onions
$1/4$ cup finely chopped green bell pepper
2 garlic cloves, minced
$1/2$ cup coconut
$1/4$ cup slivered almonds
$1/4$ cup raisins
$1/4$ to $1/2$ cup chopped pimiento-stuffed green olives
2 tablespoons capers, if desired

Prepare pie crust according to package directions for *two-crust pie* using 9-inch pie pan. Heat oven to 400° F.

Melt 1 tablespoon margarine in small saucepan. Blend in cornstarch, ginger, pepper, mustard, soy sauce and Worcestershire sauce. Gradually add orange juice. Bring to a boil; cook until mixture thickens, stirring constantly. Set aside.

Melt 2 tablespoons margarine in large skillet. Cook chicken, onions, bell pepper and garlic over medium heat until chicken is completely cooked. Stir in coconut, almonds, raisins, olives, capers and the orange sauce. Continue to cook until thoroughly heated, stirring occasionally. Spoon into pie crust-lined pan. Top with second crust and flute; cut slits in several places.

Bake at 400° F. for 30 to 40 minutes or until golden brown. Cover edge of crust with strips of foil after 15 to 20 minutes of baking to prevent excessive browning. Let stand 5 minutes before serving.

Yield: 8 servings

Nutrition Per Serving: Calories 470; Protein 21g; Carbohydrate 37g; Fat 26g; Sodium 680mg

Italian Cheese Rustica Pie

Gloria T. Bove *Bethlehem, Pennsylvania*
Bake-Off® Contest 32, 1986 Prize Winner

Pillsbury Refrigerated Pie Crusts were introduced in the thirty-second Bake-Off® Contest. This is one of the creative recipes submitted. For an extraordinary luncheon, serve this cheesy pie with a refreshing fruit salad.

1 (15-oz.) pkg. refrigerated pie crusts
3 eggs
1 cup cubed cooked ham
1 cup ricotta or small-curd cottage cheese
4 oz. (1 cup) shredded mozzarella cheese
4 oz. (1 cup) cubed provolone or Swiss cheese
4 tablespoons grated Parmesan cheese
1 tablespoon finely chopped fresh parsley or 1/2 teaspoon dried parsley flakes
1/4 teaspoon dried oregano leaves
Dash pepper
Beaten egg, if desired

Prepare pie crust according to package directions for *two-crust pie* using 9-inch pie pan. Place oven rack at lowest position. Heat oven to 375° F.

In large bowl, slightly beat 3 eggs. Add ham, ricotta cheese, mozzarella cheese, provolone cheese, 3 tablespoons of the Parmesan cheese, parsley, oregano and pepper; blend well. Spoon filling mixture into crust-lined pan. Top with second crust; seal edges and flute. Cut slits in crust in several places. Brush beaten egg over crust. Sprinkle with remaining 1 tablespoon Parmesan cheese. Bake at 375° F. on lowest oven rack for 50 to 60 minutes or until golden brown. Cover edge of crust with strips of foil after 15 to 20 minutes of baking if necessary to prevent excessive browning. Let stand 10 minutes before serving.

Yield: 8 servings

Nutrition Per Serving: Calories 450; Protein 20g; Carbohydrate 27g; Fat 29g; Sodium 860mg

Bean Picadillo Tortillas

Gilbert J. Soucy *Lowell, Massachusetts*
Bake-Off® Contest 35, 1992 Prize Winner

These Spanish-inspired tortillas contain many favorite flavors of picadillo stew, such as tomato, raisins, onions and olives.

6 (6- or 8-inch) corn tortillas or 8-inch flour tortillas

PICADILLO
2 tablespoons margarine or butter
1/2 cup finely chopped onion
1 (15.5-oz.) can light red kidney beans, drained, slightly mashed
1 (15.5-oz.) can pinto beans, drained, slightly mashed
1/2 cup picante salsa
1 teaspoon chili powder
1/4 teaspoon cumin
Dash cinnamon
1/4 cup raisins

SALSA
1 1/2 cups chunky-style salsa
1 cup frozen whole kernel corn (from 1-lb. pkg.), thawed, drained

GARNISH
6 pitted ripe olives, sliced
1 tomato, cut into 6 wedges

Heat oven to 350° F. Wrap tortillas in foil; heat at 350° F. for 15 minutes. Meanwhile, melt margarine in large skillet over medium heat. Add onion; cook and stir until tender, about 5 minutes. Stir in all remaining picadillo ingredients. Bring to a boil. Reduce heat to low; cover and simmer 12 minutes or until thoroughly heated, stirring occasionally.

In small saucepan, combine salsa ingredients; bring to a boil. Reduce heat to low; cover and simmer 10 minutes or until thoroughly heated, stirring occasionally.

To serve, spread $^1/_2$ cup hot picadillo on each tortilla to within 1 inch of edges; roll up, enclosing filling. Top with hot salsa mixture. Garnish with sliced ripe olives and tomato wedges.

Yield: 6 servings

Nutrition Per Serving: Calories 290; Protein 11g; Carbohydrate 54g; Fat 7g; Sodium 1170mg

Gilbert (Gil) Soucy: Bean Picadillo Tortillas

A good number of the men who come to the Bake-Off® Contest do so from the army, or from a similar situation in which they've been cooking for their coworkers. Firefighter Gil Soucy works "saving lives, saving homes, saving and helping my brother firefighters." But when times are quiet, Gil doesn't let them stay that way, spicing things up by cooking for the firemen at his station and trying new dishes on them. "It makes for great fun. One time I made some venison, telling them it was steak. It came out good, and I never told them what it was." His fellow firefighters may not always appreciate Gil's mischief, but they always come running when a lively dish like Bean Picadillo Tortillas is served.

Enchilada-Style Chicken Pie

Nancy Jo Mathison *Chico, California*
Bake-Off® Contest 32, 1986 Prize Winner

Contemporary microwave preparation and a refrigerated pie crust are featured in this delicious Mexican-flavored pie. A microwave cooking category at the thirty-second Bake-Off® Contest brought in this Mexican-inspired main dish pie. The entire recipe, from refrigerated pie crust to spicy chicken filling, is quickly prepared in the microwave.

CRUST
1 **refrigerated pie crust (from 15-oz. pkg.)**
1 **egg**
1 **teaspoon Worcestershire sauce**

FILLING
1 **cup chopped onions**
1 **(5-oz.) can chunk chicken, drained, flaked, or 1 cup cubed cooked chicken**
1 **(4.5-oz.) can chopped green chiles, well drained**
$^3/_4$ **cup sliced ripe olives, drained**
4 **oz. (1 cup) shredded Monterey Jack or Cheddar cheese***
$^1/_2$ **cup milk**
3 **eggs**
$^1/_2$ **teaspoon salt, if desired**
$^1/_4$ **teaspoon cumin**
$^1/_8$ **teaspoon garlic powder**
$^1/_8$ **teaspoon pepper**
3 **drops hot pepper sauce**

TOPPINGS
Salsa, dairy sour cream, avocado slices and parsley, if desired

Microwave Directions: Prepare pie crust according to package directions for *one-crust baked shell* using 9-inch microwave-safe pie pan or 10-inch microwave-safe tart pan. Flute, if desired. Generously prick crust with fork.

In medium bowl, combine 1 egg and Worcestershire sauce; blend well. Brush lightly over pie crust. (Reserve any remaining egg mixture for filling.) Microwave on HIGH for 6 to 8 minutes, rotating pan $^1/_2$ turn every 2 minutes. Crust is done when surface appears dry and flaky.

Place onions in small microwave-safe bowl. Cover with microwave-safe plastic wrap. Microwave on HIGH for 3 minutes or until crisp-tender. Drain well.

To assemble pie, layer chicken, cooked onions, chiles, olives and cheese in cooked pie shell. In medium bowl, combine milk, 3 eggs, salt, cumin, garlic powder, pepper, hot pepper sauce and any remaining egg mixture; blend well. Pour mixture slowly over cheese.

Microwave on HIGH for 8 to 11 minutes or until knife inserted near center comes out clean, rotating pan once halfway through cooking. Let stand on flat surface 5 minutes before serving. Cut into wedges to serve; top each serving with salsa, sour cream, avocado slice and parsley.

Yield: 8 servings

***Tip:** A colby-Monterey Jack cheese blend can be substituted for Monterey Jack or Cheddar cheese.

Nutrition Per Serving: Calories 340; Protein 14g; Carbohydrate 20g; Fat 22g; Sodium 600mg

Italian Country Loaf Rustica

Miranda Desantis *East Windsor, New Jersey*
Bake-Off® Contest 33, 1988 Prize Winner

Savory Italian sausage, cheese and red pepper are baked inside batter bread to make a hearty, attractive main dish. Surprisingly easy to prepare, it is sliced into wedges to serve.

FILLING
1 lb. sweet Italian sausage
1/2 cup chopped onion
2 to 4 garlic cloves, minced
8 oz. (2 cups) cubed
   mozzarella cheese
1 (7-oz.) jar mild roasted red
   peppers, drained, chopped*

BREAD
1 1/2 cups all-purpose flour
1/2 cup whole wheat flour
1/2 cup yellow cornmeal
1 tablespoon sugar
1/2 teaspoon salt
1 pkg. fast-acting dry yeast
1 1/4 cups water, heated to
   120 to 130° F.
2 teaspoons margarine or
   butter, softened
1 egg, beaten
2 to 3 teaspoons sesame seed

If sausage comes in casing, remove casing; break up. In large skillet, brown sausage, onion and garlic.** Drain; set aside.

   For the bread, in large bowl, combine 1/2 cup of the all-purpose flour, whole wheat flour, cornmeal, sugar, salt and yeast; blend well. Stir in hot water and margarine; mix well. Stir in remaining 1 cup all-purpose flour to form a stiff batter. Cover; let rest 10 minutes.

Grease 9- or 10-inch springform pan. Stir down dough. Spread about 2/3 of dough in bottom and 2 inches up sides of greased pan. Add cheese and peppers to meat mixture; spoon over dough. Gently pull dough on sides over meat mixture. Drop tablespoonfuls of remaining dough over filling. With back of spoon or buttered fingers, carefully spread to cover. (Top will appear rough.) Cover loosely with plastic wrap and cloth towel. Let rise in warm place (80 to 85° F.) until light, 20 to 30 minutes.

   Heat oven to 400° F. Brush top of dough with beaten egg; sprinkle with sesame seed. Bake at 400° F. for 25 to 35 minutes or until bread begins to pull away from sides of pan and edges are deep golden brown. Cool 5 minutes. Loosen edges with knife; remove sides of pan. To serve, cut into wedges. Store in refrigerator.

Yield: 8 servings

*Tips: Two medium chopped red bell peppers (1 1/4 cups) can be substituted for roasted red peppers.

   **If using chopped red bell peppers, cook with sausage, onion and garlic. Continue as directed above.

High Altitude—Above 3,500 feet: No change.

Nutrition Per Serving: Calories 350; Protein 19g; Carbohydrate 35g; Fat 15g; Sodium 550mg

Italian Zucchini Crescent Pie

Millicent Caplan *Tamarac, Florida*
Bake-Off® Contest 29, 1980 Grand Prize Winner

This fresh-from-the-garden pie is a wonderful main dish, or cut it into small slices to serve as an appetizer.

4 cups thinly sliced zucchini
1 cup chopped onions
2 tablespoons margarine or
   butter
2 tablespoons dried parsley
   flakes
1/2 teaspoon salt
1/2 teaspoon pepper
1/4 teaspoon garlic powder
1/4 teaspoon dried basil leaves
1/4 teaspoon dried oregano
   leaves
2 eggs, well beaten
8 oz. (2 cups) shredded
   Muenster or mozzarella
   cheese
1 (8-oz.) can refrigerated
   crescent dinner rolls
2 teaspoons prepared mustard

Heat oven to 375° F. In large skillet over medium-high heat, cook zucchini and onions in margarine until tender, about 8 minutes. Stir in parsley flakes, salt, pepper, garlic powder, basil and oregano. In large bowl, combine eggs and cheese; mix well. Stir in cooked vegetable mixture.

   Separate dough into 8 triangles. Place in ungreased 10-inch pie pan, 12×8-inch (2-quart) baking dish or 11-inch quiche pan; press over bottom and up sides to form

Italian Zucchini Crescent Pie

crust.* Firmly press perforations to seal. Spread crust with mustard. Pour egg mixture evenly into crust-lined pan.

Bake at 375°F. for 18 to 22 minutes or until knife inserted near center comes out clean.** Let stand 10 minutes before serving.

Yield: 6 servings

*Tips: If using 12×8-inch (2-quart) baking dish, unroll dough into 2 long rectangles; press over bottom and 1 inch up sides to form crust. Firmly press perforations to seal. Continue as directed above.

**Cover edge of crust with strips of foil during last 10 minutes of baking if necessary to prevent excessive browning.

Nutrition Per Serving: Calories 360; Protein 15g; Carbohydrate 21g; Fat 25g; Sodium 820mg

Gorgonzola and Onion Pie

Roberta Mintz Levine *Pittsburgh, Pennsylvania*
Bake-Off® Contest 35, 1992 Prize Winner

Sweet onions add special flavor to this pie. Use any variety of sweet onions, such as Spanish, Bermuda, Vidalia or Walla Walla.

CRUST
1 refrigerated pie crust (from 15-oz. pkg.)
1 tablespoon grated Parmesan cheese

FILLING
2 tablespoons olive oil or vegetable oil
2 1/3 cups coarsely chopped sweet onions

1 tablespoon olive oil or vegetable oil
2 garlic cloves, minced
1 (28-oz.) can whole tomatoes, drained, quartered
1/2 teaspoon dried oregano leaves
1/4 teaspoon salt
1/8 teaspoon pepper
4 oz. (1 cup) shredded mozzarella cheese
4 oz. (1 cup) crumbled gorgonzola or blue cheese

Heat oven to 450°F. Prepare pie crust according to package directions for *one-crust baked shell* using 9-inch pie pan. Bake at 450°F. for 9 to 11 minutes or until lightly browned. Sprinkle with Parmesan cheese; set aside.

Reduce oven temperature to 425°F. Heat 2 tablespoons oil in large skillet over medium-low heat until hot. Add onions; cook and stir until onions are soft and golden, about 15 minutes.

Heat 1 tablespoon oil in large saucepan over medium heat until hot. Add garlic; cook and stir until garlic is softened. Stir in tomatoes, oregano, salt and pepper. Cook for 10 minutes or until slightly thickened, stirring occasionally. Spoon tomato mixture into partially baked shell; spoon onion mixture over tomatoes. Sprinkle with mozzarella and gorgonzola cheeses.

Bake at 425°F. for 10 to 20 minutes or until crust is golden brown. Cover edge of pie crust with strips of foil after 15 to 20 minutes of baking to prevent excessive browning. Let stand 10 minutes before serving.

Yield: 8 servings

Nutrition Per Serving: Calories 290; Protein 9g; Carbohydrate 19g; Fat 19g; Sodium 390mg

Italian-Style Fish and Vegetables

Louise Bobzin *Park, Florida*
Bake-Off® Contest 33, 1988

Most catfish are freshwater fish, and channel catfish are considered to be the best eating. They are low in fat and mild in flavor.

2 tablespoons olive oil or vegetable oil
1 medium onion, sliced
1 (2.5-oz.) jar sliced mushrooms, drained
1/2 teaspoon dried basil leaves
1/2 teaspoon fennel seed

Roberta Mintz Levine: Gorgonzola and Onion Pie

More and more people are becoming vegetarians— both for reasons of health and concern for the environment— and increasingly hosts want to accommodate their vegetarian guests without cooking things that are less than thrilling. "As a vegetarian since 1971," Roberta Mintz Levine says, "I have enjoyed coming up with dinner menus that include no meat, but do not leave meat eaters feeling deprived. I like strong-flavored dishes—hence the gorgonzola and onions—and often season additionally with chili powder or cayenne pepper."

2 cups frozen mixed
   vegetables (from 1-lb. pkg.)
1¹/₂ lb. fresh or frozen catfish,
   orange roughy or sole fillets,
   thawed
¹/₄ teaspoon salt
¹/₄ teaspoon pepper
2 medium tomatoes, sliced
¹/₃ cup grated Parmesan
   cheese

Heat oil in large skillet over
medium heat. Add onion, mushrooms, basil and fennel seed; cook
4 minutes or until onion is tender.
Stir in frozen vegetables. Place fish
over vegetables; sprinkle with salt
and pepper. Arrange tomato slices
over fish. Reduce heat to low;
cover and cook 12 to 16 minutes or
until fish flakes easily with fork.
Remove from heat; sprinkle with
Parmesan cheese. Cover; let stand
about 3 minutes or until Parmesan
cheese is melted.

Yield: 6 servings

Nutrition Per Serving: Calories 240;
Protein 25g; Carbohydrate 11g; Fat 10g;
Sodium 400mg

Crab Meat Salad Pie

Evelyn Robinson *Bellevue, Washington*
Bake-Off® Contest 11, 1959

*When this tempting pie was a finalist,
the filling was spooned into a made-
from-scratch pie shell. In this updated
version, the idea remains the same but
it all goes together in a flash using the
convenience of a refrigerated pie crust.*

Hardware: It's Not Just for Carpenters Anymore

Everyone knows that cooks are handy—but some are downright creative in
finding the perfect kitchen utensil for every task.

• A teenage contestant from Texas brought a hammer from home, and, to the
  amazement of all, shattered mints on her range top with mighty smacks.
  (Good thing her neighbors weren't baking soufflés!)

• In 1980, a man submitted a bread recipe—but he wasn't content with a
  mixer, blender, food processor or wooden spoon. He specified that a drill
  with a ³/₈-inch bit should be used to mix the bread.

• One exacting finalist removed a lucky charm, a carpenter's level, from her
  apron pocket—and carefully sighted her cake along it before consigning
  it to the oven.

CRUST
1 refrigerated pie crust (from
   15-oz. pkg.)

FILLING
³/₄ cup dry bread crumbs
1 cup chopped celery
1 tablespoon finely chopped
   onion
1 tablespoon finely chopped
   green bell pepper
1 tablespoon lemon juice
1 (6-oz.) can crab meat,
   drained
³/₄ to 1 cup mayonnaise or
   salad dressing
2 oz. (¹/₂ cup) shredded
   Cheddar cheese

Heat oven to 450°F. Prepare and
bake pie crust according to package
directions for *one-crust baked shell*
using 9-inch pie pan. Bake at
450°F. for 9 to 11 minutes or until
light golden brown. Cool completely.
   Reserve 2 tablespoons of the
bread crumbs. In large bowl, combine remaining bread crumbs, celery, onion, bell pepper, lemon juice
and crab meat; toss lightly. Add
enough mayonnaise for desired
consistency; mix well. Spoon into
cooled baked shell. Sprinkle with
reserved 2 tablespoons bread
crumbs and cheese. Bake at
450°F. for 8 to 10 minutes or until
cheese is melted.

Yield: 6 servings

Nutrition Per Serving: Calories 390;
Protein 10g; Carbohydrate 28g; Fat 26g;
Sodium 600mg

Black Bean Mexican Pizza

David Schmitt *Phoenix, Arizona*
Bake-Off® Contest 35, 1992 Prize Winner

Also called turtle beans, black beans have long been a staple in Mexico, Central and South America, the Caribbean and the Southern United States. They have black skin, cream-colored flesh and a sweet flavor that is complemented by a variety of seasonings.

1 (10-oz.) can refrigerated
   pizza crust

TOPPING
1 (15-oz.) can black beans,
   drained, rinsed
3 tablespoons olive oil or
   vegetable oil
2 tablespoons chopped fresh
   cilantro or parsley
1 teaspoon cumin
1 teaspoon hot pepper sauce
1/2 teaspoon minced garlic
4 oz. (1 cup) shredded
   Monterey Jack cheese
4 oz. (1 cup) shredded
   Cheddar cheese

1 (21/4-oz.) can sliced ripe
   olives, drained
1/2 cup diced red bell pepper
1/4 cup sliced green onions
1/2 cup dairy sour cream
1/4 cup green taco sauce or
   taco sauce
1 cup chunky-style salsa

Heat oven to 425° F. Lightly grease 12-inch pizza pan or 13×9-inch pan. Unroll dough and place in greased pan; starting at center, press out with hands. Bake at 425° F. for 7 to 10 minutes or until light golden brown.

In food processor bowl with metal blade, combine black beans, oil, cilantro, cumin, hot pepper sauce and garlic; process until smooth, frequently scraping down sides of bowl.* Spread bean mixture over partially baked crust. Sprinkle with cheeses, olives, bell pepper and green onions.

Bake at 425° F. for 7 to 12 minutes or until crust is deep golden brown and cheese is melted. In small bowl, combine sour cream and taco sauce; blend well. Serve pizza with sour cream mixture and salsa.

Yield: 8 servings

*Tip: Bean mixture can be mashed with fork or potato masher, but it will not be as smooth.

Nutrition Per Serving: Calories 340; Protein 14g; Carbohydrate 29g; Fat 19g; Sodium 830mg

Chicken Fajita Pizza

Elizabeth Daniels *Kula, Maui, Hawaii*
Bake-Off® Contest 34, 1990

Salsa comes in varying degrees of hotness. For a "hotter" pizza, use the variety you prefer.

1 (10-oz.) can refrigerated
   pizza crust
1 tablespoon olive oil or
   vegetable oil
4 boneless, skinless chicken
   breast halves, cut into thin,
   bite-sized strips
1 to 2 teaspoons chili powder
1/2 to 1 teaspoon salt
1/2 teaspoon garlic powder
1 cup thinly sliced onions
1 cup green or red bell pepper
   strips (2×1/4-inch)
1/2 cup mild picante salsa
8 oz. (2 cups) shredded
   Monterey Jack cheese

Heat oven to 425° F. Spray 12-inch pizza pan or 13×9-inch pan with nonstick cooking spray. Unroll dough; place in sprayed pan. Starting at center, press out with hands. Bake at 425° F. for 7 to 9 minutes or until very light golden brown.

David Schmitt: Black Bean Mexican Pizza

"A host is like a general: It takes a mishap to reveal his genius." So said the Roman poet Horace, even before there was pasta to have misadventures with. However, most hosts would prefer not to be tested. "My specialty is home-made pasta," David Schmitt says, "but the first time I made it, it came out as hard as a rock. It never got soft. But I served it anyway because we had company and because it was the main course. Everyone ate it, and never complained." The genius in David's evening? Surrounding himself with friends and loved ones, who can be depended upon to smile even when they sample his less-than-perfect creations.

Chicken Fajita Pizza

Meanwhile, heat oil in large skillet over medium-high heat until hot. Add chicken; sprinkle with chili powder, salt and garlic powder. Cook and stir 3 to 5 minutes or until lightly browned. Add onions and bell pepper strips; cook and stir an additional 2 to 3 minutes or until chicken is no longer pink and vegetables are crisp-tender.

Remove crust from oven. Spoon chicken mixture evenly over partially baked crust. Spoon salsa over chicken. Sprinkle with cheese.

Return to oven; bake an additional 14 to 18 minutes or until crust is golden brown.

Yield: 8 servings

Nutrition Per Serving: Calories 290; Protein 24g; Carbohydrate 20g; Fat 13g; Sodium 830mg

Hearty Reuben Pizza

Marie Mickelson *Columbia Heights, Minnesota*
Bake-Off® Contest 34, 1990 Prize Winner

Seven pizzas inspired by cuisines from around the world were among the 100 Bake-Off® finalists in 1990. This was one that also won a cash prize. Reuben sandwich lovers will agree it was an excellent choice.

1 (10-oz.) can refrigerated pizza crust
1 cup sliced onions
1 to 2 tablespoons margarine or butter
¹/₂ cup salad dressing or mayonnaise
4¹/₂ teaspoons Dijon or Viennese mustard

8 oz. (2 cups) shredded Swiss cheese
8 oz. thinly sliced deli corned beef
1 cup sauerkraut, drained, squeezed dry
¹/₂ to 1 teaspoon caraway seed
1 dill pickle, cut crosswise into thin slices

Heat oven to 425°F. Lightly grease 12-inch pizza pan or 13×9-inch pan. Unroll dough; place in greased pan. Starting at center, press out with hands. Bake at 425°F. for 9 to 12 minutes or until golden brown.

In large skillet, cook onions in margarine until tender. In small bowl, combine salad dressing and mustard; blend well. Spread ¹/₄ cup dressing mixture over partially baked crust. Sprinkle with ¹/₂ cup of the Swiss cheese. Overlap corned beef slices over cheese and

dressing, covering completely. Spread remaining dressing mixture over corned beef. Top evenly with cooked onion slices, sauerkraut and remaining 1¹/₂ cups Swiss cheese. Sprinkle with caraway seed. Bake at 425°F. for an additional 10 minutes or until thoroughly heated and cheese is melted. Garnish with dill pickle slices.

Yield: 8 servings

Nutrition Per Serving: Calories 360; Protein 17g; Carbohydrate 23g; Fat 22g; Sodium 1040mg

Teresa Hannan Smith: Deluxe Turkey Club Pizza

Cooks tend to be a generous lot, and Teresa Hannan Smith makes a point of sharing the bounty of her life not just with guests at her table but with four-legged folk wherever she is. "I carry three kinds of dog and cat food in my car and feed strays everywhere I go." While she never gets the raves from her animal guests that she got from the Bake-Off® Contest judges, Teresa considers cats and dogs among the most gratifying of her diners.

Deluxe Turkey Club Pizza

Teresa Hannan Smith *Sacramento, California*
Bake-Off® Contest 35, 1992 Prize Winner

These classic sandwich ingredients also make an exceptionally good pizza topping.

1 (10-oz.) can refrigerated pizza crust
2 teaspoons sesame seed

TOPPING
¹/₄ cup reduced-calorie mayonnaise or regular mayonnaise
1 teaspoon grated lemon peel
4 oz. (1 cup) shredded Monterey Jack cheese
1 tablespoon thinly sliced fresh basil or 1 teaspoon dried basil leaves
4 oz. deli turkey breast slices, cut into 1-inch strips
6 slices bacon, cut into 1-inch pieces, cooked
2 small Italian plum tomatoes or 1 small tomato, thinly sliced

2 oz. (¹/₂ cup) shredded Swiss
  cheese
Fresh basil leaves

Heat oven to 425° F. Lightly grease
12-inch pizza pan or 13×9-inch
pan. Unroll dough and place in
greased pan; starting at center,
press out with hands. Sprinkle
sesame seed evenly over dough.
Bake at 425° F. for 10 to 12 minutes or until crust is light golden
brown.

Meanwhile, in small bowl, combine mayonnaise and lemon peel;
blend well. Spread mixture over
partially baked crust. Top with
Monterey Jack cheese, 1 tablespoon basil, turkey strips, cooked
bacon and tomatoes. Sprinkle with
Swiss cheese. Bake at 425° F. for 7
to 9 minutes or until crust is
golden brown and cheese is
melted. Garnish with fresh basil
leaves.

Yield: 8 servings

Nutrition Per Serving: Calories 220;
Protein 13g; Carbohydrate 18g; Fat 13g;
Sodium 550mg

Hearty Mexican Pizza

Linda Loda *Elk Grove Village, Illinois*
Bake-Off® Contest 33, 1988

*Tender crust and irresistible Mexican
toppings are a winning combination
in this south-of-the-border pizza.*

CRUST
1 tablespoon cornmeal
1 to 1¹/₂ cups all-purpose flour
1 cup whole wheat flour
2 teaspoons baking powder
¹/₂ teaspoon salt

More Celebrity Notes

Academy Award–winning Best Actresses Greer Garson (1942, *Mrs.
Miniver*) and Helen Hayes (1932, *The Sin of Madelon Claudet*) smiled
as other women received what some have called the Oscars of the kitchen in
1958 and 1959. Movie stars Irene Dunne, of the classic *My Favorite Wife*
(with Cary Grant), and Jeanette MacDonald, best known for her musical films
with Nelson Eddy (*Love Me Tonight*), floated through the crowds in the 1950s
too, delighted to pose with the finalists who were the stars of their own
kitchens. Television hosts have always paid an important role in the Bake-
Off® Contest. Art Linkletter's antics provided thousands of wonderful Bake-
Off® moments. Later, Bob Barker hosted eleven ceremonies. Recent years
have seen television personalities Gary Collins, Willard Scott and Alex
Trebek leading the festivities. Celebrities and diamond-clad stars aside, the
joy of the Bake-Off® contestants always shines the brightest.

³/₄ **cup beer, room**
  temperature
¹/₄ **cup oil**

TOPPING
1 (16-oz.) can refried beans
1 lb. ground beef
¹/₃ **cup chopped onion**
1 (8-oz.) can tomato sauce
**1 (4.5-oz.) can chopped green
  chiles, undrained**
**8 oz. (2 cups) shredded
  Cheddar, Monterey Jack or
  mozzarella cheese**
**1 medium red or green bell
  pepper, cut into strips**
**3 to 4 pitted ripe olives,
  sliced, if desired**

Dairy sour cream, if desired
**Taco sauce or picante salsa, if
  desired**

Heat oven to 400° F. Grease
14-inch pizza pan or 15×10×1-
inch baking pan; sprinkle with
cornmeal. In large bowl, combine
¹/₂ cup of the all-purpose flour,
whole wheat flour, baking powder,
salt, beer and oil; mix well. By

hand, stir in ¹/₄ to ¹/₂ cup all-
purpose flour to form a stiff dough.
On floured surface, knead in
remaining all-purpose flour until
dough is smooth and elastic, 2 to
3 minutes. On lightly floured surface, roll dough to 14-inch circle.
Place over cornmeal in greased
pan; press dough to fit pan evenly.

Spread refried beans over
dough. In large skillet, brown
ground beef until thoroughly
cooked; drain well. Add onion,
tomato sauce and green chiles;
blend well. Spoon meat mixture
over refried beans; top with cheese,
bell pepper and olives. Bake at
400° F. for 25 to 35 minutes or
until crust is light golden brown.
Let stand 5 minutes before serving.
Garnish with sour cream or taco
sauce.

Yield: 8 servings

High Altitude—Above 3,500 feet: No
change.

Nutrition Per Serving: Calories 560; Protein 25g;
Carbohydrate 42g; Fat 31g; Sodium 1100mg

Polish Pizza

Norma Eckhoff *Cleveland, Ohio*
Bake-Off® Contest 36, 1994 Prize Winner

Kielbasa, a smoked pork sausage, is sometimes called Polish sausage. It is delicious in this hearty pizza.

CRUST
1 tablespoon cornmeal or caraway seed
1 (10-oz.) can refrigerated pizza crust
4 oz. (1 cup) shredded Swiss cheese

TOPPING
1/2 cup chopped onion
3 slices bacon, cut into 1/2-inch pieces
1 (16-oz.) jar or can sauerkraut, well drained
1 tablespoon caraway seed
1 (4.5-oz.) jar sliced mushrooms, well drained
6 oz. (1 1/2 cups) shredded Swiss cheese
1/2 lb. Polish kielbasa sausage, cut into 1/8-inch slices
1 tablespoon chopped fresh parsley or 1 teaspoon dried parsley flakes

Heat oven to 425° F. Lightly grease 13×9-inch pan or 12-inch pizza pan; sprinkle with cornmeal. Unroll dough and place in greased pan; starting at center, press out with hands. Sprinkle with 1 cup cheese. Bake at 425° F. for 5 to 8 minutes or until light golden brown.

Meanwhile, in medium saucepan over medium-high heat, cook onion and bacon until light brown, stirring frequently. Reduce heat to low. Add sauerkraut and 1 tablespoon caraway seed; simmer 3 minutes or until thoroughly heated. Stir in mushrooms. Spread over partially baked crust. Sprinkle with 1 1/2 cups cheese. Top with sausage slices; sprinkle with parsley.

Bake at 425° F. for 12 to 15 minutes or until edges of crust are deep golden brown and cheese is melted.

Yield: 8 servings

Nutrition Per Serving: Calories 350; Protein 19g; Carbohydrate 22g; Fat 20g; Sodium 950mg

Hungry Boys' Casserole

Mira Walilko *Detroit, Michigan*
Bake-Off® Contest 15, 1963 Grand Prize Winner

This hearty casserole was inspired by the contestant's three hungry boys.

CASSEROLE
1 1/2 lb. ground beef
1 cup chopped celery
1/2 cup chopped onion
1/2 cup chopped green bell pepper
1 garlic clove, minced
1 (6-oz.) can tomato paste
3/4 cup water
1 teaspoon paprika
1/2 teaspoon salt
1 (16-oz.) can pork and beans or baked beans, undrained
1 (15-oz.) can garbanzo beans, drained*

BISCUITS
1 1/2 cups all-purpose flour
2 teaspoons baking powder
1/2 teaspoon salt
1/4 cup margarine or butter
1/2 to 3/4 cup milk
2 tablespoons sliced stuffed green olives
1 tablespoon slivered almonds

In large skillet, combine ground beef, celery, onion, bell pepper and garlic. Cook over medium-high heat until beef is thoroughly cooked and vegetables are tender; drain. Reduce heat to low. Stir in tomato paste, water, paprika and 1/2 teaspoon salt. Add pork and beans and garbanzo beans; simmer while preparing biscuits, stirring occasionally.

Heat oven to 425° F. In large

Norma Eckhoff: Polish Pizza

P oland and Italy have at least a few things in common: a love of food, a bounty of descendants in the United States and now Norma Eckhoff's Polish Pizza. "All of my grandparents were from Poland," says Norma. "We still practice many Polish customs, especially those pertaining to food." Norma was a volunteer for a group that taught English to newcomers to America. "It felt wonderful to be able to 'return the favor' that was done for my grandparents so many years ago."

bowl, combine flour, baking powder and ¹/₂ teaspoon salt; mix well. Using pastry blender or fork, cut in margarine until mixture resembles coarse crumbs. Gradually stir in enough milk until mixture leaves sides of bowl and forms a soft, moist dough. On floured surface, gently knead dough 8 times. Roll dough to ¹/₄-inch thickness; cut with floured 2¹/₂-inch doughnut cutter. Reroll dough to cut additional biscuits.

Hungry Boys' Casserole

Reserve dough centers.

Reserve ¹/₂ cup of hot meat mixture. Pour remaining hot meat mixture into ungreased 13×9-inch (3-quart) baking dish. Arrange biscuits without centers over hot meat mixture. Stir olives and almonds into reserved ¹/₂ cup meat mixture; spoon into center of each biscuit. Top each with biscuit centers.

Bake at 425° F. for 15 to 25 minutes or until biscuits are golden brown.

Yield: 8 servings

*Tips: One 15-oz. can lima beans, drained, can be substituted for the garbanzo beans.

To make ahead, cook meat mixture; refrigerate. Just before serving, reheat meat mixture; top with biscuits. Bake as directed above.

High Altitude—Above 3,500 feet: No change.

Nutrition Per Serving: Calories 470; Protein 23g; Carbohydrate 44g; Fat 22g; Sodium 1000mg

Oriental Stir-Fry Pizza

Barbara Benton *Ormond Beach, Florida*
Bake-Off® Contest 35, 1992

You'll like the sweet and spicy flavor in this zesty oriental-style pizza. It's a real change of pace!

1 (10-oz.) can refrigerated pizza crust

CHICKEN
2 whole chicken breasts, skinned, boned, cut into 2×1/4-inch strips
1/2 cup purchased zesty Italian salad dressing

SAUCE
1/3 cup plum jelly or apricot preserves
1/4 cup chili sauce
2 tablespoons white wine or chicken broth
1 teaspoon lemon juice
1/2 teaspoon allspice
1/4 teaspoon instant minced onion

TOPPING
1 cup sliced fresh mushrooms
1 medium green bell pepper, cut into 1/4-inch strips
1 medium onion, halved top to bottom, cut into 1/4-inch strips
4 oz. (1 cup) shredded Monterey Jack cheese with jalapeño peppers
4 oz. (1 cup) shredded mozzarella cheese

Heat oven to 425° F. Lightly grease 15×10×1-inch baking pan. Unroll dough and place in greased pan; starting at center, press out with hands. Bake at 425° F. for 7 to 10 minutes or until light golden brown.

In medium bowl, combine chicken and Italian dressing; set aside. In small saucepan, combine all sauce ingredients. Bring to a boil. Reduce heat to medium; simmer 5 minutes, stirring frequently. Spread sauce on partially baked crust to within 1 inch of edges.

Drain chicken; discard marinade. In large skillet over medium-high heat, cook and stir chicken for 3 minutes. Add mushrooms, bell pepper and onion; cook and stir until vegetables are crisp-tender and chicken is no longer pink, 3 to 5 minutes. Drain well. Spread chicken mixture over sauce; sprinkle with cheeses. Bake at 425° F. for 7 to 12 minutes or until crust is golden brown and cheese is melted.

Yield: 8 servings

Nutrition Per Serving: Calories 320; Protein 25g; Carbohydrate 31g; Fat 11g; Sodium 510mg

Barbara Benton: Oriental Stir-Fry Pizza

Some old saws never die. "I am living proof that the best way to a man's heart is his stomach," says Barbara Benton. "After our first blind date, Don called the very next evening—a Friday night—to ask me out over the weekend. I was going out of town, so he asked me for that same night. I couldn't because I was right in the middle of making cinnamon rolls. 'Homemade cinnamon rolls?' 'Yes,' I said, 'and you're welcome to come over and try some.' So he did, and to this day he tells everyone that he was already attracted to me, but after tasting the cinnamon rolls he knew it could be a lot more. A year and a half later we were married." As the French say, "without bread, love is nothing."

Spinach Pierogi Pizza

Rebecca Jo Verdone *Greensburg, Pennsylvania*
Bake-Off® Contest 36, 1994 Prize Winner

The stuffed noodle dumplings called pierogi are a Polish specialty. Pizzerias in Becky Verdone's area use the same stuffing ingredients on Pierogi Pizza. After enjoying commercial ones, she decided to create her own, combining two popular toppings, spinach and mashed potatoes.

1 (10-oz.) can refrigerated pizza crust
1 (9-oz.) pkg. frozen spinach in a pouch, thawed, squeezed to drain
1/2 cup chopped onion

2 tablespoons butter or
    margarine
1 1/2 cups mashed potatoes
2 tablespoons oil
1/2 teaspoon garlic salt
4 oz. (1 cup) shredded
    mozzarella cheese
2 oz. (1/2 cup) shredded
    Cheddar cheese
1 small onion, sliced,
    separated into rings

Heat oven to 425°F. Grease
13×9-inch pan. Unroll dough;
place in greased pan. Starting at
center, press out with hands. Bake
at 425°F. for 7 to 9 minutes or
until light golden brown.

Meanwhile, in large skillet,
cook spinach and onion in butter
until onion is crisp-tender. Stir in
potatoes; mix well. In small bowl,
combine oil and garlic salt; mix

well. Brush over partially baked
crust; top with spinach mixture.
Sprinkle with mozzarella cheese
and then Cheddar cheese. Top with
onion rings.

Bake at 425°F. for 15 to 20 minutes or until cheese is melted and
edges of crust are golden brown.

Yield: 8 servings

Nutrition Per Serving: Calories 260; Protein 11g;
Carbohydrate 27g; Fat 12g; Sodium 520m

Former First Lady and Prominent First Bake-Off® Celebrity

Eleanor Roosevelt was a prominent champion of women's achievements throughout her husband's political career and after his passing. She attended the first Bake-Off® Contest and wrote about it in her newspaper column, "My Day." "This is a healthy contest and a highly American one. It may sell Pillsbury flour but it also reaches far down into the lives of the housewives of America. These were women who ran their homes and cooked at home," she told her readers, "they were not professional cooks." Mrs. Roosevelt, champion of the underdog, meant so much to Bake-Off® contestants that many counted her presence as one of the highlights of the event.

Chapter 3

Side Dishes and Salads

It's hard to believe that only a generation ago dinners and lunches were built almost exclusively around a meat entree, usually beef. Steaks, chops, roasts and potatoes were followed by ice cream or pie—the food of a prosperous and bountiful land, but unfortunately not the healthiest meals. Now we know how important a variety of vegetables and grains is in our diet and have altered our eating habits accordingly. Americans are eating more pasta and more salads than ever before, and these trends are represented in the recipes cooks are sending to the Bake-Off®.

Whole grains such as bulgur and corn, vitamin-rich vegetables such as spinach and broccoli, uncommon fruits like mangoes and a large assortment of nutritious beans, all add up to a menu as rich in nutrition as it is in diversity. Of course, variety is one of the chief virtues of living and eating in the present age, since so many fruits, vegetables and grains are now so widely available. And when featured in creative and delicious side dishes and salads, these foods play a strong supporting role in meals, and sometimes take star billing.

So add color to your plate with Southwestern Couscous Salad or introduce crisp texture with Cabbage Salad Vinaigrette with Crunchy Noodles. Or let one of these recipes take center stage, such as Chicken 'n Corn Tostada Salad or Potato Corn Bake for a vegetarian meal that everyone will love. However you serve them, these dishes will get noticed and be thoroughly enjoyed.

Grilled Chicken and Mango Corn Salad, page 110

Chicken 'n Corn Tostada Salad

Karen S. Casillas *Corona Hills, California*
Bake-Off® Contest 35, 1992

This Southwestern-style main-dish salad is brimming with vibrant colors and flavors.

DRESSING
1/4 cup cider vinegar or vinegar
3 tablespoons honey
1 1/2 teaspoons cumin
1/4 teaspoon salt
1/8 teaspoon pepper

SALAD
1 tablespoon olive oil or vegetable oil
2 whole chicken breasts, skinned, boned, cut into 2 × 1/2-inch strips
1/2 teaspoon garlic salt
1 (1-lb.) pkg. frozen extra sweet whole kernel corn
1 cup chopped seeded Italian plum tomatoes or tomatoes
1 (15-oz.) can black beans, drained, rinsed
5 green onions, thinly sliced, including tops
2 medium avocados, peeled, chopped
1 head butterhead, Boston or Bibb lettuce, torn into bite-sized pieces
1 small red bell pepper, chopped
8 oz. (2 cups) shredded Monterey Jack cheese
3 cups slightly crushed blue corn tortilla chips or tortilla chips

GARNISH, IF DESIRED
1 1/4 cups picante salsa
1 1/4 cups dairy sour cream

In small jar with tight-fitting lid, combine all dressing ingredients; shake well. Set aside.

Heat oil in large skillet over medium-high heat until hot. Add chicken; cook until no longer pink, about 5 minutes. Transfer chicken to very large bowl; sprinkle with garlic salt. Prepare corn according to package directions; drain. Stir into chicken. Cover; refrigerate about 30 minutes.

Add tomatoes, black beans, green onions, avocados, lettuce and bell pepper to chicken mixture; toss to combine. Shake dressing and pour over salad mixture; toss lightly.* Just before serving, add cheese and tortilla chips; toss gently.

Garnish with salsa and sour cream. Serve immediately.

Yield: 10 (1 1/2-cup) servings

*Tip: To make ahead, recipe can be prepared to this point. Cover; store in refrigerator.

Nutrition Per Serving: Calories 480; Protein 24g; Carbohydrate 39g; Fat 26g; Sodium 640mg

Karen Casillas: Chicken 'n Corn Tostada Salad

Life is not easy for any of us. But what of that? We must have perseverance and, above all, confidence in ourselves," said the scientist Marie Curie. Karen Casillas certainly took this adage to heart after an early disaster. "I made an orange cake with orange frosting when I was six, from a mix." The cake did not turn out well. "My mom gave it to our dog! And six years later we dug up a complete piece—whole!—when putting in a garden. No kidding!" Karen persevered, however, mastered cooking and got herself in the Bake-Off® Contest. Marie Curie would have been impressed.

Island Paradise Salad

Judith Mettlin *Snyder, New York*
Bake-Off® Contest 39, 2000 Prize Winner

Make mealtime festive with a tropical taste adventure you can make in a hurry. Mango, coconut, avocado, sugar snap peas and red onion tossed with a fresh honey-lime dressing create a colorful combination of exciting flavors.

DRESSING
1 teaspoon grated lime peel
3 tablespoons honey
2 tablespoons fresh lime juice
1 tablespoon canola or vegetable oil

SALAD
2 cups frozen sugar snap peas (from 1-lb. pkg.)
3 cups torn romaine lettuce
3 cups torn Bibb lettuce
1 avocado, peeled, pitted and cut into 1/2-inch cubes
1 large ripe mango, peeled, seed removed and cut into 1/2-inch cubes

**1 small red onion, thinly
    sliced, separated into rings**
**½ cup unsweetened or regular
    shredded coconut**

In small bowl, combine all dressing ingredients; mix well.

Cook sugar snap peas as
directed on package. Drain. Rinse
with cold water to cool. Drain well.

In large bowl, combine cooked
sugar snap peas and all remaining
salad ingredients except coconut.

Add dressing; toss to coat. Sprinkle
with coconut.

Yield: 8 (1¼-cup) servings

Nutrition Per Serving: Calories 160; Protein 2g;
Carbohydrate 18g; Fat 9g; Sodium 10mg

Island Paradise Salad

Bean and Pepper Salad with Citrus Dressing

Judith Mettlin *Snyder, New York*
Bake-Off® Contest 35, 1992

Gorgonzola cheese, a rich, slightly pungent blue cheese, tops this colorful salad.

SALAD
1 (15.5-oz.) can great
  northern beans, drained,
  rinsed
1 cup red bell pepper strips
  (2×¹/₄-inch)
1 cup yellow bell pepper strips
  (2×¹/₄-inch)
¹/₂ cup sliced green onions
¹/₄ cup crumbled gorgonzola
  or blue cheese

CITRUS DRESSING
2 to 4 tablespoons olive oil or
  vegetable oil
2 tablespoons orange juice
1 tablespoon red wine vinegar
1 tablespoon finely chopped
  fresh basil or 1 teaspoon
  dried basil leaves
1 teaspoon grated orange peel
¹/₄ teaspoon salt

Lettuce leaves

In medium bowl, combine all salad ingredients; toss to combine. In small jar with tight-fitting lid, combine all dressing ingredients; shake well. Pour over salad; toss gently to coat. Cover; refrigerate 1 hour to blend flavors.

Line 8 individual serving plates with lettuce leaves; spoon salad onto lettuce.

Yield: 8 (¹/₂-cup) servings

Nutrition Per Serving: Calories 120; Protein 4g; Carbohydrate 10g; Fat 8g; Sodium 210mg

Annette Erbeck: Easy Vegetable Bulgur Salad

There's wisdom in trying the different paths that life sets out before us. "I was born and raised in New York City, but now thoroughly enjoy living on a sixty-acre farm in a small town," Annette Erbeck says. "We raise, process and freeze our own beef, and raise and can many vegetables." She hasn't changed herself unrecognizably though, says Annette. "I plead incompetence when it comes to operating tractors, preferring the kitchen." And there's wisdom in knowing your limits, too.

Easy Vegetable Bulgur Salad

Annette Erbeck *Mason, Ohio*
Bake-Off® Contest 33, 1988

Enjoy the tender, nutty texture of nutritious bulgur in this colorful salad. Bulgur is kernels of whole wheat that have been steamed, dried and crushed.

1 cup uncooked bulgur
  (cracked wheat)
2 cups boiling water
1 (1-lb.) pkg. frozen broccoli,
  cauliflower and carrots
¹/₂ cup chopped fresh parsley
¹/₄ cup sliced green onions
¹/₂ to 1 cup purchased Italian
  salad dressing

In medium bowl, combine bulgur and boiling water. Let stand 1 hour. Drain well. To thaw vegetables, place in colander under cold running water for 6 minutes. Drain well.

In large bowl, combine softened bulgur, thawed vegetables, parsley, green onions and Italian dressing; blend well. Cover; refrigerate 1 to 2 hours to blend flavors. Store in refrigerator.

Yield: 12 (¹/₂-cup) servings

Nutrition Per Serving: Calories 160; Protein 2g; Carbohydrate 15g; Fat 10g; Sodium 170mg

Top to bottom: **Southwestern Couscous Salad, page 106, Bean and Pepper Salad with Citrus Dressing**

Southwestern Couscous Salad

Rocky Brown *Carmichaels, Pennsylvania Bake-Off® Contest 35, 1992*

Serve this light and refreshing salad with grilled chicken.

SALAD
1¹/₂ cups water
1 cup uncooked couscous
1¹/₂ cups frozen corn (from 1-lb. pkg.), cooked, cooled
1 (15-oz.) can black beans, drained, rinsed
¹/₄ cup chopped seeded tomato
¹/₄ cup chopped green bell pepper
¹/₄ cup chopped red bell pepper
2 tablespoons sliced green onions
2 tablespoons chopped fresh cilantro or parsley

DRESSING
¹/₃ cup olive oil or vegetable oil
¹/₄ to ¹/₃ cup lime juice
¹/₄ teaspoon salt, if desired
¹/₄ teaspoon garlic powder
¹/₄ teaspoon cumin
¹/₈ teaspoon ground red pepper (cayenne)

GARNISH, IF DESIRED
Lettuce leaves
Fresh cilantro
Lime slices

Bring water to a boil in small saucepan; remove from heat. Stir in couscous. Cover; let stand 5 minutes. Cool completely.

In large bowl, combine all salad ingredients; toss to combine. In small jar with tight-fitting lid, combine all dressing ingredients; shake well. Pour over salad; toss to coat. Cover; refrigerate 1 hour to blend flavors.

Line serving platter with lettuce leaves; spoon salad over lettuce leaves. Garnish with cilantro and lime slices.

Yield: 12 (¹/₂-cup) servings

Nutrition Per Serving: Calories 150; Protein 4g; Carbohydrate 21g; Fat 6g; Sodium 120mg

Spicy Corn and Black Bean Salad

Marlys Ward *Mankato, Minnesota Bake-Off® Contest 34, 1990*

The Mexican flavors in this salad are enhanced when the salad is refrigerated for at least one hour.

SALAD
2 (11-oz.) cans vacuum-packed whole kernel corn with red and green sweet peppers, drained
1 (15-oz.) can black beans, drained, rinsed
1 (4.5-oz.) jar sliced mushrooms, drained
¹/₂ cup sliced green onions
¹/₂ cup peeled, thinly sliced cucumber
2 tablespoons finely chopped fresh jalapeño pepper

DRESSING
¹/₃ cup oil
¹/₄ cup rice wine vinegar or white vinegar
¹/₄ cup orange juice
1 teaspoon finely chopped garlic
¹/₂ teaspoon salt

¹/₄ cup chopped fresh cilantro
1 tablespoon grated orange peel
1 to 2 teaspoons cumin seed
Lettuce leaves

In large bowl, combine all salad ingredients; blend well. In small bowl using wire whisk, blend oil, vinegar, orange juice, garlic and salt. Pour over salad; toss gently. Cover; refrigerate 1 to 2 hours to blend flavors.

Just before serving, drain salad. Stir in cilantro, orange peel and cumin seed. Serve in lettuce-lined bowl or on lettuce-lined plates. Store in refrigerator.

Yield: 11 (¹/₂-cup) servings

Nutrition Per Serving: Calories 110; Protein 4g; Carbohydrate 18g; Fat 2g; Sodium 200mg

Top to bottom: **Spicy Corn and Black Bean Salad, Cabbage Salad Vinaigrette with Crunchy Noodles, page 112**

Texas Two-Step Slaw

Betty Schroedl *Jefferson, Wisconsin*
Bake-Off® Contest 38, 1998 Prize Winner

Enjoy Tex-Mex flavor with this color-fully zesty coleslaw sure to win the favor of kids and adults alike. Cheddar cheese, corn and jalapeño chiles make an ordinary slaw extraordinary.

SALAD
4 cups shredded green cabbage
1 cup shredded red cabbage
¼ cup chopped red onion
2 jalapeño chiles, seeded, finely chopped*
2 tablespoons chopped fresh cilantro
1 (11-oz.) can vacuum-packed whole kernel corn with red and green peppers, drained
4 oz. (1 cup) shredded Cheddar cheese
Fresh cilantro sprigs

DRESSING
¾ cup purchased ranch salad dressing
1 tablespoon fresh lime juice
1 teaspoon cumin

In large bowl, combine all salad ingredients except cilantro sprigs; mix well.

In small bowl, combine all dressing ingredients; blend well. Pour over salad; toss to coat. Serve immediately or refrigerate until serving time. Garnish with cilantro sprigs.

Yield: 8 (1-cup) servings

*****Tip:** When handling jalapeño chiles, wear plastic or rubber gloves to protect hands. Do not touch face or eyes.

Nutrition Per Serving: Calories 240; Protein 5g; Carbohydrate 12g; Fat 19g; Sodium 410mg

Fiesta Chicken Salad

Greta Eberhardt *San Pedro, California*
Bake-Off® Contest 37, 1996 Prize Winner

Flavorful, crumb-coated, baked chicken slices are served on a bed of mixed salad greens and chopped tomatoes. This warm main-dish salad is ready to eat in just 30 minutes.

¼ cup margarine or butter, cut into 4 pieces
6 boneless, skinless chicken breast halves
2 eggs
1¼ cups medium chunky-style picante
1⅓ cups unseasoned bread crumbs
1 teaspoon salt
1 teaspoon cumin
1 teaspoon chili powder
½ teaspoon ground oregano
4 green onions, sliced
1 (16-oz.) pkg. mixed salad greens
3 medium tomatoes, chopped
1 (8-oz.) bottle red wine vinegar and oil salad dressing
1 avocado, peeled, sliced
1 cup sour cream

Heat oven to 400° F. Place margarine in 15×10×1-inch baking pan. Place pan in oven; heat 3 minutes or until margarine is melted. Tilt pan to coat with margarine.

Meanwhile, cut chicken breast halves in half lengthwise. Cut crosswise into ½-inch slices. In large bowl, beat eggs; stir in chicken and ¼ cup of the picante.

In shallow bowl, combine bread crumbs, salt, cumin, chili powder and oregano; mix well. Add chicken pieces to bread crumb mixture, a few at a time; turn to coat. Place coated chicken in margarine-coated pan. Bake at 400° F. for 15 to 20 minutes or until chicken is no longer pink.

Reserve 1 tablespoon of the green onions for garnish. In large bowl, combine remaining onions, salad greens and tomatoes; toss gently. Pour half of the dressing over salad; toss to coat. Arrange evenly on 8 individual plates.

Spoon chicken into center of each salad. Top each with 1 tablespoon sour cream and about ½ teaspoon reserved green onions. Garnish each plate with avocado slices. Serve with remaining half of salad dressing, ½ cup sour cream and 1 cup picante.

Yield: 8 servings

Nutrition Per Serving: Calories 530; Protein 27g; Carbohydrate 25g; Fat 36g; Sodium 740mg

Fiesta Chicken Salad

PROFILE

KAREN KWAN

A special challenge of the modern age is to have holidays that are consistently meaningful, not ones that are dictated by window displays and the calendar. Karen Kwan has met that challenge: She and her mother play host to an extended family in a Christmas-season tea.

They invite about thirty women over: "It's sort of like *The Joy Luck Club*," Karen says, "where I call most of the women 'Auntie,' even though we're not blood-related. My mother and I usually try to split the cooking up, and do about half each. First we do miniatures—about twenty to twenty-five items—like individual cakes, cookies, tartlets and sandwiches. It's quite an elaborate thing. We usually do two kinds of scones, a variety of tartlets—fruit tarts, chocolate ganache, lemon meringue and custard—and then we'll do little cakes, like a cake roll with mocha cream, and then a

variety of traditional tea sandwiches, like smoked chicken or smoked salmon and cucumber. We try to keep it traditional. We get out all the tea services. It's really fun."

Karen, a newlywed and art director for an advertising agency, says her mother prepared her daughters for this kind of delicate work from an early age. "She had us in the kitchen from age three on, helping her roll out pie crusts. She had a philosophy about kids doing the pie crusts— because we had really tiny hands and a light touch, she thought the crusts worked out better than those made with adult-sized hands."

As Karen has proved with her Grilled Chicken and Mango Corn Salad, some cooks never lose their delicate touch, lacing together inspiration and tradition for exciting meals.

Grilled Chicken and Mango Corn Salad

Karen Kwan *Saratoga, California*
Bake-Off® Contest 36, 1994

Mangoes are an oval-shaped tropical fruit that, when ripe, have a red and yellow skin and bright orange-yellow flesh. Mangoes have a sweet peach-pineapple flavor with a hint of spiciness.

CHICKEN
4 boneless, skinless chicken
    breast halves
$^1/_2$ cup purchased teriyaki
    marinade and sauce

DRESSING
1 (0.4-oz.) pkg. buttermilk
    ranch salad dressing mix
$^1/_2$ cup skim milk
$^1/_2$ cup light sour cream
1 cup reduced-calorie
    mayonnaise

SALSA
1 (11-oz.) can white corn,
    drained
1 (15-oz.) can black beans,
    drained, rinsed
$^1/_2$ cup chopped red bell
    pepper
$^1/_2$ cup chopped green bell
    pepper
$^1/_2$ avocado, peeled, cubed
$^1/_2$ medium cucumber,
    quartered, thinly sliced
1 medium tomato, cubed
1 ripe mango, peeled, cubed

4 oz. (1 cup) shredded
   Monterey Jack cheese
1 tablespoon olive oil or
   vegetable oil
4 teaspoons white wine vinegar
   or rice wine vinegar

SALAD
4 cups thin, crisp corn chips
   or corn chips
6 cups green leaf lettuce, torn
   into bite-sized pieces
1/2 avocado, peeled, sliced

Grill Directions: In 12×8-inch
(2-quart) baking dish or resealable
plastic bag, place chicken and
marinade; turn to coat. Cover dish
or seal bag; refrigerate 1 hour.

Meanwhile, in small bowl, combine all dressing ingredients; blend
well. Refrigerate to blend flavors.
In large bowl, combine all salsa
ingredients; gently toss to combine.

Heat grill. Drain chicken,
reserving marinade. Place chicken
on gas grill over medium heat or on
charcoal grill 4 to 6 inches from
medium coals. Cook 10 to 15 minutes or until chicken is no longer
pink, turning and brushing with
reserved marinade. Discard any
remaining marinade. Cool. Cut
chicken into 1/2-inch cubes; stir
into salsa.

Just before serving, combine
salsa mixture and corn chips; toss
gently. Place 1 cup lettuce on each
of 6 serving plates. Top each with
1/6 of salsa mixture. Garnish with
sliced avocado. Serve immediately
with dressing.

Broiler Directions: Marinate chicken
as directed above and drain, reserving marinade. Place chicken on
broiler pan. Broil 4 to 6 inches from
heat for 10 to 15 minutes or until
chicken is no longer pink, turning

and brushing with reserved marinade. Discard any remaining marinade. Continue as directed above.

Yield: 6 servings

Nutrition Per Serving: Calories 760;
Protein 35g; Carbohydrate 61g; Fat 42g;
Sodium 1130mg

Mediterranean Corn Salad

Ellen Nishimura *Fair Oaks, California
Bake-Off® Contest 34, 1990 Prize Winner*

*Mozzarella cheese, olives, basil and
garlic are ingredients commonly used
in Mediterranean cuisine. You'll enjoy
their combined flavors in this salad.*

SALAD
1 (15.25-oz.) can whole
   kernel corn, drained
8 oz. mozzarella cheese, cut
   into 1/4-inch cubes
1 (2 1/4-oz.) can sliced ripe
   olives, drained
1 large tomato, seeded, cut
   into 1/2-inch pieces
1/4 cup chopped fresh basil
   leaves
1/4 cup chopped fresh parsley

DRESSING
1/4 cup olive oil
3 tablespoons cider vinegar
1 teaspoon grated lemon peel
1 large garlic clove, minced
Salt
Pepper

Fresh spinach leaves, if
   desired
Toasted pine nuts, if desired*

In large bowl, combine all salad
ingredients; mix well. In small bowl

using wire whisk, blend olive oil,
vinegar, lemon peel and garlic. Pour
over corn mixture; toss gently. Salt
and pepper to taste. Refrigerate 1 to
2 hours to blend flavors. Serve on
spinach-lined plates. Sprinkle each
serving with pine nuts.

Yield: 8 (1/2-cup) servings

*Tip: To toast pine nuts, spread
evenly in shallow pan; bake at
375° F. for 3 to 5 minutes or until
light golden brown, stirring
occasionally.

Nutrition Per Serving: Calories 190; Protein 9g;
Carbohydrate 10g; Fat 13g; Sodium 310mg

Ellen Nishimura: Mediterranean Corn Salad

Asked about a memorable
cooking experience, Ellen
Nishimura supplied this tale:
"Three years ago my husband
trained for a marathon. The day
before the race, it started to rain.
He was determined to run no
matter what. That night the rain
developed into one of the worst
storms all winter. I was so worried
I couldn't sleep, and at three in
the morning I got up and started
to bake cookies to try to relax. My
husband slept through the storm
—and my baking—and at six
o'clock in the morning, he found
me in the kitchen—with over
nine dozen cookies. I took them
to work. Lou ran the marathon in
the storm and hasn't run another
since—but my coworkers keep
encouraging him to try again."

Cabbage Salad Vinaigrette with Crunchy Noodles

Birdie Casement *Denver, Colorado*
Bake-Off® Contest 34, 1990 Prize Winner

Ingredients for this salad are available year-round, so you can make this colorful side dish often.

SALAD

4¹⁄₂ cups (1 medium head) shredded red or green cabbage
5 green onions, thinly sliced (including tops)
1 (11-oz.) can vacuum-packed whole kernel corn, drained
1¹⁄₂ cups frozen sweet peas (from 1-lb. pkg.), cooked, drained
1 (4.5-oz.) jar sliced mushrooms, undrained

DRESSING

1 (3-oz.) pkg. instant Oriental noodles with chicken-flavor seasoning packet
¹⁄₄ cup tarragon vinegar
¹⁄₄ cup oil
3 tablespoons sugar
¹⁄₂ teaspoon pepper

¹⁄₂ cup slivered almonds, toasted*
2 tablespoons sesame seed, toasted**

In large bowl, combine all salad ingredients. In small bowl, combine contents of seasoning packet from noodles, vinegar, oil, sugar and pepper; blend well. Pour dressing over salad ingredients; toss to coat. Refrigerate at least 2 hours to chill.

Break noodles into ³⁄₄-inch pieces. Before serving, stir noodles, almonds and sesame seed into salad mixture. Store in refrigerator.

Yield: 16 (¹⁄₂-cup) servings

*Tips: To toast almonds, spread on cookie sheet; bake at 375° F. for 5 to 6 minutes or until light golden brown, stirring occasionally. Or spread in thin layer in microwave-safe pie pan and microwave on HIGH for 6 to 7 minutes or until light golden brown, stirring frequently.

**To toast sesame seed, spread in baking pan; bake at 375° F. for 5 to 7 minutes or until light golden brown. Or spread in medium skillet and stir over medium heat for 8 to 10 minutes or until light golden brown.

Nutrition Per Serving: Calories 130; Protein 3g; Carbohydrate 14g; Fat 7g; Sodium 210mg

Garden Chicken Salad

Edith Shulman *Grapevine, Texas*
Bake-Off® Contest 33, 1988

Mango chutney is the unique ingredient in this main-dish salad. It is a chunky condiment made from a mixture of mango, garlic, shallots, pimiento, apple, mustard, brown sugar and vinegar.

SALAD

2 cups frozen cut broccoli (from 1-lb. pkg.)
4 cups cubed cooked chicken
¹⁄₃ cup chopped red or green bell pepper
3 tablespoons sliced ripe olives
2 tablespoons finely chopped red onion
1 large orange, peeled, chopped

Birdie Casement: Cabbage Salad Vinaigrette with Crunchy Noodles

If anyone ever asks you what it was like to live richly through the twentieth century, direct them to the story of Birdie Casement. "I married Russ," Birdie says, "then World War II changed our lives. We found ourselves wrestling with gas rationing, sugar stamps, tire shortages, among other shortages, and two wee tots. . . . The following years were a merry-go-round of PTA, fund-raising, cake bakes, Brownies, Cub Scouts, car pooling, measles, trips to the zoo, picnics and all the fun, tears, brawls and challenges that go hand in hand with parenthood. Time flies, and soon no one was hurrying home for that noontime sandwich." Birdie became a kindergarten teacher and was nominated for Colorado teacher of the year. At the Bake-Off® Contest, she wowed everybody with her ebullience, her wisdom and, of course, her salad.

DRESSING

3 tablespoons purchased mango chutney

^{2}/3 cup reduced-calorie mayonnaise or regular mayonnaise

1 tablespoon dry sherry, if desired

2^1/2 teaspoons garlic-flavored wine vinegar or red wine vinegar

^{1}/4 cup sesame seed, toasted*

^{1}/8 teaspoon pepper

Lettuce leaves

Cook broccoli as directed on package until crisp-tender. Drain; cool. In large bowl, combine cooked broccoli and remaining salad ingredients; blend well.

Place chutney in small bowl. Remove any large pieces and finely chop; return to bowl. Stir in remaining dressing ingredients; blend well. Pour dressing over salad; toss gently. Serve on lettuce leaves or in lettuce-lined bowl. Store in refrigerator.

Yield: 6 (1^1/4-cup) servings

*Tip: To toast sesame seed, spread in baking pan; bake at 350° F. for 6 to 8 minutes or until golden brown, stirring occasionally. Or spread in medium skillet; stir over medium heat for 8 to 10 minutes or until golden brown.

Nutrition Per Serving: Calories 340; Protein 30g; Carbohydrate 14g; Fat 18g; Sodium 290mg

Hot 'n Spicy Sautéed Mushrooms

Gladys Randall *Houston, Texas*
Bake-Off® Contest 33, 1988

This spicy mushroom-vegetable side dish will add zest to any meal. Try serving it on top of steaks or chops. It's sure to please your family or guests.

^{1}/2 cup margarine or butter

^{1}/2 cup chopped green bell pepper

^{1}/2 cup chopped red bell pepper

^{1}/4 cup sliced green onions

2 garlic cloves, minced

3 (6-oz.) jars sliced mushrooms, drained*

^{1}/4 cup sherry

^{1}/2 teaspoon Creole or Cajun seasoning

^{1}/4 teaspoon ground red pepper (cayenne)

^{1}/4 teaspoon pepper

Melt margarine in large skillet. Add bell peppers, green onions and garlic; cook and stir over medium heat until tender. Stir in mushrooms, sherry, Creole seasoning, ground red pepper and pepper. Simmer for 2 to 3 minutes or until thoroughly heated, stirring occasionally.

Yield: 6 (^{1}/2-cup) servings

*Tip: Four (4.5-oz.) jars sliced mushrooms, drained, can be substituted for 3 (6-oz. jars).

Nutrition Per Serving: Calories 180; Protein 3g; Carbohydrate 6g; Fat 15g; Sodium 660mg

Gladys Randall: Hot 'n Spicy Sautéed Mushrooms

Cooking is very much a chicken-and-egg sort of endeavor. If you've never had a good meat loaf, how can you know if yours is any good? Gladys Randall figured out this principle when she was a young child, the hard way. "I would see a baked pie on top of the stove. I tried to bake a lemon pie by putting it on top of the burner. I thought that was the way it's done." Gladys kept trying, her adventurous spirit intact. "It took me two years to learn how to make a traditional Italian stuffing. One day a guest at Christmas, who was ninety-two years old, said 'Very good—but too loose. You make it together, like a meatball.' Then I knew what I was doing wrong!" Gladys listened, learned and today is master of her kitchen.

Potato Corn Bake

Marion Bedient *Cameron, Wisconsin*
Bake-Off® Contest 34, 1990

This make-ahead side dish can ease your last-minute meal preparation for relaxed entertaining.

^{1}/$_2$ **lb. bacon, cut into** ^{3}/$_4$**-inch pieces**
^{1}/$_2$ **cup finely chopped green bell pepper**
^{1}/$_3$ **cup finely chopped onion**
1 (15-oz.) can cream-style corn
2 cups milk
3 tablespoons margarine or butter
^{3}/$_4$ **teaspoon salt, if desired**
^{1}/$_8$ **teaspoon pepper**
2 cups mashed potato flakes
^{1}/$_2$ **cup dairy sour cream**
^{1}/$_4$ **cup grated Parmesan cheese**
2 tablespoons finely chopped green onion tops, if desired

Heat oven to 375°F. Grease 11×7-inch or 9-inch square pan. Cook bacon in large saucepan until crisp. Drain, reserving 1 tablespoon bacon drippings. Set bacon aside. Return 1 tablespoon bacon drippings to saucepan. Add bell pepper and onion to drippings. Cook over medium heat until tender.

Stir in corn, milk, margarine, salt and pepper; cook over medium heat until mixture is hot and bubbly. Remove from heat; stir in potato flakes and sour cream until well blended. Spoon mixture into greased pan. Top with bacon, Parmesan cheese and green onions. Bake at 375°F. for 20 to 25 minutes or until thoroughly heated.

Yield: 6 servings

Tip: To make ahead, prepare, cover and refrigerate up to 4 hours before baking. Bake at 375°F. for 25 to 30 minutes or until thoroughly heated.

Nutrition Per Serving: Calories 360; Protein 11g; Carbohydrate 33g; Fat 21g; Sodium 860mg

Antipasto Tortellini Salad

Vickie Cox *Wilkes-Barre, Pennsylvania*
Bake-Off® Contest 35, 1992 Prize Winner

An assortment of antipasti, *or cold appetizers including marinated vegetables and salami, are combined with tortellini and Italian dressing.*

1 (16-oz.) pkg. fresh or frozen uncooked cheese tortellini
4 oz. (1 cup) chopped salami
4 oz. provolone cheese, cut into 2×^{1}/$_4$×^{1}/$_4$-inch strips
1 (11-oz.) can vacuum-packed whole kernel corn, drained
1 (9-oz.) pkg. frozen spinach in a pouch, thawed, squeezed to drain
1 (6-oz.) jar marinated artichoke hearts, drained, chopped
1 (6-oz.) can (1^1/$_2$ cups) pitted ripe olives, drained, sliced
1^1/$_2$ cups purchased creamy Italian salad dressing
1 teaspoon Dijon mustard
^{1}/$_2$ **cup grated Parmesan cheese**
1 (2-oz.) jar diced pimiento, drained, if desired

Cook tortellini to desired doneness as directed on package. Drain; rinse with cold water.

In very large bowl, combine tortellini, salami, provolone cheese, corn, spinach, artichoke hearts and 1 cup of the olives. In small bowl, combine salad dressing, mustard and ^{1}/$_4$ cup of the Parmesan cheese; blend well. Pour dressing over salad; toss gently. Top with remaining olives and Parmesan cheese. Cover; refrigerate 1 to 2 hours to blend flavors. Just before serving, garnish with pimiento.

Yield: 12 (1-cup) servings

Nutrition Per Serving: Calories 350; Protein 13g; Carbohydrate 28g; Fat 21g; Sodium 910mg

Broccoli Cauliflower Tetrazzini

Barbara Van Itallie *Poughkeepsie, New York*
Bake-Off® Contest 33, 1988

Tetrazzini was originally a main dish made with spaghetti and chicken. Thanks to today's creative cooks, we see many exciting variations. This one is a saucy vegetable and spaghetti side dish that will complement any meal.

8 oz. uncooked spaghetti, broken into thirds
1 (1-lb.) pkg. frozen broccoli, cauliflower and carrots
2 tablespoons margarine or butter
3 tablespoons all-purpose flour
2 cups milk
1/2 cup grated Parmesan cheese
Dash pepper
1 (4.5-oz.) jar sliced mushrooms, drained
2 tablespoons grated Parmesan cheese

Cook spaghetti to desired doneness as directed on package. Drain; rinse with hot water. Keep warm. Set aside. Cook vegetables until crisp-tender as directed on package. Drain; set aside.

Heat oven to 400°F. Grease 13×9-inch pan. Melt margarine in medium saucepan.

Stir in flour until smooth. Gradually add milk; blend well. Cook over medium heat for 6 to 10 minutes or until mixture thickens and boils, stirring constantly. Stir in 1/2 cup Parmesan cheese and pepper.

Spoon cooked spaghetti into greased pan. Top with cooked vegetables and sliced mushrooms. Pour milk mixture over mushrooms; sprinkle with 2 tablespoons Parmesan cheese.

Bake at 400°F. for 15 to 20 minutes or until mixture bubbles at edges and is thoroughly heated.

Yield: 6 servings

Nutrition Per Serving: Calories 310; Protein 14g; Carbohydrate 41g; Fat 9g; Sodium 380mg

Savory Mashed Potato Pie

Chris Hurst *Atlanta, Georgia*
Bake-Off® Contest 37, 1996 Prize Winner

While savory vegetable pies are not as well known in this country as meat pies, they offer a creative way to dress up everyday foods. Serve a wedge of this attractive tomato-topped pie as a side dish for a company dinner or as a light luncheon main dish.

CRUST
1 refrigerated pie crust (from 15-oz. pkg.)

FILLING
2 cups water
3 tablespoons butter or margarine
1/2 teaspoon salt, if desired
1/2 teaspoon garlic powder
1/8 teaspoon white pepper
2 1/2 cups mashed potato flakes
1/2 cup sour cream
1/4 cup purchased real bacon bits, or 4 slices bacon, cooked, crumbled
1/2 cup thinly sliced green onions

4 oz. (1 cup) shredded Cheddar cheese
2 small tomatoes, thinly sliced
1 tablespoon olive oil or vegetable oil

GARNISH
2 tablespoons thinly sliced green onions
1/2 cup sour cream

Heat oven to 450°F. Prepare pie crust according to package directions for *one-crust baked shell* using 9-inch deep-dish pie pan or 9-inch pie pan. Bake at 450°F. for 9 to 11 minutes or until light golden brown. Cool while preparing mashed potatoes.

Meanwhile, in large saucepan, combine water, butter, salt, garlic powder and pepper. Bring to a boil. Remove from heat; stir in potato flakes, 1/2 cup sour cream and bacon bits; mix well.

Sprinkle 1/2 cup onions over bottom of cooled baked shell; sprinkle with cheese. Spoon and spread potato mixture evenly over cheese. Arrange tomatoes around edge, overlapping if necessary. Brush potato mixture and tomatoes with oil.

Reduce oven temperature to 400°F. Bake pie for 15 to 20 minutes or until thoroughly heated in center. Cool 5 minutes. To serve, sprinkle with 2 tablespoons onions. Cut into wedges; top each serving with 1 tablespoon sour cream.

Yield: 8 servings

Nutrition Per Serving: Calories 390; Protein 9g; Carbohydrate 33g; Fat 25g; Sodium 590mg

Savory Mashed Potato Pie

Mexican Fiesta Biscuit Bake

Madge Savage *Mount Vernon, Ohio*
Bake-Off® Contest 36, 1994 Prize Winner

Madge Savage lives in Ohio, but her favorite cuisines are Tex-Mex and Mexican. She puts these spicy flavors in her hot bread by tossing biscuit pieces with salsa, spooning the mixture into a baking dish and topping it with a layer of Monterey Jack cheese.

2 tablespoons margarine or butter
1 (1 lb. 0.3-oz.) can large refrigerated buttermilk biscuits
1 (10.8-oz.) can large refrigerated buttermilk biscuits
1 (16-oz.) jar (1³/₄ cups) medium thick and chunky salsa
12 oz. (3 cups) shredded Monterey Jack cheese
¹/₂ cup chopped green bell pepper
¹/₂ cup sliced green onions
1 (2¹/₄-oz.) can sliced ripe olives, drained
1 cup picante salsa, if desired

Heat oven to 375° F. Melt margarine in oven in 13×9-inch (3-quart) glass baking dish or non-aluminum baking pan. Tilt to evenly coat dish. Separate dough into 13 biscuits; cut each biscuit into eighths. Place biscuit pieces in large bowl; toss with 1³/₄ cups salsa. Spoon evenly into margarine-coated dish. Sprinkle with cheese, bell pepper, green onions and ripe olives.

Bake at 375° F. for 35 to 45 minutes or until edges are deep golden brown and center is set. Let stand 15 minutes. Cut into squares; serve with 1 cup picante salsa.

Yield: 15 servings

Nutrition Per Serving: Calories 280; Protein 9g; Carbohydrate 25g; Fat 16g; Sodium 1050mg

Saucy Bean 'n Bacon Bake

Joy Ann Kidder *Gainesville, Florida*
Bake-Off® Contest 35, 1992

In the South, lima beans are commonly referred to as butter beans, so use whichever bean is available for this recipe.

¹/₂ lb. bacon, cut into ³/₄-inch pieces
3 (15.5-oz.) cans butter beans, drained
1 (2-oz.) jar sliced pimiento, drained
1 cup chopped green onions
³/₄ cup dairy sour cream
¹/₃ cup firmly packed brown sugar
1 to 2 teaspoons dry mustard
1 teaspoon garlic powder
¹/₈ teaspoon ground red pepper (cayenne)
2 tablespoons chopped green onion tops

Heat oven to 350° F. Cook bacon in large skillet until crisp; drain. Set aside. In large bowl, combine all remaining ingredients except green onion tops; mix well. Pour into ungreased 8-inch square (1¹/₂-quart) baking dish or 2-quart casserole.

Bake uncovered at 350° F. for 25 minutes. Sprinkle with cooked bacon and 2 tablespoons green onion tops; bake an additional 10 to 15 minutes or until thoroughly heated.

Yield: 8 (¹/₂-cup) servings

Nutrition Per Serving: Calories 220; Protein 10g; Carbohydrate 29g; Fat 9g; Sodium 43

Black Bean Mole and Coconut Couscous

Virginia Moon *Harvest, Alabama*
Bake-Off® Contest 37, 1996 Prize Winner

Mole is a complex sauce supposedly created two centuries ago by nuns in a Mexican convent in honor of a visiting dignitary. Although there are many variations, it always includes the flavors of chili plus a touch of chocolate.

COUSCOUS
1 cup uncooked couscous
¹/₂ cup coconut, toasted*
¹/₂ teaspoon cinnamon

MOLE
1 tablespoon olive oil or vegetable oil
2 teaspoons purchased minced garlic
2 (15-oz.) cans black beans, drained, rinsed
1 (16-oz.) jar mild homestyle salsa or chunky-style salsa
1¹/₂ teaspoons unsweetened cocoa
1 teaspoon chili powder
¹/₂ teaspoon cumin
¹/₄ teaspoon cinnamon

TOPPING

3 oz. (³/₄ cup) shredded colby–Monterey Jack cheese blend

6 tablespoons sour cream

¹/₄ to ¹/₂ cup thinly sliced green onions

1 medium tomato, seeded, chopped

Cook couscous as directed on package. Stir in toasted coconut and ¹/₂ teaspoon cinnamon. Cover to keep warm.

Heat oil in medium saucepan over medium heat until hot. Add garlic; cook and stir 1 minute. Stir in all remaining mole ingredients. Reduce heat to low; simmer 5 minutes or until thoroughly heated, stirring occasionally.

To serve, fluff couscous with fork; spoon onto serving platter. Spoon mole mixture over couscous. Top with cheese, sour cream, onions and tomato.

Yield: 6 (1¹/₂-cup) servings

*Tip: To toast coconut, place in small skillet; cook and stir over low heat for 6 to 8 minutes or until light golden brown.

Nutrition Per Serving: Calories 400; Protein 16g; Carbohydrate 55g; Fat 13g; Sodium 760mg

Black Bean Mole and Coconut Couscous

Santa Fe Corn and Cheese Bake

Alda Menoni *Santa Barbara, California*
Bake-Off® Contest 33, 1988

Although this is usually served as a side dish, for a change of pace, serve the flavorful casserole as a meatless main dish. You'll enjoy the popular Southwestern flavor.

2 eggs, beaten
1 cup creamed cottage cheese
$1/2$ cup dairy sour cream
$1/3$ cup chopped green chiles, drained
3 tablespoons all-purpose flour
3 tablespoons milk
2 to 3 teaspoons sugar
1 teaspoon onion salt
$1/4$ to $1/2$ teaspoon pepper
1 (15.25-oz.) can whole kernel corn, drained
3 tablespoons chopped ripe olives
1 oz. ($1/4$ cup) shredded Cheddar cheese

Heat oven to 350°F. In large bowl, combine eggs and cottage cheese; blend well. Add sour cream and chiles; mix well. In small bowl, combine flour and milk; beat until smooth. Add to cottage cheese mixture. Stir in sugar, onion salt, pepper and corn; blend well. Pour into ungreased 8-inch square ($1\frac{1}{2}$-quart) baking dish or 2-quart casserole.

Bake at 350°F. for 30 to 40 minutes or until knife inserted near center comes out clean. Sprinkle top with olives and Cheddar cheese. Bake an additional 1 to 2 minutes or until cheese is melted.

Yield: 8 servings

Tip: To make individual corn and cheese bakes, pour mixture into ungreased 6-oz. custard cups. Fill cups $3/4$ full, place on cookie sheet and bake according to recipe directions.

Nutrition Per Serving: Calories 160; Protein 8g; Carbohydrate 15g; Fat 8g; Sodium 580mg

Alda Menoni: Santa Fe Corn and Cheese Bake

Alda Menoni is no newcomer to the art of novel recipes. When she was a girl helping out her father in his ice cream business, she says, "Several batches of fresh ice cream were ready for an added touch of color. My brother and I, in our youthful enthusiasm, inadvertently switched colorings. Plop—the green coloring went into a container of fresh strawberry ice cream, while the pink went into the pistachio! What to do?" Alda's father made tricolor bricks with the strawberry, pistachio and vanilla ice cream. "No one ever mentioned the nutty taste of the pink ice cream or the fruity flavor of the green, and all the bricks sold!" As they say, when life gives you lemons, make lemonade!

Turkey and Pasta Coleslaw

Nancy E. Smith *The Woodlands, Texas*
Bake-Off® Contest 35, 1992

This unique salad has plenty of crunch! Serve it with crusty hard rolls and fruit.

1 (1-lb.) pkg. frozen pasta, broccoli, corn and carrots in a garlic-seasoned sauce
3 cups finely shredded green cabbage
1 cup cubed cooked turkey
$1/2$ cup shredded carrot
1 green onion, chopped
$1/3$ cup purchased reduced-calorie coleslaw salad dressing
5 lettuce leaves
5 lime slices
5 fresh parsley sprigs

Prepare frozen vegetables and pasta according to package directions until vegetables are crisp-tender. Place in large bowl. Cool 15 minutes in refrigerator.

Add cabbage, turkey, carrot and green onion to vegetable and pasta mixture; mix well. Pour dressing over salad; toss gently to combine. Cover; refrigerate at least 1 hour to blend flavors. Serve on 5 lettuce-lined plates; garnish with lime slices and parsley.

Yield: 5 ($1\frac{1}{2}$-cup) servings

Nutrition Per Serving: Calories 210; Protein 13g; Carbohydrate 26g; Fat 8g; Sodium 560mg

Chapter 4

Breads

Tortillas, matzos, pita, biscuits, muffins, sourdough—all are varieties of bread. Bread is such a versatile and basic food, coming in such an amazing variety of shapes and sizes, and from such a kaleidoscope of traditions, that it's no wonder bread is known as the staff of life.

The first Bake-Off® Contest required only that a minimum of one-half cup of flour be used in every recipe. Almost all the submitted recipes were from "scratch," reflecting the way families had cooked for hundreds of years. Heirloom recipes—those handed down through several generations of a family—were common. Pillsbury asked its earliest Bake-Off® contestants how much time they spent baking for their families every week, and a response of twelve hours was not uncommon. However, the ensuing years brought a change in family life, and people no longer had time to devote to from-scratch yeast breads. Women became busy in ways unimaginable to their grandparents: working, volunteering, shepherding their children to a complex variety of activities. Families relied more and more on mixes and refrigerated dough to provide the building blocks for sophisticated breads, getting them out of the kitchen faster, but still providing the high-quality results they desired.

In these pages you'll find breads plain and fancy, sweet and savory, made from scratch and from convenience ingredients, for all occasions and all delicious.

Clockwise from right: **Cheddar Thyme Casserole Bread, page 142, Cheese-Filled Parmesan Biscuit Loaves, page 150, Biscuit Mini Focaccia, page 45**

Easy English Muffins

Julia Hauber *Winfield, Kansas*
Bake-Off® Contest 19, 1968

These homemade English muffins are baked on the griddle, then toasted to perfection. Spread them with butter and marmalade or jam for a wonderfully delicious breakfast accompaniment.

2 pkg. active dry yeast
2 cups warm water
5 to 6 cups all-purpose flour
1 tablespoon sugar
3 teaspoons salt
¹/₂ cup shortening
Cornmeal
Margarine or butter

In large bowl, dissolve yeast in warm water (105 to 115°F.). Add 3 cups flour, sugar, salt and shortening to yeast mixture, stirring by hand until moistened. Stir vigorously by hand until smooth. Gradually add remaining 2 to 3 cups flour to form a stiff dough, beating well after each addition. On floured surface, gently knead dough 5 to 6 times until no longer sticky. Roll dough to ¹/₄- to ³/₈-inch thickness; cut with 3- to 4-inch floured round cutter.

Sprinkle cornmeal evenly over 2 ungreased cookie sheets. Place cut-out dough on cornmeal; sprinkle with additional cornmeal. Cover loosely with plastic wrap and cloth towel. Let rise in warm place until light, 30 to 45 minutes.

Heat griddle to 350°F. With wide spatula, invert dough onto ungreased griddle. Bake 5 to 6 minutes on each side or until light golden brown; cool. Split, toast and butter.

Yield: 26 servings
(1 muffin per serving)

High Altitude—Above 3,500 feet: No change.

Nutrition Per Serving: Calories 149; Protein 3g; Carbohydrate 23g; Fat 4g; Sodium 250mg

Lemon Raspberry Muffins

Stephanie Luetkehans *Chicago, Illinois*
Bake-Off® Contest 33, 1988 Prize Winner

"After buying and eating dozens of bakery muffins, I decided to make my own," said the finalist who created these prize-winning muffins. They are so rich and flavorful that they can easily be served for dessert.

2 cups all-purpose flour
1 cup sugar
3 teaspoons baking powder
¹/₂ teaspoon salt
1 cup half-and-half
¹/₂ cup oil
1 teaspoon lemon extract
2 eggs
1 cup fresh or frozen raspberries without syrup (do not thaw)

Heat oven to 425°F. Line 12 muffin cups with paper baking cups. In large bowl, combine flour, sugar, baking powder and salt; mix well. In small bowl, combine half-and-half, oil, lemon extract and eggs; blend well. Add to dry ingredients; stir just until ingredients are moistened. Carefully fold in raspberries. Divide batter evenly into paper-lined muffin cups. Bake at 425°F. for 18 to 23 minutes or until golden brown. Cool 5 minutes; remove from pans.

Yield: 12 servings
(1 muffin per serving)

High Altitude—Above 3,500 feet: Line 16 muffin cups with paper baking cups. Decrease baking powder to 2 teaspoons. Bake as directed above. Yield: 16 muffins.

Nutrition Per Serving: Calories 260; Protein 4g; Carbohydrate 35g; Fat 12g; Sodium 230mg

Julia Hauber: Easy English Muffins

Grace under pressure—one of a cook's most necessary gifts. That's where the saying "If you can't take the heat, get out of the kitchen" comes from. "A tornado alert once sent us to the basement for an hour," Julia Hauber remembers. "Everyone else worried about being killed. I just worried about my rare roast beef, and kept running upstairs to check it." Despite the approaching storm, Julia's guests arrived. "We had our first course, hors d'oeuvres and drinks, in the southwest (safest) corner of the basement . . . which unfortunately was the powder room." Amazingly, the roast turned out perfect, and grace was triumphant.

Quick Apple Cranberry Pear Muffins

Joyce L. Bowman *Raleigh, North Carolina. Bake-Off® Contest 37, 1996 Prize Winner*

Joyce Bowman takes classes in Asian cuisines, but an All-American fruit muffin brought her to the 1996 contest. Judged the best recipe in the quick treats and snacks category, it was one of the four contenders for the million-dollar grand prize.

Quick Apple Cranberry Pear Muffins

1 pkg. apple cinnamon bread mix*
³/₄ cup buttermilk**
3 tablespoons oil
1 egg
1 cup fresh or frozen cranberries, thawed
³/₄ cup coarsely chopped walnuts
1 large firm pear, peeled, cut into ¹/₂-inch pieces

Heat oven to 400°F. Line with paper baking cups or grease 18 muffin cups. In large bowl, combine quick bread mix, buttermilk, oil and egg. Stir 50 to 75 strokes with spoon until mix is moistened. Stir in cranberries, walnuts and pear. Spoon batter into paper-lined muffin cups. (Cups will be full.)

Bake at 400°F. for 18 to 25 minutes or until golden brown. Serve warm or cool.

Yield: 18 servings
(1 muffin per serving)

*Tips: Date bread mix can be substituted.

**To substitute for buttermilk, use 2 teaspoons vinegar or lemon juice plus milk to make ³/₄ cup.

High Altitude—Above 3,500 feet: Add ¹/₄ cup flour to dry bread mix. Bake as directed above.

Nutrition Per Serving: Calories 170; Protein 3g; Carbohydrate 24g; Fat 7g; Sodium 125mg

Chocolate Chunk Pistachio Muffins

Sally Vog *Springfield, Oregon*
Bake-Off® Contest 34, 1990

A pocket of raspberry jam is hidden inside each of these indulgent muffins.

2 cups all-purpose flour
³/4 cup sugar
2 teaspoons baking powder
¹/2 teaspoon cinnamon
¹/4 teaspoon baking soda
¹/4 teaspoon salt
6 oz. sweet cooking chocolate, coarsely chopped
¹/2 cup coarsely chopped pistachios
1 cup milk
¹/2 cup margarine or butter, melted
1 teaspoon grated lemon peel
1 teaspoon vanilla
1 egg, slightly beaten
¹/3 cup seedless raspberry jam

Heat oven to 375° F. Line with paper baking cups or grease bottoms only of 10 jumbo muffin cups. In large bowl, combine flour, sugar, baking powder, cinnamon, baking soda and salt; mix well. Reserve ¹/3 cup of the largest pieces of chopped chocolate; reserve 2 tablespoons of the pistachios. Stir remaining chopped chocolate and pistachios into dry ingredients. In small bowl, combine milk, margarine, lemon peel, vanilla and egg; blend well. Add to dry ingredients all at once; stir just until dry ingredients are moistened.

Fill each paper-lined muffin cup with 2 heaping tablespoons batter. Spoon rounded teaspoon jam into center of batter in each cup. Spoon about 1 heaping tablespoon of the remaining batter over jam in each cup. Top each with reserved chopped chocolate and pistachios.

Bake at 375° F. for 20 to 25 minutes or until toothpick inserted in center comes out clean. Cool 5 minutes; remove from pan. Serve warm or cool.

Yield: 10 servings
(1 muffin per serving)

Tip: For regular-sized muffins, line 20 regular-sized muffin cups with paper baking cups or grease bottoms only. Prepare batter as directed above. Fill each paper-lined muffin cup with 1 tablespoon batter. Place rounded ¹/2 teaspoon jam in center of batter in each cup. Spoon remaining batter evenly over each filled cup, covering jam. Top each with reserved chopped chocolate and pistachios. Bake at 375° F. for 15 to 20 minutes or until toothpick inserted in center comes out clean. Cool 5 minutes; remove from pan.

High Altitude—Above 3,500 feet: Increase flour to 2¹/4 cups. Bake as directed above.

Nutrition Per Serving: Calories 420; Protein 6g; Carbohydrate 54g; Fat 20g; Sodium 260mg

---

Top to bottom: **Tropical Oat Bran Muffins, page 129, Chocolate Chunk Pistachio Muffins**

Dairyland Date Muffins

Phyllis Saevre *Janesville, Wisconsin*
Bake-Off® Contest 20, 1969

What a wonderful idea—secret centers of cream cheese enclosed in a delicious, tender muffin. These are excellent served warm or cold.

1 cup shreds of whole bran cereal
¹/2 cup milk
2 (3-oz.) pkg. cream cheese
1 cup dairy sour cream
1 pkg. date bread mix
2 eggs

Heat oven to 400° F. Line with paper baking cups or grease bottoms only of 16 muffin cups. In large bowl, combine bran cereal and milk; let stand 10 minutes to soften. Cut each package of cream cheese into 8 equal cubes; set aside.

Add sour cream, bread mix and eggs to bran mixture; stir 50 to 75 strokes until dry particles are moistened. Divide batter evenly in paper-lined muffin cups. Press cube of cream cheese into batter in each cup; spread batter to completely cover cream cheese. Bake at 400° F. for 19 to 21 minutes or until golden brown. Cool 1 minute; remove from pan.

Yield: 16 servings
(1 muffin per serving)

High Altitude—Above 3,500 feet: Add 1 tablespoon flour to dry bread mix. Bake as directed above.

Nutrition Per Serving: Calories 200; Protein 4g; Carbohydrate 29g; Fat 7g; Sodium 160mg

The Giant's Corn Muffins

Irene McEwen *West Lafayette, Indiana*
Bake-Off® Contest 33, 1988

These are picture-perfect, moist, tender muffins that are chock-full of healthful ingredients. Treat yourself to one of these giant-sized beauties made in custard cups.

MUFFINS
1 cup cornmeal
1/2 cup all-purpose flour
1/2 cup whole wheat flour
1 teaspoon baking powder
1 teaspoon baking soda
1/2 teaspoon salt
1/4 teaspoon nutmeg
1 cup plain yogurt or buttermilk
1/4 cup margarine or butter, melted
3 tablespoons honey
1 egg
1 green onion, sliced
1 (11-oz.) can vacuum-packed whole kernel corn with red and green peppers, drained

TOPPING
1 tablespoon all-purpose flour
1 tablespoon cornmeal
2 teaspoons sugar
Dash salt
4 teaspoons margarine or butter

Heat oven to 400° F. Grease bottoms only of six 6-oz. custard cups; place custard cups on 15×10×1-inch baking pan. In large bowl, combine 1 cup cornmeal, 1/2 cup all-purpose flour, whole wheat flour, baking powder, baking soda, 1/2 teaspoon salt and nutmeg; blend well. In medium bowl, combine yogurt, 1/4 cup margarine, honey, egg, green onion and corn; mix well. Add to dry ingredients; stir just until dry ingredients are moistened. Spoon batter evenly into greased custard cups. (Cups will be full.) In small bowl, combine all topping ingredients; mix well. Crumble evenly over muffins.

Bake at 400° F. for 20 to 30 minutes or until toothpick inserted in center comes out clean. Cool 1 minute; remove from custard cups. Serve warm.

Yield: 6 servings
(1 muffin per serving)

High Altitude—Above 3,500 feet: No change.

Nutrition Per Serving: Calories 380; Protein 9g; Carbohydrate 56g; Fat 13g; Sodium 760mg

Middleberry Scones

Lisa Keys *Middlebury, Connecticut*
Bake-Off® Contest 36, 1994 Prize Winner

A traditional Scottish quick bread, scones come in a variety of shapes and flavors. This jam-filled whole wheat version is served in wedges. Scones are usually served for breakfast or tea.

SCONES
1 1/2 cups all-purpose flour
1/2 cup whole wheat flour
2 tablespoons sugar
1 tablespoon baking powder
1/2 teaspoon salt
1/2 teaspoon cinnamon
1 teaspoon grated orange peel
1/4 cup butter or margarine
2/3 cup half-and-half
1 egg
1/3 cup raspberry or strawberry preserves
1 teaspoon sugar

SPREAD AND GARNISH
1 (3-oz.) pkg. cream cheese, softened
16 fresh raspberries or strawberries, if desired
1 teaspoon grated orange peel, if desired

Heat oven to 425° F. Lightly grease cookie sheet. In large bowl, combine all-purpose flour, whole wheat flour, 2 tablespoons sugar, baking powder, salt, cinnamon and 1 teaspoon orange peel; mix well. Using fork or pastry blender, cut in butter until mixture resembles coarse crumbs.

In small bowl, combine half-and-half and egg; blend well. Add to flour mixture. Stir just until dry ingredients are moistened. Turn dough out onto well-floured surface; knead lightly 4 times. Divide in half; pat each half into 8-inch circle. Place 1 circle on greased cookie sheet; spread preserves to within 1 inch of edge. Place remaining circle over preserves; pinch edges to seal. Sprinkle top with 1 teaspoon sugar. Cut into 8 wedges; do not separate.

Bake at 425° F. for 15 to 18 minutes or until edges are golden. Cut through scones. Serve warm with cream cheese; garnish with berries and 1 teaspoon orange peel.

Yield: 8 servings (1 scone per serving)

High Altitude—Above 3,500 feet: No change.

Nutrition Per Serving: Calories 290; Protein 6g; Carbohydrate 38g; Fat 13g; Sodium 350mg

Tropical Oat Bran Muffins

Claudia Howe *Hickory Hills, Illinois*
Bake-Off® Contest 34, 1990

These muffins are full of coconut, macadamia nuts, bananas and pineapple. Serve them warm with the light and fluffy fruit spread.

MUFFINS
2 cups all-purpose flour
3/4 cup fortified whole bran cereal with oat bran or fortified whole bran cereal
1/2 cup coconut
2 teaspoons baking powder
1 teaspoon cinnamon
1 (3 1/2-oz.) jar macadamia nuts, chopped, if desired
1/2 cup margarine or butter, softened
1 cup sugar
1/4 cup firmly packed brown sugar
3 eggs
3/4 cup (about 2 medium) mashed ripe bananas
2 teaspoons vanilla
1 (8-oz.) can crushed pineapple in unsweetened juice, drained

FRUIT SPREAD*
1/2 cup margarine or butter, softened
1/3 cup low-calorie pineapple fruit spread, preserves or jam

Heat oven to 350°F. Line with paper baking cups or grease bottoms only of 22 regular-sized muffin cups or 12 jumbo muffin cups. In large bowl, combine flour, cereal, coconut, baking powder, cinnamon and macadamia nuts; mix well.

In another large bowl, combine 1/2 cup margarine, sugar and brown sugar; beat until light and fluffy. Add eggs; blend well. Stir in mashed bananas, vanilla and pineapple; blend well. Add to dry ingredients all at once; stir until dry ingredients are just moistened. Fill greased muffin cups 2/3 full.

Bake at 350°F. for 20 to 30 minutes or until light golden brown and toothpick inserted in center comes out clean. Cool 2 minutes; remove from pans. In small bowl, combine fruit spread ingredients at low speed until well blended. Serve with muffins.

Yield: 22 servings
(1 muffin per serving)

*Tip: To make cream-cheese fruit spread, substitute 8-oz. pkg. reduced-fat cream cheese, softened, for margarine. Increase pineapple spread to 1/2 cup. Prepare as directed above.

High Altitude—Above 3,500 feet: Decrease sugar to 3/4 cup. Bake as directed above.

Nutrition Per Serving: Calories 240; Protein 3g; Carbohydrate 28g; Fat 13g; Sodium 160mg

Lemon Nutmeg Scones

Anita Atoulikian *Parma, Ohio*
Bake-Off® Contest 34, 1990 Prize Winner

A lemony cream cheese spread adds the finishing touch to these company-special scones. Serve them for a brunch, a weekend breakfast or a coffee klatch.

1 3/4 cups all-purpose flour
1/4 cup cornstarch
1 teaspoon baking soda
1/4 teaspoon nutmeg
6 tablespoons margarine or butter
1 (8-oz.) container lemon yogurt
1/3 cup golden raisins
2 eggs
4 1/2 teaspoons sugar
1/8 teaspoon nutmeg
1 (3-oz.) pkg. cream cheese, softened

Heat oven to 450°F. Grease cookie sheet. In large bowl, combine flour, cornstarch, baking soda and 1/4 teaspoon nutmeg; blend well.

Lisa Keys: Middleberry Scones

Scones were popular in the last half of the nineteenth century, when baking powder became readily available. Perhaps that is why we associate them most with Victorian teatime. However, scones are almost exactly like biscuits —a simple quick bread that can be dressed up with spices and additions until they are quite extravagant. "Cinnamon and orange flavors are my favorite," Lisa Keys says. "I love the smell of my kitchen when these scones are baking. They are fragrant and special indeed, yet simple and quick." Cooks everywhere are thankful for the indispensable combination of sodium bicarbonate and acid salt—otherwise known as baking powder.

Using pastry blender or fork, cut in margarine until mixture resembles coarse crumbs.

In small bowl, combine $1/2$ cup of the lemon yogurt, raisins and eggs. Add to dry ingredients all at once; stir until dry ingredients are just moistened. (Dough will be sticky.) On floured surface, shape dough into ball. On greased cookie sheet, press dough into 9-inch circle, about $3/4$ inch thick.

In small bowl, combine sugar and $1/8$ teaspoon nutmeg; sprinkle over top of dough. Cut into 12 wedges; separate so wedges are 1 inch apart. Bake at 450°F. for 7 to 10 minutes or until very light golden brown.

Meanwhile, in small bowl, combine remaining lemon yogurt and cream cheese; beat until well blended. Serve with warm scones.

Yield: 12 servings
(1 scone per serving)

High Altitude—Above 3,500 feet: Increase flour to $2^{1}/4$ cups. Bake as directed above.

Nutrition Per Serving: Calories 200; Protein 5g; Carbohydrate 25g; Fat 9g; Sodium 200mg

Orange-Glazed Tropical Fruit Scones

Fran Neavoll *Salem, Oregon*
Bake-Off® Contest 37, 1996 Prize Winner

Followers of the Oregon State Fair know Fran Neavoll as one of the top blue-ribbon winners in baking. Although her fair specialty is cookies, her glazed fruit-filled scones were good enough to make her one of the four contenders for the million-dollar grand prize in 1996.

SCONES
2 cups all-purpose flour
2 tablespoons sugar
3 teaspoons baking powder
1 teaspoon salt
1$1/2$ teaspoons grated orange peel
$1/4$ cup butter or margarine
$1/3$ cup milk
2 eggs, beaten
1 cup tropical medley dried fruit or dried fruit bits
$1/2$ cup white vanilla chips

GLAZE
1 cup powdered sugar
2 to 3 tablespoons orange juice

SPREAD
$1/3$ cup apricot-pineapple or apricot preserves

Heat oven to 400°F. In large bowl, combine flour, sugar, baking powder, salt and orange peel; mix well. With pastry blender or fork, cut in butter until mixture resembles coarse crumbs. Add milk and eggs; blend well. Stir in dried fruit and white vanilla chips until well mixed.

On lightly floured surface, knead dough 6 or 7 times until smooth. Divide dough in half. Pat each half into a 6-inch circle. With floured knife, cut each circle into 4 wedges. Place wedges 2 inches apart on ungreased cookie sheet.

Bake at 400°F. for 12 to 16 minutes or until golden brown. Cool 1 minute.

Meanwhile, in small bowl, combine powdered sugar and enough orange juice for desired drizzling consistency; blend until smooth. Drizzle mixture over top and sides of each scone. Cool 5 minutes. If desired, split each scone and spread with 2 teaspoons preserves, or serve preserves with scones. Serve warm.

Yield: 8 servings (1 scone per serving)

High Altitude—Above 3,500 feet: Increase flour to 2 cups plus 2 tablespoons. Bake at 400°F. for 14 to 19 minutes or until golden brown.

Nutrition Per Serving: Calories 430; Protein 7g; Carbohydrate 70g; Fat 14g; Sodium 550mg

Graham Cracker Brown Bread

Grace M. Kain *West Boothbay Harbor, Maine*
Bake-Off® Contest 10, 1958

The secret ingredient in this unusual bread is graham crackers—they add color, texture and flavor appeal. The recipe makes two loaves. Have one now and freeze one to serve later.

2 cups graham cracker crumbs or finely crushed graham crackers (30 squares)

^{1}/$_2$ **cup shortening**
1^3/$_4$ cups buttermilk*
^{3}/$_4$ **cup molasses**
2 eggs, slightly beaten
1^3/$_4$ cups all-purpose flour
2 teaspoons baking soda
1 teaspoon salt
^{1}/$_4$ to ^{1}/$_2$ teaspoon nutmeg
1 cup raisins

Heat oven to 375°F. Grease and flour bottoms only of two 8×4-inch loaf pans. In large bowl, combine graham cracker crumbs and shortening; beat until well blended. Add buttermilk, molasses and eggs; blend well. In small bowl, combine flour, baking soda, salt and nutmeg; mix well. Add to graham cracker mixture; mix at low speed until well blended. Fold in raisins. Pour batter into greased and floured pans.

Bake at 375°F. for 35 to 40 minutes or until toothpick inserted in center comes out clean. Cool 5 minutes; remove from pans. Cool on wire racks. Wrap tightly and store in refrigerator.

Yield: 32 servings
(1 slice per serving)

***Tip:** To substitute for buttermilk, use 5 teaspoons vinegar or lemon juice plus milk to make 1^3/$_4$ cups.

High Altitude—Above 3,500 feet: Increase flour to 2^1/$_4$ cups. Bake as directed above.

Nutrition Per Serving: Calories 110; Protein 2g; Carbohydrate 17g; Fat 4g; Sodium 180mg

Orange-Glazed Tropical Fruit Scones

Pepper Biscuit Pull-Apart

Julie Ann Robasse *Big Lake, Minnesota*
Bake-Off® Contest 34, 1990

A kissing cousin to pizza, serve as a snack or with soup or salad.

1/4 **teaspoon garlic powder**
1/4 **teaspoon salt, if desired**
1/4 **teaspoon dried basil leaves, crushed**
1/4 **teaspoon dried oregano leaves, crushed**
1 **(12-oz.) can refrigerated flaky biscuits**
41/2 **teaspoons olive oil**
1/4 **cup chopped green bell pepper**
1/4 **cup chopped red bell pepper**
1 **oz. (1/4 cup) shredded mozzarella cheese**
2 **tablespoons grated Romano or Parmesan cheese**

Heat oven to 400° F. In small bowl, combine garlic powder, salt, basil and oregano; blend well. Set aside.

Separate dough into 10 biscuits. Place 1 biscuit in center of ungreased cookie sheet. Arrange remaining biscuits in circle, edges slightly overlapping, around center biscuit. Gently press out to 10-inch circle. Brush with olive oil; top with bell peppers and cheeses. Sprinkle garlic powder mixture over top. Bake at 400° F. for 12 to 15 minutes or until golden brown. To serve, pull apart warm biscuits.

Yield: 10 servings
(1 biscuit per serving)

Nutrition Per Serving: Calories 130; Protein 3g; Carbohydrate 14g; Fat 7g; Sodium 450mg

Easy Baked Onion Rings

Kevin Koors *Lafayette, Indiana*
Bake-Off® Contest 35, 1992

These quick and easy dinner rolls taste like a soft onion-filled bagel!

1/3 **cup chopped onion**
2 **tablespoons margarine or butter, melted**
1 **tablespoon grated Parmesan cheese**
1/2 **teaspoon poppy seed**
1/4 **teaspoon chili powder**
1/4 **teaspoon garlic powder**
1/8 **teaspoon pepper**
1 **(8-oz.) can refrigerated crescent dinner rolls**
1/4 **cup seasoned dry bread crumbs**
1/4 **teaspoon chili powder**
1 **egg, beaten**

Heat oven to 375° F. In small bowl, combine onion, margarine, Parmesan cheese, poppy seed, 1/4 teaspoon chili powder, garlic powder and pepper; mix well. Separate dough into 4 rectangles; firmly press perforations to seal. Cut each rectangle lengthwise into 2 strips, forming 8 strips. Spoon about 2 teaspoons onion mixture down center of each strip. Bring long sides of dough together over filling; firmly pinch edges to seal. Twist each filled dough strip; form into a ring. Pinch ends of strips together to seal.

In small bowl, combine bread crumbs and 1/4 teaspoon chili powder. Dip tops and sides of rings in beaten egg and then in bread crumb mixture. Place crumb side up on ungreased cookie sheet. Bake at 375° F. for 10 to 15 minutes or until deep golden brown. Serve warm.

Yield: 8 servings (1 roll per serving)

Nutrition Per Serving: Calories 150; Protein 3g; Carbohydrate 14g; Fat 9g; Sodium 330mg

Kevin Koors: Easy Baked Onion Rings

Cooking brings friends together, although sometimes in odd ways. "The first time that I boiled rice in a bag, just after college, it bothered me that the bag would float to the top," Kevin Koors says. "Afraid that the rice wouldn't cook, I asked a friend what to do. Following her directions, I went to the grocery in search of a 'cooking rock,' to hold the bag down. An amused clerk informed me that there was no such thing, and I had a good laugh at my friend's prank." And Kevin's rice cooked perfectly well, even without the mythical cooking rock.

Pepper Biscuit Pull-Apart

Banana-Wheat Quick Bread

Barbara Goldstein *New York, New York*
Bake-Off® Contest 24, 1973

You'll like the down-home goodness of this version of wholesome banana bread.

1¼ cups all-purpose flour
½ cup whole wheat flour
1 cup sugar
1 teaspoon baking soda
1 teaspoon salt
1½ cups (3 medium) mashed
   ripe bananas
¼ cup margarine or butter,
   softened
2 tablespoons orange juice
¼ teaspoon lemon juice, if
   desired
1 egg
¼ to ½ cup raisins

Heat oven to 350°F. Grease and flour bottom only of 9×5- or 8×4-inch loaf pan.

In large bowl, combine all ingredients except raisins; beat 3 minutes at medium speed. Fold in raisins. Pour batter into greased and floured pan.

Bake at 350°F. for 55 to 65 minutes or until toothpick inserted in center comes out clean. Cool 10 minutes; remove from pan. Cool on wire rack. Wrap tightly and store in refrigerator.

Yield: 16 servings (1 slice per serving)

High Altitude—Above 3,500 feet: Increase all-purpose flour to 1½ cups. Bake as directed above.

Nutrition Per Serving: Calories 160; Protein 2g; Carbohydrate 31g; Fat 3g; Sodium 250mg

Golden Sesame Loaves

Grayce Berggren *State College, Pennsylvania*
Bake-Off® Contest 33, 1988 Prize Winner

Reflecting the growing interest in more nutritious yeast breads in the 1980s, this rich, moist loaf also gets a flavor boost from the addition of oat bran, honey and toasted sesame seed.

5 to 6 cups all-purpose flour
½ cup instant nonfat dry milk
½ cup oat bran
½ cup sesame seed, toasted*
1½ teaspoons salt
1 teaspoon sugar
2 pkg. active dry yeast
1¾ cups water
¼ cup oil
¼ cup honey
1 egg
1 egg white, beaten
1 tablespoon sesame seed

In large bowl, combine 2 cups flour, dry milk, oat bran, ½ cup toasted sesame seed, salt, sugar and yeast; blend well. In small saucepan, heat water, oil and honey until very warm (120 to 130°F.). Add warm liquid and 1 egg to flour mixture. Blend at low speed until moistened; beat 3 minutes at medium speed. Stir in an additional 2¾ to 3½ cups flour until dough pulls cleanly away from sides of bowl.

On floured surface, knead in remaining ¼ to ½ cup flour until dough is smooth and elastic, about 10 minutes. Place dough in greased bowl; cover loosely with plastic wrap and cloth towel. Let rise in warm place (80 to 85°F.) until light and doubled in size, 45 to 55 minutes.

Grease two 9×5- or three 7×3-inch loaf pans. Punch down dough several times to remove all air bubbles. Divide dough in half; shape into balls. Shape into loaves by rolling each half into 12×8-inch rectangle. Starting with shortest side, roll up; pinch edges firmly to seal. Place seam side down in greased pans. Cover; let rise in warm place until dough fills pans

Original Autographs

The creative abilities of Bake-Off® finalists extend beyond the kitchen; they have a certain flair when asking for autographs as well!

- In 1960, Ivy Baker Priest, then the Treasurer of the United States, was the Bake-Off® Contest's guest of honor. She signed dollar bills for the finalists —since she was the only person legally allowed to do so.

- Television host Art Linkletter was the Bake-Off® Contest's emcee 19 times, making him the most frequent participant, except for contest founder Philip Pillsbury. Linkletter got a big kick out of circulating on the Bake-Off® Contest floor, and was seen autographing everything from program books to flour bags, to the occasional egg!

and tops of loaves are about 1 inch-above pan edges, 30 to 35 minutes.

Heat oven to 350°F. Uncover dough. Carefully brush loaves with egg white; sprinkle with 1 tablespoon sesame seed. Bake at 350°F. for 30 to 40 minutes or until loaves sound hollow when lightly tapped. Immediately remove from pans; cool on wire racks.

Yield: 32 servings (1 slice per serving)

*Tip: To toast sesame seed, spread on cookie sheet; bake at 375°F. for about 5 minutes to until light golden brown, stirring occasionally. Or, spread in medium skillet and stir over medium heat for about 10 minutes or until light golden brown.

High Altitude—Above 3,500 feet: Decrease each rise time by about 15 minutes. Bake at 350°F. for 25 to 35 minutes.

Nutrition Per Serving: Calories 130; Protein 4g; Carbohydrate 22g; Fat 3g; Sodium 110mg

Whole Wheat Raisin Loaf

Lenora Smith *Harahan, Louisiana*
Bake-Off® Contest 27, 1976 Grand Prize Winner

As a grand prize winner in 1976, this hearty loaf introduced thousands to the joys of making their own whole-grain bread. You'll find the raisins and spices have a natural affinity with the nut-like flavors of rolled oats and whole wheat.

Recipe Swapping

Cookbooks were not always as common as they are today. In fact, most recipes were recorded on index cards and stored in boxes and drawers. Family cooks would get together and copy one another's cards. The Bake-Off® Contest sprung from this tradition. "Pillsbury's Bake-Off® is actually a 'back fence,' and over it America's best recipes and ideas are exchanged in a true neighbor-to-neighbor fashion," as described in the first Bake-Off® recipe booklet in 1949. Early entry forms were accompanied by text that advised, "All you have to do is swap your recipe. Don't miss out on the greatest cooking event and exchange of recipes in America." Nearly fifty years later, this recipe swapping is still going strong.

2 to 3 cups all-purpose flour
¹⁄₂ cup sugar
3 teaspoons salt
1 teaspoon cinnamon
¹⁄₂ teaspoon nutmeg
2 pkg. active dry yeast
2 cups milk
³⁄₄ cup water
¹⁄₄ cup oil
4 cups whole wheat flour
1 cup rolled oats
1 cup raisins
1 tablespoon margarine or butter, melted
1 teaspoon sugar, if desired

In large bowl, combine 1¹⁄₂ cups all-purpose flour, ¹⁄₂ cup sugar, salt, cinnamon, nutmeg and yeast; mix well. In medium saucepan, heat milk, water and oil until very warm (120 to 130°F.). Add warm liquid to flour mixture. Blend at low speed until moistened; beat 3 minutes at medium speed. By hand, stir in whole wheat flour, rolled oats, raisins and an additional ¹⁄₄ to ³⁄₄ cup all-purpose flour until dough pulls cleanly away from sides of bowl.

On floured surface, knead in remaining ¹⁄₄ to ³⁄₄ cup all-purpose flour until dough is smooth and elastic, about 5 minutes. Place dough in greased bowl; cover loosely with greased plastic wrap and cloth towel. Let rise in warm place (80 to 85°F.) until light and doubled in size, 20 to 30 minutes.

Grease two 9×5- or 8×4-inch loaf pans. Punch down dough several times to remove all air bubbles. Divide dough in half; shape into loaves. Place in greased pans.

Cover; let rise in warm place until light and doubled in size, 30 to 45 minutes.

Heat oven to 375°F. Uncover dough. Bake 40 to 50 minutes or until deep golden brown and loaves sound hollow when lightly tapped. If loaves become too brown, cover loosely with foil last 10 minutes of baking. Immediately remove from pans; cool on wire racks. Brush tops of loaves with margarine; sprinkle with 1 teaspoon sugar.

Yield: 32 servings (1 slice per serving)

High Altitude—Above 3,500 feet: No change.

Nutrition Per Serving: Calories 160; Protein 5g; Carbohydrate 29g; Fat 3g; Sodium 210mg

Dilly Casserole Bread

Leona Schnuelle *Crab Orchard, Nebraska*
Bake-Off® Contest 12, 1960 Grand
Prize Winner

This dill and onion–flavored bread is
made with cottage cheese and baked
in a round casserole. It's easy, deli-
cious and a Pillsbury favorite!

2 to 2²/₃ cups all-purpose flour
2 tablespoons sugar
2 to 3 teaspoons instant
   minced onion
2 teaspoons dill seed
1 teaspoon salt
¹/₄ teaspoon baking soda
1 pkg. active dry yeast
¹/₄ cup water
1 tablespoon margarine or
   butter
1 cup creamed cottage cheese
1 egg

2 teaspoons margarine or
   butter, melted
¹/₄ teaspoon coarse salt, if
   desired

In large bowl, combine 1 cup flour,
sugar, onion, dill seed, 1 teaspoon
salt, baking soda and yeast; mix
well. In small saucepan, heat
water, 1 tablespoon margarine and

Left to right: **Golden Gate Snack Bread,
page 145, Dilly Casserole Bread,
Muffin Mix Buffet Bread, page 145**

cottage cheese until very warm (120 to 130°F.). Add warm liquid and egg to flour mixture. Blend at low speed until moistened; beat 3 minutes at medium speed. By hand, stir in remaining 1 to 1²/₃ cups flour to form a stiff batter. Cover loosely with greased plastic wrap and cloth towel. Let rise in warm place (80 to 85°F.) until light and doubled in size, 45 to 60 minutes.

Generously grease 1½- or 2-quart casserole. Stir down dough to remove all air bubbles. Turn into greased casserole. Cover; let rise in warm place until light and doubled in size, 30 to 45 minutes.

Heat oven to 350°F. Uncover dough. Bake 30 to 40 minutes or until deep golden brown and loaf sounds hollow when lightly tapped. Immediately remove from casserole; cool on wire rack. Brush warm loaf with melted margarine; sprinkle with coarse salt.

Yield: 18 servings (1 slice per serving)

Food Processor Directions: In small bowl, soften yeast in ¼ cup *warm* water (105 to 115°F.). In food processor bowl with metal blade, combine 2 cups flour, sugar, onion, dill seed, 1 teaspoon salt, baking soda and 1 tablespoon margarine. Cover; process 5 seconds. Add cottage cheese and egg. Cover; process about 10 seconds or until blended. With machine running, pour yeast mixture through feed tube. Continue processing until blended, about 20 seconds or until mixture pulls away from sides of bowl and forms a ball, adding additional flour if necessary. Carefully scrape dough from blade and bowl; place in lightly greased bowl. Cover loosely with greased plastic wrap and cloth towel. Let rise in warm place (80 to 85°F.) until light and doubled in size, 45 to 60 minutes. Continue as directed above.

High Altitude—Above 3,500 feet: Bake at 375°F. for 35 to 40 minutes.

Nutrition Per Serving: Calories 100; Protein 4g; Carbohydrate 16g; Fat 2g; Sodium 230mg

Leona Schnuelle: Dilly Casserole Bread

When Leona Schnuelle captured the Grand Prize in the twelfth Bake-Off® Contest, she suddenly found herself a celebrity in her small town of Crab Orchard, Nebraska. "Everyone seems happier when I arrive, even at the square dances. They say 'Hi, Mrs. Pillsbury!' Even though I miss a *do-si-do* now and then—they think I can bake a dilly of a bread! And all the fan mail I receive! It's exciting to hear from all the different people with all their different ways of life, yet they all seem so interested in a bread recipe." Especially with a loaf like Dilly Casserole Bread to pique their interest.

Easy Cheese Batter Bread

Frances Sisinni *Milwaukee, Wisconsin*
Bake-Off® Contest 23, 1972

Batter breads are among the simplest to prepare because they aren't kneaded or shaped. This moist and chewy version is even better the second day.

2½ cups all-purpose flour
2 teaspoons sugar
1½ teaspoons salt
1 pkg. active dry yeast
4 oz. (1 cup) shredded Cheddar cheese
¾ cup milk
½ cup margarine or butter
3 eggs

In large bowl, combine 1½ cups flour, sugar, salt and yeast; blend well. Stir in cheese. In small saucepan, heat milk and margarine until very warm (120 to 130°F.). Add warm liquid and eggs to flour mixture. Blend at low speed until moistened; beat 3 minutes at medium speed. By hand, stir in remaining 1 cup flour. Cover loosely with plastic wrap and cloth towel. Let rise in warm place (80 to 85°F.) until light and doubled in size, 45 to 60 minutes.

Generously grease 1½- or 2-quart casserole or 9×5-inch loaf pan. Stir down dough to remove all air bubbles. Turn into greased casserole. Cover; let rise in warm place until light and doubled in size, 20 to 25 minutes.

Heat oven to 350°F. Uncover dough. Bake 40 to 45 minutes or until deep golden brown. Immediately remove from casserole; cool on wire rack.

Yield: 18 servings (1 slice per serving)

High Altitude—Above 3,500 feet: Bake at 375°F. for 40 to 45 minutes.

Nutrition Per Serving: Calories 150; Protein 5g; Carbohydrate 15g; Fat 8g; Sodium 290mg

Southwestern Pockets of Cheese Bread

Mariette Deutsch *Cedarburg, Wisconsin*
Bake-Off® Contest 36, 1994

This intensely seasoned black bean bread is especially delicious when served warm.

1/2 cup sun-dried tomatoes without oil, chopped
1 (15-oz.) can black beans, drained
1/2 cup nonfat plain yogurt
2 teaspoons cumin
1 teaspoon dried oregano leaves
1 teaspoon dried parsley flakes
1 garlic clove, minced, or
    1 teaspoon garlic powder
5 1/2 to 6 1/2 cups all-purpose flour
2 tablespoons sugar
1 tablespoon salt
2 pkg. fast-acting dry yeast
1 cup water
1/2 cup canola oil or other vegetable oil
1 egg
1 (4.5-oz.) can chopped green chiles, drained, or 2 tablespoons finely chopped jalapeño pepper
8 oz. Monterey Jack cheese, cut into 1/2-inch cubes (2 cups)

In blender container or food processor bowl with metal blade, finely chop tomatoes. Add beans, yogurt, cumin, oregano, parsley and garlic; process 10 to 15 seconds or until beans are mashed. Set aside.

In large bowl, combine 1 1/2 cups flour, sugar, salt and yeast; mix well. In small saucepan, heat water and oil until very warm (120 to 130° F.). Add warm liquid and egg to flour mixture. Blend at low speed until moistened; beat 3 minutes at medium speed. Add bean mixture; beat until well mixed. By hand, stir in green chiles and an additional 3 1/2 to 4 cups flour to form a stiff dough.

On floured or cornmeal-coated surface, knead in 1/2 to 1 cup flour for about 5 minutes or until dough is smooth and elastic. Place dough in greased bowl; cover loosely with greased plastic wrap and cloth towel. Let rise in warm place (80 to 85° F.) for 45 to 60 minutes or until light and doubled in size.

Grease two 8- or 9-inch round cake pans or 1 large cookie sheet. Punch down dough. Divide dough in half; shape each half into 6-inch round loaf. Place in greased pans. Using sharp knife, 1 1/2 inches from edge, cut 2 1/2-inch-deep ring around each loaf. Cut another 2 1/2-inch-deep ring 1 inch inside of first cut. Insert cheese in cuts; pinch cut edges to seal. Cover; let rise in warm place 30 to 40 minutes or until light and almost doubled in size.

Heat oven to 375° F. Uncover dough. Bake 35 to 45 minutes or until loaves are deep golden brown and sound hollow when lightly tapped. Immediately remove from pans; cool on wire racks.

Yield: 32 servings (1 slice per serving)

Tip: Bread can be frozen. Thaw at room temperature. To reheat, heat oven to 375° F. Wrap loaf in foil; bake at 375° F. for 30 to 40 minutes or until hot.

High Altitude—Above 3,500 feet: No change.

Nutrition Per Serving: Calories 170; Protein 6g; Carbohydrate 24g; Fat 6g; Sodium 270mg

Salsa Bread Olé

Cindy Atwood *Taunton, Massachusetts*
Bake-Off® Contest 37, 1996

Bring out the maracas and prepare for a fiesta. Your family will want to say "Olé!" after one bite of this hearty cornbread bursting with a blend of cheeses, ripe olives and salsa.

3 eggs
1/2 cup cornmeal
2/3 cup buttermilk*
1/2 cup butter or margarine, softened
1 (16-oz.) jar mild salsa, well drained
1/2 cup chopped ripe olives
1/4 cup chopped green onions
1 tablespoon chopped fresh parsley
5 oz. (1 1/4 cups) shredded Cheddar cheese
1 oz. (1/4 cup) shredded Monterey Jack cheese, if desired
2 cups all-purpose flour
1 cup mashed potato flakes
4 teaspoons taco seasoning mix
3 teaspoons baking powder
1 teaspoon baking soda
1/4 teaspoon salt
1/4 teaspoon pepper

Heat oven to 350° F. Grease and flour 10-inch tube or 12-cup Bundt® pan. In large bowl, beat eggs at high speed for 1 minute. Add cornmeal, buttermilk, butter and salsa; beat 1 minute at medium speed or until well blended. With spoon, stir in olives, onions, parsley and cheeses.

In medium bowl, combine flour and all remaining ingredients; mix well. Add to salsa mixture; stir

until well blended. Spoon batter into greased and floured pan.

Bake at 350° F. for 45 to 50 minutes or until toothpick inserted in center comes out clean. Cool 15 minutes. Remove from pan. Cool 20 minutes. Serve warm.

Yield: 1 (24-slice) loaf

*Tip: To substitute for buttermilk, use 2 teaspoons vinegar or lemon juice plus milk to make ⅔ cup.

High Altitude—Above 3,500 feet: No change.

Nutrition Per Serving: Calories 140; Protein 4g; Carbohydrate 14g; Fat 7g; Sodium 360mg

Salsa Bread Olé

Onion Lover's Twist

Nan Robb *Huachucha City, Arizona*
Bake-Off® Contest 21, 1970 Grand Prize Winner

This no-knead bread features fresh chopped onions rolled in strips of dough that are braided together to create a light-textured onion bread. Serve it warm or cold with a favorite chicken or beef main dish and see why it took top honors!

BREAD
3¹/₂ to 4¹/₂ cups all-purpose
   flour
¹/₄ cup sugar
1¹/₂ teaspoons salt
1 pkg. active dry yeast
³/₄ cup water
¹/₂ cup milk
¹/₄ cup margarine or butter
1 egg

FILLING
¹/₄ cup margarine or butter
1 cup finely chopped onions
   or ¹/₄ cup instant minced
   onion
1 tablespoon grated Parmesan
   cheese
1 tablespoon sesame or poppy
   seed
¹/₂ to 1 teaspoon garlic salt
1 teaspoon paprika

In large bowl, combine 2 cups of the flour, sugar, salt and yeast; blend well. In small saucepan, heat water, milk and ¹/₄ cup margarine until very warm (120 to 130° F.). Add warm liquid and egg to flour mixture. Blend at low speed until

Left to right: **Onion Lover's Twist, Whole Wheat Raisin Loaf, page 135**

moistened; beat 3 minutes at medium speed. By hand, stir in remaining 1¹/₂ to 2¹/₂ cups flour to form a soft dough. Cover loosely with greased plastic wrap and cloth towel. Let rise in warm place (80 to 95° F.) until light and doubled in size, 45 to 60 minutes.

Grease large cookie sheet. Melt ¹/₄ cup margarine in small saucepan; stir in remaining filling ingredients. Set aside. Stir down dough to remove all air bubbles. On floured surface, toss dough until no longer sticky. Roll dough into 18×12-inch rectangle. Cut rectangle in half crosswise to make two 12×9-inch rectangles; cut each rectangle into three 9×4-inch strips. Spread about 2 tablespoons onion mixture over each strip to ¹/₂ inch of edges. Bring lengthwise edges of each strip together to enclose filling; pinch edges and ends to seal.

On greased cookie sheet, braid 3 rolls together; pinch ends to seal. Repeat with remaining 3 rolls for second loaf. Cover; let rise in warm place until light and doubled in size, 25 to 30 minutes.

Heat oven to 350° F. Uncover dough. Bake 27 to 35 minutes or until golden brown and loaves sound hollow when lightly tapped. Immediately remove from cookie sheet; cool on wire racks.

Yield: 32 servings (1 slice per serving)

High Altitude—Above 3,500 feet: No change.

Nutrition Per Serving: Calories 130; Protein 3g; Carbohydrate 16g; Fat 6g; Sodium 230mg

Golden Party Loaves

Effie Cato *San Antonio, Texas*
Bake-Off® Contest 31, 1984

In this recipe, six wholesome mini loaves are baked side by side in two loaf pans and served with a tangy apricot spread.

BREAD
4¹/₂ to 5¹/₂ cups all-purpose
   flour
1¹/₂ cups finely shredded
   carrots
1 teaspoon salt
1 pkg. active dry yeast
³/₄ cup apricot nectar
¹/₂ cup plain low-fat yogurt
¹/₄ cup honey
¹/₄ cup margarine or butter
1 egg
Margarine or butter, softened

SPREAD
1 (8-oz.) pkg. cream cheese,
   softened
¹/₂ cup apricot preserves

In large bowl, combine 2 cups flour, carrots, salt and yeast; blend well. In small saucepan, heat apricot nectar, yogurt, honey and ¹/₄ cup margarine until very warm (120 to 130° F.). Add warm liquid and egg to flour mixture. Blend at low speed until moistened; beat 3 minutes at medium speed. By hand, stir in an additional 2 to 2¹/₂ cups flour to form a stiff dough.

On floured surface, knead in remaining ¹/₂ to 1 cup flour until dough is smooth and elastic, about 5 minutes. Place dough in greased bowl; cover loosely with plastic wrap and cloth towel. Let rise in warm place (80 to 85° F.) until light and doubled in size, about 1 hour.

Grease and flour two 9×5- or 8×4-inch loaf pans. Punch down dough several times to remove all air bubbles. Divide dough in half. Work dough with hands to remove large air bubbles. Divide each half into thirds. Shape each third into a small loaf. Spread sides of loaves with softened margarine. Place 3 loaves crosswise in each greased and floured pan. Cover; let rise in warm place until light and doubled in size, about 45 minutes.

Heat oven to 375° F. Uncover dough. Bake 30 to 35 minutes or until loaves are deep golden brown and sound hollow when lightly tapped. Immediately remove from pans; cool on wire racks. Brush warm loaves with softened margarine. In small bowl, combine spread ingredients; blend well. Serve with bread.

Yield: 42 servings (1 slice per serving)

High Altitude—Above 3,500 feet: No change.

Nutrition Per Serving: Calories 120; Protein 3g; Carbohydrate 18g; Fat 4g; Sodium 90mg

Honey Granola Bread

Gloria Kirchman *Mankato, Minnesota*
Bake-Off® Contest 30, 1982

Whole wheat flour, honey and granola make this a wholesome tasty sandwich bread for the school lunchbox. Lower fat granola cereal is now available and can be used to make the bread.

5 to 5½ cups all-purpose flour
1 cup granola cereal
2 teaspoons salt
2 pkg. active dry yeast
1½ cups water
1 cup low-fat plain yogurt
½ cup honey
¼ cup oil or shortening
2 eggs
2 cups whole wheat flour

In large bowl, combine 3 cups all-purpose flour, granola cereal, salt and yeast; blend well. In medium saucepan, heat water, yogurt, honey and oil until very warm (120 to 130° F.). Add warm liquid and eggs to flour mixture; blend at low speed until moistened. Beat 3 minutes at medium speed. By hand, stir in whole wheat flour and an additional 1 cup all-purpose flour to form a stiff dough.

On floured surface, knead in remaining 1 to 1½ cups all-purpose flour until dough is smooth and elastic, about 10 minutes. Place dough in greased bowl; cover loosely with plastic wrap and cloth towel. Let rise in warm place (80 to 85° F.) until light and doubled in size, about 1 hour.

Generously grease two 9×5- or 8×4-inch loaf pans. Punch down dough several times to remove all air bubbles. Divide dough in half; shape into loaves. Place in greased pans. Cover; let rise in warm place until light and doubled in size, 30 to 45 minutes.

Heat oven to 350° F. Uncover dough. Bake 30 to 40 minutes or until loaves sound hollow when lightly tapped. Immediately remove from pans; cool on wire racks. If desired, brush loaves with melted margarine.

Yield: 2 (17-slice) loaves

High Altitude—Above 3,500 feet: Bake at 350° F. for 40 to 50 minutes.

Nutrition Per Serving: Calories 150; Protein 4g; Carbohydrate 27g; Fat 3g; Sodium 135mg

Cheddar Thyme Casserole Bread

Denny Gross *Troy, Michigan*
Bake-Off® Contest 37, 1996

Get them to say "cheese" in a snap with this casserole bread covered by a cheese-coated crust. You can skip the kneading step and go right to making this cheesiest of breads instead.

8 oz. (2 cups) shredded sharp Cheddar cheese
2½ cups all-purpose flour
1 tablespoon sugar
1 teaspoon salt
1 teaspoon onion powder
¾ teaspoon dried thyme leaves
1 pkg. fast-acting dry yeast
1¼ cups buttermilk*
2 tablespoons margarine or butter
1 egg

Grease 2-quart round casserole. Press ½ cup of the cheese onto sides and bottom of dish.

In large bowl, combine 1½ cups of the flour, sugar, salt, onion powder, thyme and yeast; mix well. In small saucepan, heat buttermilk and margarine until very warm (120 to 130° F.). Add warm liquid and egg to flour mixture; beat at medium speed for 3 minutes.

By hand, stir in remaining flour; mix well. Stir in remaining cheese. Spoon batter into cheese-coated dish. Cover loosely with greased plastic wrap and cloth towel. Let rise in warm place (80 to 85° F.) until light and doubled in size, 45 to 60 minutes.

Heat oven to 350° F. Uncover dough. Bake 30 to 40 minutes or until golden brown and loaf sounds hollow when lightly tapped. Cool 30 minutes; invert bread onto serving platter. (Bread will release from casserole in 45 to 60 seconds.) Remove casserole; cool 15 minutes before slicing. If desired, serve warm with butter.

Yield: 1 (12-slice) loaf

*Tip: To substitute for buttermilk, use 4 teaspoons vinegar or lemon juice plus milk to make 1¼ cups.

High Altitude—Above 3,500 feet: No change.

Nutrition Per Serving: Calories 210; Protein 9g; Carbohydrate 23g; Fat 9g; Sodium 350mg

Mexican Cilantro Batter Bread

Frances Sheppard *Corsicana, Texas*
Bake-Off® Contest 35, 1992

Cilantro and green chiles accent the flavor of this easy and unique batter bread.

4½ cups all-purpose flour
2 tablespoons sugar
1 teaspoon salt
1 teaspoon garlic powder
1 pkg. active dry yeast
1 cup water
1 cup milk
2 tablespoons margarine or butter
½ cup chopped fresh cilantro
3 teaspoons freeze-dried chopped chives
1 (4.5-oz.) can chopped green chiles, drained
1 tablespoon poppy seed

In large bowl, combine 2 cups flour, sugar, salt, garlic powder and yeast; blend well. In small saucepan, heat water, milk and margarine until very warm (120 to 130° F.). Add warm liquid to flour mixture; beat 2 minutes at medium speed. By hand, stir in remaining 2½ cups flour, cilantro, chives and green chiles to form a stiff batter. Cover; let rise in warm place (80 to 85° F.) until light and doubled in size, 45 to 60 minutes.

Generously grease 12-cup Bundt pan or 10-inch tube pan. Sprinkle bottom and sides of pan with poppy seed. Stir down dough to remove all air bubbles. Carefully spoon into greased pan. Cover loosely with greased plastic wrap and cloth towel. Let rise in warm place until light and doubled in size, 30 to 45 minutes.

Heat oven to 375° F. Uncover dough. Bake 35 to 40 minutes or until deep golden brown. Cool 5 minutes; remove from pan. Serve warm or cool.

Yield: 1 (16-slice) loaf

High Altitude—Above 3,500 feet: No change.

Nutrition Per Serving: Calories 160; Protein 5g; Carbohydrate 30g; Fat 2g; Sodium 200mg

Italian Cheese Bread Ring

Kayleen L. Sloboden *Puyallup, Washington*
Bake-Off® Contest 31, 1984

Try this exceptional no-knead, cheese-filled loaf any time you're in the mood for something special. It's almost like a sandwich in a loaf!

BREAD
4¹/₂ to 5¹/₄ cups all-purpose
    flour
¹/₄ cup sugar
1¹/₂ teaspoons salt
2 pkg. active dry yeast
1 cup milk
1 cup water
¹/₂ cup margarine or butter
2 eggs
2 tablespoons sesame seed

FILLING
4 oz. (1 cup) shredded
    mozzarella cheese
¹/₂ teaspoon dried Italian
    seasoning
¹/₄ teaspoon garlic powder
¹/₄ cup margarine or butter,
    softened

In large bowl, combine 2¹/₂ cups flour, sugar, salt and yeast; blend well. In small saucepan, heat milk, water and ¹/₂ cup margarine until very warm (120 to 130° F.). Add warm liquid and eggs to flour mixture. Blend at low speed until moistened; beat 3 minutes at medium speed. By hand, stir in remaining 2 to 2³/₄ cups flour to form a stiff batter.

Generously grease 12-cup Bundt or 10-inch tube pan; sprinkle with sesame seed. In small bowl, combine all filling ingredients; mix well. Spoon half of batter into greased pan; spoon filling mixture evenly over batter to within ¹/₂ inch of sides of pan. Spoon remaining batter over filling. Cover loosely with plastic wrap and cloth towel. Let rise in warm place (80 to 85° F.) until light and doubled in size, about 30 minutes.

Heat oven to 350° F. Uncover dough. Bake 30 to 40 minutes or until golden brown and loaf sounds hollow when lightly tapped. Immediately remove from pan; cool on wire rack. Serve warm or cool.

Yield: 24 servings (1 slice per serving)

High Altitude—Above 3,500 feet: No change.

Nutrition Per Serving: Calories 190; Protein 5g; Carbohydrate 24g; Fat 8g; Sodium 240mg

Oat Bran Potato Buns

Darlene Herrick *Le Mars, Iowa*
Bake-Off® Contest 34, 1990

These nutty, moist buns are made with oat bran and potato flakes. Enjoy them as dinner rolls or as sandwich buns.

3¹/₂ to 4¹/₂ cups all-purpose
    flour
1 cup mashed potato flakes
1 cup instant nonfat dry milk
1 cup oat bran
2 teaspoons salt
2 pkg. active dry yeast
2¹/₂ cups water
¹/₄ cup shortening
3 tablespoons honey
Margarine or butter, melted

In large bowl, combine 1 cup flour, potato flakes, dry milk, oat bran, salt and yeast; blend well. In small saucepan, heat water, shortening and honey until very warm (120 to 130° F.). Add warm liquid to flour mixture; blend at low speed until moistened. Beat 3 minutes at medium speed. By hand, stir in an additional 1¹/₂ to 2 cups flour until dough pulls cleanly away from sides of bowl.

On floured surface, knead in remaining 1 to 1¹/₂ cups flour until dough is smooth and elastic, about 5 minutes. Place dough in greased bowl; cover loosely with plastic wrap and cloth towel. Let rise in warm place (80 to 85° F.) until light and doubled in size, 45 to 60 minutes.

Grease cookie sheets. Punch down dough several times to remove all air bubbles. On floured surface, roll out dough to ³/₄-inch thickness; cut with floured 2- to 2¹/₂-inch round cutter.* Place 2 inches apart on greased cookie sheets. Cover; let rise in warm place until light and doubled in size, about 30 minutes.

Heat oven to 375° F. Uncover dough. Bake 12 to 16 minutes or until golden brown. Immediately remove from cookie sheets; place on wire racks. Brush tops of warm rolls with melted margarine. Serve warm or cool.

Yield: 30 servings (1 roll per serving)

*Tip: For sandwich-sized rolls, cut dough with floured 3-inch round cutter. Makes about twelve 3-inch rolls.

High Altitude—Above 3,500 feet: No change.

Nutrition Per Serving: Calories 120; Protein 4g; Carbohydrate 21g; Fat 3g; Sodium 160mg

Golden Gate Snack Bread

Mari Jane Petrelli *Las Vegas, Nevada*
Bake-Off® Contest 17, 1966 Grand Prize Winner

The seventeenth Bake-Off® Contest was designated the "Busy Lady Bake-Off®." This streamlined, no-knead cheese bread with its zesty onion filling and easy, innovative shaping still is a big winner with busy people who like to bake.

BREAD
3¹/₂ cups all-purpose flour
2 tablespoons sugar
2 pkg. active dry yeast
1 cup warm water
2 tablespoons margarine or butter
1 (8-oz.) jar pasteurized process cheese spread

FILLING
¹/₄ cup margarine or butter, softened
3 tablespoons dry onion soup mix

In large bowl, combine 1¹/₂ cups flour, sugar and yeast; blend well. In small saucepan, heat water and 2 tablespoons margarine until very warm (120 to 130°F.). Add warm liquid to flour mixture. Blend at low speed until moistened; beat 2 minutes at medium speed. Beat in cheese until blended. By hand, stir in remaining 2 cups flour to make a stiff dough. Cover loosely with greased plastic wrap and cloth towel. Let rise in warm place (80 to 85°F.) until light and doubled in size, about 30 minutes.

In small bowl, combine ¹/₄ cup margarine and onion soup mix; blend well. Set aside.

Heat oven to 350°F. Grease cookie sheet. Punch down dough. On floured surface, roll out dough to a 20×14-inch rectangle. (Be sure sides are straight before rolling.) Spread with filling. Starting with 14-inch side, roll up, pressing edges and ends to seal. Using knife, carefully cut lengthwise down center to form 2 loaves. Place cut side up on greased cookie sheet. Cover; let rise in warm place until light and doubled in size, about 20 minutes.

Bake at 350°F. for 15 to 25 minutes or until golden brown.

Yield: 16 servings (1 slice per serving)

High Altitude—Above 3,500 feet: No change.

Nutrition Per Serving: Calories 190; Protein 6g; Carbohydrate 25g; Fat 8g; Sodium 350mg

Muffin Mix Buffet Bread

Maxine Bullock *Topeka, Kansas*
Bake-Off® Contest 18, 1967 Grand Prize Winner

The original recipe called for cream of vegetable soup, which is no longer available, so we now use Cheddar cheese soup to make the bread. Updated and revised, this moist batter bread is slightly sweet, perfect as part of a brunch selection, and just as delicious as the original was in 1967.

1 (8¹/₂-oz.) pkg. corn muffin mix
2 pkg. active dry yeast
³/₄ cup warm water
4 cups all-purpose flour
1 (10³/₄-oz.) can condensed Cheddar cheese soup
¹/₂ cup butter or margarine, melted

Grease two 8- or 9-inch square pans. Set aside 2 tablespoons of the dry muffin mix. In large bowl, dissolve yeast in warm water (105 to 115°F.). Add remaining dry muffin mix, 2 cups of the flour, soup and ¹/₄ cup of the melted butter; mix just until dry ingredients are moistened. Gradually stir in remaining 2 cups flour to form a stiff dough. Knead on floured surface until smooth, about 1 minute. Cover; let rest 15 minutes.

Heat oven to 375°F. Divide dough in half; press into greased pans. Cut each into 8 strips. Drizzle remaining ¹/₄ cup melted butter over loaves; sprinkle with reserved muffin mix. Cover; let rise in warm place 12 to 15 minutes or until light.

Bake at 375°F. for 18 to 25 minutes or until golden brown. Immediately remove from pans. Break apart or cut with knife. Serve warm.

Yield: 16 servings (1 slice per serving)

High Altitude—Above 3,500 feet: No change.

Nutrition Per Serving: Calories 250; Protein 5g; Carbohydrate 36g; Fat 9g; Sodium 370mg

Potato Chive Rolls

Susan Cox *Unionville, Pennsylvania*
Bake-Off® Contest 27, 1976 Prize Winner

America's Bicentennial set the theme for the 1976 contest and brought out updated versions of heirloom recipes. Sour cream gives these tender, no-knead rolls a hint of sourdough flavor, and mashed potato flakes eliminate the need to cook a potato.

$4^{1}/_{2}$ **to 5 cups all-purpose flour**
1 cup mashed potato flakes
1 tablespoon sugar
3 to 4 teaspoons chopped fresh or freeze-dried chives
2 teaspoons salt
2 pkg. active dry yeast
2 cups milk
$^{1}/_{2}$ **cup dairy sour cream**
2 eggs

In large bowl, combine $1^{1}/_{2}$ cups flour, potato flakes, sugar, chives, salt and yeast; blend well. In small saucepan, heat milk and sour cream until very warm (120 to 130° F.). Add warm liquid and eggs to flour mixture. Blend at low speed until moistened; beat 3 minutes at medium speed. By hand, stir in remaining 3 to $3^{1}/_{2}$ cups flour to form a stiff dough. Cover loosely with plastic wrap and cloth towel. Let rise in warm place (80 to 85° F.) until light and doubled in size, 45 to 55 minutes.

Generously grease 13×9-inch pan. On floured surface, knead dough gently until no longer sticky. Divide into 24 pieces; shape into balls. Place in greased pan. Cover; let rise in warm place until light

and doubled in size, 30 to 35 minutes.

Heat oven to 375° F. Uncover dough. Bake 25 to 35 minutes or until golden brown. Immediately remove from pan; cool on wire rack. If desired, lightly dust tops of rolls with flour.

Yield: 24 servings (1 roll per serving)

High Altitude—Above 3,500 feet: No change.

Nutrition Per Serving: Calories 130; Protein 4g; Carbohydrate 24g; Fat 2g; Sodium 200mg

Susan Cox: Potato Chive Rolls

The inventing and testing of their recipes often provides Bake-Off® Contest entrants with their fondest memories. "My husband and I became very close friends with a student from Rhodesia," Susan Cox says. "He and my husband were my official Bake-Off® critics for one month. Each week they were served a special meal with Potato Chive Rolls as the highlight. The first time I was told they greatly resembled sour wallpaper paste. I finally came up with a roll that received their seal of approval. Our beloved friend returned to his native land, but before he boarded his plane he presented me with a sterling silver roll basket." Now Susan's prize-winning rolls are proudly served in silver, but she treasures the memories of perfecting her Bake-Off® recipe most of all.

Garden Pepper Bread

Marlys Stover *Boca Raton, Florida*
Bake-Off® Contest 34, 1990

This bountiful bread has tasty bits of colorful peppers dotting every slice. The recipe makes two hearty loaves. Plan to freeze one for later. Serve the bread warm or cool.

2 tablespoons margarine or butter
$^{1}/_{2}$ **cup chopped onion**
$^{1}/_{3}$ **cup chopped red bell pepper**
$^{1}/_{3}$ **cup chopped green bell pepper**
7 to 8 cups all-purpose flour
$^{1}/_{2}$ **cup sugar**
$^{1}/_{2}$ **to 1 teaspoon salt**
$^{1}/_{8}$ **teaspoon pepper**
2 pkg. active dry yeast
1 cup milk
$^{3}/_{4}$ **cup water**
$^{1}/_{3}$ **cup margarine or butter**
6 egg whites or 3 whole eggs

Melt 2 tablespoons margarine in small skillet over medium heat. Add onion and bell peppers; cook 4 to 5 minutes or until vegetables are tender, stirring occasionally. Set aside.

In large bowl, combine 2 cups flour, sugar, salt, pepper and yeast; blend well. In small saucepan, heat milk, water and $^{1}/_{3}$ cup margarine until very warm (120 to 130° F.). Add warm liquid to flour mixture. Blend at low speed until moistened; beat 3 minutes at medium speed. Add egg whites, cooked vegetable mixture and 1 cup flour; beat at medium speed 3 minutes. By hand, stir in an additional 3 to

3½ cups flour to make a stiff dough.

On floured surface, knead in remaining 1 to 1½ cups flour until dough is smooth and elastic, about 10 minutes. (Dough will be slightly sticky.) Place dough in greased bowl; cover loosely with plastic wrap and cloth towel. Let rise in warm place (80 to 85°F.) until light and doubled in size, about 40 minutes.

Grease two 9×5- or three 8×4-inch loaf pans. Punch down dough several times to remove all air bubbles. Divide dough in half; shape into loaves. Place in greased pans. Cover with greased plastic wrap and cloth towel; let rise in warm place until light and doubled in size, about 40 minutes.

Heat oven to 375°F. Uncover dough. Bake 30 to 40 minutes or until loaves are deep golden brown and sound hollow when lightly tapped. Cover with foil during last 10 minutes of baking if necessary to avoid excessive browning. Immediately remove from pans; cool on wire racks.

Yield: 2 (15-slice) loaves

High Altitude—Above 3,500 feet: No change.

Nutrition Per Serving: Calories 170; Protein 5g; Carbohydrate 30g; Fat 3g; Sodium 120mg

Swedish Whole Wheat Dinner Rolls

Patty Entringer *Marshall, Minnesota*
Bake-Off® Contest 32, 1986

Fast-acting dry yeast allows bread to rise in about one-third less time than with regular yeast. In this recipe, because of the fast-acting yeast, there is only one rise.

1 cup whole wheat flour
½ cup mashed potato flakes
2 tablespoons brown sugar
2 teaspoons salt
1 teaspoon anise seed, crushed
1 teaspoon fennel seed, crushed
1½ teaspoons grated orange peel
1 pkg. fast-acting dry yeast
1⅓ cups water
¼ cup margarine or butter
1 tablespoon instant coffee granules or crystals
2 tablespoons molasses
1 teaspoon orange extract, if desired
1 egg
2½ to 3½ cups all-purpose flour
1 tablespoon margarine or butter, softened
½ teaspoon grated orange peel, if desired

Grease two 8- or 9-inch round cake pans. In large bowl, combine whole wheat flour, potato flakes, brown sugar, salt, anise seed, fennel seed, 1½ teaspoons orange peel and yeast; blend well. In small saucepan, heat water, ¼ cup margarine, instant coffee, molasses and

orange extract until very warm (120 to 130°F.). Add warm liquid and egg to flour mixture. Blend at low speed until moistened; beat 3 minutes at medium speed. Stir in 2 to 2½ cups all-purpose flour until dough pulls cleanly away from sides of bowl.

On floured surface, knead in remaining ½ to 1 cup all-purpose flour until dough is smooth and elastic, about 5 minutes. Divide dough in half. Divide each half into 8 equal pieces; shape into balls. Place 8 balls in each greased pan. Cover loosely with plastic wrap and cloth towel. Let rise in warm place (80 to 85°F.) until light and doubled in size, about 1 hour.

Heat oven to 375°F. Uncover dough. Bake 20 to 25 minutes or until rolls are golden brown and sound hollow when lightly tapped. Immediately remove from pans; place on wire racks. Brush warm rolls with 1 tablespoon margarine; sprinkle with ½ teaspoon orange peel.

Yield: 16 servings (1 roll per serving)

High Altitude—Above 3,500 feet: No change.

Nutrition Per Serving: Calories 180; Protein 5g; Carbohydrate 31g; Fat 4g; Sodium 320mg

Savory Cheese and Scallion Scones

Susan Brinkley *Eminence, Missouri*
Bake-Off® Contest 37, 1996

Scones are usually made with butter. These use cream cheese instead for a tender texture. Everyone will love them.

SCONES
2¾ **cups all-purpose flour**
5 **teaspoons baking powder**
½ **teaspoon salt, if desired**
4 **oz. (1 cup) crumbled feta cheese**
4 **oz. cream cheese or ⅓-less-fat cream cheese (Neufchatel), cut into 1-inch cubes**

4 **scallions or green onions, chopped**
1 **cup half-and-half or milk**
1 **egg**

GLAZE, IF DESIRED
1 **egg**
2 **tablespoons milk**

Heat oven to 400° F. Grease large cookie sheet. In large bowl, combine flour, baking powder and salt; mix well. With pastry blender or fork, cut in feta cheese and cream cheese until mixture is crumbly. Add scallions; toss gently until combined. In small bowl, combine half-and-half and 1 egg; blend well. Add half-and-half mixture to flour mixture; stir lightly, just until soft dough forms.

Turn dough out onto well-floured surface; knead lightly 5 or 6 times. Pat or press dough into

1-inch-thick round. With floured knife, cut into 8 wedges. Place wedges 2 inches apart on greased cookie sheet. In small bowl, combine glaze ingredients; blend well. Brush over tops of wedges.

Bake at 400° F. for 25 to 30 minutes or until golden brown. Remove scones from cookie sheet. Cool 5 minutes. Serve warm or cool. Store in refrigerator.

Yield: 8 scones

High Altitude—Above 3,500 feet: No change.

Nutrition Per Serving: Calories 310; Protein 10g; Carbohydrate 37g; Fat 13g; Sodium 670mg

Savory Cheese and Scallion Scones

Half-Time Spoon Rolls

Virginia Walker *Kenosha, Wisconsin*
Bake-Off® Contest 2, 1950 Prize Winner

Created in the 1950s, this recipe is convenience-oriented for the 1990s. These moist and light dinner rolls use just one bowl for both mixing and rising and require no kneading, rolling or shaping.

3 to 3¹/₂ cups all-purpose flour
¹/₄ cup sugar
1 teaspoon salt
1 pkg. active dry yeast
³/₄ cup milk
³/₄ cup water
¹/₃ cup margarine or butter
1 egg

In large bowl, combine 1¹/₂ cups flour, sugar, salt and yeast; blend well. In small saucepan, heat milk, water and margarine until very warm (120 to 130°F.). Add warm liquid and egg to flour mixture. Blend at low speed until moistened; beat 3 minutes at medium speed. By hand, stir in remaining 1¹/₂ to 2 cups flour to form a stiff batter. Cover loosely with plastic wrap and cloth towel. Let rise in warm place (80 to 85°F.) until light and doubled in size, 45 to 50 minutes.

Grease 18 muffin cups. Stir down dough to remove all air bubbles. Spoon into greased muffin cups, filling about ²/₃ full. Cover loosely with greased plastic wrap and cloth towel; let rise in warm place until light and doubled in size, 25 to 35 minutes.

Heat oven to 400°F. Uncover dough. Bake 15 to 20 minutes or until golden brown. Remove from pans immediately; cool on wire racks.

Yield: 18 servings (1 roll per serving)

High Altitude—Above 3,500 feet: No change.

Nutrition Per Serving: Calories 140; Protein 3g; Carbohydrate 22g; Fat 4g; Sodium 170mg

Old Plantation Rolls

Mrs. William Edwin Baker *Colorado Springs, Colorado*
Bake-Off® Contest 1, 1949

The first Bake-Off® Contest, in 1949, was called Pillsbury's Grand National Recipe and Baking Contest. It was launched by First Lady Eleanor Roosevelt. These no-knead rolls from almost fifty years ago continue to be a natural for today's busy cooks.

5 to 6 cups all-purpose flour
¹/₄ cup sugar
1 teaspoon baking powder
1 teaspoon salt
¹/₂ teaspoon baking soda
1 pkg. active dry yeast
1 cup water
1 cup milk
¹/₂ cup shortening
1 egg

Grease 24 muffin cups. In large bowl, combine 3 cups flour, sugar, baking powder, salt, baking soda and yeast; blend well. In small saucepan, heat water, milk and shortening until very warm (120 to 130°F.). Add warm liquid and egg to flour mixture. Blend at low speed until moistened; beat 3 minutes at medium speed. By hand, stir in remaining 2 to 3 cups flour to form a stiff dough. Cover loosely with greased plastic wrap and cloth towel. Let rise in warm place (80 to 85°F.) until light and doubled in size, about 1 hour.

Punch down dough several times to remove all air bubbles.* On well-floured surface, toss dough until no longer sticky. Divide dough into 24 equal pieces; shape into balls.** Place 1 ball in each greased muffin cup. With scissors or sharp knife, make X-shaped cut in each ball, forming 4 equal pieces. Cover; let rise in warm place until light and doubled in size, 35 to 45 minutes.

Heat oven to 400°F. Uncover dough. Bake 13 to 15 minutes or until golden brown. Remove from pans immediately.

Yield: 24 servings (1 roll per serving)

*Tips: Rolls can be prepared to this point, covered and refrigerated overnight. Increase second rise time to 1¹/₄ hours.

****For a more traditional cloverleaf shape, divide dough into 72 pieces; shape into balls. Place 3 balls in each greased muffin cup. Cover; let rise in warm place until light and doubled in size, 35 to 45 minutes. Bake as directed above.

High Altitude—Above 3,500 feet: No change.

Nutrition Per Serving: Calories 160; Protein 4g; Carbohydrate 25g; Fat 5g; Sodium 135mg

Cheese-Filled Parmesan Biscuit Loaves

Eileen M. Watson *Oviedo, Florida*
Bake-Off® Contest 37, 1996

Fresh basil brings fantastic flavor to cream cheese–filled biscuits rolled in an enticing cheese-walnut crust. Make these for a quick snack, an elegant appetizer or as part of a Sunday brunch.

¾ **cup grated Parmesan cheese**
⅓ **cup finely chopped walnuts**
2 **oz. cream cheese, softened**
1½ **tablespoons finely chopped fresh basil**
1 **garlic clove, minced**
1 **(1 lb. 0.3-oz.) can large refrigerated buttermilk biscuits**
¼ **cup butter or margarine, melted**

Heat oven to 350° F. Lightly grease two 9×5- or 8×4-inch loaf pans. In small bowl, combine Parmesan cheese and walnuts; mix well. In another small bowl, combine cream cheese, basil and garlic; mix well.

Separate dough into 8 biscuits. Spoon 1 teaspoon cream cheese mixture on half of each biscuit. Fold biscuit over cream cheese; press edges to seal.

Dip each biscuit in melted butter; coat with cheese-walnut mixture. Arrange 4 biscuits, seam side down, in each greased pan. Drizzle any remaining butter over biscuits; sprinkle with any remaining cheese mixture.

Bake at 350° F. for 25 to 35 minutes or until golden brown. Immediately remove from pan. Serve warm. Store in refrigerator.

Yield: 8 servings

Nutrition Per Serving: Calories 350; Protein 9g; Carbohydrate 26g; Fat 23g; Sodium 850mg

Cheese-Crusted Flat Bread

Lois Mattson *Duluth, Minnesota*
Bake-Off® Contest 16, 1964

Enliven a weeknight spaghetti dinner with this warm cheese bread. It's similar to the cheese focaccia found in many bakeries today.

BREAD
2½ **to 3 cups all-purpose flour**
1 **tablespoon sugar**
1 **teaspoon salt**
1 **pkg. active dry yeast**
¾ **cup milk**
¼ **cup water**
2 **tablespoons butter or margarine**

TOPPING
¼ **cup butter or margarine, melted**
2 **tablespoons chopped onion**
½ **teaspoon dried oregano leaves**
½ **teaspoon paprika**
¼ **teaspoon garlic salt**
¼ **teaspoon celery seed**
4 **oz. (1 cup) shredded Cheddar cheese**

In large bowl, combine 2 cups flour, sugar, salt and yeast; mix well. In small saucepan, combine milk, water and 2 tablespoons butter. Heat until very warm (120 to 130° F.). Add warm liquid to flour mixture; mix well. Stir in remaining ½ to 1 cup flour to form a stiff dough.

On lightly floured surface, knead dough until smooth, about 5 minutes. Place dough in greased bowl. Cover loosely with greased plastic wrap and cloth towel. Let rise in warm place (80 to 85° F.) until light and doubled in size, 45 to 60 minutes.

Grease two 9-inch round cake or pie pans. Divide dough in half; press each half in greased pan. In small bowl, combine ¼ cup butter, onion, oregano, paprika, garlic salt and celery seed; mix well. Spread mixture over dough. Prick tops generously with fork. Sprinkle evenly with cheese. Cover; let rise in warm place until light and doubled in size, 30 to 45 minutes.

Heat oven to 375° F. Uncover dough. Bake 20 to 25 minutes or until golden brown. Serve warm.

Yield: 16 servings

High Altitude—Above 3,500 feet: No change.

Nutrition Per Serving: Calories 160; Protein 5g; Carbohydrate 20g; Fat 7g; Sodium 260mg

Cheese-Crusted Flat Bread

Chapter 5

Sweet Rolls and Coffee Cakes

Mornings bring out the best or the worst in people. Some spring out of bed with a smile on their face, ready to get things done. Others are grumpy, pale shadows of their ordinary selves—until after their third cup of coffee.

Probably none of this has to do with breakfast itself, for although breakfast has changed, chances are that people haven't. Breakfasts of old were the biggest meal of the day—several kinds of meat, cheeses, breads and hot cereals were common, as farmers and laborers filled up for a long laborious day. The Industrial Revolution brought desk jobs, mornings grew more rushed and cold cereal or a store-bought muffin became standard breakfasts. Thankfully, brunch sprang up to preserve the foods and traditions of breakfast, and the leisurely weekend meal has become an important one for many families and a special time for entertaining.

Sweet rolls and coffee cakes have always been a prominent part of the Bake-Off® Contest and have remained fairly traditional. Early recipes like 1949's No-Knead Water-Rising Twists and 1955's Ring-A-Lings call for the most basic pantry ingredients: flour, leavening, a sweetener, shortening and nuts. Today even the most sophisticated recipes, such as the 1990's Blueberry Poppy Seed Brunch Cake, require nothing more extraordinary than contemporary common pantry ingredients, in this case poppy seed and lemon peel.

Despite how breakfasts, lifestyles or tastes change, people still prefer not to be surprised too much in the morning. If breakfast routines have borne out anything over the years, it is that no matter whether people are at their best or worst at the start of the day, they can't help but be encouraged by something a bit traditional, and a little sweet, in the morning.

Ring-A-Lings, page 154

Maple Pecan Crescent Twists

Jean K. Olson *Wallingford, Iowa*
Bake-Off® Contest 35, 1992

A unique shape plus a crunchy sugar-nut filling makes this sweet roll a winner!

TWISTS
1/2 **cup chopped pecans**
3 **tablespoons sugar**
1 **teaspoon cinnamon**
1/8 **teaspoon nutmeg**
2 **(8-oz.) cans refrigerated crescent dinner rolls**
2 **tablespoons margarine or butter, melted**

GLAZE
1/2 **cup powdered sugar**
1/4 **teaspoon maple extract**
2 **to 3 teaspoons milk**

Heat oven to 375°F. Lightly grease 1 large or 2 small cookie sheets. In small bowl, combine pecans, sugar, cinnamon and nutmeg; mix well. Separate dough into 8 rectangles; firmly press perforations to seal. Brush each rectangle with margarine. Sprinkle 1 tablespoon sugar-nut mixture evenly over each rectangle, pressing in lightly. Starting at longer side, roll up each rectangle, pinching edges to seal. With sharp knife, cut 1 roll in half lengthwise, forming 2 strips. With cut side up, carefully overlap strips 2 times to form twist. Press ends together to seal. Place on greased cookie sheet. Repeat with remaining dough. Sprinkle with any remaining sugar-nut mixture.

Bake at 375°F. for 10 to 15 minutes or until golden brown. In small bowl, blend all glaze ingredients,

adding enough milk for desired drizzling consistency. Drizzle over warm rolls. Serve warm.

Yield: 8 servings (1 roll per serving)

Nutrition Per Serving: Calories 320; Protein 4g; Carbohydrate 36g; Fat 19g; Sodium 500mg

Ring-A-Lings

Bertha Jorgensen *Portland, Oregon*
Bake-Off® Contest 7, 1955 Grand Prize Winner

Bertha Jorgensen's method of filling, twisting and shaping her orange-flavored yeast rolls has been copied in many recipes since 1955. Judges that year were so impressed with the eating quality of her hazelnut-filled rolls and innovative shaping, they picked hers as the best recipe in America's premier cooking event.

DOUGH
4 **to** 4 1/2 **cups all-purpose flour**
1/3 **cup sugar**
2 **teaspoons salt**
2 **teaspoons grated orange peel**
2 **pkg. active dry yeast**
1 **cup milk**
1/3 **cup margarine or butter**
2 **eggs**

FILLING
1 **cup powdered sugar**
1/3 **cup margarine or butter, softened**
1 **cup hazelnuts (filberts), pecans or walnuts, ground**

GLAZE
3 **tablespoons sugar**
1/4 **cup orange juice**

In large bowl, combine 2 cups of the flour, 1/3 cup sugar, salt, orange peel and yeast; mix well. In small

saucepan, heat milk and 1/3 cup margarine until very warm (120 to 130°F.). Add warm liquid and eggs to flour mixture. Blend at low speed until moistened; beat 3 minutes at medium speed. By hand, stir in remaining 2 to 2 1/2 cups flour to form a stiff dough. Place dough in greased bowl; cover loosely with plastic wrap and cloth towel. Let rise in warm place (80 to 85°F.) until light and doubled in size, 35 to 50 minutes.

In small bowl, blend powdered sugar and 1/3 cup margarine until smooth. Stir in hazelnuts; set aside. In second small bowl, blend glaze ingredients; set aside.

Grease 2 large cookie sheets. Stir down dough to remove all air bubbles. On floured surface, roll dough to 22×12-inch rectangle. Spread filling mixture lengthwise over half of dough. Fold dough over filling. Cut crosswise into 1-inch strips; twist each strip 4 to 5 times. To shape rolls, hold folded end of strip down on greased cookie sheet to form center; coil strip around center. Tuck loose end under. Repeat with remaining twisted strips. Cover; let rise in warm place until light and doubled in size, 30 to 45 minutes.

Heat oven to 375°F. Uncover dough. Bake 9 to 12 minutes or until light golden brown. Brush tops of rolls with glaze. Bake an additional 3 to 5 minutes or until golden brown. Immediately remove from cookie sheets; cool on wire racks. Serve warm.

Yield: 22 servings (1 roll per serving)

High Altitude—Above 3,500 feet: No change.

Nutrition Per Serving: Calories 230; Protein 5g; Carbohydrate 32g; Fat 10g; Sodium 270mg

Easy Crescent Danish Rolls

Barbara S. Gibson *Ft. Wayne, Indiana Bake-Off® Contest 26, 1975 Grand Prize Winner*

These Danish pastries can be made to suit everyone's taste by just changing the flavor of preserves.

1 (8-oz.) pkg. cream cheese, softened
¹/₂ cup sugar
1 tablespoon lemon juice
2 (8-oz.) cans refrigerated crescent dinner rolls

4 teaspoons preserves or jam

GLAZE
¹/₂ cup powdered sugar
1 teaspoon vanilla
2 to 3 teaspoons milk

Heat oven to 350° F. In small bowl, combine cream cheese, sugar and lemon juice; beat until smooth. Separate dough into 8 rectangles; firmly press perforations to seal. Spread each rectangle with about 2 tablespoons cream cheese mixture. Starting at longer side, roll up each rectangle, firmly pinching edges and ends to seal. Gently stretch each roll to about 10 inches. Coil each roll into a spiral with seam on the inside, tucking end under. Make deep indentation in center of each roll; fill with ¹/₂ teaspoon preserves. Place on ungreased large cookie sheet.

Bake at 350° F. for 20 to 25 minutes or until deep golden brown. In small bowl, blend all glaze ingredients, adding enough milk for desired drizzling consistency. Drizzle over warm rolls.

Yield: 8 servings (1 roll per serving)

Nutrition Per Serving: Calories 390; Protein 6g; Carbohydrate 45g; Fat 21g; Sodium 550mg

Easy Crescent Danish Rolls

Danish Almond Cream Rolls

Donna Hilgendorf *Waunakee, Wisconsin*
Bake-Off® Contest 35, 1992

Donna Hilgendorf likes to bake yeast rolls, but making Danish pastry was too time-consuming. She used flaky crescent roll dough to get a similar effect in a short time. The big almond cream-filled rolls were such a hit, friends urged her to enter them in the Bake-Off® Contest.

ROLLS
2 (3-oz.) pkg. cream cheese, softened
¹/₂ to 1 teaspoon almond extract
¹/₂ cup powdered sugar
¹/₂ cup finely chopped almonds
2 (8-oz.) cans refrigerated crescent dinner rolls
1 egg white
1 teaspoon water
¹/₄ cup sliced almonds

GLAZE
²/₃ cup powdered sugar
¹/₄ to ¹/₂ teaspoon almond extract
3 to 4 teaspoons milk

Heat oven to 350° F. In small bowl, beat cream cheese, ¹/₂ teaspoon almond extract and ¹/₂ cup powdered sugar until fluffy. Stir in chopped almonds. Separate 1 can of dough into 4 rectangles; firmly press perforations to seal. Press or roll each to form 7×4-inch rectangle; spread each with about 2 tablespoons of the cream cheese filling to within ¹/₄ inch of edges. Starting at longer side, roll up each rectangle, firmly pinching edges and ends to seal. Gently stretch each roll to 10 inches. Coil each roll into a spiral with the seam on the inside, tucking ends under. Place on ungreased cookie sheets. Repeat with remaining can of dough and cream cheese filling.

In small bowl, combine egg white and water; brush over rolls. Sprinkle with sliced almonds.

Bake at 350° F. for 17 to 23 minutes or until deep golden brown. In small bowl, blend all glaze ingredients, adding enough milk for desired drizzling consistency; drizzle over warm rolls. Serve warm.

Yield: 8 servings (1 roll per serving)

Nutrition Per Serving: Calories 410; Protein 8g; Carbohydrate 42g; Fat 24g; Sodium 540mg

Quick Praline Rolls

Alice Houghtaling *San Diego, California*
Bake-Off® Contest 14, 1962 Prize Winner

The combined leavening action of yeast and baking powder gives these rolls a biscuitlike texture. After mixing and shaping, the dough rises only once before baking.

FILLING
³/₄ cup firmly packed brown sugar
¹/₃ cup margarine or butter, softened
¹/₂ cup chopped walnuts

ROLLS
1³/₄ to 2³/₄ cups all-purpose flour
2 tablespoons sugar
1 teaspoon baking powder
¹/₂ teaspoon salt
1 pkg. active dry yeast
¹/₃ cup milk
¹/₄ cup water
¹/₃ cup margarine or butter
1 egg
¹/₄ cup chopped walnuts

In small bowl, combine brown sugar and margarine; beat until light and fluffy. Stir in ¹/₂ cup nuts; set aside. In large bowl, combine 1 cup flour, sugar, baking powder, salt and yeast; blend well. In small saucepan, heat milk, water and margarine until very warm (120 to 130° F.). Add warm liquid and egg to flour mixture. Blend at low speed until moistened; beat 3 minutes at medium speed. By hand, stir in remaining ³/₄ to 1³/₄ cups flour to form a soft dough.

Grease cookie sheet. On floured surface, toss dough until no longer sticky. Roll into 15×10-inch rectangle; spread with half of filling mixture. Starting with 15-inch side, roll up tightly, pressing edges to seal. Cut into 15 slices. Place cut side down on greased cookie sheet; flatten to ¹/₂ inch. Spread tops of rolls with remaining filling. Sprinkle with ¹/₄ cup nuts. Cover loosely with greased plastic wrap and cloth towel. Let rise in warm place (80 to 85° F.) until light, about 45 minutes.

Heat oven to 400° F. Uncover dough. Bake 10 to 12 minutes or until light golden brown. Immediately remove from cookie sheet; place on wire racks. Serve warm.

Yield: 15 servings (1 roll per serving)

High Altitude—Above 3,500 feet: No change.

Nutrition Per Serving: Calories 260; Protein 4g; Carbohydrate 32g; Fat 13g; Sodium 200mg

Bohemian Raisin Biscuit Kolachy

Margaret Kramer *Forestville, Wisconsin*
Bake-Off® Contest 30, 1982 Prize Winner

Adaptations of ethnic recipes were much in evidence at the 1982 contest. This winner simplified the preparation of a traditional Old World pastry by using refrigerated flaky biscuits instead of a rich yeast dough.

ROLLS
1 cup raisins or dried currants
¹/₄ cup firmly packed brown sugar
¹/₄ cup water
1 to 2 teaspoons lemon juice
1 (12-oz.) can refrigerated flaky biscuits
¹/₂ cup sugar
¹/₂ teaspoon cinnamon
¹/₄ cup margarine or butter, melted

GLAZE
¹/₂ cup powdered sugar
2 to 4 teaspoons milk
¹/₂ teaspoon vanilla

Heat oven to 375°F. In small saucepan, combine raisins, brown sugar, water and lemon juice. Cook over medium heat 7 minutes or until mixture thickens, stirring occasionally. Cool. Separate dough into 10 biscuits. Combine sugar and cinnamon. Dip both sides of each biscuit in melted margarine, then in sugar mixture. Place rolls, sides touching, in ungreased 15×10×1-inch baking pan or 13×9-inch pan. With thumb, make wide imprint in center of each roll; fill with 1 rounded tablespoon raisin mixture.

Bake at 375°F. for 15 to 20 minutes or until golden brown. In small bowl, combine glaze ingredients until smooth; drizzle over warm rolls.

Yield: 10 servings (1 roll per serving)

Nutrition Per Serving: Calories 280; Protein 3g; Carbohydrate 47g; Fat 9g; Sodium 420mg

Orangeasy Pastries

Lynette K. Dahlman *Chatsworth, California*
Bake-Off® Contest 35, 1992 Prize Winner

As a busy intensive care nurse and active volunteer, Lynette Dahlman likes recipes for great-tasting food that's quick to prepare. Her simply shaped flaky rolls with their orange-cream cheese filling turn ordinary ingredients into something special.

ROLLS
¹/₂ (8-oz.) pkg. (4 oz.) cream cheese, softened
¹/₃ cup orange marmalade
¹/₃ cup chopped pecans
1 tablespoon sugar

2 (8-oz.) cans refrigerated crescent dinner rolls
1 egg white, beaten
¹/₃ cup sliced almonds

GLAZE
³/₄ cup powdered sugar
1 teaspoon grated orange peel
3 to 4 teaspoons orange juice

Heat oven to 375°F. In small bowl, combine cream cheese, orange marmalade, pecans and sugar; mix well. Separate dough into 8 rectangles; firmly press perforations to seal. Spread orange filling on half of each rectangle to within ¹/₄ inch of edges. To make each pastry, bring unfilled half of dough over filling; pinch edges to seal. Place on ungreased cookie sheet. Brush with beaten egg white; sprinkle with almonds.

Bake at 375°F. for 13 to 18 minutes or until golden brown. Cool. In small bowl, blend all glaze ingredients, adding enough orange juice for desired drizzling consistency; drizzle over rolls.

Yield: 8 servings (1 roll per serving)

Nutrition Per Serving: Calories 390; Protein 6g; Carbohydrate 47g; Fat 21g; Sodium 520mg

Margaret Kramer:
Bohemian Raisin Biscuit Kolachy

Cooking is largely a matter of addition. Margaret Kramer noticed an analogy at an early age. "My parents deserve a lot of credit for conveying to me their philosophy of life, which is 'you get out of life just what you put into it.'" Of course, that holds true whether you're talking about honey, raisins, salt or care.

Magic Marshmallow Crescent Puffs

Edna (Holmgren) Walker *Hopkins, Minnesota*
Bake-Off® Contest 20, 1969 Grand
Prize Winner

"Such a simple way to get great taste," people exclaim when they try this Bake-Off® Contest classic recipe. It is created by wrapping refrigerated crescent-roll dough around cinnamon-sugar-coated marshmallows. The marshmallows melt during baking, forming a sweet, hollow puff.

PUFFS
1/4 **cup sugar**
2 **tablespoons all-purpose flour**
1 **teaspoon cinnamon**
2 **(8-oz.) cans refrigerated crescent dinner rolls**
16 **large marshmallows**
1/4 **cup margarine or butter, melted**

GLAZE
1/2 **cup powdered sugar**
1/2 **teaspoon vanilla**
2 **to 3 teaspoons milk**
1/4 **cup chopped nuts, if desired**

Heat oven to 375°F. Spray 16 muffin cups with nonstick cooking spray. In small bowl, combine sugar, flour and cinnamon. Separate dough into 16 triangles. Dip 1 marshmallow in margarine; roll in sugar mixture. Place marshmallow on shortest side of triangle. Roll up starting at shortest side of triangle and rolling to opposite point. Completely cover marshmallow with dough; firmly pinch edges to seal. Dip 1 end in remaining margarine; place margarine side down in sprayed muffin cup. Repeat with remaining marshmallows.

Bake at 375°F. for 12 to 15 minutes or until golden brown. (Place foil or cookie sheet on rack below muffin cups to guard against spills.) Remove from oven; cool 1 minute. Remove from muffin cups; place on wire racks set over waxed paper. In small bowl, blend powdered sugar, vanilla and enough milk for desired drizzling consistency. Drizzle over warm rolls. Sprinkle with nuts.

Yield: 16 servings (1 roll per serving)

Nutrition Per Serving: Calories 200; Protein 2g; Carbohydrate 25g; Fat 10g; Sodium 250mg

Edna (Holmgren) Walker: Magic Marshmallow Crescent Puffs

The nineteenth Bake-Off® Contest saw the introduction of refrigerated fresh dough as a contest category, mirroring changes in the way Americans were cooking. Who had time anymore to spend a day wrestling with pastry? The next year, Magic Marshmallow Crescent Puffs won the grand prize and became the "little black dress" of desserts: easy to make, always appropriate, a crowd pleaser. It's said that the hardest thing to achieve is simplicity, but these puffs are the exception to the rule.

Orange Date Crescent Claws

Barbara Rhea *Beavercreek, Ohio*
Bake-Off® Contest 33, 1988 Prize Winner

Like bakery bear claws with a moist date-nut filling, these rolls are fun to shape and a treat to eat.

1/2 **cup chopped walnuts or pecans**
1/4 **cup sugar**
1 **teaspoon grated orange peel**
1/2 **cup chopped dates**
1 **(8-oz.) can refrigerated crescent dinner rolls**
2 **tablespoons margarine or butter, melted**

Heat oven to 375°F. In small bowl, combine walnuts, sugar and orange peel; blend well. Reserve 1/4 cup of mixture for topping. Stir dates into remaining mixture; set aside.

Separate dough into 4 rectangles; firmly press perforations to seal. Cut each rectangle in half crosswise; press or roll out each to form eight 4-inch squares. Brush each with margarine. Spoon about 2 teaspoons date mixture across center 1/3 of each square to within 1/4 inch of edges. Fold sides of dough over filling; pinch center seam and ends to seal. Place seam side down on ungreased cookie sheet.

Using scissors or sharp knife, make three 1/2-inch cuts in one folded edge. To form claws, separate cut sections of each roll by gently curving into crescent shape. Brush top of each claw with remaining margarine; sprinkle with reserved sugar-nut mixture. Bake at 375° F. for 8 to 12 minutes or until golden brown.

Yield: 8 servings (1 roll per serving)

Nutrition Per Serving: Calories 240; Protein 3g; Carbohydrate 27g; Fat 13g; Sodium 260mg

Lemon Nut Rolls

Betty May *Sykesville, Maryland*
Bake-Off® Contest 10, 1958 Prize Winner

Flour still was the only eligible product in the 1958 contest, and recently married women between ages nineteen and thirty-one could enter a special Bride Award category. These light, tender potato rolls won first prize for a newly married contestant.

ROLLS
2¹/₂ to 3¹/₂ cups all-purpose flour
¹/₃ cup mashed potato flakes
¹/₃ cup sugar
1 teaspoon salt
¹/₂ teaspoon grated lemon peel
1 pkg. active dry yeast
³/₄ cup water
¹/₂ cup milk
¹/₃ cup margarine or butter
1 tablespoon lemon juice
1 egg

FILLING
2 tablespoons margarine or butter, softened
³/₄ cup sugar
¹/₂ cup chopped pecans
1 teaspoon grated lemon peel

GLAZE
¹/₂ cup powdered sugar
¹/₂ teaspoon grated lemon peel
¹/₂ teaspoon lemon juice
2 to 3 teaspoons half-and-half or milk

In large bowl, combine 1 cup flour, potato flakes, ¹/₃ cup sugar, salt, ¹/₂ teaspoon lemon peel and yeast; blend well. In small saucepan, heat water, milk and ¹/₃ cup margarine until very warm (120 to 130° F.). Add warm liquid, lemon juice and egg to flour mixture. Blend at low speed until moistened; beat 2 minutes at medium speed. By hand, stir in remaining 1¹/₂ to 2¹/₂ cups flour to form a stiff dough. Cover loosely with plastic wrap and cloth towel. Let rise in warm place (80 to 85° F.) until light and doubled in size, about 1 hour.

Grease two 8- or 9-inch round cake pans. On floured surface, toss dough until no longer sticky. Roll into 16×12-inch rectangle; spread with 2 tablespoons margarine. In small bowl, combine remaining filling ingredients; sprinkle over dough. Starting with 16-inch side, roll up tightly, pressing edges to seal. Cut into 16 slices; place in greased pans. Cover; let rise in warm place (80 to 85° F.) until light and doubled in size, 30 to 40 minutes.

Heat oven to 375° F. Uncover dough. Bake 20 to 30 minutes or until light golden brown. Immediately remove from pans; cool on wire racks. In small bowl, blend all glaze ingredients adding enough half-and-half for desired drizzling consistency. Drizzle over warm rolls.

Yield: 16 servings (1 roll per serving)

High Altitude—Above 3,500 feet: No change.

Nutrition Per Serving: Calories 250; Protein 4g; Carbohydrate 40g; Fat 9g; Sodium 210mg

Beehive Buns

Janis Chudleigh *Bethany, Connecticut*
Bake-Off® Contest 32, 1986 Prize Winner

These honey-flavored raisin buns are shaped like miniature beehives. Serve them fresh from the oven with butter.

ROLLS
2 cups whole wheat flour
2 pkg. active dry yeast
1 teaspoon salt
1 cup raisins
1 cup very hot water
1 cup milk
¹/₃ cup honey
¹/₃ cup margarine or butter
2 eggs
2 to 3¹/₄ cups all-purpose flour

GLAZE
3 tablespoons honey
3 tablespoons margarine or butter
1¹/₄ cups powdered sugar
1 teaspoon vanilla

In large bowl, combine whole wheat flour, yeast and salt; set aside. Cover raisins with water for 1 minute; drain. In small saucepan, heat milk, ¹/₃ cup honey and ¹/₃ cup

Janis Chudleigh: Beehive Buns

I developed this recipe to help my children appreciate their rich Utah pioneer heritage," says Janis Chudleigh. "The pioneers called Utah 'the land of milk and honey,' and 'Deseret,' meaning honey bee, was their symbol for industry." Honey is a food rich in symbolism. The ancient Greeks thought that honey fell to earth from the tables of the gods, and some ancient Romans thought that honey was juice that dripped down from the stars, which the bees gathered up.

margarine until very warm (120 to 130° F.). Add warm mixture to flour mixture. Beat in eggs 1 at a time; stir in drained raisins. By hand, stir in 1 1/2 to 2 cups all-purpose flour until dough pulls cleanly away from sides of bowl.

On floured surface, knead in an additional 1/2 to 1 1/4 cups all-purpose flour until dough is smooth and elastic, about 5 minutes. Place dough in greased bowl; cover loosely with plastic wrap and cloth towel. Let rise in warm place (80 to 85° F.) until light and doubled in size, 45 to 60 minutes.

Grease 24 muffin cups. Punch down dough several times to remove all air bubbles. Divide dough into 24 pieces. (Cover dough pieces with inverted bowl to prevent drying out.) Using 1 piece of dough at a time, roll to form 10- to 12-inch rope. Coil rope in muffin cup, tucking end into top center to form beehive shape. Repeat with remaining pieces. Cover; let rise in warm place until light and doubled in size, about 30 to 45 minutes.

Heat oven to 350° F. Uncover dough. Bake 15 to 20 minutes or until golden brown. Immediately remove from muffin cups; place on wire racks. In small saucepan, heat

3 tablespoons each honey and margarine. Stir in powdered sugar and vanilla until smooth. Drizzle over warm rolls.

Yield: 24 servings (1 roll per serving)

High Altitude—Above 3,500 feet: No change.

Nutrition Per Serving: Calories 210; Protein 4g; Carbohydrate 37g; Fat 5g; Sodium 150mg

Country Blueberry Coffee Cake

Wendy L. Hart *Ray City, Georgia*
Bake-Off® Contest 38, 1998

This scrumptious coffee cake, bursting with blueberries, is a perfect appetite-pleaser at any time of the day.

1/2 **cup firmly packed brown sugar**
1/2 **teaspoon cinnamon**
1 **(12-oz.) can refrigerated fluffy buttermilk biscuits**
1/4 **cup butter or margarine, melted**

1 **cup quick-cooking rolled oats**
1 1/2 **cups fresh or frozen blueberries**
1/4 **cup sugar**
2 **tablespoons butter or margarine, cut into small pieces**

Heat oven to 375° F. Generously grease 8- or 9-inch square (2-quart) glass baking dish. In small bowl, combine brown sugar and cinnamon; mix well with fork.

Separate dough into 10 biscuits. Cut each biscuit into quarters. Dip each piece in melted butter; coat with brown sugar mixture. Arrange in single layer in greased baking dish. Sprinkle with 1/2 cup of the oats.

In medium bowl, combine blueberries and sugar; toss to coat. Spoon over oats and biscuits; sprinkle with remaining 1/2 cup oats. Top with butter pieces.

Bake at 375° F. for 30 to 35 minutes or until coffee cake is golden brown and center is done. Cool 20 minutes. Serve warm.

Yield: 9 servings

Nutrition Per Serving: Calories 300; Protein 4g; Carbohydrate 42g; Fat 13g; Sodium 420mg

Maple Cream Coffee Treat

Reta Ebbink *Torrance, California*
Bake-Off® Contest 28, 1978 Prize Winner

Friends and family will praise the baker who serves these cream-filled, caramel-topped sweet rolls, named because they're perfect with coffee.

1 cup firmly packed brown sugar
1/2 cup chopped nuts
1/3 cup maple-flavored syrup or dark corn syrup
1/4 cup margarine or butter, melted
1 (8-oz.) pkg. cream cheese, softened
1/4 cup powdered sugar
2 tablespoons margarine or butter, softened
1/2 cup coconut
2 (12-oz.) cans refrigerated flaky biscuits

Heat oven to 350°F. In ungreased 13×9-inch pan, combine brown sugar, nuts, syrup and 1/4 cup margarine; spread evenly in bottom of pan. In small bowl, blend cream cheese, powdered sugar and 2 tablespoons margarine until smooth; stir in coconut.

Separate dough into 20 biscuits. Press or roll each to a 4-inch circle. Spoon 1 tablespoon of cream cheese mixture down center of each circle to within 1/4 inch of edge. Overlap sides of dough over filling, forming finger-shaped rolls. Arrange rolls seam side down in 2 rows of 10 rolls each over brown sugar mixture in pan.

Bake at 350°F. for 25 to 30 minutes or until deep golden brown. Cool 3 to 5 minutes; invert onto foil, waxed paper or serving platter.

Yield: 20 servings (1 roll per serving)

Nutrition Per Serving: Calories 270; Protein 3g; Carbohydrate 32g; Fat 14g; Sodium 450mg

Quick Apple Pancake

Eileen Thorston *Springfield, Minnesota*
Bake-Off® Contest 31, 1984 Prize Winner

This recipe, a microwave winner, can also be prepared in a conventional oven. It makes a great dessert when topped with ice cream.

1/4 cup margarine or butter
1 1/2 cups thinly sliced, peeled apples
1/2 cup sugar
1/2 teaspoon cinnamon
1/4 teaspoon nutmeg

BATTER
1 cup complete or buttermilk pancake mix
1/2 teaspoon cinnamon
1/4 teaspoon nutmeg
3/4 cup water
1 teaspoon vanilla

TOPPING
1 tablespoon sugar
1/4 teaspoon cinnamon

Microwave Directions: In 9-inch microwave-safe pie pan or round cake pan, microwave margarine on HIGH for 30 to 45 seconds or until margarine is melted. Stir in apples, 1/2 cup sugar, 1/2 teaspoon cinnamon and 1/4 teaspoon nutmeg. Cover; microwave on HIGH for 3 to 4 minutes or until apples are tender.

In medium bowl, combine all batter ingredients; blend well. Pour evenly over cooked apples. In small bowl, combine all topping ingredients; sprinkle over batter. Microwave on HIGH for 3 to 5 minutes or until toothpick inserted 1 1/2 to 2 inches from edge comes out clean. Let stand 5 minutes on flat surface. Invert onto serving plate.

Yield: 6 servings

Conventional Directions: Heat oven to 350°F. In 9-inch pie pan or round cake pan, melt margarine in oven. Stir in apples, 1/2 cup sugar, 1/2 teaspoon cinnamon and 1/4 teaspoon nutmeg. Bake at 350°F. for 10 minutes.

In medium bowl, combine all batter ingredients; blend well. Pour evenly over cooked apples. In small bowl, combine topping ingredients; sprinkle over batter. Bake an additional 15 to 20 minutes or until toothpick inserted in center comes out clean. Let stand 2 minutes. Invert onto serving plate. To serve, cut into wedges; top with cheese slice or ice cream, if desired.

Yield: 6 servings

High Altitude—Above 3,500 feet: No change.

Nutrition Per Serving: Calories 240; Protein 2g; Carbohydrate 39g; Fat 9g; Sodium 390mg

Maple Cream Coffee Treat

Orange Pineapple Muffin Cake

Nancy Labrie *Rye, New Hampshire*
Bake-Off® Contest 34, 1990

Whole wheat flour adds texture and wholesomeness to this muffinlike cake.

CAKE
1¹/₂ cups all-purpose flour
1 cup whole wheat flour
¹/₃ cup firmly packed brown
   sugar
3 teaspoons baking powder
¹/₂ teaspoon baking soda
¹/₄ teaspoon salt
1 (8¹/₄-oz.) can crushed
   pineapple, drained
¹/₂ cup orange juice
¹/₃ cup margarine or butter,
   melted
¹/₂ to 1 teaspoon grated
   orange peel
1 egg, slightly beaten

GLAZE
¹/₂ cup powdered sugar
¹/₂ teaspoon grated orange
   peel
1 to 2 tablespoons orange juice

GARNISH
Fresh orange slices
Mint leaves

Heat oven to 400° F. Grease bottom only of 9-inch springform pan or 9-inch round cake pan. In large bowl, combine all-purpose flour, whole wheat flour, brown sugar, baking powder, baking soda and salt; mix well. In medium bowl, combine all remaining cake ingredients; blend well. Add to dry ingredients all at once; stir just

until dry ingredients are moistened. Spread dough in greased pan.

Bake at 400° F. for 22 to 27 minutes or until light golden brown and toothpick inserted in center comes out clean. Cool 1 minute; remove from pan. In small bowl, combine all glaze ingredients, adding enough orange juice for desired drizzling consistency. Drizzle over warm cake. Garnish with orange slices and mint leaves. Serve warm.

Yield: 12 servings

High Altitude—Above 3,500 feet: Decrease baking powder to 2 teaspoons. Bake as directed above.

Nutrition Per Serving: Calories 200; Protein 4g; Carbohydrate 34g; Fat 6g; Sodium 230mg

No-Knead Water-Rising Twists

Theadora Smafield *Detroit, Michigan*
Bake-Off® Contest 1, 1949 Grand Prize Winner

This first Bake-Off® Contest winner originally had a unique rising method. In that procedure, the dough was wrapped in a tea towel and submerged in warm water to rise. In this updated version, we have streamlined the preparation of the dough and the rising method.

2¹/₂ to 3¹/₂ cups all-purpose
   flour
¹/₂ cup sugar
1 teaspoon salt
1 pkg. active dry yeast
³/₄ cup milk

¹/₂ cup margarine or butter
1 teaspoon vanilla
2 eggs
¹/₂ cup chopped nuts
¹/₂ cup sugar
1 teaspoon cinnamon

In large bowl, combine 1 cup flour, ¹/₂ cup sugar, salt and yeast; blend well.

In small saucepan, heat milk and margarine until very warm (120 to 130° F.). Add warm liquid, vanilla and eggs to flour mixture. Blend at low speed until moistened; beat 2 minutes at medium speed. By hand, stir in remaining 1¹/₂ to 2¹/₂ cups flour to form a soft dough. Cover loosely with greased plastic wrap and cloth towel. Let rise in warm place (80 to 85° F.) until light and doubled in size, 30 to 40 minutes. (Dough will be sticky.)

Grease 2 large cookie sheets. In small bowl, combine nuts, ¹/₂ cup sugar and cinnamon; blend well. Drop about ¹/₄ cup dough into nut mixture; thoroughly coat. Stretch dough to about 8 inches in length; twist into desired shape. Place on greased cookie sheets. Repeat with remaining dough. Cover; let rise in warm place, about 15 minutes.

Heat oven to 375° F. Uncover dough. Bake 8 to 16 minutes or until light golden brown. Immediately remove from cookie sheets; cool on wire racks. Serve warm.

Yield: 12 servings (1 roll per serving)

High Altitude—Above 3,500 feet: No change.

Nutrition Per Serving: Calories 320; Protein 6g; Carbohydrate 47g; Fat 12g; Sodium 290mg

Top to bottom: **Orange Pineapple Muffin Cake, Raspberry-Filled Jelly Doughnuts, page 170**

Delivering the News

- A call to a Wyoming finalist was answered by her husband—who was on top of the telephone pole, fixing their line. He told Pillsbury that his wife "couldn't come to the phone, because she was at the bottom of the pole."
- One contestant was traveling around the country in an RV with no itinerary and no plans to contact her family for several weeks. Pillsbury enlisted the help of the highway patrols, forest rangers and park officials from several states to let this contestant know the good news.
- After a few days of trying to notify a San Jacinto contestant, Pillsbury became concerned. Calls to the Chamber of Commerce and other city offices didn't provide any clues, but the local newspaper yielded a reporter that personally knew the contestant. That led Pillsbury to one of the contestant's neighbors, who said that the contestant was visiting her family in another part of the state. Much of San Jacinto knew about the contestant's good luck before she did!

Twist-of-Honey Orange Rolls

Roxanne Frisbie *Tigard, Oregon*
Bake-Off® Contest 33, 1988

The best blend of orange and honey flavors these sticky rolls. On-hand ingredients make them quick to make anytime.

**3 tablespoons margarine or
　butter, softened
1 tablespoon finely chopped
　nuts
1 tablespoon grated orange
　peel
1 tablespoon honey
1 (12-oz.) can refrigerated
　flaky biscuits
1/2 cup sugar
1/4 cup orange juice
1 teaspoon vanilla**

Heat oven to 400°F. In small bowl, combine margarine, nuts, orange

peel and honey; mix well. Separate dough into 10 biscuits. Separate each biscuit into 2 layers. Spread top of 10 layers with 1 teaspoon of honey-orange mixture. Top each with remaining layers; press together to form 10 filled biscuits. Gently pull and twist each filled biscuit 4 or 5 times to form 3 1/2-inch twisted roll. Place rolls in ungreased 8- or 9-inch square pan.

　In small saucepan, combine sugar, orange juice and vanilla. Cook over high heat until sugar is melted and syrup begins to boil, stirring constantly. Spoon over rolls. (Mixture will glaze rolls while baking.)

　Bake at 400°F. for 16 to 22 minutes or until golden brown. Cool in pan 2 minutes; invert onto serving plate. Serve warm.

Yield: 10 servings (1 roll per serving)

Nutrition Per Serving: Calories 190; Protein 2g; Carbohydrate 27g; Fat 8g; Sodium 400mg

Apricot Pecan Biscuit Pull-Apart

Thelma Zieammermann *Newton, Kansas*
Bake-Off® Contest 37, 1996 Prize Winner

In 1966 Thelma Zieammermann was a finalist in the Busy Lady Bake-Off® Contest. Now retired, this winner from the seventeenth contest is still busy. She created this quick pull-apart coffee cake as a delicious substitute for time-consuming pecan sweet rolls.

**3/4 cup chopped pecans
2/3 cup firmly packed brown
　sugar
1/2 cup chopped dried apricots
1/2 cup butter, melted
1/2 cup dairy sour cream
1 teaspoon maple flavor
2 (12-oz.) cans refrigerated
　buttermilk flaky biscuits**

Heat oven to 350°F. Grease 12-cup Bundt pan or *one-piece* 10-inch tube pan. In large bowl, combine all ingredients except biscuits; mix well.

　Separate dough into 10 biscuits. Cut each biscuit into 4 pieces; place in bowl with pecan mixture. Toss gently to coat. Spoon biscuit mixture into greased pan.

　Bake at 350°F. for 30 to 40 minutes or until deep golden brown. Immediately invert onto serving plate; cool 10 minutes. Serve warm.

Yield: 12 servings

Nutrition Per Serving: Calories 380; Protein 5g; Carbohydrate 41g; Fat 22g; Sodium 690mg

Apricot Pecan Biscuit Pull-Apart

Lemon Almond Breakfast Pastry

Sharon Richardson *Dallas, Texas*
Bake-Off® Contest 33, 1988 Prize Winner

This large, round pastry, filled with a light lemony almond paste, is similar to pastries found in France and Switzerland. Cut in thin wedges to serve.

FILLING
$1/2$ **cup butter or margarine, softened**
1 (7-oz.) tube almond paste, broken into small pieces
2 eggs
5 teaspoons all-purpose flour
1 to 2 teaspoons grated lemon peel

CRUST
1 (15-oz.) pkg. refrigerated pie crusts
1 teaspoon all-purpose flour
1 egg, beaten
1 tablespoon milk
2 tablespoons sugar

In small bowl or food processor bowl with metal blade, combine butter and almond paste; beat or process until smooth. Add 2 eggs; mix well. By hand, stir in 5 teaspoons flour and lemon peel until just blended. Cover; place in freezer for 20 to 30 minutes or until mixture is thick.

Allow both crust pouches to stand at room temperature for 15 to 20 minutes. Heat oven to 400° F. Remove 1 crust from pouch; unfold. Press out fold lines; sprinkle with 1 teaspoon flour. Place floured side down on ungreased 12-inch pizza pan or cookie sheet. Spread cold filling over crust to within 2 inches of edge. Brush edge with beaten egg. Refrigerate while preparing top crust.

Remove remaining crust from pouch; unfold. Press out fold lines; cut 1-inch circle from center of crust. Using very sharp knife, and curving motions, decoratively score crust in pinwheel design. (Do not cut through crust or filling will leak out.) Carefully place over filled bottom crust. Press edges to seal; flute. In small bowl, combine remaining beaten egg and milk. Brush over pastry; sprinkle with sugar.

Bake at 400° F. for 22 to 27 minutes or until golden brown. Serve warm.

Yield: 16 servings

Nutrition Per Serving: Calories 250; Protein 3g; Carbohydrate 20g; Fat 18g; Sodium 240mg

Blueberry Poppy Seed Brunch Cake

Linda Rahman *Petaluma, California*
Bake-Off® Contest 34, 1990 Grand Prize Winner

Serve it as dessert or let it play the leading role at a special breakfast or brunch. Either way this rich poppy seed coffee cake topped with a layer of blueberries will win compliments.

CAKE
$2/3$ **cup sugar**
$1/2$ **cup margarine or butter, softened**
2 teaspoons grated lemon peel
1 egg
$1^1/2$ cups all-purpose flour
2 tablespoons poppy seed
$1/2$ **teaspoon baking soda**
$1/4$ **teaspoon salt**
$1/2$ **cup dairy sour cream**

FILLING
2 cups fresh or frozen blueberries, thawed, drained on paper towels
$1/3$ **cup sugar**
2 teaspoons all-purpose flour
$1/4$ **teaspoon nutmeg**

GLAZE
$1/3$ **cup powdered sugar**
1 to 2 teaspoons milk

Heat oven to 350° F. Grease and flour bottom and sides of 9- or 10-inch springform pan. In large bowl, beat $2/3$ cup sugar and margarine until light and fluffy. Add lemon peel and egg; beat 2 minutes at medium speed. In medium bowl, combine $1^1/2$ cups flour, poppy seed, baking soda and salt; add to margarine mixture alternately with sour cream. Spread batter over bottom and 1 inch up sides of greased and floured pan, making sure batter on sides is $1/4$ inch thick. In medium bowl, combine all filling ingredients; spoon over batter.

Bake at 350° F. for 45 to 55 minutes or until crust is golden brown. Cool slightly. Remove sides of pan.

In small bowl, combine powdered sugar and enough milk for desired drizzling consistency. Drizzle over warm cake. Serve warm or cool.

Yield: 8 servings

High Altitude—Above 3,500 feet: Increase flour in cake to $1^3/4$ cups. Bake as directed above.

Nutrition Per Serving: Calories 380; Protein 5g; Carbohydrate 55g; Fat 17g; Sodium 300mg

PROFILE

LINDA RAHMAN

When Linda Rahman grew up in the small logging town of Deming, Washington, she cooked in cast-iron pans on a wood stove. "You could hear the cedar crackling; I always loved that." But it wasn't just ham and eggs young Linda was cooking. "My father was always fascinated with foods, exotic foods. He introduced us to bouillabaisse back in the fifties when everyone was eating just meat and potatoes. He had a real appetite for food and its history, and he taught my family to be interested in and excited about food."

That curiosity didn't end with European food. "Shortly after my husband and I were married, we borrowed his parents' boat and spent six weeks sailing. We set out to find out what Native Americans had eaten—on the beach, out of the water, plant life. We had books with us to guide us, but there's not too much you can pick along the beach that is very harmful, so we tried just about everything in a shell, and all kinds of grasses and vegetation along the beach—some we liked and some were not very interesting." Among the interesting ones? Prized mushrooms like morels and chanterelles: "As the snowline moves up, and the bleeding heart flowers bloom, up

come the morels, and now we know right where to go out at Thanksgiving to pick the chanterelles."

Mushrooms aren't the only thing Linda gathers. "Foraging really helps me keep things in perspective. Today life is so hectic, I think we've lost track of some of the basics. People used to work hard with their hands, and appreciate a final product because they worked on it; today we pay money and instantly have it. Unless you've made things from scratch you may not have the full appreciation of what goes into making anything, like jelly. Early in my marriage, before I was caught up in the hustle and bustle of a career, I noticed a fence line covered with grapes. My husband came home from work, and I showed him the pints of grape jelly I made. A lot of the work we do today in the workplace does not give you the same kind of satisfaction as a simple thing like picking grapes and making jelly while your kids are playing." Whether bringing wild mushrooms or her Bake-Off® Grand Prize–winning Blueberry Poppy Seed Brunch Cake to the table, Linda's gathering yields both a sense of accomplishment and extraordinary meals.

Quick Cheese Coffee Cake

Johanna Yoakum *Lake Isabelle, California Bake-Off® Contest 30, 1982 Prize Winner*

With few ingredients and quick to make, this rich, creamy cheese-filled coffee cake is delicious any time.

1 (8-oz.) pkg. cream cheese, softened
$1/2$ cup sugar
1 tablespoon all-purpose flour
1 egg
1 (12-oz.) can refrigerated flaky biscuits
$1^1/2$ teaspoons sugar
$1/4$ teaspoon cinnamon

Heat oven to 350° F. In small bowl, combine cream cheese, $1/2$ cup sugar, flour and egg until smooth. Separate dough into 10 biscuits. Place in ungreased 8- or 9-inch round cake pan; press over bottom and 1 inch up sides to form crust. Pour cream cheese mixture over crust. Combine $1^1/2$ teaspoons sugar and cinnamon; sprinkle over top.

Bake at 350° F. for 24 to 30 minutes or until filling is set and crust is deep golden brown. Cool 20 minutes. Serve warm or cool. Store in refrigerator.

Yield: 8 servings

Nutrition Per Serving: Calories 300; Protein 6g; Carbohydrate 32g; Fat 16g; Sodium 540mg

Blueberry Poppy Seed Brunch Cake, page 168

Raspberry-Filled Jelly Doughnuts

Ted Viveiros *Sunnyvale, California Bake-Off® Contest 34, 1990*

Here's a bakery-shop treat you can make in your own kitchen!

6 tablespoons margarine or butter, melted
³/4 cup sugar
³/4 teaspoon cinnamon

¹/2 cup raspberry jelly
1 (12-oz.) can refrigerated buttermilk fluffy biscuits

Heat oven to 375° F. Place melted margarine in small bowl. In another small bowl, combine sugar and cinnamon; set aside. Stir jelly until smooth. Seal tip of large baster with foil. Remove rubber bulb. Spoon jelly into baster; replace bulb.

Prepare and bake biscuits according to package directions. Immediately dip each hot biscuit in melted margarine, coating all sides. Roll in sugar mixture, heavily coating all sides of each biscuit. Remove foil from tip of baster. Insert baster in side of each biscuit; squeeze small amount of jelly into center. (Refill baster as needed.) Serve warm or cold.

Yield: 10 servings

Tip: To reheat, wrap loosely in foil; heat at 350° F. for 5 to 10 minutes or until warm.

Nutrition Per Serving: Calories 260; Protein 2g; Carbohydrate 36g; Fat 12g; Sodium 430mg

Ted Viveiros: Raspberry-Filled Jelly Doughnuts

When young Ted Viveiros's father passed away, his mother went to work and he had to learn to cook. "I made an apple pie—apples, sugar, crust—and it was awful. The apples were undercooked and the crust was really tough." But Ted toughed it out himself, and grew to be an innovative, no-nonsense cook. Doughnut cravings lead most people to a store, but not Ted. He was in the mood for doughnuts one night, so he just made his own. "By the way," he says, "I now make darn good apple pies, and know enough to add cinnamon and butter." Sometimes our early mistakes provide thought to fuel a lifetime of productive, and sometimes tasty, work.

Raspberry Ripple Crescent Coffee Cake

Priscilla Yee *Concord, California*
Bake-Off® Contest 32, 1986

The cut wedges of this coffee cake show berry pinwheels reminiscent of an Austrian linzer torte.

COFFEE CAKE
³/₄ **cup sugar**
¹/₄ **cup margarine or butter, softened**
2 eggs
³/₄ **cup ground almonds**
¹/₄ **cup all-purpose flour**
1 teaspoon grated lemon peel
1 (8-oz.) can refrigerated crescent dinner rolls
8 teaspoons raspberry preserves
¹/₄ **cup sliced almonds**

GLAZE
¹/₃ **cup powdered sugar**
1 to 2 teaspoons milk

Heat oven to 375° F. Grease 9-inch round cake pan or 9-inch pie pan. In small bowl, beat sugar, margarine and eggs until smooth. Stir ground almonds, flour and lemon peel into sugar mixture. Set aside.

Separate dough into 8 triangles. Spread 1 teaspoon of the preserves on each triangle. Roll up, starting at shortest side of triangle, rolling to opposite point. Place rolls in greased pan in 2 circles, arranging 5 rolls around outside edge and 3 in center. Pour and carefully spread almond mixture evenly over rolls; sprinkle with almonds.

Bake at 375° F. for 27 to 37 minutes or until deep golden brown and center is set. (If necessary, cover coffee cake with foil during last 5 to 10 minutes of baking to prevent excessive browning.) In small bowl, blend glaze ingredients, adding enough milk for desired drizzling consistency. Drizzle over warm cake. Serve warm.

Yield: 8 servings

Nutrition Per Serving: Calories 380; Protein 6g; Carbohydrate 45g; Fat 19g; Sodium 300mg

Whole Wheat Caramel Rolls

Lorraine Edie *Hamburg, New York*
Bake-Off® Contest 9, 1957

These sensational whole wheat rolls form their own gooey caramel topping as they bake.

1 to 2 cups all-purpose flour
1 cup whole wheat flour
3 tablespoons sugar
1 teaspoon salt
1 pkg. active dry yeast
³/₄ **cup milk**
¹/₄ **cup water**
2 tablespoons shortening
1 cup firmly packed brown sugar
¹/₃ **cup margarine or butter, melted**
¹/₂ **cup chopped nuts**

In large bowl, combine ¹/₂ cup of the all-purpose flour, whole wheat flour, sugar, salt and yeast; blend well. In small saucepan, heat milk, water and shortening until very warm (120 to 130° F.). Add warm liquid to flour mixture.

Stir by hand until dry ingredients are moistened. Stir in an additional $^1/_4$ to $^3/_4$ cup all-purpose flour to form a stiff dough.

On floured surface, knead in remaining $^1/_4$ to $^3/_4$ cup all-purpose flour until dough is smooth and elastic, about 5 minutes. Place dough in greased bowl; cover loosely with plastic wrap and cloth towel. Let rise in warm place (80 to 85° F.) until light and doubled in size, about $1^1/_4$ hours.

Grease 9-inch square pan. Punch down dough several times to remove all air bubbles. On lightly floured surface, roll into 16×12-inch rectangle. In small bowl, combine brown sugar and margarine; blend well. Spread evenly over dough; sprinkle with nuts. Starting with 16-inch side, roll up tightly, pressing edge to seal. Cut into 16 slices; place cut side down in greased pan. Cover; let rise in warm place until light and doubled in size, about 45 to 60 minutes.

Heat oven to 350° F. Uncover dough. Bake 25 to 30 minutes or until golden brown. Cool 2 minutes; turn onto serving plate or foil.

Yield: 16 servings (1 roll per serving)

High Altitude—Above 3,500 feet: Bake at 375° F. for 25 to 30 minutes.

Nutrition Per Serving: Calories 210; Protein 3g; Carbohydrate 31g; Fat 8g; Sodium 190mg

One-Step Tropical Coffee Cake

Sharon Schubert *Mentor, Ohio*
Bake-Off® Contest 24, 1973 Prize Winner

Pineapple yogurt, coconut and cinnamon are teamed together in a deliciously different coffee cake that won first prize in the Flour category. Serve it warm from the oven.

COFFEE CAKE
$1^1/_2$ cups all-purpose flour
1 cup sugar
2 teaspoons baking powder
$^1/_2$ teaspoon salt
1 (8-oz.) container pineapple or unflavored yogurt
$^1/_2$ cup oil
2 eggs

TOPPING
1 cup coconut
$^1/_3$ cup sugar
1 teaspoon cinnamon

Heat oven to 350° F. Grease 9-inch square or 11×7-inch pan. In large bowl, combine all coffee cake ingredients; stir 70 to 80 strokes until well blended. Pour into greased pan. In small bowl, combine all topping ingredients. Sprinkle over batter.

Bake at 350° F. for 35 to 40 minutes or until toothpick inserted in center comes out clean.

Yield: 9 servings

High Altitude—Above 3,500 feet: Decrease sugar to $^3/_4$ cup plus 2 tablespoons; decrease baking powder to $1^1/_2$ teaspoons. Bake as directed above.

Nutrition Per Serving: Calories 390; Protein 5g; Carbohydrate 54g; Fat 17g; Sodium 220mg

More Delivering-the-News Stories

- Arriving at her bank to make a deposit, one contestant found, strangely, that her husband was on the phone. He told her to call Pillsbury immediately, and she did, from the bank lobby. Her shrieks of joy resounded through the bank lobby, and she promised to bring her winning dish in for the tellers to taste.

- One contestant without a phone luckily "had her ears on" and learned the good news via a citizens-band message broadcast by her town's postmistress.

- A severe blizzard enveloped one contestant's town during notification and the contestant's phone was out. Pillsbury contacted another finalist who lived in the same town; she was so excited that she drove across town in the storm and scaled a snowdrift to deliver the news.

Sugar-Crusted Almond Pastries

Sugar-Crusted Almond Pastries

Karla Kunoff *Bloomington, Indiana*
Bake-Off® Contest 37, 1996 Prize Winner

The 1996 contest encouraged the creation of quick and simple recipes that fit the way busy people are cooking. Working on this theme, Karla Kunoff developed a super-easy variation of a pastry she remembered from her native Germany.

2 (8-oz.) cans refrigerated crescent dinner rolls
1/2 cup butter
2 cups slivered almonds
1 1/3 cups sugar

Heat oven to 375° F. Unroll dough into 2 large rectangles. Place in ungreased 15×10×1-inch baking pan; press over bottom to form crust. Seal perforations.

Melt butter in medium saucepan over low heat. Cook and stir 4 to 5 minutes or until light golden brown. Add almonds and sugar; stir to coat. Spoon and spread mixture evenly over dough.

Bake at 375° F. for 11 to 16 minutes or until crust is deep golden brown. Cool 30 minutes. Cut into squares. Serve warm or cool.

Yield: 24 servings

Nutrition Per Serving: Calories 210; Protein 3g; Carbohydrate 20g; Fat 13g; Sodium 180mg

Apple Coffee Cake Supreme

Nicole Plaut *Madison, Wisconsin*
Bake-Off® Contest 32, 1986

Savor the down-home goodness of apples in this delicious coffee cake, baked in a tart pan for an elegant look.

COFFEE CAKE
$1/2$ cup sugar
2 eggs
1 to 2 teaspoons grated lemon peel
$1/2$ cup plain yogurt
3 tablespoons margarine or butter, melted
$1^1/3$ cups all-purpose flour
2 teaspoons baking powder
$1/2$ teaspoon salt

3 to 4 cups thinly sliced, peeled apples (3 to 4 medium)
2 tablespoons sugar
$1/2$ to 1 cup sliced almonds

GLAZE
$1/3$ cup sugar
$1/3$ cup margarine or butter, melted
1 egg, beaten

Heat oven to 375°F. Grease 10-inch tart pan with removable bottom or 8-inch square pan. In small bowl, beat $1/2$ cup sugar and 2 eggs; stir in lemon peel, yogurt and 3 tablespoons margarine. Add flour, baking powder and salt to egg mixture; blend well. Pour into greased pan. Arrange apple slices on top of dough, overlapping slightly. Sprinkle with 2 table-spoons sugar and almonds.

Bake at 375°F. for 35 to 45 minutes or until golden brown and toothpick inserted in center comes out clean.*

Meanwhile, in small bowl, combine all glaze ingredients; blend well. Slowly pour over almonds and allow mixture to soak into hot cake. Broil 5 to 6 inches from heat for 1 to 2 minutes or until bubbly. Serve warm. Store in refrigerator.

Yield: 8 servings

*Tip: If using 8-inch square pan, increase baking time 5 minutes.

High Altitude—Above 3,500 feet: No change.

Nutrition Per Serving: Calories 400; Protein 8g; Carbohydrate 49g; Fat 21g; Sodium 380mg

Country Apple Coffee Cake

Country Apple Coffee Cake

Susan Porubcan *Whitewater, Wisconsin Bake-Off® Contest 31, 1984 Grand Prize Winner*

The flavors are down-home, but the innovative shaping of this refrigerated biscuit coffee cake gives it a pastry shop look that's easy to duplicate.

COFFEE CAKE
1 tablespoon margarine or butter, softened
1¹/₂ cups chopped peeled apples
1 (12-oz.) can refrigerated flaky biscuits
1 tablespoon margarine or butter, softened
¹/₃ cup firmly packed brown sugar
¹/₄ teaspoon cinnamon
¹/₃ cup light corn syrup
1¹/₂ teaspoons whiskey, if desired
1 egg
¹/₂ cup pecan halves or pieces

GLAZE
¹/₃ cup powdered sugar
¹/₄ teaspoon vanilla
1 to 2 teaspoons milk

Heat oven to 350°F. Using 1 tablespoon margarine, generously grease 9-inch round cake pan or 8-inch square pan. Spread 1 cup of the apples in greased pan. Separate dough into 10 biscuits; cut each into quarters. Arrange biscuit pieces, points up, over apples. Top with remaining ¹/₂ cup apples.

In small bowl, combine 1 tablespoon margarine, brown sugar, cinnamon, corn syrup, whiskey and egg; beat 2 to 3 minutes or until sugar is partially dissolved. Stir in pecans; spoon over biscuit pieces and apples.

Bake at 350°F. for 35 to 45 minutes or until deep golden brown. Cool 5 minutes. In small bowl, blend all glaze ingredients, adding enough milk for desired drizzling consistency. Drizzle over warm cake. Serve warm or cool. Store in refrigerator.

Yield: 8 servings

Nutrition Per Serving: Calories 330; Protein 4g; Carbohydrate 47g; Fat 14g; Sodium 510mg

Susan Porubcan: Country Apple Coffee Cake

Susan Porubcan's apple cake is certainly as American as apple pie. In it she uses bourbon, the liquor with the distinction of being the only true American spirit. It's distilled from corn—that most American of grains—and can, by law, have only limestone-filtered spring water added to lower its proof. Bourbon was first made in 1789 (in what was originally Virginia but later became Kentucky) by a Baptist minister, Elijah Craig, who would doubtless have approved this creative use of the potent beverage.

Chocolate Almond Crescent Braid

Susie P. Dempsey *Deerfield, Illinois Bake-Off® Contest 29, 1980*

Sour cream, chocolate and almonds in flaky pastry are a top-notch combination. Serve on a dessert plate with a fork, or simply pick up a slice and pass the napkins. When working with crescent-roll dough, keep it refrigerated until needed. Rolls and coffee cakes will be flaky and tender and will rise nicely.

2 oz. semi-sweet chocolate, melted, cooled
¹/₃ cup sugar
¹/₄ cup dairy sour cream
2 tablespoons chopped almonds, toasted*
1 (8-oz.) can refrigerated crescent dinner rolls

GLAZE
¹/₂ cup powdered sugar
¹/₄ teaspoon almond extract
3 to 4 teaspoons milk
2 tablespoons sliced or slivered almonds, toasted*

Heat oven to 350°F. In small bowl, combine chocolate, sugar and sour cream; blend until smooth. Stir in 2 tablespoons chopped almonds. On ungreased cookie sheet, unroll dough into 2 long rectangles. Overlap long sides to form 14×7-inch rectangle; firmly press perforations and edges to seal. Spread chocolate mixture in 2-inch strip lengthwise down center of dough to within ¹/₂ inch of ends. Make cuts 2 inches apart on each side of rectangle just to edge of filling. To

LOIS ANN GROVES

Creativity is one of the keys to creating a Bake-Off® Contest winning recipe—but so is following through with your inspiration. Just ask Lois Ann Groves, who was a Bake-Off® Contest finalist twice before she took the crown, as Grand Prize Winner in Bake-Off® Contest 27, in 1976.

The idea of entering the Pillsbury Bake-Off® was instilled long ago, remembers Lois Ann. "As I was growing up, my mother would occasionally have a successful recipe she had created or revised and comment, 'I'll have to send that in to the Pillsbury Bake-Off!' However, I guess my mother was so busy rearing her family that she never got her recipes written down and sent to Pillsbury." Many years later, Lois Ann came across a Bake-Off® entry blank on the very day of the postmark deadline. She had never actually made the recipe she had in mind but felt strongly she should enter. After getting her young children to bed, she made the recipe as her husband helped type the directions. At 11:00 P.M., they loaded the children into the car and drove twenty miles to the downtown post office to mail it.

Several months later, she received word that she was indeed one of the finalists and to Hawaii she would go! The entertainment and meals were so fabulous she wanted to return to a future Bake-Off®, so she began incorporating Pillsbury products into many of her recipes. "This caused me to become much more creative in the kitchen as well as in other areas." Her creativity in the kitchen paid off: In 1976, she won a trip to Boston. Her easy and spectacular nutty Crescent Caramel Swirl captured the Grand Prize, winning $25,000. Lois Ann is now a successful public speaker who has shared her personal experience and inspirational message with thousands of women.

Her children also enjoy creativity in the kitchen and other areas. "There is a lot that is passed down from mothers to children while you are doing something as simple as preparing a meal or making bread. Some people consider kitchen work wasted time, but if you think about creativity and the attitude of carrying something through, then you realize recipes are not the only things that get passed on in the kitchen."

give braided appearance, fold strips of dough at an angle halfway across filling, alternating from sides. Fold ends under to seal.

Bake at 350°F. for 18 to 23 minutes or until golden brown. Cool 5 minutes. Remove from cookie sheet. Cool on wire rack.

In small bowl, combine powdered sugar, almond extract and enough milk for desired drizzling consistency; blend until smooth. Drizzle over warm braid. Sprinkle with 2 tablespoons almonds. Cool slightly; cut into 8 slices. Store in refrigerator.

Yield: 8 servings (1 slice per serving)

*Tip: To toast almonds, spread on cookie sheet; bake at 375°F. for 3 to 5 minutes or until light golden brown, stirring occasionally. Or spread in thin layer in microwave-safe pie pan. Microwave on HIGH for 2 to 4 minutes or until light golden brown, stirring frequently.

Nutrition Per Serving: Calories 240; Protein 3g; Carbohydrate 33g; Fat 12g; Sodium 240mg

Crescent Caramel Swirl

Lois Ann Groves *San Antonio, Texas*
Bake-Off® Contest 27, 1976 Grand
Prize Winner

The recipe is simple—only five ingre-dients—but the result was worthy of a grand prize. Crescent roll dough, filled with caramel and cut into pinwheels, is layered and baked into a gorgeous Bundt coffee cake.

^{1}/$_2$ **cup butter (do not use margarine)**
^{1}/$_2$ **cup chopped nuts**
^{3}/$_4$ **cup firmly packed brown sugar**
1 tablespoon water
2 (8-oz.) cans refrigerated crescent dinner rolls

Crescent Caramel Swirl

Heat oven to 350° F. Melt butter in small saucepan. Coat bottom and sides of 12-cup Bundt pan with 2 tablespoons of the melted butter; sprinkle pan with 3 tablespoons of the nuts. Add remaining nuts, brown sugar and water to remaining 6 tablespoons melted butter. Bring to a boil, stirring occasionally. Boil 1 minute, stirring constantly.

Remove dough from cans; do not unroll. Cut each roll into 4 slices (for total of 16 slices). Arrange 8 slices, cut side down, in nut-lined pan; separate layers of each pinwheel slightly. Spoon half of brown sugar mixture over dough. Place remaining dough slices alternately over bottom layer. Spoon remaining brown sugar mixture over slices.

Bake at 350° F. for 23 to 33 minutes or until deep golden brown. Cool 3 minutes. Invert onto serving platter or waxed paper.

Yield: 12 servings

Nutrition Per Serving: Calories 280; Protein 3g; Carbohydrate 29g; Fat 18g; Sodium 400mg

Chocolate Crescent Twist

Steve Grieger *Oceanside, California*
Bake-Off® Contest 38, 1998

Willy Wonka will be sorry his chocolate factory didn't think of this chocolate-filled crescent twist first. However, your family will be the first to say "thank you" when you make them this chocolate delight.

STREUSEL
3 tablespoons all-purpose flour
3 tablespoons sugar
1 tablespoon butter or margarine

TWIST
1 (8-oz.) can refrigerated crescent dinner rolls
⅔ cup semi-sweet chocolate chips
1 tablespoon sugar
1 to 3 teaspoons cinnamon
1 tablespoon butter or margarine, melted
1 tablespoon semi-sweet chocolate chips

Heat oven to 375° F. Grease and flour 8×4- or 7×3-inch loaf pan. In small bowl, combine flour and 3 tablespoons sugar. With fork, cut in 1 tablespoon butter until crumbly.

Unroll dough to form 12×8-inch rectangle; firmly press perforations to seal. Sprinkle with ⅔ cup chocolate chips, 1 tablespoon sugar, cinnamon and half of the streusel mixture.

Starting at long side of rectangle, roll up; pinch edge to seal. Join ends to form ring; pinch to seal. Gently twist ring to form fig-

ure 8; place in greased and floured pan. Brush with melted butter; sprinkle with remaining half of streusel. Sprinkle with 1 tablespoon chocolate chips; press lightly into dough.

Bake at 375° F. for 30 to 40 minutes or until deep golden brown. Cool on wire rack for 20 minutes. Remove from pan. Serve warm.

Yield: 6 servings

Nutrition Per Serving: Calories 340; Protein 4g; Carbohydrate 40g; Fat 18g; Sodium 330mg

Lemon-Pecan Sunburst Coffee Cake

Jennifer Peterson *Lincoln City, Oregon*
Bake-Off® Contest 38, 1998

Award-winning flavor baked into a delightful sunburst coffee cake will make "more coffee cake, please" a popular household phrase.

COFFEE CAKE
1 (1 lb. 1.3-oz.) can large refrigerated flaky biscuits
¼ cup finely chopped pecans
¼ cup sugar
2 teaspoons grated lemon peel
2 tablespoons butter or margarine, melted

GLAZE
½ cup powdered sugar
1½ oz. cream cheese (from 3-oz. pkg.), softened
2½ to 3 teaspoons lemon juice

Heat oven to 375°F. Grease 9- or 8-inch round cake pan. Separate dough into 8 biscuits. Place 1 biscuit in center of greased pan. Cut remaining biscuits in half, forming 14 half rounds. Arrange pieces around center biscuit in sunburst pattern with cut sides facing same direction.

In small bowl, combine pecans, sugar and lemon peel; mix well. Brush butter over top of biscuits; sprinkle with pecan mixture.

Bake at 375°F. for 20 to 25 minutes or until golden brown.

Meanwhile, in small bowl, combine all glaze ingredients, adding enough lemon juice for desired drizzling consistency; blend until smooth. Drizzle over warm coffee cake. Cool 10 minutes. Serve warm.

Yield: 8 servings

Nutrition Per Serving: Calories 320; Protein 5g; Carbohydrate 40g; Fat 16g; Sodium 620mg

Lemon-Pecan Sunburst Coffee Cake

Chapter 6

Cookies and Bars

Cookies are one of the few topics on which adults and children see eye to eye. Adults may lose their taste for certain pleasures of childhood—marshmallows squished between their fingers until they resemble "taffy," sugar right out of the bowl and it's the rare child who appreciates a good rack of lamb or a perfectly seasoned bowl of soup. But young and old think alike on the subject of cookies.

Rich cookies, light cookies, wholesome cookies, simple cookies, unusual cookies, even downright decadent cookies have all brought their creators to the Bake-Off® Contest. Recipe histories run the gamut from Old World cookies like the 1957 winner, Accordion Treats, to absolutely American concoctions like Cherry Winks, which are coated with crushed cornflakes, to Old World–New World hybrids like Quick Crescent Baklava.

Some Bake-Off® cookies, like Peanut Blossoms and Snappy Turtle Cookies, have gone on to become American classics. They have become classics because they are festive, tasty, fun to make and, of course because they're cookies—which means they're great dessert, snacks, gifts and holiday activities. If enthusiasm is the province of youth, and wisdom the gift of maturity, isn't it nice that the two can meet for cookies? Cookies truly are food for the young and the young at heart.

Clockwise from left: **Lemon-Go-Lightly Cookies, page 187, Rocky Road Fudge Bars, page 219, Peanut Blossoms, page 192 (HERSHEY®'S KISSES® milk chocolates and the Conical Configuration are registered trademarks of The Hershey Food Corporation).**

Choconut Chippers

Deborah Anderson *Fairborn, Ohio*
Bake-Off® Contest 32, 1986 Prize Winner

Here's a chocolate chip cookie that pulls out all the stops. The rich chocolate dough also is loaded with rolled oats and pecans. Judges agreed this chewy drop cookie was a winner.

3/4 **cup sugar**
3/4 **cup firmly packed brown sugar**
1/4 **cup oil**
1 **teaspoon vanilla**
2 **egg whites or 1 whole egg**
1 **(5-oz.) pkg. chocolate fudge pudding and pie filling mix (6-serving size; not instant)**
1 **(8-oz.) container dairy sour cream**
2 **cups all-purpose flour**
1 1/2 **cups rolled oats**
1 **teaspoon baking soda**
1/2 **teaspoon salt**
2 **cups chopped pecans**
1 **(12-oz.) pkg. (2 cups) semi-sweet chocolate chips**

Heat oven to 375°F. Grease cookie sheets. In large bowl, combine sugar, brown sugar, oil, vanilla, egg whites, pudding mix and sour cream at low speed until moistened; beat 2 minutes at medium speed. Add flour, rolled oats, baking soda and salt; mix at low speed until blended. By hand, stir in pecans and chocolate chips.* Drop by rounded tablespoonfuls 2 inches apart onto greased cookie sheets.

Betty Chromzack: Chocolate Coconut Crunchers

Betty Chromzack joined the WACs during World War II and was a cook in New Guinea and the Philippines until she was wounded. "I spent the following three and a half years in army and VA hospitals . . . where I learned that no matter how bad things get, they could be a lot worse." Betty's indomitable spirit led her through these trials, and she subsequently raised a family—and became a great baker. Betty bought a car with her prize money: "I call it the 'Chocolate Coconut Cruncher.'" Driven by strength and spirit like Betty's, no doubt the Cruncher will go far.

Bake at 375°F. for 6 to 7 minutes or until set. DO NOT OVERBAKE. Cool 1 minute; remove from cookie sheets.

Yield: 72 servings (1 cookie per serving)

*Tip: If dough is too soft, cover with plastic wrap and refrigerate about 1 hour, or stir in an additional 1/4 cup flour for easier handling.

High Altitude—Above 3,500 feet: No change.

Nutrition Per Serving: Calories 100; Protein 1g; Carbohydrate 13g; Fat 5g; Sodium 45mg

Chocolate Coconut Crunchers

Betty Chromzack *Northlake, Illinois*
Bake-Off® Contest 36, 1994 Prize Winner

Chewy, crunchy and chocolaty describe these family-pleasing drop cookies. Because they start with cake mix, you can have homemade cookies in a hurry.

1 **(1 lb. 2.25-oz.) pkg. pudding-included German chocolate cake mix**
1 **cup margarine or butter, softened**
2 **eggs**
1 **cup coconut**
1 **cup chopped walnuts**
1 **cup crushed cornflakes cereal or other cereal flakes**
1 **cup rolled oats**
1 **(6-oz.) pkg. (1 cup) semi-sweet chocolate chips**
1 **to 2 tablespoons sugar**

Heat oven to 350°F. In large bowl, combine cake mix, margarine and eggs; mix well. Add coconut, walnuts, cereal, oats and chocolate chips; mix well. Drop dough by rounded teaspoonfuls 2 inches apart onto ungreased cookie sheets. Flatten with glass dipped in sugar.

Bake at 350°F. for 8 to 10 minutes or until set. Cool 1 minute; remove from cookie sheets.

Yield: 60 servings (1 cookie per serving)

High Altitude—Above 3,500 feet: No change.

Nutrition Per Serving: Calories 120; Protein 1g; Carbohydrate 12g; Fat 7g; Sodium 110mg

Crickets

Deborah Zurow *Lombard, Illinois*
Bake-Off® Contest 18, 1967

Similar to chocolate chip cookies in texture and appearance, these cookies are dotted with chocolate-covered raisins.

1/2 cup margarine or butter, softened
1/3 cup sugar
1/4 cup firmly packed brown sugar
1 teaspoon vanilla
1 egg
1 cup all-purpose flour
1/2 teaspoon baking soda
1/2 teaspoon salt
1/2 cup chopped toasted almonds, if desired*
1 (7-oz.) pkg. (1 cup) chocolate-covered raisins

Heat oven to 375°F. In large bowl, beat margarine, sugar and brown sugar until light and fluffy. Add vanilla and egg; beat well. Stir in flour and remaining ingredients; mix well. Drop by teaspoonfuls 2 inches apart onto ungreased cookie sheets.

Bake at 375°F. for 8 to 10 minutes or until light golden brown. Cool 1 minute; remove from cookie sheets.

Yield: 30 servings (1 cookie per serving)

*Tip: To toast almonds, spread on cookie sheet; toast at 375°F. for 5 to 10 minutes or until light golden brown, stirring occasionally.

High Altitude—Above 3,500 feet: Decrease sugar to 1/4 cup; increase flour to 1 1/4 cups. Bake as directed above.

Nutrition Per Serving: Calories 100; Protein 1g; Carbohydrate 12g; Fat 6g; Sodium 95mg

Maple Oat Chewies

Kitty Cahill *St. Paul, Minnesota*
Bake-Off® Contest 32, 1986

A favorite breakfast cereal adds crispness to these chewy cookies with a fun crunch. They are sure to be a family favorite.

1 cup sugar
1 cup firmly packed brown sugar
1 cup margarine or butter, softened
1 tablespoon molasses
2 teaspoons maple extract
2 eggs
1 3/4 cups all-purpose flour
2 teaspoons baking powder
1 teaspoon cinnamon
1/2 teaspoon salt
2 cups rolled oats
2 cups crisp rice cereal

Heat oven to 350°F. Grease cookie sheets. In large bowl, beat sugar, brown sugar and margarine until light and fluffy. Add molasses, maple extract and eggs; blend well. Add flour, baking powder, cinnamon and salt; beat at medium speed until well blended. Stir in rolled oats and cereal. Drop by heaping teaspoonfuls 2 inches apart onto greased cookie sheets.

Bake at 350°F. for 8 to 12 minutes or until light golden brown. Cool 2 minutes; remove from cookie sheets.

Yield: 60 servings (1 cookie per serving)

Tip: One cup butterscotch chips can be added with rolled oats and cereal, if desired.

High Altitude—Above 3,500 feet: No change.

Nutrition Per Serving: Calories 80; Protein 1g; Carbohydrate 13g; Fat 3g; Sodium 80mg

Kitty Cahill: Maple Oat Chewies

Parenthood has been called the toughest job on earth, because parents have to provide equally for the bodies and souls of their children. "I've been a counselor for the YWCA, a lifeguard and a police officer for a large metropolitan city," Kitty Cahill says. "Being a full-time homemaker is the toughest of all. On an average income it requires endless creativity, resourcefulness and stamina." Of course, easy cookies like Maple Oat Chewies provide energy for the long stretch from lunch to dinner, so that parents can gear up for whatever follows.

Accordion Treats

Gerda Roderer *Berkeley, California*
Bake-Off® Contest 9, 1957 Grand Prize Winner

This uniquely shaped cookie is an old family recipe that originated in Alsace-Lorraine.

2 (1-yard) sheets heavy-duty foil
¾ cup margarine or butter, softened
¾ cup sugar
1 teaspoon vanilla
2 eggs
1 cup all-purpose flour
¼ teaspoon salt
½ cup chopped walnuts, if desired

Heat oven to 325°F. Fold 1 sheet of foil in half lengthwise. Fold the double-thickness foil crosswise into 1-inch pleats to make an "accordion-pleated" pan. Place on ungreased cookie sheet. Repeat with second sheet of foil.

In large bowl, beat margarine and sugar until light and fluffy. Add vanilla and eggs; beat well. Add flour and salt; mix well. Stir in walnuts. Drop 1 rounded teaspoon of dough into each fold of foil. (Dough spreads during baking to form 4½- to 5-inch-long cookies.)

Bake at 325°F. for 18 to 26 minutes or until golden brown. Remove cookies from foil; cool completely. Turn foil over for second baking.

Yield: 48 servings (1 cookie per serving)

Tips: If desired, baked cookies can be sprinkled with powdered sugar or frosted with a powdered sugar glaze.

For flavor variations, substitute one of the following for the walnuts or vanilla. Replace walnuts with 1 teaspoon cardamom, caraway seed, anise seed, or grated orange or lemon peel. Replace vanilla with ½ teaspoon rum flavor or almond, orange or lemon extract.

High Altitude—Above 3,500 feet: Decrease sugar to ⅔ cup; increase flour to 1¼ cups. Bake as directed above.

Nutrition Per Serving: Calories 60; Protein 1g; Carbohydrate 5g; Fat 4g; Sodium 45mg

Cherry Winks

Ruth Derousseau *Rice Lake, Wisconsin*
Bake-Off® Contest 2, 1950 Prize Winner

The cherry pressed in the top of each cookie gives these ever-popular cookies their name. Their crunchy texture, with cornflakes cereal on the outside and pecans, dates and cherries hidden inside, appeals to young and old alike.

1 cup sugar
¾ cup shortening
2 tablespoons milk
1 teaspoon vanilla
2 eggs
2¼ cups all-purpose flour
1 teaspoon baking powder
½ teaspoon baking soda
½ teaspoon salt
1 cup chopped pecans
1 cup chopped dates
⅓ cup chopped maraschino cherries, well drained
1½ cups coarsely crushed cornflakes cereal
15 maraschino cherries, quartered

Heat oven to 375°F. Grease cookie sheets. In large bowl, combine sugar, shortening, milk, vanilla and eggs; beat well. Stir in flour, baking powder, baking soda, salt, pecans, dates and ⅓ cup chopped cherries; mix well.*

Drop by rounded teaspoonfuls into cereal; thoroughly coat. Form into balls; place 2 inches apart on greased cookie sheets. Lightly press maraschino cherry piece into top of each ball.

Bake at 375°F. for 10 to 15 minutes or until light golden brown.

Yield: 60 servings (1 cookie per serving)

*Tip: If desired, cover with plastic wrap and refrigerate dough for easier handling.

High Altitude—Above 3,500 feet: No change.

Nutrition Per Serving: Calories 90; Protein 1g; Carbohydrate 12g; Fat 4g; Sodium 55mg

Brownie Macaroons

Ronald Grasgreen *Sugarland, Texas*
Bake-Off® Contest 39, 2000

An explosion of moist flavor with each crunchy-chewy bite—coconut and chocolate baked into a tantalizing cookie that may just win you a standing ovation.

1 (15.5-oz.) pkg. fudge
   brownie mix with chocolate
   chunks
2 cups coconut
2 tablespoons water
1 tablespoon oil
1 egg

Heat oven to 350° F. Lightly grease cookie sheets or line with parchment paper. In large bowl, combine all ingredients; beat 50 strokes with spoon. Shape dough into 1½-inch balls. Place 3 inches apart on greased cookie sheet; flatten slightly.

Bake at 350° F. for 12 to 15 minutes or until edges are set. (Centers will be soft.) Remove from cookie sheets.

Yield: 24 servings (1 cookie per serving)

High Altitude—Above 3,500 feet: No change.

Nutrition Per Serving: Calories 120; Protein 1g; Carbohydrate 18g; Fat 5g; Sodium 75mg

Fudgy Bonbons

Mary Anne Tyndall *Whiteville, North Carolina Bake-Off® Contest 36, 1994 Grand Prize Winner*

Serve these incredibly delicious cookies in miniature paper cups for a dazzling presentation. They make a lovely holiday care package.

1 (12-oz.) pkg. (2 cups) semi-
   sweet chocolate chips
¼ cup butter or margarine
1 (14-oz.) can sweetened
   condensed milk (not
   evaporated)
2 cups all-purpose flour
½ cup finely chopped nuts, if
   desired
1 teaspoon vanilla
60 milk chocolate candy drops
   or pieces, unwrapped
2 oz. white baking bar or
   white candy coating
1 teaspoon shortening or oil

Heat oven to 350° F. In medium saucepan, combine chocolate chips and butter; cook and stir over very low heat until chips are melted and smooth. Add sweetened condensed milk; mix well.

In medium bowl, combine flour, nuts, chocolate mixture and vanilla; mix well. Shape 1 tablespoon dough (use measuring spoon) around each milk chocolate, covering completely. Place 1 inch apart on ungreased cookie sheets.

Bake at 350° F. for 6 to 8 minutes. DO NOT OVERBAKE. Cookies will be soft and appear shiny but will become firm as they cool. Remove from cookie sheets; cool.

In small saucepan, combine white baking bar and shortening; cook and stir over low heat until melted and smooth. Drizzle over cookies. Store in tightly covered container.

Yield: 60 servings (1 cookie per serving)

High Altitude—Above 3,500 feet: Increase flour to 2¼ cups. Bake as directed above.

Nutrition Per Serving: Calories 110; Protein 2g; Carbohydrate 14g; Fat 5g; Sodium 20mg

Mary Anne Tyndall: Fudgy Bonbons

Bonbon is a corruption of the French for "good-good"—and what more, really, is there to be said about these rich chocolate cookies? Mary Anne Tyndall reported that her husband found her work very good indeed. "My husband has always supported, praised and eaten my kitchen creations. In fact, he appreciated them so much he gained thirty-five pounds the first year we were married. The more praise I received, the more I cooked, and the more I cooked the more he ate. That was twenty-seven years ago, and since then we have learned the meaning of moderation!"

Funfetti Cookies

Molly Taylor *Maryville, Tennessee*
Bake-Off® Contest 34, 1990

Children will love to sprinkle the candy bits on these fast and fun cookies. Because they're so festive, they make a perfect birthday party treat.

1 (1 lb. 2.9-oz.) pkg. pudding-included white cake mix with candy bits
^{1}/$_3$ cup oil
2 eggs
^{1}/$_2$ (15.6-oz.) can pink vanilla frosting with candy bits

Heat oven to 375°F. In large bowl, combine cake mix, oil and eggs; stir by hand until thoroughly moistened. Shape dough into 1-inch balls. Place 2 inches apart on ungreased cookie sheets. Flatten to ^{1}/$_4$-inch thickness with bottom of glass dipped in flour.

Bake at 375°F. for 6 to 8 minutes or until edges are light golden brown. Cool 1 minute; remove from cookie sheets. Spread frosting over warm cookies. Immediately sprinkle each with candy bits from frosting. Allow frosting to set before storing. Store in tightly covered container.

Yield: 36 servings (1 cookie per serving)

High Altitude—Above 3,500 feet: Add ^{1}/$_2$ cup flour to dry cake mix. Bake as directed above.

Nutrition Per Serving: Calories 100; Protein 1g; Carbohydrate 15g; Fat 4g; Sodium 100mg

Lemon-Go-Lightly Cookies

Margaret Conway *Oceano, California*
Bake-Off® Contest 27, 1976 Prize Winner

Potato flakes are the secret ingredient in these soft, chewy, delicately flavored cookies.

2 cups all-purpose flour
2 cups mashed potato flakes
1 cup sugar
1 cup firmly packed brown sugar
^{1}/$_2$ to ^{3}/$_4$ cup finely chopped nuts
1 teaspoon baking soda
^{3}/$_4$ cup margarine or butter, melted
1 teaspoon grated lemon peel
2 eggs
^{1}/$_4$ cup sugar

Heat oven to 350°F. In large bowl, combine all ingredients except ^{1}/$_4$ cup sugar; blend well. (Mixture will be crumbly.) Firmly press into 1-inch balls; roll in ^{1}/$_4$ cup sugar. Place 2 inches apart on ungreased cookie sheets.

Bake at 350°F. for 9 to 12 minutes or until golden brown. Cool 1 minute; remove from cookie sheets.

Yield: 72 servings (1 cookie per serving)

High Altitude—Above 3,500 feet: No change.

Nutrition Per Serving: Calories 70; Protein 1g; Carbohydrate 11g; Fat 3g; Sodium 45mg

Moonbeam Cookies

Janice Oeffler *Danbury, Wisconsin*
Bake-Off® Contest 39, 2000

Seedless raspberry preserves can be used in place of the lemon curd to fill these simple thumbprint cookies made with refrigerated dough.

1 (18-oz.) pkg. refrigerated sugar cookies
1 cup coconut
^{1}/$_2$ cup lemon curd (from 10-oz. jar)*
2 oz. vanilla-flavored candy coating, chopped, or ^{1}/$_3$ cup white vanilla chips

Heat oven to 350°F. Break up cookie dough into large bowl. Stir in coconut. Shape dough into 1-inch balls. Place 2 inches apart on ungreased cookie sheets. With thumb or handle of wooden spoon, make indentation in center of each cookie. Spoon about ^{1}/$_2$ teaspoon lemon curd into each indentation.

Bake at 350°F. for 10 to 13 minutes or until edges are light golden brown. Remove from cookie sheets. Cool 5 minutes.

Microwave candy coating in small microwave-safe bowl on MEDIUM for 2 minutes. Stir well. Drizzle over cookies.

Yield: 3 dozen cookies

*Tip: Lemon pie filling can be substituted for the lemon curd.

Nutrition Per Serving: Calories 90; Protein 1g; Carbohydrate 13g; Fat 4g; Sodium 60mg

Apricot Snowcaps

Virginia Johnson *Blanchardville, Wisconsin*
Bake-Off® Contest 35, 1992

A drizzle of white chocolate adds a special touch to these thumbprint-style cookies.

COOKIES
¹/₂ **cup sugar**
¹/₂ **cup firmly packed brown sugar**
¹/₄ **cup margarine or butter, softened**
¹/₄ **cup shortening**
¹/₂ **teaspoon vanilla**
1 **egg**
1 **cup all-purpose flour**
¹/₂ **teaspoon baking powder**
¹/₂ **teaspoon baking soda**
¹/₂ **teaspoon salt**
1 **cup quick-cooking rolled oats**
¹/₂ **cup purchased apricot filling**

GLAZE
1 **(6-oz.) pkg. white baking bars, chopped**
2 **tablespoons shortening**

Heat oven to 350° F. In large bowl, beat sugar, brown sugar, margarine and ¹/₄ cup shortening until light and fluffy. Add vanilla and egg; blend well. Add flour, baking powder, baking soda and salt; mix well. Stir in rolled oats. Shape dough into 1-inch balls; place 2 inches apart on ungreased cookie sheets. Make a small indentation in each cookie; fill each indentation with ¹/₂ teaspoon apricot filling.

Bake at 350° F. for 9 to 13 minutes or until light golden brown. Cool 1 minute; remove from cookie sheets. Meanwhile, in small saucepan over very low heat, melt glaze ingredients. Spoon or drizzle over warm cookies. Cool completely.

Yield: 36 servings (1 cookie per serving)

***Left to right:** Apricot Snowcaps,*
Tropical Pineapple Coconut Bars, page 220

High Altitude—Above 3,500 feet: Decrease sugar to ¹/₃ cup; increase flour to 1¹/₃ cups. Bake as directed above.

Nutrition Per Serving: Calories 110; Protein 1g; Carbohydrate 14g; Fat 5g; Sodium 70mg

White Chocolate Chunk Cookies

Dottie Due *Edgewood, Kentucky*
Bake-Off® Contest 33, 1988 Prize Winner

Dottie Due wanted to duplicate cookies from a trendy cookie shop at a time when white chocolate was still new. After twelve variations on the recipe, family and friends agreed this tender drop cookie was the best.

1 cup shortening
³/₄ cup sugar
³/₄ cup firmly packed brown sugar
3 eggs
1 teaspoon vanilla
2¹/₂ cups all-purpose flour
1 teaspoon baking powder
1 teaspoon baking soda
¹/₂ teaspoon salt
1 cup flaked coconut
¹/₂ cup rolled oats
¹/₂ cup chopped walnuts
2 (6-oz.) pkg. white baking bars, cut into ¹/₄- to ¹/₂-inch chunks*

Heat oven to 350°F. In large bowl, beat shortening, sugar and brown sugar until light and fluffy. Add eggs 1 at a time, beating well after each addition. Add vanilla; blend well. Stir in flour, baking powder,

baking soda and salt; mix well. Stir in remaining ingredients. Drop by rounded tablespoonfuls 2 inches apart onto ungreased cookie sheets.

Bake at 350°F. for 10 to 15 minutes or until light golden brown. Cool 1 minute; remove from cookie sheets.

Yield: 60 servings (1 cookie per serving)

*Tip: One (12-oz.) pkg. white vanilla chips can be substituted for 2 (6-oz.) pkg. white baking bars. Do not substitute almond bark or vanilla-flavored candy coating.

High Altitude—Above 3,500 feet: Decrease baking powder to ¹/₂ teaspoon; decrease baking soda to ¹/₂ teaspoon. Bake at 375°F. for 8 to 12 minutes.

Nutrition Per Serving: Calories 120; Protein 1g; Carbohydrate 14g; Fat 6g; Sodium 60mg

Caramel-Filled Chocolate Cookies

Jean Olson *Wallingford, Iowa*
Bake-Off® Contest 34, 1990 Prize Winner

These look like a chocolate crinkle cookie, but the delicious surprise is a baked-in caramel filling.

2¹/₂ cups all-purpose flour
³/₄ cup unsweetened cocoa
1 teaspoon baking soda
1 cup sugar
1 cup firmly packed brown sugar
1 cup margarine or butter, softened

2 teaspoons vanilla
2 eggs
1 cup chopped pecans
48 Rolo® Chewy Caramels in Milk Chocolate (13-oz. pkg.), unwrapped
1 tablespoon sugar
4 oz. vanilla-flavored candy coating, if desired

In small bowl, combine flour, cocoa and baking soda; blend well. In large bowl, beat 1 cup sugar, brown sugar and margarine until light and fluffy. Add vanilla and eggs; beat well. Add flour mixture; blend well. Stir in ¹/₂ cup of the pecans. If necessary, cover with plastic wrap; refrigerate 30 minutes for easier handling.

Heat oven to 375°F. For each cookie, with floured hands shape about 1 tablespoon dough around 1 caramel candy, covering completely.

In small bowl, combine remaining ¹/₂ cup pecans and 1 tablespoon sugar. Press one side of each ball into pecan mixture. Place nut side up 2 inches apart on ungreased cookie sheets.

Bake at 375°F. for 7 to 10 minutes or until set and slightly cracked. Cool 2 minutes; remove from cookie sheets. Cool completely on wire rack.

Melt candy coating in small saucepan over low heat, stirring constantly until smooth. Drizzle over cookies.

Yield: 48 servings (1 cookie per serving)

High Altitude—Above 3,500 feet: Increase flour to 2³/₄ cups. Bake as directed above.

Nutrition Per Serving: Calories 160; Protein 2g; Carbohydrate 20g; Fat 8g; Sodium 90mg

German Chocolate Thumbprint Cookies

Frances Sheppard *Corsicana, Texas*
Bake-Off® Contest 34, 1990 Prize Winner

This quick cookie features a thumb-print filled with a coconut mixture typical of German chocolate desserts.

TOPPING
1 cup sugar
1 cup evaporated milk
1/2 cup unsalted butter, butter
 or margarine, softened
1 teaspoon vanilla
3 egg yolks, beaten
1 1/2 cups flaked coconut
1 1/2 cups chopped pecans

COOKIES
1 (1 lb. 2.25-oz.) pkg.
 pudding-included German
 chocolate cake mix
1/3 cup unsalted butter, butter
 or margarine, melted

In heavy 2-quart saucepan, combine sugar, evaporated milk, 1/2 cup butter, vanilla and egg yolks; blend well. Cook over medium heat for 10 to 13 minutes or until thickened and bubbly, stirring frequently. Remove from heat. Stir in coconut and pecans. Cool to room temperature.

Reserve 1 1/4 cups of the topping mixture; set aside. In large bowl, combine cookie ingredients and remaining topping mixture; stir by hand until thoroughly moistened. Cover with plastic wrap; refrigerate 30 minutes for easier handling.

Heat oven to 350° F. Shape dough into 1-inch balls. Place 2 inches apart on ungreased cookie sheets. With thumb, make an indentation in center of each ball. Fill each indentation with rounded 1/2 teaspoon reserved topping mixture.

Bake at 350° F. for 10 to 13 minutes or until set. Cool 5 minutes; remove from cookie sheets. Cool completely.

Yield: 60 servings (1 cookie per serving)

High Altitude—Above 3,500 feet: Add 1/2 cup flour to dry cake mix. Bake as directed above.

Nutrition Per Serving: Calories 110; Protein 1g; Carbohydrate 12g; Fat 6g; Sodium 65mg

Praline Cookies

Cheryl Dean Matthews *Charlotte, North Carolina*
Bake-Off® Contest 11, 1959 Prize Winner

This contestant was a fourteen-year-old Junior Second Prize winner. She did her recipe testing on a range that her mother won as a finalist in the fourth Bake-Off® Contest! Praline, a mixture of pecans and caramelized sugar, flavors the frosting on these irresistible cookies.

COOKIES
1 1/2 cups firmly packed brown
 sugar
1/2 cup margarine or butter,
 softened
1 teaspoon vanilla
1 egg
1 1/2 cups all-purpose flour
1 1/2 teaspoons baking powder
1/2 teaspoon salt

FROSTING
1/2 cup firmly packed brown
 sugar
1/4 cup half-and-half
1 cup powdered sugar
1/2 cup coarsely chopped
 pecans

Heat oven to 350° F. Grease cookie sheets. In large bowl, beat 1 1/2 cups brown sugar and margarine until light and fluffy. Add vanilla and egg; blend well. Stir in flour, baking powder and salt; mix well. Drop dough by rounded teaspoonfuls 2 inches apart onto greased cookie sheets.

Bake at 350° F. for 10 to 12 minutes or until light golden brown. Cool 1 minute; remove from cookie sheets.

In small saucepan, combine 1/2 cup brown sugar and half-and-half. Bring to a boil over medium heat; boil 2 minutes, stirring constantly. Remove from heat. Stir in powdered sugar; beat until smooth. Place about 1/2 teaspoon of the pecans on each cookie; drizzle with frosting, covering pecans. Let stand until set.

Yield: 36 servings (1 cookie per serving)

High Altitude—Above 3,500 feet: No change.

Nutrition Per Serving: Calories 120; Protein 1g; Carbohydrate 20g; Fat 4g; Sodium 80mg

Pistachio Pecan Party Cookies

Karla Johnson *St. Paul, Minnesota*
Bake-Off® Contest 31, 1984

Tender and flavorful, these cookies make a wonderful addition to a tray of festive cookies. For paler green cookies, use the smaller amount of green food color.

¹/₂ cup powdered sugar
¹/₂ cup margarine or butter, softened
¹/₂ cup oil
1 teaspoon almond extract
2 eggs
1 (3.4-oz.) pkg. instant pistachio pudding and pie filling mix
1 to 3 drops green food color
2 cups all-purpose flour
¹/₂ teaspoon baking soda
¹/₂ teaspoon cream of tartar
¹/₈ teaspoon salt
¹/₂ cup chopped pecans
Sugar

In large bowl, combine powdered sugar, margarine, oil, almond extract, eggs, pudding mix and food color; mix well. Add flour, baking soda, cream of tartar and salt; mix well. Stir in pecans. Cover with plastic wrap; refrigerate 1 hour for easier handling.

Heat oven to 375°F. Shape dough into 1-inch balls; roll in sugar. Place 2 inches apart on ungreased cookie sheets. Bake at 375°F. for 10 to 15 minutes or until edges are light golden brown. Immediately remove from cookie sheets.

Yield: 54 servings (1 cookie per serving)

High Altitude—Above 3,500 feet: No change.

Nutrition Per Serving: Calories 70; Protein 1g; Carbohydrate 7g; Fat 5g; Sodium 45mg

Nutmeg Cookie Logs

Julia Woods *South Charleston, West Virginia*
Bake-Off® Contest 8, 1956

Nutmeg comes from the fruit of a tropical evergreen called a nutmeg tree. The orange fleshy fruit is split to reveal the nutmeg seed, which can be purchased whole or ground. These cookies have a delicately warm, spicy-sweet flavor.

COOKIES
³/₄ cup sugar
1 cup margarine or butter, softened
2 teaspoons vanilla
2 teaspoons rum extract
1 egg
3 cups all-purpose flour
1 teaspoon nutmeg

FROSTING
2 cups powdered sugar
3 tablespoons margarine or butter, softened
³/₄ teaspoon rum extract
¹/₄ teaspoon vanilla
2 to 3 tablespoons half-and-half or milk
Nutmeg

In large bowl, beat sugar, 1 cup margarine, 2 teaspoons vanilla, 2 teaspoons rum extract and egg until light and fluffy. Stir in flour and 1 teaspoon nutmeg; mix well. Cover with plastic wrap; refrigerate 30 to 45 minutes for easier handling.

Heat oven to 350°F. Divide dough into 12 pieces. On lightly floured surface, shape each piece of dough into long rope, ¹/₂ inch in diameter and about 15 inches long. Cut into 3-inch lengths; place on ungreased cookie sheets. Bake at 350°F. for 12 to 15 minutes or until light golden brown. Immediately remove from cookie sheets. Cool completely.

In small bowl, combine all frosting ingredients except nutmeg, adding enough half-and-half for desired spreading consistency. Spread on top and sides of cookies. If desired, mark frosting with tines of fork to resemble bark. Sprinkle lightly with nutmeg. Let stand until frosting is set. Store in tightly covered container.

Yield: 60 servings (1 cookie per serving)

High Altitude—Above 3,500 feet: No change.

Nutrition Per Serving: Calories 80; Protein 1g; Carbohydrate 11g; Fat 4g; Sodium 45mg

Molasses Oat Bran Cookies

Constance Dudley *Stanardsville, Virginia*
Bake-Off® Contest 34, 1990 Prize Winner

These spicy cookies have a full-bodied molasses flavor. Coating them with sugar gives them a wonderful, crackly appearance.

1 cup sugar
³/4 cup oil
¹/4 cup refrigerated or frozen fat-free egg product, thawed, or 1 egg
¹/4 cup molasses
1¹/2 cups whole wheat flour
1¹/2 cups quick-cooking rolled oats
¹/2 cup oat bran
2 teaspoons baking soda
1 teaspoon cinnamon
¹/2 teaspoon ginger
¹/4 teaspoon salt
¹/4 teaspoon cloves
¹/4 cup sugar

In large bowl, combine 1 cup sugar, oil, egg product and molasses; mix well. By hand, stir flour, rolled oats, oat bran, baking soda, cinnamon, ginger, salt and cloves into sugar mixture until well blended. Cover with plastic wrap; refrigerate at least 1 hour for easier handling.

Heat oven to 375°F. Spray cookie sheets with nonstick cooking spray. Shape dough into 1-inch balls; roll in ¹/4 cup sugar. Place 2 inches apart on sprayed-coated cookie sheets. With bottom of glass dipped in sugar, flatten balls slightly.

Bake at 375°F. for 7 to 10 minutes or until cookies are set and tops are cracked. Cool 1 minute; remove from cookie sheets.

Yield: 60 servings (1 cookie per serving)

High Altitude—Above 3,500 feet: Increase flour to 1³/4 cups. Bake as directed above.

Nutrition Per Serving: Calories 60; Protein 1g; Carbohydrate 8g; Fat 3g; Sodium 50mg

Peanut Blossoms

Freda Smith *Gibsonburg, Ohio*
Bake-Off® Contest 9, 1957

Have you ever wondered where old-fashioned cookie favorites such as these originated? This popular cookie made its first appearance as an entry in a Bake-Off® Contest. They have sometimes been called Brown-Eyed Susans.

1³/4 cups all-purpose flour
¹/2 cup sugar
¹/2 cup firmly packed brown sugar
1 teaspoon baking soda
¹/2 teaspoon salt
¹/2 cup shortening
¹/2 cup peanut butter
2 tablespoons milk
1 teaspoon vanilla
1 egg
Sugar
About 48 milk chocolate candy drops or pieces, unwrapped

Heat oven to 375°F. In large bowl, blend flour, ¹/2 cup sugar, brown sugar, baking soda, salt, shortening, peanut butter, milk, vanilla and egg at low speed until stiff dough forms. Shape into 1-inch balls; roll in sugar. Place 2 inches apart on ungreased cookie sheets.

Bake at 375°F. for 10 to 12 minutes or until golden brown. Immediately top each cookie with 1 milk chocolate, pressing down firmly so cookie cracks around edge; remove from cookie sheets.

Yield: 48 servings (1 cookie per serving)

High Altitude—Above 3,500 feet: No change.

Nutrition Per Serving: Calories 100; Protein 2g; Carbohydrate 12g; Fat 5g; Sodium 65mg

Swedish Heirloom Cookies

Bernice Wheaton *Hopkins, Minnesota*
Bake-Off® Contest 3, 1951

The earliest contests were designed to collect treasured family recipes. Originality was not a requirement. These buttery Swedish molded cookies are similar to Mexican wedding cakes and Russian tea cakes.

2 cups all-purpose flour
1 cup powdered sugar
¹/4 teaspoon salt
1 cup butter or margarine
1 tablespoon vanilla
1 cup finely chopped almonds
2 to 3 tablespoons powdered sugar

Heat oven to 325°F. In large bowl, combine flour, 1 cup powdered sugar and salt. Using pastry blender or fork, cut in butter until mixture resembles coarse crumbs. Add vanilla and almonds; knead by hand to form a smooth dough. Shape rounded teaspoonfuls of dough into balls or crescents. Place 1 inch apart on ungreased cookie sheets.

Bake at 325°F. for 12 to 15 minutes or until set; do not brown. Remove from cookie sheets. Roll in powdered sugar.

Yield: 60 servings (1 cookie per serving)

High Altitude—Above 3,500 feet: No change.

Nutrition Per Serving: Calories 60; Protein 1g; Carbohydrate 6g; Fat 4g; Sodium 40mg

Maple Peanut Yummies

Judith Korbey *Methuen, Massachusetts*
Bake-Off® Contest 10, 1958

This traditional peanut butter cookie is deliciously flavored with maple syrup. Instead of flattening the balls with a fork, try using a decorative cookie stamp purchased from a kitchen specialty shop.

¹/₂ cup firmly packed brown sugar
¹/₂ cup margarine, softened, or shortening
¹/₂ cup peanut butter
¹/₂ cup maple-flavored syrup or real maple syrup
1 egg yolk
1¹/₂ cups all-purpose flour
¹/₂ teaspoon baking soda
¹/₂ teaspoon salt
¹/₄ teaspoon baking powder
Sugar

Heat oven to 350°F. In large bowl, beat brown sugar, margarine and peanut butter until light and fluffy. Add syrup and egg yolk; beat well. Stir in flour, baking soda, salt and baking powder; mix well. If necessary, refrigerate 15 to 30 minutes for easier handling.

Shape dough into 1-inch balls; place 2 inches apart on ungreased cookie sheets. With fork dipped in sugar, flatten balls in crisscross pattern. Bake at 350°F. for 8 to 12 minutes or until golden brown.

Yield: 48 servings (1 cookie per serving)

High Altitude—Above 3,500 feet: Decrease brown sugar to ¹/₄ cup; increase flour to 2 cups. Bake as directed above.

Nutrition Per Serving: Calories 70; Protein 1g; Carbohydrate 8g; Fat 3g; Sodium 75mg

Sachertorte Cookies

Phyllis Wolf *Salem, Oregon*
Bake-Off® Contest 30, 1982 Prize Winner

Elegant yet easy, these chocolate cookies are filled with apricot or cherry preserves and drizzled with a chocolate glaze.

1 cup margarine or butter, softened
1 (3.9-oz.) pkg. instant chocolate pudding and pie filling mix
1 egg
2 cups all-purpose flour

3 tablespoons sugar
²/₃ cup apricot or cherry preserves
¹/₂ cup semi-sweet chocolate chips
3 tablespoons margarine or butter

Heat oven to 325°F. In large bowl, beat 1 cup margarine and pudding mix until light and fluffy. Add egg; blend well. Gradually add flour; mix well. Shape dough into 1-inch balls; roll in sugar. Place 2 inches apart on ungreased cookie sheets. With thumb, make indentation in center of each cookie.

Bake at 325°F. for 15 to 18 minutes or until firm to touch. Immediately remove from cookie sheets. Cool completely. Fill each indentation with ¹/₂ teaspoon preserves. In small saucepan over low heat, melt chocolate chips and 3 tablespoons margarine, stirring until smooth. Drizzle ¹/₂ teaspoon glaze over each cookie.

Yield: 48 servings (1 cookie per serving)

High Altitude—Above 3,500 feet: Bake at 350°F. for 12 to 15 minutes.

Nutrition Per Serving: Calories 90; Protein 1g; Carbohydrate 11g; Fat 5g; Sodium 90mg

BEATRICE HARLIB

Beatrice Harlib's twin sons, Sam and Joel, helped her come up with her Snappy Turtle Cookies—the famous combination of chocolate, caramel and pecans. "I have always had a very loving family, always," Beatrice says. After winning the Grand Prize in the fourth Bake-Off® Contest, and after being welcomed back to Chicago by the mayor and a police escort, and being congratulated in public ceremonies with thousands of spectators, Beatrice found "I had been called upon to make so many appearances . . . that I have become quite at ease before groups and enjoy speaking, whereas previously I was very shy and timid and dreaded talking before a crowd."

Beatrice went on to become president of the Children's Asthma Research Institute and later became a key executive in an early feminist group, Women's Share in Public Service, which helped to promote women in public office and worked to advance women's political and economic status. Beatrice reports that her Bake-Off® experience gave her just enough celebrity to be noticed and the confidence to move into these highly visible offices.

It's incredible how much happiness can be achieved through the simple addition of caramel to chocolate, of cookies to a lunchbox or of public confidence to an already special woman.

Snappy Turtle Cookies

Beatrice Harlib *Chicago, Illinois*
Bake-Off® Contest 4, 1952 Grand Prize Winner

These rich brown sugar cookies resemble the well-known turtle-shaped candies. This recipe has earned the rank of a Bake-Off® Contest classic.

COOKIES
$^1/_2$ **cup firmly packed brown sugar**
$^1/_2$ **cup margarine or butter, softened**
$^1/_4$ **teaspoon vanilla**
$^1/_8$ **teaspoon maple flavor, if desired**
1 **whole egg**
1 **egg, separated**
$1^1/_2$ **cups all-purpose flour**
$^1/_4$ **teaspoon baking soda**
$^1/_4$ **teaspoon salt**
$1^1/_2$ **to 2 cups pecan halves, split lengthwise**

FROSTING
$^1/_3$ **cup semi-sweet chocolate chips**
3 **tablespoons milk**
1 **tablespoon margarine or butter**
1 **cup powdered sugar**

In large bowl, combine brown sugar and $^1/_2$ cup margarine; beat until light and fluffy. Add vanilla, maple flavor, 1 whole egg and 1 egg yolk; beat well. Stir in flour, baking soda and salt; mix well. Cover with plastic wrap; refrigerate about 1 hour for easier handling.

Heat oven to 350° F. Grease cookie sheets. Arrange pecan pieces in groups of 5 on greased cookie sheets to resemble head and legs of turtle. In small bowl, beat egg white. Shape dough into 1-inch

Top to bottom: **Mardi Gras Party Cake, page 236, Snappy Turtle Cookies**

balls. Dip bottoms in beaten egg white; press lightly onto pecans. (Tips of pecans should show.)

Bake at 350° F. for 10 to 12 minutes or until edges are light golden brown. Immediately remove from cookie sheets. Cool completely.

In small saucepan, combine chocolate chips, milk and 1 tablespoon margarine; cook over low heat, stirring constantly until melted and smooth. Remove from heat; stir in powdered sugar. Add more powdered sugar if necessary for desired spreading consistency. Frost cooled cookies. Allow frosting to set before storing. Store in airtight container.

Yield: 42 servings (1 cookie per serving)

High Altitude—Above 3,500 feet: No change.

Nutrition Per Serving: Calories 100; Protein 1g; Carbohydrate 11g; Fat 6g; Sodium 55mg

Starlight Mint Surprise Cookies

Laura Rott *Naperville, Illinois*
Bake-Off® Contest 1, 1949 Prize Winner

The idea for this cookie came to the originator when she was given a package of mint-flavored chocolate candies. Brown sugar cookie dough is pressed around each candy so each cookie has a surprise chocolate mint in the center.

1 cup sugar
1/2 cup firmly packed brown sugar
3/4 cup margarine or butter, softened
2 tablespoons water
1 teaspoon vanilla
2 eggs
3 cups all-purpose flour
1 teaspoon baking soda
1/2 teaspoon salt
2 (6-oz.) pkg. solid chocolate mint candy wafers
60 walnut halves or pieces

In large bowl, combine sugar, brown sugar, margarine, water, vanilla and eggs; blend well. In medium bowl, combine flour, baking soda and salt; mix well. Add to sugar mixture; mix at low speed until well blended. Cover with plastic wrap; refrigerate at least 2 hours for easier handling.

Heat oven to 375° F. Using about 1 tablespoon dough, press dough around each candy wafer to cover completely. Place 2 inches apart on ungreased cookie sheets. Top each with walnut half.

Bake at 375° F. for 7 to 9 minutes or until light golden brown. Immediately remove from cookie sheets.

Yield: 60 servings (1 cookie per serving)

High Altitude—Above 3,500 feet: No change.

Nutrition Per Serving: Calories 110; Protein 2g; Carbohydrate 14g; Fat 6g; Sodium 65mg

Cookie Tips

- Don't substitute a low-fat spread for butter or margarine, or the cookies will tend to turn out dense and may not brown.
- Unbaked cookie dough can be wrapped in airtight, freezer-weight plastic or foil and frozen for up to one year.
- You can freeze cookies, wrapping them in airtight plastic or foil, for up to four months. For iced cookies, it's best to frost cookies after they've thawed.
- Always use the pan size specified for bar cookies. If the pan is too small, your cookies may end up gummy; if it is too big, they may turn out dry.
- Always preheat the oven for ten to fifteen minutes before baking cookies.
- Don't store soft and crisp cookies together; the crisp ones will get soft.
- Cookies have to be completely cool before you store them, or they will "sweat" and get soggy.

Big Wheels

Mrs. Alfred O. Williams *Richland, Michigan*
Bake-Off® Contest 8, 1956

These super-sized cookies are great for picnics, parties or just for a special treat—one will satisfy any sweet tooth. Flavored with malted milk powder and frosted with an easy icing, they are truly scrumptious.

COOKIES
4 cups all-purpose flour
3/4 cup plain malted milk powder
2 teaspoons baking powder
1/2 teaspoon baking soda
1/2 teaspoon salt
1 cup margarine or butter, softened

2 cups firmly packed brown
  sugar
2 eggs
1/3 cup dairy sour cream
2 teaspoons vanilla
1 cup chopped almonds or
  peanuts

FROSTING
1/4 cup margarine or butter,
  softened
1/4 cup half-and-half
1/2 cup firmly packed brown
  sugar
1/3 cup plain malted milk powder
1/2 teaspoon vanilla
2 to 2 1/2 cups powdered sugar

GARNISH
90 whole almonds (about
  1 1/4 cups)*
18 chocolate chips (about
  1 tablespoon)

In medium bowl, combine flour,
3/4 cup malted milk powder, baking
powder, baking soda and salt; set
aside. In large bowl, beat 1 cup
margarine and 2 cups brown sugar
until light and fluffy. Add eggs;
beat well. Add half of dry ingredients; mix well. Blend in sour cream
and 2 teaspoons vanilla. Stir in
remaining dry ingredients and
chopped almonds; mix well. Cover
with plastic wrap; refrigerate at
least 4 hours.

Heat oven to 375°F. On well-
floured surface, roll out half of
dough at a time to 1/4-inch thickness. Cut into 5-inch circles using
empty 14-oz. coffee can as cutter
or small bowl or plate as pattern,
cutting around pattern with knife.
Using pancake turner, transfer
dough circles to ungreased cookie
sheets. Bake at 375°F. for 10 to
14 minutes or until light golden
brown. Cool 2 minutes; remove

from cookie sheets. Cool completely on wire racks.

In medium saucepan, combine
1/4 cup margarine, half-and-half
and 1/2 cup brown sugar; cook and
stir until sugar dissolves. Remove
from heat; stir in 1/3 cup malted
milk powder and 1/2 teaspoon
vanilla. Gradually beat in enough
powdered sugar for desired spreading consistency. Frost cooled cookies. Decorate each with 5 whole
almonds in "spoke" design; place
chocolate chip in center. Allow
frosting to set before storing.

Yield: 18 servings (1 cookie per serving)

*Tip: Slivered almonds or whole
peanuts can be substituted for the
whole almonds.

High Altitude—Above 3,500 feet:
Decrease brown sugar in cookies to
1 1/2 cups. Bake as directed above.

Nutrition Per Serving: Calories 520; Protein 8g;
Carbohydrate 74g; Fat 23g; Sodium 330mg

Lemon Kiss Cookies

Sandi Lamberton *Solvang, California*
Bake-Off® Contest 33, 1988 Prize Winner

*Delicate lemon-flavored cookie dough
wraps up a milk chocolate candy to
make these cookies. They are special
enough for entertaining, and children
love them.*

1 1/2 cups butter or margarine,
  softened
3/4 cup sugar
1 tablespoon lemon extract
2 3/4 cups all-purpose flour

1 1/2 cups finely chopped
  almonds
1 (13-oz.) pkg. milk chocolate
  candy drops or pieces,
  unwrapped
Powdered sugar
1/2 cup semi-sweet chocolate
  chips
1 tablespoon shortening

In large bowl, beat butter, sugar
and lemon extract until light and
fluffy. Add flour and almonds; beat
at low speed until well blended.
Cover; refrigerate at least 1 hour
for easier handling.

Heat oven to 375°F. Shape
1 scant tablespoon dough around
each milk chocolate, covering completely. Roll in hands to form ball.
Place on ungreased cookie sheets.

Bake at 375°F. for 8 to 12 minutes or until set and bottom edges
are light golden brown. Cool 1
minute; remove from cookie sheets.
Cool completely.

Lightly sprinkle cooled cookies
with powdered sugar. In small
saucepan over low heat, melt
chocolate chips and shortening,
stirring until smooth. Drizzle over
each cookie.

Yield: 72 servings (1 cookie per serving)

High Altitude—Above 3,500 feet:
Decrease butter to 1 1/4 cups. Bake
as directed above.

Nutrition Per Serving: Calories 110; Protein 1g;
Carbohydrate 10g; Fat 7g; Sodium 45mg

Praline Apple Waffle Cookies

Jone Schumacher *Chapin, Illinois*
Bake-Off® Contest 36, 1994 Prize Winner

These tasty cookies with a charming shape have a delectable praline flavor.

COOKIES
1¼ cups firmly packed brown
   sugar
½ cup butter or margarine,
   softened
2 eggs
1 teaspoon vanilla
1½ cups all-purpose flour
1 teaspoon baking powder
1 teaspoon cinnamon
½ teaspoon salt
⅛ teaspoon nutmeg
½ cup shredded peeled apples
½ cup finely chopped pecans

TOPPING
½ cup powdered sugar
¼ teaspoon cinnamon

Heat waffle iron to medium-low. In large bowl, beat brown sugar and butter until blended. Add eggs and vanilla; beat well. Add flour, baking powder, 1 teaspoon cinnamon, salt and nutmeg; mix well. Stir in apples and pecans.

Spray waffle iron with nonstick cooking spray. Drop dough by heaping teaspoonfuls 2 inches apart onto waffle iron. Bake 1½ to 2 minutes or until cookies are deep golden brown. Immediately remove from waffle iron; cool 1 minute on wire rack. Repeat with remaining dough.

In small bowl, combine powdered sugar and ¼ teaspoon cinnamon; mix well. Dip or dust both sides of slightly warm cookies using powdered sugar mixture. Serve warm or cool. Store in tightly covered container.

Yield: 36 servings (1 cookie per serving)

High Altitude—Above 3,500 feet: Decrease brown sugar to 1 cup. Bake as directed above.

Nutrition Per Serving: Calories 90; Protein 1g; Carbohydrate 14g; Fat 4g; Sodium 70mg

Texan-Sized Almond Crunch Cookies

Barbara Hodgson *Elkhart, Indiana*
Bake-Off® Contest 30, 1982 Prize Winner

You'll have a hard time keeping the cookie jar filled with these giant-sized crunchy treats!

1 cup sugar
1 cup powdered sugar
1 cup margarine or butter,
   softened
1 cup oil
1 teaspoon almond extract
2 eggs
3½ cups all-purpose flour
1 cup whole wheat flour
1 teaspoon baking soda
1 teaspoon cream of tartar
1 teaspoon salt

2 cups coarsely chopped
   almonds
1 cup toffee bits (from 10-oz.
   pkg.)
Sugar

Heat oven to 350° F. In large bowl, combine sugar, powdered sugar, margarine and oil; beat until well blended. Add almond extract and eggs; mix well. In second large bowl, combine all-purpose flour, whole wheat flour, baking soda, cream of tartar and salt; mix well. Add to sugar mixture; mix at low speed until well blended. By hand, stir in almonds and toffee bits. If necessary, cover with plastic wrap and refrigerate dough about 30 minutes for easier handling.

Using large tablespoonfuls of dough, shape into balls. Roll in sugar. Place 5 inches apart on ungreased cookie sheets. With fork dipped in sugar, flatten each in crisscross pattern.

Bake at 350° F. for 12 to 18 minutes or until light golden brown around edges. Cool 1 minute; remove from cookie sheets.

Yield: 42 servings (1 cookie per serving)

High Altitude—Above 3,500 feet: No change.

Nutrition Per Serving: Calories 230; Protein 3g; Carbohydrate 23g; Fat 14g; Sodium 170mg

Top to bottom: **Texan-Sized Almond Crunch Cookies, Maple Oat Chewies, page 183**

Blond Brownie Caramel Cups

Alberta Richter *Lockport, Illinois*
Bake-Off® Contest 34, 1990

These creative brownies are made in muffin cups. They're not only clever but decadent!

CUPS
1/2 cup butter or margarine
1 cup firmly packed brown
    sugar
1 teaspoon vanilla
1 egg
1 cup all-purpose flour
1 teaspoon baking powder
1/4 teaspoon salt
1/2 cup chopped nuts

TOPPING
20 caramels, unwrapped
1 tablespoon water
1/2 cup semi-sweet chocolate chips
1/4 to 1/2 cup finely chopped nuts

Heat oven to 350° F. Line 16 muffin cups with foil or paper baking cups. Melt butter in medium saucepan over low heat. Remove from heat; stir in brown sugar. Add vanilla and egg; mix well. Add flour, baking powder and salt; blend well. Stir in 1/2 cup chopped nuts. Divide batter evenly into lined muffin cups. Bake at 350° F. for 16 to 20 minutes or until golden brown.

    Meanwhile, in small saucepan over low heat, melt caramels with water; stir constantly until smooth.* Immediately after pans are removed from oven, place chocolate chips evenly into middle of each brownie. Spoon 1 scant tablespoon of caramel over chocolate chips in each cup. If necessary, stir additional water into melted caramels to maintain spoon-

able consistency. Sprinkle 1/4 cup finely chopped nuts evenly over brownies. Cool completely. Store in tightly covered container.

Yield: 16 servings
(1 brownie per serving)

*Tip: To melt caramels in microwave, place in small microwave-safe bowl with 1 tablespoon water. Microwave on HIGH for 2 to 3 minutes, stirring occasionally.

High Altitude—Above 3,500 feet: Increase flour to 1 1/4 cups. Bake as directed above.

Nutrition Per Serving: Calories 270; Protein 3g; Carbohydrate 33g; Fat 14g; Sodium 140mg

Poppy Seed Sugar Cookies

Jolene Braddy *Greeley, Colorado*
Bake-Off® Contest 32, 1986

Orange and almond flavors and a poppy seed glaze combine to create a new version of the rolled sugar cookie. Cut them large for the cookie jar or small and dainty for parties.

COOKIES
1 1/4 cups sugar
2/3 cup margarine or butter,
    softened
1 teaspoon almond extract
1 teaspoon vanilla
1 teaspoon butter flavor, if
    desired
1 tablespoon orange juice
2 eggs
3 cups all-purpose flour
2 tablespoons poppy seed
2 teaspoons baking powder
1/2 to 1 teaspoon salt

GLAZE
1/3 cup sugar
1/4 teaspoon poppy seed
2 tablespoons orange juice
1/4 teaspoon almond extract
1/4 teaspoon vanilla
1/4 teaspoon butter flavor, if
    desired

In large bowl, beat 1 1/4 cups sugar, margarine, 1 teaspoon almond extract, 1 teaspoon vanilla and 1 teaspoon butter flavor until light and fluffy. Add 1 tablespoon orange juice and eggs; blend well. By hand, stir in flour, 2 tablespoons poppy seed, baking powder and salt until well blended. If necessary, refrigerate soft dough for easier handling or stir in small amount of flour until no longer sticky.

    Heat oven to 350° F. On lightly floured surface, roll out 1/3 of dough at a time to 1/8- to 1/4-inch thickness. Keep remaining dough refrigerated. Cut with 2 1/2- to 3-inch cookie cutter of desired shape. Place 2 inches apart on ungreased cookie sheets.

    Bake at 350° F. for 9 to 12 minutes or until light golden brown. While cookies are baking, combine all glaze ingredients; mix well. Immediately brush baked cookies with glaze, stirring glaze occasionally. Cool 1 minute; remove from cookie sheets. Let stand until glaze is set.

Yield: 36 servings (1 cookie per serving)

High Altitude—Above 3,500 feet: No change.

Nutrition Per Serving: Calories 110; Protein 2g; Carbohydrate 17g; Fat 4g; Sodium 120mg

Top to bottom: **Blond Brownie Caramel Cups, Caramel-Filled Chocolate Cookies, page 189**

Hawaiian Cookie Tarts

Elizabeth Zemelko *Knox, Indiana*
Bake-Off® Contest 34, 1990

These melt-in-your-mouth cookies are perfect for party trays. They are like miniature pineapple pies.

COOKIES
1³/₄ **cups all-purpose flour**
¹/₂ **cup powdered sugar**
2 **tablespoons cornstarch**
1 **cup margarine or butter, softened**
1 **teaspoon vanilla**

FILLING
1 **cup pineapple preserves**
¹/₂ **cup sugar**
1 **egg**
1¹/₂ **cups coconut**
Powdered sugar

Heat oven to 350°F. In large bowl, combine flour, ¹/₂ cup powdered sugar and cornstarch; blend well. Add margarine and vanilla. By hand, blend until soft dough forms. Shape dough into 1-inch balls. Place 1 ball in each of 36 ungreased miniature muffin cups;

press in bottom and up sides of each cup.*

Spoon 1 teaspoon pineapple preserves into each dough-lined cup. In small bowl, combine sugar and egg. Using fork, beat until well blended. Stir in coconut until well coated with egg mixture. Spoon 1 teaspoon coconut mixture over pineapple preserves in each cup.

Bake at 350°F. for 23 to 33 minutes or until crusts are very light golden brown. Cool 20 minutes. To release cookies from cups, hold muffin pan upside down at an angle over wire rack. Using handle of table knife, firmly tap bottom of each cup until cookie releases. Cool completely. Just before serving, sprinkle with powdered sugar.

Yield: 36 servings (1 cookie per serving)

*Tip: If only 1 muffin pan is available, keep remaining cookie dough refrigerated until ready to bake.

Nutrition Per Serving: Calories 130; Protein 1g; Carbohydrate 17g; Fat 6g; Sodium 55mg

Elizabeth Zemelko: Hawaiian Cookie Tarts

Cooking for a large family is one of the most absorbing and challenging kinds of work, and Elizabeth Zemelko has been involved with food and cooking from an early age. "I grew up in a Slovak-speaking home, with Ma, Pa, ten kids, and three boarders. We ate in three shifts: those who worked, those who went to school, and then us little ones, with Ma, had the leftovers. What a beautiful survival, now that I look back on everything. Once Ma said to me, 'I can't believe how much these hands have done in work.'" When the work is raising and feeding a family, it is a labor of love and the rewards are profound.

Orange and Oats Chewies

Maryann Goschka *St. Charles, Michigan*
Bake-Off® Contest 31, 1984

Maryann Goscha kept tinkering with a favorite oatmeal cookie recipe from her mother until she came up with this chewy drop cookie with a fresh orange flavor. These are great to keep in the cookie jar for between-meal snacks.

2 **cups firmly packed brown sugar**
1 **cup shortening**
3 **tablespoons frozen orange juice concentrate, thawed**
1 **tablespoon grated orange peel**
2 **eggs**
2 **cups all-purpose flour**
1 **teaspoon baking soda**
³/₄ **teaspoon salt**
2 **cups rolled oats**
1 **cup chopped nuts**
¹/₃ **cup coconut**

Heat oven to 350°F. Grease cookie sheets. In large bowl, combine brown sugar, shortening, orange juice, orange peel and eggs; mix well. Add flour, baking soda and salt; mix well. By hand, stir in oats, nuts and coconut. Drop by rounded teaspoonfuls 2 inches apart onto greased cookie sheets.

Bake at 350°F. for 10 to 12 minutes or until light golden brown. Cool cookies 1 minute; remove from cookie sheets.

Yield: 60 servings (1 cookie per serving)

High Altitude—Above 3,500 feet: Increase flour to 2¹/₂ cups. Bake at 375°F. for 9 to 12 minutes.

Nutrition Per Serving: Calories 100; Protein 1g; Carbohydrate 13g; Fat 5g; Sodium 75mg

Cherry Truffle Squares

Catherine Stovern *Veteran, Wyoming*
Bake-Off® Contest 39, 2000

Starting with a sugar cookie base, this rich confection is made with a medley of chocolate chips, vanilla chips and maraschino cherries. Don't wait too long to have seconds, or they may be gone!

BASE
1 (18-oz.) pkg. refrigerated
   sugar cookies

FILLING
1/3 cup semi-sweet chocolate
   chips
1/4 cup butter or margarine
1/4 cup unsweetened cocoa
3 tablespoons light corn syrup
1 tablespoon milk
2 cups powdered sugar
1 (10-oz.) jar maraschino
   cherries, drained, chopped
   (about 30 cherries)

TOPPING
1 cup white vanilla chips
2 tablespoons shortening

GARNISH, IF DESIRED
Chocolate shavings or curls

Heat oven to 350°F. Cut cookie dough in half crosswise. Cut each section in half lengthwise. With floured fingers, press dough in bottom of ungreased 13×9-inch pan to form base. Bake at 350°F. for 12 to 16 minutes or until light golden brown. Remove from oven. Cool 45 minutes or until completely cooled.

In medium microwave-safe bowl, combine chocolate chips and butter. Microwave on HIGH for 1 to 2 minutes or until melted and smooth, stirring every 30 seconds. Add cocoa, corn syrup and milk; blend well. Add powdered sugar; mix until smooth. Press over cooled base. Top with cherries; gently press into filling.

In small microwave-safe bowl, combine vanilla chips and shortening. Microwave on HIGH for 1 to 2 minutes or until melted and smooth, stirring every 30 seconds. Spoon and spread over filling. Refrigerate 20 minutes or until set. Cut into squares or diamond-shaped pieces. Garnish with chocolate shavings.

Yield: 48 servings (1 bar per serving)

Nutrition Per Serving: Calories 110; Protein 1g; Carbohydrate 16g; Fat 5g; Sodium 55mg

The Technical Side of Judging

It's no small responsibility to pick the United States' most important new recipes, and Bake-Off® Contest judges don't take their responsibilities lightly.

• Judges sip ginger ale, water, coffee, tea or broth, or nibble on celery and carrot sticks between tastings.

• A guard is posted at the door of the judges' room to prevent anyone from entering.

• Judges are forbidden to have any conversations with contestants or other judges about any recipes or contestants.

• The judges don't attend any functions with the contestants until after the winners are announced.

• Judges pick the winners almost eighteen hours before they are told at the awards luncheon—but they are sworn to secrecy.

• The more things change, the more they stay the same. The judges in the first years of the Bake-Off® Contest were professional home economists—people who wrote about food for newspapers and magazines. Today the judges are food editors—people who write about food for newspapers and magazines.

Candy Bar Cookies

Alice Reese *Minneapolis, Minnesota Bake-Off® Contest 13, 1961 Grand Prize Winner*

Try our quick bar variation using a press-in-the-pan crust.

BASE
³/₄ **cup powdered sugar**
³/₄ **cup margarine or butter, softened**
2 **tablespoons whipping cream**
1 **teaspoon vanilla**
2 **cups all-purpose flour**

FILLING
28 **caramels, unwrapped**
¹/₄ **cup whipping cream**
¹/₄ **cup margarine or butter**
1 **cup powdered sugar**
1 **cup chopped pecans**

GLAZE
¹/₂ **cup semi-sweet chocolate chips**
2 **tablespoons whipping cream**
1 **tablespoon margarine or butter**
¹/₄ **cup powdered sugar**
1 **teaspoon vanilla**
48 **pecan halves (²/₃ cup), if desired**

In large bowl, combine all base ingredients except flour; blend well. Stir in flour; mix well. If necessary, refrigerate dough for easier handling.

Heat oven to 325°F. On well-floured surface, roll half of dough to 12×8-inch rectangle. Using pastry wheel or knife, cut into 2-inch squares. Place ¹/₂ inch apart on ungreased cookie sheets. Bake at 325°F. for 12 to 16 minutes or until set. Cool on wire racks. Repeat with remaining dough.

In medium saucepan, combine caramels, ¹/₄ cup whipping cream and ¹/₄ cup margarine; cook over low heat, stirring frequently, until caramels are melted and mixture is smooth. Remove from heat; stir in 1 cup powdered sugar and chopped pecans. (Add additional whipping cream a few drops at a time, if needed for desired spreading consistency.) Spread 1 teaspoon of warm filling on each cookie square.

In small saucepan, combine chocolate chips, 2 tablespoons whipping cream and 1 tablespoon margarine; cook over low heat, stirring frequently, until chocolate chips are melted and mixture is smooth. Remove from heat; stir in ¹/₄ cup powdered sugar and 1 teaspoon vanilla. Spread glaze over caramel filling. Top each cookie with pecan half.

Yield: 48 servings (1 cookie per serving)

Tip: To make bars, in large bowl, blend all base ingredients at low speed until crumbly. Press in bottom of ungreased 15×10×1-inch baking pan. Bake at 325°F. for 15 to 20 minutes or until light golden brown. Cool. Prepare filling as directed above; spread over base. Prepare glaze; drizzle over filling. Top bars with pecan halves, forming 8 rows of 6 pecans each. Allow glaze to set. Cut into bars.

Yield: 48 servings (1 bar per serving)

High Altitude—Above 3,500 feet: No change.

Nutrition Per Serving: Calories 130; Protein 1g; Carbohydrate 14g; Fat 8g; Sodium 60mg

Top to bottom: **Choco-Nut Sweet Treats, page 206, Candy Bar Cookies**

Split Seconds

Karin Fellows *Silver Spring, Maryland Bake-Off® Contest 6, 1954 Prize Winner*

This contestant learned to cook in Sweden, where she was born, and this was one of her mother's family recipes. You'll enjoy the unique method for making these delicious shortbread cookies. Choose your favorite flavor of jelly or preserves to make this Bake-Off® Contest classic.

³/₄ **cup margarine or butter, softened**
²/₃ **cup sugar**
2 **teaspoons vanilla**
1 **egg**
2 **cups all-purpose flour**
¹/₂ **teaspoon baking powder**
¹/₂ **cup red jelly or preserves**

Heat oven to 350°F. In large bowl, beat margarine and sugar until light and fluffy. Add vanilla and egg; blend well. Stir in flour and baking powder; mix well. Divide dough into 4 equal parts. On lightly floured surface, shape each part into 12×³/₄-inch roll; place on ungreased cookie sheets. Using handle of wooden spoon or finger, make depression about ¹/₂ inch wide and ¹/₄ inch deep lengthwise down center of each roll. Fill each roll with 2 tablespoons jelly.

Bake at 350°F. for 15 to 20 minutes or until light golden brown. Cool slightly; cut diagonally into bars. Cool on wire racks.

Yield: 48 servings (1 cookie per serving)

High Altitude—Above 3,500 feet: No change.

Nutrition Per Serving: Calories 70; Protein 1g; Carbohydrate 9g; Fat 3g; Sodium 40mg

Apricot Almond Squares

Sandy Munson *LaJunta, Colorado*
Bake-Off® Contest 32, 1986

A delicate fruit flavor and a streusel topping make this bar a luscious choice for a party tray.

BASE
1 (1 lb. 2.25-oz.) pkg. pudding-included yellow or white cake mix
1/2 cup margarine or butter, melted
1/2 cup finely chopped almonds
1 cup apricot preserves

FILLING
1 (8-oz.) pkg. cream cheese, softened
1/4 cup sugar
2 tablespoons all-purpose flour
1/8 teaspoon salt
1 teaspoon vanilla
1 egg
1/3 cup apricot preserves
1/2 cup coconut

Heat oven to 350° F. Generously grease 13×9-inch pan. In large bowl, combine cake mix and margarine; mix at low speed until crumbly. Stir in almonds. Reserve 1 cup base mixture. Press remaining mixture in bottom of greased pan. Carefully spread 1 cup preserves over base.*

In same bowl, beat cream cheese, sugar, flour, salt, vanilla and egg until well blended. Beat in 1/3 cup preserves at low speed. Carefully spread mixture over base. Combine reserved 1 cup base mixture and coconut; sprinkle over filling.

Bake at 350° F. for 30 to 40 minutes or until golden brown and center is set. Cool completely. Cut into bars. Store in refrigerator.

Yield: 36 servings (1 bar per serving)

*Tip: For ease in spreading, preserves can be warmed slightly.

High Altitude—Above 3,500 feet: No change.

Nutrition Per Serving: Calories 160; Protein 2g; Carbohydrate 22g; Fat 7g; Sodium 160mg

Choco-Nut Sweet Treats

Agatha L. Roth *Indianapolis, Indiana*
Bake-Off® Contest 37, 1996 Prize Winner

Using refrigerated cookie dough as a crust was an idea that appealed to a number of contestants at the 1996 contest. With a creamy coconut pecan filling and chocolate nut icing, these wonderfully rich bars indeed are a sweet treat.

CRUST
1 (18-oz.) pkg. refrigerated chocolate chip cookies, well chilled

FILLING
2 eggs
2 teaspoons vanilla
1 (15-oz.) can coconut pecan frosting
1 (14-oz.) can sweetened condensed milk (not evaporated)

TOPPING
1 1/2 cups semi-sweet chocolate chips
3 tablespoons oil
1 cup coarsely chopped pecans or walnuts

Heat oven to 350° F. Cut cookie dough into 1/2-inch slices. Arrange slices in bottom of ungreased 15×10×1-inch baking pan. Using floured fingers, press dough evenly in pan to form crust. Bake at 350° F. for 8 to 12 minutes or until light golden brown. Cool 5 minutes.

Meanwhile, in large bowl, beat eggs until foamy. Add all remaining filling ingredients; beat 1 minute at medium speed or until well blended. Spoon and spread filling evenly over partially baked crust.

Bake an additional 20 to 25 minutes or until top is deep golden brown and center is set. Cool 5 minutes.

In small saucepan, combine chocolate chips and oil. Cook over medium heat until chips are melted, stirring constantly. Carefully pour over filling; gently spread to cover. Sprinkle with pecans. Refrigerate 1 1/2 hours or until chocolate is set. Cut into bars. Store in refrigerator.

Yield: 48 servings (1 bar per serving)

Nutrition Per Serving: Calories 170; Protein 2g; Carbohydrate 19g; Fat 10g; Sodium 65mg

Apricot Almond Squares

Caramel Layer Choco-Squares

Joan Adler *Marshfield, Wisconsin*
Bake-Off® Contest 21, 1970

Recipes using convenience products to achieve homemade results were especially popular in 1970. The cookie layer and topping for these luscious bars calls for chocolate cake mix. The easily made caramel filling uses caramel candies.

1 (5-oz.) can evaporated milk
1 (14-oz.) pkg. caramels, unwrapped
1 (1 lb. 2.25-oz.) pkg. pudding-included German chocolate cake mix
1 cup chopped nuts
1/2 cup margarine or butter, softened
1 (6-oz.) pkg. (1 cup) semi-sweet chocolate chips

Heat oven to 350° F. Reserve 2 tablespoons evaporated milk for cake mixture. In medium saucepan, combine caramels with remaining evaporated milk. Cook over low heat, stirring frequently, until caramels are melted and mixture is smooth. Remove from heat.

In large bowl, combine cake mix, nuts, margarine and reserved 2 tablespoons evaporated milk; mix at low speed until crumbly. Press half of dough mixture in bottom of ungreased 13×9-inch pan; reserve remaining dough mixture for topping.

Bake at 350° F. for 8 minutes. Sprinkle chocolate chips evenly over partially baked crust. Carefully spread caramel mixture over chocolate chips. Crumble reserved dough mixture over caramel mixture. Return to oven; bake an additional 15 to 18 minutes or until filling is set. Cool completely; cut into bars.

Yield: 36 servings (1 bar per serving)

High Altitude—Above 3,500 feet: No change.

Nutrition Per Serving: Calories 190; Protein 2g; Carbohydrate 24g; Fat 9g; Sodium 150mg

Quick Crescent Baklava

Annette Erbeck *Mason, Ohio*
Bake-Off® Contest 29, 1980

This ingenious contestant borrowed an idea from the Greeks, simplified it by using refrigerated crescent roll dough instead of fragile phyllo and created a delightful dessert bar.

2 (8-oz.) cans refrigerated crescent dinner rolls
3 to 4 cups walnuts, finely chopped
1/2 cup sugar
1 teaspoon cinnamon

GLAZE
1/4 cup sugar
1/2 cup honey
2 tablespoons margarine or butter
2 teaspoons lemon juice

Heat oven to 350° F. Unroll 1 can of dough into 2 long rectangles. Place in ungreased 13×9-inch pan; press over bottom and 1/2 inch up sides to form crust. Firmly press perforations to seal. Bake at 350° F. for 5 minutes. Remove from oven.

In large bowl, combine walnuts, 1/2 cup sugar and cinnamon; mix well. Spoon walnut mixture evenly over partially baked crust. Unroll remaining can of dough into 2 long rectangles. Place over walnut mixture; press out to edges of pan. With tip of sharp knife, score dough with 5 lengthwise and 7 diagonal markings to form 28 diamond-shaped pieces, using dough edges and perforations as a guide.

In small saucepan, combine all glaze ingredients. Bring to a boil; remove from heat. Spoon half of glaze evenly over dough. Return to oven; bake an additional 25 to 30 minutes or until golden brown. Spoon remaining glaze evenly over hot baklava. Cool completely. Refrigerate until thoroughly chilled. Cut into diamond-shaped pieces.

Yield: 28 servings (1 bar per serving)

Nutrition Per Serving: Calories 210; Protein 4g; Carbohydrate 19g; Fat 15g; Sodium 140mg

Chocolate Raspberry Vanilla Cream Bars

Deborah Glick *Missoula, Montana*
Bake-Off® Contest 37, 1996

When it comes to delectable desserts, this one gets a gold medal. Rich chocolate glaze, a cream cheese and raspberry filling, and devil's food cake make this recipe simply irresistible.

BASE
1 (1 lb. 2.25-oz.) pkg. pudding-included devil's food cake mix
⅓ cup butter or margarine, softened
1 egg

FILLING
1 cup raspberry preserves
1 (8-oz.) pkg. cream cheese, softened
¼ cup milk
1 (12-oz.) pkg. (2 cups) white vanilla chips, melted

GLAZE
½ cup semi-sweet chocolate chips
2 tablespoons butter or margarine

Heat oven to 350° F. Grease 15×10×1-inch baking pan. In large bowl, combine all base ingredients; mix until crumbly. Press in bottom of greased pan.

Bake at 350° F. for 8 to 12 minutes or until crust puffs and appears dry. Cool 5 minutes. Spread preserves over base. Cool

25 minutes or until completely cooled.

In small bowl, combine cream cheese and milk; beat until smooth. Add warm melted vanilla chips; beat until smooth. Carefully spread over preserves.

In small saucepan, combine glaze ingredients; melt over low heat, stirring constantly until smooth. Drizzle over filling.* Refrigerate 1 hour. Cut into bars. Serve chilled. Store in refrigerator.

Yield: 48 servings (1 bar per serving)

*Tip: To evenly drizzle, transfer chocolate mixture to small resealable plastic bag; seal tightly. Cut off a tiny corner to create a small opening. Squeeze bag to drizzle glaze over bars.

High Altitude—Above 3,500 feet: No change.

Nutrition Per Serving: Calories 140; Protein 2g; Carbohydrate 18g; Fat 7g; Sodium 125mg

Peanut Butter Carrumba Bars

Virginia Moon *Harvest, Alabama*
Bake-Off® Contest 36, 1994

For everyday meals Virginia Moon likes nutritious "old standby" recipes. But for special occasions, she knows dessert lovers crave rich treats. Her layered bars combine chocolate, peanuts, peanut butter and caramel.

CRUST
1 (1 lb. 2.25-oz.) pkg. pudding-included yellow cake mix

½ cup butter or margarine, melted
1 egg
1 (6-oz.) pkg. (ten .6-oz. cups) chocolate-covered peanut butter cups, chopped

FILLING
1 (12.5-oz.) jar (1 cup) caramel ice cream topping
¼ cup peanut butter
2 tablespoons cornstarch
½ cup salted cocktail peanuts

TOPPING
1 (16-oz.) can milk chocolate frosting
2 tablespoons mocha-flavored instant coffee beverage powder
½ cup salted cocktail peanuts, chopped

Heat oven to 350° F. Grease 13×9-inch pan. In large bowl, combine all crust ingredients; beat at low speed until well blended. Lightly press in greased pan. Bake at 350° F. for 18 to 22 minutes or until light golden brown.

In small saucepan, combine all filling ingredients except peanuts. Cook and stir over low heat until peanut butter is melted. Remove from heat; stir in ½ cup peanuts. Spread evenly over crust. Return to oven and bake an additional 5 to 7 minutes or until almost set. Cool completely.

In small bowl, combine frosting and beverage powder; mix well. Spread over filling; sprinkle with chopped peanuts.

Yield: 36 servings (1 bar per serving)

High Altitude—Above 3,500 feet: No change.

Nutrition Per Serving: Calories 230; Protein 3g; Carbohydrate 30g; Fat 11g; Sodium 220mg

So-Easy Sugar Cookies

Kathryn Blackburn *National Park, New Jersey*
Bake-Off® Contest 30, 1982

The name says it all—and they're so good, they'll become a family favorite! Instead of rolling out the dough, it's baked in a pan, then cut into squares.

³/₄ cup sugar
¹/₃ cup margarine or butter,
   softened, or shortening
¹/₃ cup oil
1 tablespoon milk
1 to 2 teaspoons almond
   extract
1 egg
1¹/₂ cups all-purpose flour
1¹/₂ teaspoons baking powder
¹/₄ teaspoon salt
1 tablespoon sugar

Heat oven to 375° F. In large bowl, beat ³/₄ cup sugar, margarine, oil, milk, almond extract and egg until light and fluffy. Stir in flour, baking powder and salt; blend well. Spread evenly in ungreased 15×10×1-inch baking pan; sprinkle with 1 tablespoon sugar.

Bake at 375° F. for 10 to 12 minutes or until light golden brown. Cool 5 minutes. Cut into bars.

Yield: 48 servings (1 cookie per serving)

Food Processor Directions: Place ³/₄ cup sugar, margarine, oil, milk, almond extract and egg in food processor bowl with metal blade. Cover; process until light and fluffy. Add flour, baking powder and salt.

Cover; process using on/off turns just until flour is well blended. (Do not overprocess or cookies will be tough.) Continue as directed above.

High Altitude—Above 3,500 feet: Decrease baking powder to 1 teaspoon. Bake as directed above.

Nutrition Per Serving: Calories 50; Protein 1g; Carbohydrate 6g; Fat 3g; Sodium 35mg

Coconut Lemon Crescent Bars

Marilyn Blankschien *Clintonville, Wisconsin*
Bake-Off® Contest 30, 1982 Prize Winner

Cookie and bar making has been revolutionized with the introduction of refrigerated dough products. In this recipe, lemon and coconut combine with an easy crescent crust to make these refreshing bars.

CRUST
1 (8-oz.) can refrigerated
   crescent dinner rolls

FILLING
1 cup sugar
1 cup flaked coconut
2 tablespoons all-purpose flour
¹/₂ teaspoon baking powder
¹/₂ teaspoon grated lemon peel
¹/₄ teaspoon salt
2 tablespoons lemon juice
2 tablespoons margarine or
   butter, melted
2 eggs, slightly beaten

Heat oven to 375° F. Unroll dough into 2 long rectangles. Place in ungreased 13×9-inch pan; press over bottom and ¹/₂ inch up sides to form crust. Firmly press perforations to seal. Bake at 375° F. for 5 minutes.

Meanwhile, in medium bowl, combine all filling ingredients; mix well. Pour over partially baked crust. Return to oven; bake an additional 12 to 17 minutes or until light golden brown. Cool completely. Cut into bars.

Yield: 36 servings (1 bar per serving)

Nutrition Per Serving: Calories 70; Protein 1g; Carbohydrate 9g; Fat 3g; Sodium 80mg

Kathryn Blackburn: So-Easy Sugar Cookies

Time. You can save it, savor it, spend it or even waste it. With three young children, Kathryn Blackburn found herself baking every day. "To save time I developed a sugar cookie recipe that could be made as a bar cookie." She entered her one recipe, and several months later found herself a finalist. Once at the Bake-Off® Contest, Kathryn wasn't fazed by the bustle. "Actually, it was a lot easier cooking at the Bake-Off® than in my own kitchen with my three little helpers constantly underfoot." But she acknowledges that without the little helpers, she might never have created her winning cookie recipe.

So-Easy Sugar Cookies

Chocolate Cherry Bars

Frances Jerzak *Porter, Minnesota*
Bake-Off® Contest 25, 1974 Grand Prize Winner

Cake mix and cherry pie filling make this Silver Anniversary Grand Prize winner a quick and easy recipe. Very cakelike, this bar can also be served as a dessert square.

1 (1 lb. 2.25-oz.) pkg. pudding-included devil's food cake mix
1 (21-oz.) can cherry fruit pie filling
1 teaspoon almond extract
3 eggs, beaten

FROSTING
1 cup sugar
1/3 cup milk
5 tablespoons margarine or butter
1 (6-oz.) pkg. (1 cup) semi-sweet chocolate chips

Heat oven to 350°F. Grease and flour 15×10×1-inch baking pan or 13×9-inch pan. In large bowl, combine all bar ingredients; stir until well blended. Pour into greased and floured pan.

Bake at 350°F. until toothpick inserted in center comes out clean. For 15×10×1-inch pan, bake 20 to 30 minutes; for 13×9-inch pan, bake 25 to 35 minutes.

In small saucepan, combine sugar, milk and margarine. Bring to a boil; boil 1 minute, stirring constantly. Remove from heat; stir in chocolate chips until smooth. Pour and spread over warm bars. Cool completely. Cut into bars.

Yield: 48 servings (1 bar per serving)

High Altitude—Above 3,500 feet: Add 1/4 cup flour to dry cake mix. For either size pan, bake at 375°F. for 25 to 35 minutes.

Nutrition Per Serving: Calories 110; Protein 1g; Carbohydrate 18g; Fat 4g; Sodium 105mg

Pecan Pie Surprise Bars

Pearl Hall *Snohomish, Washington*
Bake-Off® Contest 22, 1971 Grand Prize Winner

The taste of pecan pie in a convenient bar cookie!

BASE
1 (1 lb. 2.25-oz.) pkg. pudding-included yellow or butter flavor cake mix
1/3 cup margarine or butter, softened
1 egg

FILLING
1/2 cup firmly packed brown sugar
1 1/2 cups dark corn syrup
1 teaspoon vanilla
3 eggs
1 cup chopped pecans

Heat oven to 350°F. Grease 13×9-inch pan. Reserve 2/3 cup of the dry cake mix for filling. In large bowl, combine remaining dry cake mix, margarine and 1 egg at low speed until well blended. Press in bottom of greased pan. Bake at 350°F. for 15 to 20 minutes or until light golden brown.

In large bowl, combine reserved 2/3 cup dry cake mix, brown sugar, corn syrup, vanilla and 3 eggs at low speed until moistened. Beat 1 minute at medium speed or until well blended. Pour filling mixture over warm base; sprinkle with pecans. Bake an additional 30 to 35 minutes or until filling is set. Cool completely. Cut into bars. Store in refrigerator.

Yield: 36 servings (1 bar per serving)

High Altitude—Above 3,500 feet: Decrease brown sugar by 1 tablespoon. Bake base at 375°F. for 15 to 20 minutes and filling for 30 to 35 minutes.

Nutrition Per Serving: Calories 160; Protein 1g; Carbohydrate 26g; Fat 6g; Sodium 140mg

Ella Schulz: Cashew Caramel Yummies

Pillsbury staffers love to notify finalists, for the happiness that accompanies the news is often profound. "There I was," Ella Schulz says, "ill, feeling lonely, my famous sense of humor pretty frayed at the edges. I made up a recipe, just one, scribbled it on a piece of paper . . . and forgot about it. I really was too miserable to remember anything but my troubles. Then one Sunday, I came home from church and the phone rang! Of course, the Bake-Off® Contest was like a dream . . . Now whenever I have a setback, I always remember my happiness at the Bake-Off®."

Cashew Caramel Yummies

Ella Schulz *Racine, Wisconsin*
Bake-Off® Contest 6, 1954

These rich and chewy caramel bars have cashews inside the bars as well as in the yummy broiled topping.

BARS
¹/₂ cup sugar
¹/₂ cup firmly packed brown sugar
2 eggs
1 cup all-purpose flour
¹/₂ teaspoon baking powder
¹/₄ teaspoon salt
¹/₂ cup chopped salted cashews or peanuts

TOPPING
2 tablespoons margarine or butter
¹/₃ cup chopped salted cashews or peanuts
¹/₄ cup firmly packed brown sugar
1¹/₂ tablespoons half-and-half

Heat oven to 350° F. Grease 9-inch square pan. In large bowl, combine sugar, ¹/₂ cup brown sugar and eggs; mix well. Stir in flour, baking powder, salt and ¹/₂ cup cashews. Pour batter into greased pan. Bake at 350° F. for 20 to 25 minutes or until light golden brown.

Meanwhile, melt margarine in small saucepan; remove from heat. Add remaining topping ingredients; mix well. Immediately spread topping over baked bars. Broil about 6 inches from heat for 1 to 2 minutes or until bubbly and golden brown. Cool completely. Cut into bars.

Yield: 25 servings (1 bar per serving)

High Altitude—Above 3,500 feet: No change.

Nutrition Per Serving: Calories 100; Protein 2g; Carbohydrate 16g; Fat 4g; Sodium 45mg

Clockwise from left: **Cashew Caramel Yummies, Coconut Lemon Crescent Bars, page 211, Candy Bar Brownies, page 216**

Quick Crescent Pecan Pie Bars

Albina Flieller *Floresville, Texas*
Bake-Off® Contest 24, 1973 Grand Prize Winner

Judges were so impressed by the way this pecan bar exemplified the "Bake It Easy" theme of the twenty-fourth contest, they awarded it a grand prize. These delicious bars taste just like pecan pie but are much quicker to make.

CRUST
1 (8-oz.) can refrigerated crescent dinner rolls

FILLING
¹/₂ cup chopped pecans
¹/₂ cup sugar
¹/₂ cup corn syrup
1 tablespoon margarine or butter, melted
¹/₂ teaspoon vanilla
1 egg, beaten

Heat oven to 375°F. Unroll dough into 2 long rectangles. Place in ungreased 13×9-inch pan; press over bottom and ¹/₂ inch up sides to form crust. Firmly press perforations to seal. Bake at 375°F. for 5 minutes.

Meanwhile, in medium bowl, combine all filling ingredients. Pour over partially baked crust. Bake an additional 18 to 22 minutes or until golden brown. Cool completely. Cut into bars.

Yield: 24 servings (1 bar per serving)

Nutrition Per Serving: Calories 90; Protein 1g; Carbohydrate 14g; Fat 4g; Sodium 95mg

Top to bottom: Pecan Pie Surprise Bars, page 212, Quick Crescent Pecan Pie Bars, Quick 'n Chewy Crescent Bars

Quick 'n Chewy Crescent Bars

Isabelle Collins *Elk River, Minnesota*
Bake-Off® Contest 23, 1972 Grand Prize Winner

The frosting mix that was originally used to make these winning bars is no longer available. But you'll find this updated version to be just as delicious as the original, and just as easy.

¹/₂ cup all-purpose flour
1 cup coconut
³/₄ cup firmly packed brown sugar
¹/₂ cup chopped pecans
¹/₄ cup margarine or butter
1 (8-oz.) can refrigerated crescent dinner rolls
1 (14-oz.) can sweetened condensed milk (not evaporated)

Heat oven to 400°F. In medium bowl, combine flour, coconut, brown sugar and pecans. Using pastry blender or fork, cut in margarine until mixture resembles coarse crumbs. Set aside.

Unroll dough into 2 long rectangles. Place in ungreased 15×10×1-inch baking pan; gently press dough to cover bottom of pan. Firmly press perforations to seal. Pour condensed milk evenly over dough to within ¹/₂ inch of edges. Sprinkle coconut mixture over condensed milk; press in lightly.

Bake at 400°F. for 12 to 15 minutes or until deep golden brown. Cool. Cut into bars.

Yield: 48 servings (1 bar per serving)

Nutrition Per Serving: Calories 80; Protein 1g; Carbohydrate 12g; Fat 4g; Sodium 60mg

The Personal Side of Judging

Newspaper food editors make up the largest portion of judges. They're a generous lot, giving over a weekend to be sequestered in a hotel under high security. They have the tremendous responsibility of choosing among 100 great recipes and picking the Grand Prize winner—and all for the love of good food.

• One judge said, "There is a palpable thrill surrounding the event. I found it on the faces of finalists as they hurried between preliminary events. I could feel it on the contest floor, where I surreptitiously snooped and sniffed for a few minutes before entering the security-ringed judging room." But how do they finally choose? "Truly great dishes are almost instantly evident. You could literally smell a winner. One bite essentially confirmed or denied."

• A judge at the nineteenth Bake-Off® Contest said: "Judges of each category group choose their favorites, then present them to other judges and thus begin the long process of narrowing the field. I can say that there was no violence but there were strong arguments. The tension was great, with concern that winning recipes would be liked by everyone. I loved every part of it—even the five extra pounds I now carry."

Treasure Chest Bars

Marie Hammons *Shawnee, Kansas*
Bake-Off® Contest 14, 1962 Prize Winner

This recipe was developed by mistake by Mrs. Hammons. She was not having success with her usual cookie recipe and so decided to add fruit, nuts and candy to salvage the batter. She then baked the creation in a jelly-roll pan. The result is a delicious bar packed with a treasure of goodies!

BARS
2 cups all-purpose flour
¹/₂ cup sugar
¹/₂ cup firmly packed brown sugar
1¹/₂ teaspoons baking powder
Dash salt
¹/₂ cup margarine or butter, softened
³/₄ cup milk
1 teaspoon vanilla
2 eggs
3 (1.45-oz.) bars milk chocolate candy, cut into small pieces
1 cup maraschino cherries, drained, halved
1 cup coarsely chopped mixed nuts

ICING
¹/₄ cup butter
2 cups powdered sugar
¹/₂ teaspoon vanilla
2 to 3 tablespoons milk

Heat oven to 350°F. Grease and flour 15×10×1-inch baking pan. In large bowl, combine all bar ingredients except chocolate, cherries and nuts. Blend at medium speed until smooth, about 2 minutes. By hand, stir in chocolate, cherries and nuts; spread in greased and floured pan. Bake at 350°F. for 25 to 30 minutes or until light golden brown.

In small heavy saucepan over medium heat, brown butter until light golden brown, stirring constantly. Remove from heat. Stir in powdered sugar and ¹/₂ teaspoon vanilla. Add 2 to 3 tablespoons milk; blend until smooth and of desired spreading consistency. Spread over warm bars. Cool completely.

Yield: 48 servings (1 bar per serving)

High Altitude—Above 3,500 feet: No change.

Nutrition Per Serving: Calories 120; Protein 2g; Carbohydrate 15g; Fat 6g; Sodium 55mg

Candy Bar Brownies

Elizabeth Sedensky *Cleveland, Ohio*
Bake-Off® Contest 6, 1954

Chocolate-covered coconut candy bars are melted and baked into these brownies for a delicious twist.

2 (1.9-oz.) chocolate-covered coconut candy bars
¹/₂ cup shortening
1 cup sugar
1 teaspoon vanilla
2 eggs
1 cup all-purpose flour
¹/₂ teaspoon salt
¹/₂ cup chopped nuts

Heat oven to 350°F. Grease 9-inch square pan. In medium saucepan over low heat, melt candy bars and shortening, stirring occasionally until chocolate and shortening are melted. Add sugar and vanilla; blend well. Add eggs 1 at a time, beating well after each addition. Stir in flour, salt and nuts; mix well. Spread in greased pan.

Bake at 350°F. for 25 to 35 minutes or until top springs back when touched lightly in center. Cool completely; cut into bars.

Yield: 25 servings (1 bar per serving)

High Altitude—Above 3,500 feet: Decrease sugar to ³/₄ cup. Bake as directed above.

Nutrition Per Serving: Calories 120; Protein 2g; Carbohydrate 14g; Fat 7g; Sodium 55mg

Raspberry-Filled White Chocolate Bars

Mark Bocianski *Wheaton, Illinois*
Bake-Off® Contest 34, 1990

There is no sugar added to spreadable fruit and you'll find it in the jam and jelly section of most large grocery stores. It's delicious baked in these contemporary bars.

¹/₂ cup margarine or butter
1 (12-oz.) pkg. (2 cups) white vanilla chips or 2 (6-oz.) pkg. white baking bars, chopped
2 eggs
¹/₂ cup sugar
1 cup all-purpose flour
¹/₂ teaspoon salt
1 teaspoon amaretto or almond extract
¹/₂ cup raspberry spreadable fruit or jam
¹/₄ cup sliced almonds, toasted*

Heat oven to 325° F. Grease and flour 9-inch square pan or 8-inch square baking dish. Melt margarine in small saucepan over low heat. Remove from heat. Add 1 cup of the white vanilla chips. LET STAND; DO NOT STIR.

In large bowl, beat eggs until foamy. Gradually add sugar, beating at high speed until lemon-colored. Stir in vanilla milk chip mixture. Add flour, salt and amaretto; mix at low speed until just combined. Spread half (about 1 cup) of batter in greased and floured pan. Bake at 325° F. for 15 to 20 minutes or until light golden brown.

Stir remaining 1 cup white vanilla chips into remaining half of batter; set aside. Melt spreadable fruit in small saucepan over low heat. Spread evenly over warm, partially baked crust. Gently spoon teaspoonfuls of remaining batter over fruit spread. (Some fruit spread may show through batter.) Sprinkle with almonds.

Return to oven; bake an additional 25 to 35 minutes or until toothpick inserted in center comes out clean. Cool completely. Cut into bars.

Yield: 24 servings (1 bar per serving)

*Tip: To toast almonds, spread on cookie sheet; bake at 325° F. for 6 to 10 minutes or until light golden brown, stirring occasionally. Or spread in thin layer in microwave-safe pie pan. Microwave on HIGH for 3 to 4 minutes or until light golden brown, stirring frequently.

High Altitude—Above 3,500 feet: No change.

Nutrition Per Serving: Calories 180; Protein 2g; Carbohydrate 22g; Fat 9g; Sodium 105mg

Raspberry-Filled White Chocolate Bars

Walnut Date Snack Bars

Teresita Larcina *San Mateo, California*
Bake-Off® Contest 37, 1996 Prize Winner

Tere Larcina likes to bake with California-grown dates and walnuts. By combining these favorite ingredients with cake mix, she created a tempting bar that's ready for the oven in minutes. Either fresh or dried dates can be used in this recipe.

1 (1 lb. 2.25-oz.) pkg. pudding-included yellow cake mix
3/4 cup firmly packed brown sugar
3/4 cup margarine or butter, melted
2 eggs
2 cups chopped dates
2 cups chopped walnuts

Heat oven to 350° F. Generously grease 13×9-inch pan. In large bowl, combine cake mix and brown sugar; blend well. Add margarine and eggs; beat 2 minutes at medium speed.

In medium bowl, combine dates and walnuts; mix well. Stir date mixture into cake batter; blend well. (Batter will be stiff.) Spread evenly in greased pan.

Bake at 350° F. for 35 to 45 minutes or until edges are golden brown. Cool 10 minutes. Run knife around sides of pan to loosen. Cool 1 hour or until completely cooled. Cut into bars. Store in tightly covered container.

Yield: 24 servings (1 bar per serving)

Walnut Date Snack Bars

High Altitude—Above 3,500 feet: No change.

Nutrition Per Serving: Calories 290; Protein 3g; Carbohydrate 37g; Fat 14g; Sodium 220mg

Rocky Road Fudge Bars

Mary Wilson *Leesburg, Georgia*
Bake-Off® Contest 23, 1972 Prize Winner

This chocolate lover's delight is one of the most requested Bake-Off® Contest recipes of all time.

BASE
1/2 cup margarine or butter
1 oz. unsweetened chocolate, cut up
1 cup all-purpose flour
1 cup sugar
1 teaspoon baking powder
1 teaspoon vanilla
2 eggs
3/4 cup chopped nuts

FILLING
1 (8-oz.) pkg. cream cheese, softened, reserving 2 oz. for frosting
1/4 cup margarine or butter, softened
1/2 cup sugar
2 tablespoons all-purpose flour
1/2 teaspoon vanilla
1 egg
1/4 cup chopped nuts
1 (6-oz.) pkg. (1 cup) semi-sweet chocolate chips

FROSTING
2 cups miniature marshmallows
1/4 cup margarine or butter
1/4 cup milk

1 oz. unsweetened chocolate, cut up
2 oz. reserved cream cheese
3 cups powdered sugar, sifted
1 teaspoon vanilla

Heat oven to 350° F. Grease and flour 13×9-inch pan. In large saucepan, melt 1/2 cup margarine and 1 oz. unsweetened chocolate over low heat, stirring until smooth. Stir in 1 cup flour and remaining base ingredients; mix well. Spread into greased and floured pan.

In small bowl, combine all filling ingredients except 1/4 cup nuts and chocolate chips. Beat 1 minute at medium speed until smooth and fluffy; stir in nuts. Spread over chocolate mixture; sprinkle evenly with chocolate chips.

Bake at 350° F. for 25 to 35 minutes or until toothpick inserted in center comes out clean. Immediately sprinkle marshmallows over top. Bake at 350° F. for an additional 2 minutes.

Meanwhile, in large saucepan over low heat, combine 1/4 cup margarine, milk, 1 oz. unsweetened chocolate and reserved 2 oz. cream cheese; stir until well blended. Remove from heat; stir in powdered sugar and 1 teaspoon vanilla until smooth. Immediately pour frosting over marshmallows and lightly swirl with knife to marble. Refrigerate until firm; cut into bars. Store in refrigerator.

Yield: 48 servings (1 bar per serving)

High Altitude—Above 3,500 feet: No change.

Nutrition Per Serving: Calories 160; Protein 2g; Carbohydrate 20g; Fat 9g; Sodium 70mg

Tropical Pineapple Coconut Bars

Maureen Pinegar *Midvale, Utah*
Bake-Off® Contest 35, 1992

The tropical flavors of pineapple, macadamia nuts and coconut are blended into a pretty layered bar that will dress up any cookie tray.

BASE
1 (1 lb. 2.25-oz.) pkg. pudding-included yellow cake mix
1¹/₂ cups quick-cooking rolled oats
¹/₂ cup margarine or butter, softened
1 egg

FILLING
¹/₂ cup all-purpose flour
1 (14-oz.) can sweetened condensed milk (not evaporated)
1 (8-oz.) can crushed pineapple, well drained, reserving liquid
¹/₂ teaspoon nutmeg

TOPPING
1 cup chopped macadamia nuts
1 cup coconut
1 cup white vanilla chips

GLAZE
1 cup powdered sugar
4 to 6 teaspoons reserved pineapple liquid

Heat oven to 350° F. Lightly grease 13×9-inch pan. In large bowl, combine all base ingredients at low speed until crumbly. Reserve 1¹/₂ cups of the crumb mixture.

Press remaining crumb mixture in bottom of greased pan.

In medium bowl, combine all filling ingredients; blend well. Pour into crust-lined pan. Add all topping ingredients to reserved crumb mixture; mix well. Sprinkle evenly over filling. Bake at 350° F. for 30 to 40 minutes or until golden brown. Cool completely.

In small bowl, combine powdered sugar and enough reserved pineapple liquid for desired drizzling consistency; blend until smooth. Drizzle over bars. Store in refrigerator.

Yield: 36 servings (1 bar per serving)

High Altitude—Above 3,500 feet: No change.

Nutrition Per Serving: Calories 220; Protein 3g; Carbohydrate 29g; Fat 10g; Sodium 150mg

Oatmeal Carmelitas

Erlyce Larson *Kennedy, Minnesota*
Bake-Off® Contest 18, 1967

These rich, chewy bars have become a favorite of Pillsbury and are one of the most requested recipes ever. They will stay soft and delicious when stored tightly covered in the baking pan.

CRUST
2 cups all-purpose flour
2 cups quick-cooking rolled oats
1¹/₂ cups firmly packed brown sugar
1 teaspoon baking soda
¹/₂ teaspoon salt
1¹/₄ cups margarine or butter, softened

FILLING
1 (12.5-oz.) jar (1 cup) caramel ice cream topping
3 tablespoons all-purpose flour
1 (6-oz.) pkg. (1 cup) semi-sweet chocolate chips
¹/₂ cup chopped nuts

Heat oven to 350° F. Grease 13×9-inch pan. In large bowl, blend all crust ingredients at low speed until crumbly. Press half of crumb mixture, about 3 cups, in bottom of greased pan. Reserve remaining crumb mixture for topping.

Bake at 350° F. for 10 minutes. Meanwhile, in small bowl, combine caramel topping and 3 tablespoons flour. Remove partially baked crust from oven; sprinkle with chocolate chips and nuts. Drizzle evenly with caramel mixture; sprinkle with reserved crumb mixture.

Bake at 350° F. for an additional 18 to 22 minutes or until golden brown. Cool completely. Refrigerate 1 to 2 hours until filling is set. Cut into bars.

Yield: 36 servings (1 bar per serving)

High Altitude—Above 3,500 feet: No change.

Nutrition Per Serving: Calories 200; Protein 2g; Carbohydrate 26g; Fat 9g; Sodium 160mg

Top to bottom: **Oatmeal Carmelitas, Choconut Chippers, page 182**

Spicy Banana Bars

Margaret Cummings *Enderlin, North Dakota*
Bake-Off® Contest 6, 1954

A tangy lemon frosting tops these cakelike bars. When serving them at a party, cut them into narrow bars and garnish each with a pecan half.

BARS
1/4 **cup margarine, softened, or shortening**
1/3 **cup mashed ripe banana**
1/4 **cup milk**
1 **egg**
1 **cup all-purpose flour**
3/4 **cup sugar**
1/2 **teaspoon baking powder**
1/2 **teaspoon salt**
1/4 **teaspoon baking soda**
3/4 **teaspoon cinnamon**
1/4 **teaspoon cloves**
1/4 **teaspoon allspice**
1/3 **cup chopped pecans**

FROSTING
2 **tablespoons margarine or butter**
1 **cup powdered sugar**
2 **teaspoons lemon juice**
2 **to 4 teaspoons water**

Heat oven to 350° F. Grease and flour 13×9-inch pan. In small bowl, combine 1/4 cup margarine and banana until well blended. Add milk and egg; beat well. Stir in flour and remaining bar ingredients until well mixed. Spread in greased and floured pan. Bake at 350° F. for 20 to 25 minutes or until light golden brown.

Meanwhile, melt 2 tablespoons margarine in small saucepan. Stir in powdered sugar, lemon juice and enough water for desired spreading consistency. Spread over warm bars. Cool completely. Cut into bars. Garnish as desired.

Yield: 36 servings (1 bar per serving)

High Altitude—Above 3,500 feet: Decrease sugar to 2/3 cup. Bake as directed above.

Nutrition Per Serving: Calories 70; Protein 1g; Carbohydrate 10g; Fat 3g; Sodium 65mg

Charmin' Cherry Bars

Deanna Thompson *Alexandria, Minnesota*
Bake-Off® Contest 3, 1951

This variation of the ever-popular two-layer Dream Bars adds bright red maraschino cherries to the rich coconut-walnut filling.

CRUST
1 **cup all-purpose flour**
1/4 **cup powdered sugar**
1/2 **cup margarine or butter, softened**

FILLING
1/4 **cup all-purpose flour**
3/4 **cup sugar**
1/2 **teaspoon baking powder**
1/4 **teaspoon salt**
2 **eggs**
1/2 **cup maraschino cherries, well drained, chopped**
1/2 **cup coconut**
1/2 **cup chopped walnuts**

Heat oven to 350° F. In small bowl, combine 1 cup flour and powdered sugar. Using fork or pastry blender, cut in margarine until mixture resembles coarse crumbs. Press crumb mixture firmly in bottom of ungreased 9-inch square pan. Bake at 350° F. for 10 minutes.

Meanwhile, in same small bowl, combine 1/4 cup flour, sugar, baking powder and salt. Add eggs; beat well. Stir in cherries, coconut and walnuts. Spread over partially baked crust. Return to oven; bake an additional 25 to 30 minutes or until golden brown. Cool completely. Cut into bars.

Yield: 25 servings (1 bar per serving)

High Altitude—Above 3,500 feet: No change.

Nutrition Per Serving: Calories 120; Protein 2g; Carbohydrate 14g; Fat 6g; Sodium 75mg

Top to bottom: **Spicy Banana Bars, Charmin' Cherry Bars**

Black and White Brownies

Penelope Weiss *Pleasant Grove, Utah*
Bake-Off® Contest 35, 1992

An American favorite has just gotten even better; this medley of fudgy-chocolate flavor will tantalize taste buds. Indulge yourself and those you love with this heavenly dessert.

BROWNIES
1 (1 lb. 3.5-oz.) pkg. fudge
  brownie mix
¼ cup water
½ cup oil
2 eggs
½ cup chopped pecans
1 (6-oz.) pkg. (1 cup) semi-
  sweet chocolate chips
1 (12-oz.) pkg. (2 cups) white
  vanilla chips

FROSTING
2 cups powdered sugar
¼ cup unsweetened cocoa
3 to 4 tablespoons hot water
¼ cup margarine or butter,
  melted
1 teaspoon vanilla
½ to 1 cup pecan halves

Heat oven to 350° F. Grease bottom only of 13×9-inch pan. In large bowl, combine brownie mix, water, oil and eggs; beat 50 strokes with spoon. Add ½ cup pecans, chocolate chips and 1 cup of the vanilla chips; mix well. Spread in greased pan.

Bake at 350° F. for 28 to 34 minutes or until center is set. Remove from oven; immediately sprinkle with remaining 1 cup vanilla chips. Return to oven for 1 minute to soften chips; spread evenly over brownies with back of spoon. Cool.

In small bowl, combine all frosting ingredients except pecan halves; beat until smooth. (Mixture will be thin.) Spoon over melted white vanilla chips; spread to

cover. Arrange pecan halves over frosting. Cool 1½ hours or until completely cooled. Cut into bars.

Yield: 36 servings (1 bar per serving)

High Altitude—Above 3,500 feet: Add ⅓ cup flour to dry brownie mix. Increase water to ⅓ cup; decrease oil to ⅓ cup. Bake at 375° F. for 30 to 35 minutes.

Nutrition Per Serving: Calories 240; Protein 2g; Carbohydrate 29g; Fat 13g; Sodium 70mg

Peanut Butter 'n Fudge Brownies

Jeannie Hobel *San Diego, California Bake-Off® Contest 31, 1984 Prize Winner*

This doubly rich and delicious brownie is made with peanut butter and peanut butter chips—it's for chocolate and peanut butter lovers everywhere!

CHOCOLATE PORTION
2 cups sugar
1 cup margarine or butter, softened
4 eggs
2 teaspoons vanilla
1½ cups all-purpose flour
¾ cup unsweetened cocoa
1 teaspoon baking powder
½ teaspoon salt
1 cup peanut butter chips

PEANUT BUTTER PORTION
¾ cup peanut butter
⅓ cup margarine or butter, softened
⅓ cup sugar
2 tablespoons all-purpose flour
¾ teaspoon vanilla
2 eggs

FROSTING
3 oz. unsweetened chocolate
3 tablespoons margarine or butter
2⅔ cups powdered sugar
¼ teaspoon salt
¾ teaspoon vanilla
4 to 5 tablespoons water

Heat oven to 350° F. Grease 13×9-inch pan. In large bowl, beat 2 cups sugar and 1 cup margarine until light and fluffy. Add 4 eggs one at a time, beating well after each addition. Add 2 teaspoons vanilla; blend well. In small bowl, combine 1½ cups flour, cocoa, baking powder and ½ teaspoon salt. Gradually add flour mixture to sugar mixture; mix well. Stir in peanut butter chips.

In small bowl, beat peanut butter and ⅓ cup margarine until smooth. Add ⅓ cup sugar and 2 tablespoons flour; mix well. Add ¾ teaspoon vanilla and 2 eggs; blend well. Spread half of chocolate mixture in greased pan. Spread peanut butter mixture evenly over chocolate mixture. Spread remaining chocolate mixture evenly over peanut butter mixture. To marble, pull knife through layers in wide curves.

Bake at 350° F. for 40 to 50 minutes or until top springs back when touched lightly in center and brownies begin to pull away from sides of pan. Cool completely.

In medium saucepan over low heat, melt chocolate and 3 tablespoons margarine, stirring constantly until smooth. Remove from heat. Stir in powdered sugar, ¼ teaspoon salt, ¾ teaspoon vanilla and enough water for desired spreading consistency. Frost cooled brownies; cut into bars.

Yield: 36 servings (1 bar per serving)

High Altitude—Above 3,500 feet: No change.

Nutrition Per Serving: Calories 260; Protein 5g; Carbohydrate 30g; Fat 14g; Sodium 200mg

Black and White Brownies

Salted Peanut Chews

Gertrude M. Schweitzerhof *Cupertino, California*
Bake-Off® Contest 29, 1980

Reminiscent of a popular candy bar, these are sure to be a favorite with everyone. Our microwave directions allow the bars to be made in a smaller pan for smaller households.

CRUST
1 1/2 cups all-purpose flour
2/3 cup firmly packed brown sugar

1/2 teaspoon baking powder
1/2 teaspoon salt
1/4 teaspoon baking soda
1/2 cup margarine or butter, softened
1 teaspoon vanilla
2 egg yolks
3 cups miniature marshmallows

TOPPING
2/3 cup corn syrup
1/4 cup margarine or butter
2 teaspoons vanilla
1 (10-oz.) pkg. peanut butter chips
2 cups crisp rice cereal
2 cups salted peanuts

Heat oven to 350° F. In large bowl, combine all crust ingredients except marshmallows at low speed until crumbly. Press firmly into bottom of ungreased 13×9-inch pan.

Bake at 350° F. for 12 to 15 minutes or until light golden brown. Remove from oven. Immediately sprinkle with marshmallows. Return to oven and bake an additional 1 to 2 minutes or until marshmallows just begin to puff. Cool while preparing topping.

In large saucepan, combine all topping ingredients except cereal

Salted Peanut Chews

and peanuts. Heat just until chips are melted and mixture is smooth, stirring constantly. Remove from heat; stir in cereal and peanuts. Immediately spoon warm topping over marshmallows; spread to cover. Refrigerate until firm. Cut into bars.

Yield: 36 servings (1 bar per serving)

Microwave Directions: Halve the recipe. Combine all crust ingredients except marshmallows as directed. Press in bottom of ungreased 8-inch square (1½-quart) microwave-safe dish. Microwave on HIGH for 3½ to 4½ minutes or until crust looks dry, rotating dish ½ turn halfway through cooking. Immediately sprinkle marshmallows over top. Microwave on HIGH for 1 to 1½ minutes or until marshmallows begin to puff. Cool while preparing topping.

In 4-cup microwave-safe measuring cup, combine all topping ingredients except cereal and peanuts. Microwave on HIGH for 1 to 2 minutes or until chips are melted, stirring once halfway through cooking. Stir until smooth. Continue as directed above.

Yield: 18 servings (1 bar per serving)

High Altitude—Above 3,500 feet: No change.

Nutrition Per Serving: Calories 200; Protein 4g; Carbohydrate 23g; Fat 10g; Sodium 170mg

Truffle-Topped Amaretto Brownies

Arlene Schlotter *El Cajon, California*
Bake-Off® Contest 34, 1990.

This very rich almond-flavored, three-layered brownie will please even the most discriminating brownie lover. Serve them in miniature foil cups for a special touch on a cookie tray.

BROWNIES
1 (1 lb. 3.5-oz.) pkg. fudge brownie mix
½ cup oil
⅓ cup water
2 tablespoons amaretto or 1 teaspoon almond extract*
1 egg
¾ cup chopped almonds

FILLING
1 (8-oz.) pkg. cream cheese, softened
¼ cup powdered sugar
1 (6-oz.) pkg. (1 cup) semi-sweet chocolate chips, melted
2 to 3 tablespoons amaretto or 1 teaspoon almond extract*

TOPPING
½ cup semi-sweet chocolate chips
¼ cup whipping cream
½ cup sliced almonds, toasted**

Heat oven to 350° F. Grease 13×9-inch pan. In large bowl, combine all brownie ingredients. Beat 50 strokes by hand. Spread batter in greased pan. Bake at 350° F. for 26 to 33 minutes or until set. Cool completely.

In small bowl, beat cream cheese and powdered sugar at medium speed until smooth. Add melted chocolate chips and 2 to 3 tablespoons amaretto; beat until well blended. Spread filling mixture over top of cooled brownies. Refrigerate at least 1 hour or until firm.

In small saucepan over low heat, melt ½ cup chocolate chips with whipping cream, stirring constantly until smooth. Carefully spread topping mixture evenly over chilled filling. Sprinkle with sliced almonds. Refrigerate at least 1 hour or until set. Cut into bars. Store in refrigerator.

Yield: 54 servings (1 bar per serving)

***Tips:** If using almond extract instead of amaretto, increase water in brownies to ½ cup; use almond extract and 2 tablespoons milk in filling.

****To toast almonds, spread on cookie sheet; bake at 350° F. for 5 to 10 minutes or until light golden brown, stirring occasionally. Or spread in thin layer in microwave-safe pie pan. Microwave on HIGH for 3 to 4 minutes or until light golden brown, stirring frequently.

High Altitude—Above 3,500 feet: Add ⅓ cup flour to dry brownie mix. Bake at 350° F. for 30 to 35 minutes.

Nutrition Per Serving: Calories 130; Protein 2g; Carbohydrate 13g; Fat 8g; Sodium 40mg

Coconut Pecan Brownies

Oddny Cerisano *Houston, Texas*
Bake-Off® Contest 34, 1990

A wonderful coconut topping rises to the surface of this brownie cake during baking. It's a perfect dessert for potluck gatherings.

1 (1 lb. 3.5-oz.) pkg. fudge
 brownie mix
1/2 cup water
1/2 cup oil
1 egg
1 (15-oz.) can coconut pecan
 frosting
1 cup dairy sour cream
1/2 cup chopped pecans
1/2 cup miniature semi-sweet
 chocolate chips

Heat oven to 350° F. Grease bottom only of 13×9-inch pan. In large bowl, combine brownie mix, water, oil and egg. Beat 50 strokes by hand. Add pecan frosting and sour cream; mix well. Spread batter in greased pan. Sprinkle pecans and chocolate chips evenly over top.

 Bake at 350° F. for 42 to 52 minutes or until toothpick inserted in center comes out clean. Cool completely. Cut into bars.

Yield: 24 servings (1 bar per serving)

High Altitude—Above 3,500 feet: Add 1/2 cup flour to dry brownie mix. Bake as directed above.

Nutrition Per Serving: Calories 290; Protein 2g; Carbohydrate 31g; Fat 17g; Sodium 100mg

Chewy Peanut Brownie Bars

Helen Peach *Pensacola, Florida*
Bake-Off® Contest 34, 1990 Prize Winner

Peanut butter and chocolate are favorite flavors of brownie lovers of all ages. Press the crust evenly in the pan with your fingers or the back of a wide spatula.

CRUST
1 (1 lb. 3.5-oz.) pkg. fudge
 brownie mix
1/2 cup margarine or butter,
 melted
1 egg

FILLING
1 cup light corn syrup
3/4 cup peanut butter
1 cup unsalted peanuts
1 tablespoon margarine or
 butter, melted
1/2 teaspoon vanilla

GLAZE
1 tablespoon margarine or
 butter
1 oz. unsweetened chocolate
7 1/2 teaspoons water
1 cup powdered sugar
1/2 teaspoon vanilla

Heat oven to 350° F. In large bowl, combine all crust ingredients; mix well. Press evenly in bottom of ungreased 15×10×1-inch baking pan.

 In small bowl, beat corn syrup and peanut butter at low speed until well blended. Stir in remaining filling ingredients. Spread filling evenly over crust to within 1/2 inch of edges.

Bake at 350° F. for 18 to 20 minutes or until edges are firm and center is just firm to the touch. Cool completely.

 In small saucepan over low heat, heat 1 tablespoon margarine, chocolate and water, stirring constantly until mixture is smooth. Remove from heat. Stir in powdered sugar and 1/2 teaspoon vanilla; blend until smooth. Drizzle glaze over cooled brownies. Let stand until set. Cut into bars.

Yield: 50 servings (1 bar per serving)

High Altitude—Above 3,500 feet: Add 1/4 cup flour to dry brownie mix. Bake as directed above.

Nutrition Per Serving: Calories 140; Protein 2g; Carbohydrate 18g; Fat 7g; Sodium 85mg

Chewy Peanut Brownie Bars

Triple Espresso Brownies

Sheryl Hakko *Eugene, Oregon*
Bake-Off® Contest 34, 1990

Here's the way to give new meaning to brownies: add a dark chocolate and nut filling, glaze the bars with chocolate and accent all three layers with the rich flavor of espresso coffee granules.

BROWNIES
1 (1 lb. 3.5-oz.) pkg. fudge
   brownie mix
$1/2$ cup oil
$1/4$ cup water
2 eggs
2 teaspoons instant espresso
   coffee granules
1 teaspoon vanilla

FILLING
$1/4$ cup butter or margarine,
   softened
$1/2$ cup firmly packed brown
   sugar
1 egg
2 teaspoons instant espresso
   coffee granules
1 teaspoon vanilla
1 cup coarsely chopped
   walnuts
3 (4-oz.) bars sweet dark or
   bittersweet chocolate,
   coarsely chopped

GLAZE
$1/2$ cup semi-sweet chocolate
   chips
1 tablespoon butter or
   margarine

$1/8$ teaspoon instant espresso
   coffee granules
1 to 2 teaspoons milk or
   whipping cream

Heat oven to 350° F. Grease bottom only of 13×9-inch pan. In large bowl, combine all brownie ingredients. Beat 50 strokes with spoon. Spread in greased pan. Bake at 350° F. for 28 minutes. Remove from oven.

   Meanwhile, in small bowl, beat $1/4$ cup butter and brown sugar until light and fluffy. Add 1 egg, 2 teaspoons coffee granules and 1 teaspoon vanilla; blend well. In

Triple Espresso Brownies

medium bowl, combine walnuts and chopped chocolate. Add brown sugar mixture; blend well. Spoon and carefully spread over partially baked brownies. Bake at 350° F. for an additional 17 to 20 minutes or until light brown.

In small saucepan over low heat, melt chocolate chips and 1 tablespoon butter, stirring constantly until smooth. Remove from heat. With wire whisk, stir in $1/8$ teaspoon coffee granules and enough milk for desired drizzling consistency. Drizzle over warm brownies. Cool completely. Cut into bars.

Yield: 48 servings (1 bar per serving)

High Altitude—Above 3,500 feet: See brownie mix package for directions.

Nutrition Per Serving: Calories 160; Protein 2g; Carbohydrate 18g; Fat 9g; Sodium 50mg

1 (1 lb. 3.5-oz.) pkg. fudge brownie mix
1¹/₂ cups graham cracker crumbs
¹/₂ cup sugar
¹/₂ cup margarine or butter, melted
1 (14-oz.) pkg. caramels, unwrapped
¹/₃ cup evaporated milk
³/₄ cup peanut butter chips
³/₄ cup semi-sweet chocolate chips
1 cup chopped pecans or walnuts
¹/₄ cup water
¹/₄ cup oil
1 egg

Heat oven to 350° F. In medium bowl, combine 1¹/₂ cups of the brownie mix, graham cracker crumbs, sugar and melted margarine; mix well. Press mixture in bottom of ungreased 13×9-inch pan.

In medium saucepan, combine caramels and evaporated milk.

Cook over medium heat until caramels are melted, stirring constantly. Carefully spread melted caramel mixture over crust. Sprinkle with peanut butter chips, chocolate chips and ³/₄ cup of the chopped pecans, reserving remaining ¹/₄ cup pecans for topping.

In same medium bowl, combine remaining brownie mix, water, oil and egg. Beat 50 strokes by hand. Carefully spoon batter evenly over pecans. Sprinkle with remaining ¹/₄ cup pecans.

Bake at 350° F. for 33 to 38 minutes or until center is set. Cool completely. Cut into bars.

Yield: 24 servings (1 bar per serving)

High Altitude—Above 3,500 feet: Add 2 tablespoons flour to remaining dry brownie mix; then add water, oil and egg. Bake as directed above.

Nutrition Per Serving: Calories 360; Protein 4g; Carbohydrate 47g; Fat 17g; Sodium 200mg

Caramel Graham Fudge Brownies

Kathy (Gardner) Herdman *Middleport, Ohio Bake-Off® Contest 35, 1992 Prize Winner*

Brownie doneness is often difficult to determine. Follow the recipe time range carefully and watch for the brownies to be "set" in the center. Usually the brownies will just begin to pull away from the sides of the pan when they're done. You'll enjoy the combination of ingredients in these rich, layered brownies.

Kathy (Gardner) Herdman: Caramel Graham Fudge Brownies

Cooking is a work of the mind as much as it is a work of the hands. "I'm just a typical down-home country girl who loves to cook and cook and cook," Kathy Herdman commented, describing the abstract process that many Bake-Off® winners say they use to come up with their recipes. "I don't just start throwing food together. Visualization is the key. I add and take away ingredients in my mind. When the final product looks good in my mind, then I try out the recipe in reality. Dreams do come true," concluded Kathy, "at least sometimes." Sometimes they become so real, you can taste them!

Caramel Swirl Cheesecake Brownies

Rebecca Moe *Carmichael, California*
Bake-Off® Contest 36, 1994 Prize Winner

Swirls of caramel in a peanut butter cheesecake—these bars will become a new favorite!

BASE
1 (1 lb. 3.5-oz.) pkg. fudge brownie mix
¹/₂ cup butter or margarine, softened
¹/₄ cup creamy peanut butter
1 egg

FILLING
2 (8-oz.) pkg. cream cheese, softened
¹/₃ cup creamy peanut butter
1 cup sugar
3 tablespoons all-purpose flour
¹/₄ cup dairy sour cream
2 teaspoons vanilla
2 eggs

CARAMEL SAUCE
12 caramels, unwrapped
3 tablespoons whipping cream

GARNISH, IF DESIRED
¹/₂ cup whipping cream
1 tablespoon powdered sugar

Heat oven to 325°F. Grease bottom of 13×9-inch pan. In large bowl, combine all base ingredients; beat until dough forms. Press lightly in bottom of greased pan.

In large bowl, combine cream cheese and ¹/₃ cup peanut butter; beat at low speed until smooth. Add sugar, flour, sour cream and vanilla; beat until blended. Add 2 eggs 1 at a time, beating just until blended. Pour filling over base.

In small heavy saucepan, combine caramels and 3 tablespoons whipping cream. Cook and stir over low heat until caramels are melted and mixture is smooth. Drop spoonfuls of caramel sauce randomly over filling. For swirl effect, pull knife through batter in wide curves; turn pan and repeat.

Bake at 325°F. for 35 to 45 minutes or until center is set and edges are light golden brown. Cool 30 minutes. Refrigerate 1 hour before serving.

Just before serving, in small bowl, combine ¹/₂ cup whipping cream and powdered sugar; beat until stiff peaks form. Pipe whipped cream rosettes or spoon dollops of whipped cream on each serving. Store in refrigerator.

Yield: 24 servings (1 bar per serving)

High Altitude—Above 3,500 feet: Add 2 tablespoons flour to dry brownie mix. Bake as directed above.

Nutrition Per Serving: Calories 330; Protein 5g; Carbohydrate 33g; Fat 20g; Sodium 210mg

Caramel Swirl Cheesecake Brownies,
Fudgy Bonbons, page 186

Chapter 7

Cakes and Tortes

Cakes are a food for holidays, a food for sharing. Like a roast turkey or a barbecue, a cake is not a solitary pleasure. Cakes are a food of celebration, marking the special times in our lives with extravagance and cheer.

While some Bake-Off® prize-winning cakes, like 1950's Orange Kiss-Me Cake and 1953's "My Inspiration" Cake, were simple cakes to round out a meal, most Bake-Off® cakes have been lavish creations, the product of a homemaker's expansive love and a bit of time. The 1951 contest's Starlight Double-Delight Cake and 1959's Mardi Gras Party Cake are both beautifully frosted, elaborate cakes. The Tunnel of Fudge Cake, from the 1966 contest, may have been the ultimate home-grown extravagance, packed full of nuts and fudgy chocolate.

The 1970s marked a real change in cake baking, with more homey cakes gaining in popularity, featuring whole-food ingredients like molasses, bananas and oats, as in 1973's Banana Crunch Cake or 1978's Nutty Graham Picnic Cake. In the 1980s, cooks returned to decadence and looked to Europe for inspiration. With 1984's Dark Chocolate Sacher Torte or 1988's Almond Mocha Cake, American families were treated like European royalty.

Recently, American cooks have been displaying their increased sophistication by combining the best of European and American traditions. The Chocolate Mousse Fantasy Torte, from the 1990s contest, combined an American original—brownies—with a European classic—chocolate mousse. In 1994 Glazed Sweet Potato Mini-Cakes revealed an *haute cuisine* treatment of indigenous American ingredients: sweet potatoes, maple syrup and pecans.

While ingredients, manners of preparation and tastes have changed over the years, the reasons for presenting a special cake haven't. Celebrations find cake bakers and cake eaters in perfect agreement: cakes are the perfect food for sharing.

Tunnel of Fudge Cake, page 262

Brown Butter Apricot Cake

Shirley Sauber *Indianapolis, Indiana*
Bake-Off® Contest 32, 1986

To split the cake layers evenly, insert toothpicks around the middle as a cutting guide line and cut with a long-bladed sharp knife or a long piece of dental floss.

CAKE
1 (1 lb. 2.25-oz.) pkg. pudding-included white cake mix
$1^{1}/_{4}$ cups water
$^{1}/_{3}$ cup oil
1 tablespoon grated orange peel
1 teaspoon orange extract
3 egg whites

FROSTING AND FILLING
$^{1}/_{2}$ cup butter (do not use margarine)
3 to 4 cups powdered sugar
$^{1}/_{3}$ cup orange juice
$^{2}/_{3}$ cup apricot preserves
$^{1}/_{3}$ cup chopped walnuts or pecans

Heat oven to 350° F. Grease and flour two 8- or 9-inch round cake pans. In large bowl, combine all cake ingredients at low speed until moistened. Beat 2 minutes at high speed. Pour batter into greased and floured pans.

Bake at 350° F. for 20 to 30 minutes or until toothpick inserted in center comes out clean. Cool 15 minutes; remove from pans. Cool completely.

Meanwhile, in small heavy saucepan over medium heat, brown butter until light golden brown, stirring constantly. Remove from heat; cool completely. In large bowl, combine browned butter, 3 cups powdered sugar and orange juice at low speed until moistened. Beat 2 minutes at medium speed or until smooth and well blended. Beat in up to 1 cup additional powdered sugar if necessary for desired spreading consistency.

To assemble cake, slice each cake layer in half horizontally; remove top half from each layer. Spread $^{1}/_{3}$ cup of the preserves on bottom half of each layer; replace top half. Place 1 filled layer top side down on serving plate; spread with $^{1}/_{2}$ cup of frosting mixture. Top with second filled layer, top side up. Frost sides and top of cake with remaining frosting. Sprinkle walnuts over cake. Refrigerate until serving time. Store in refrigerator.

Yield: 12 servings

High Altitude—Above 3,500 feet: Add $^{1}/_{4}$ cup flour to dry cake mix; increase water to $1^{1}/_{3}$ cups. Bake at 375° F. for 20 to 30 minutes.

Nutrition Per Serving: Calories 540; Protein 3g; Carbohydrate 87g; Fat 20g; Sodium 370mg

Mardi Gras Party Cake

Eunice G. Surles *Lake Charles, Louisiana*
Bake-Off® Contest 11, 1959 Grand Prize Winner

The Louisiana widow who created her new version of a favorite Southern caramel cake added her own rich butterscotch-nut filling and topping. A fluffy seafoam cream frosting adds the final party touch.

CAKE
$^{2}/_{3}$ cup butterscotch chips
$^{1}/_{4}$ cup water
$2^{1}/_{4}$ cups all-purpose flour
$1^{1}/_{4}$ cups sugar
1 teaspoon baking soda
1 teaspoon salt
$^{1}/_{2}$ teaspoon baking powder
1 cup buttermilk*
$^{1}/_{2}$ cup shortening
3 eggs

FILLING
$^{1}/_{2}$ cup sugar
1 tablespoon cornstarch
$^{1}/_{2}$ cup half-and-half or evaporated milk
$^{1}/_{3}$ cup water
$^{1}/_{3}$ cup butterscotch chips
1 egg, slightly beaten
2 tablespoons margarine or butter
1 cup coconut
1 cup chopped nuts

SEAFOAM CREAM
1 cup whipping cream
$^{1}/_{4}$ cup firmly packed brown sugar
$^{1}/_{2}$ teaspoon vanilla

Heat oven to 350° F. Generously grease and flour two 9-inch round cake pans.** In small saucepan over low heat, melt $^{2}/_{3}$ cup butterscotch chips in $^{1}/_{4}$ cup water, stirring until smooth. Cool slightly. In large bowl, combine flour, remaining cake ingredients and cooled butterscotch mixture at low speed until moistened; beat 3 minutes at medium speed. Pour batter into greased and floured pans.

Bake at 350° F. for 20 to 30 minutes or until toothpick inserted in center comes out clean. Cool 10 minutes; remove from pans. Cool completely.

In medium saucepan, combine $^{1}/_{2}$ cup sugar and cornstarch; stir in half-and-half, $^1/_3$ cup water, $^1/_3$ cup butterscotch chips and 1 egg. Cook over medium heat until mixture thickens, stirring constantly. Remove from heat. Stir in margarine, coconut and nuts; cool slightly.

In small bowl, beat whipping cream until soft peaks form. Gradually add brown sugar and vanilla, beating until stiff peaks form.

To assemble cake, place 1 cake layer top side down on serving plate. Spread with half of filling mixture. Top with second layer, top side up; spread remaining filling on top to within $^1/_2$ inch of edge. Frost sides and top edge of cake with seafoam cream. Refrigerate at least 1 hour before serving. Store in refrigerator.

Yield: 16 servings

*Tips: To substitute for buttermilk, use 1 teaspoon vinegar or lemon juice plus milk to make 1 cup.

**Cake can be baked in 13×9-inch pan. Grease bottom only of pan. Bake at 350° F. for 30 to 35 minutes or until toothpick inserted in center comes out clean. Cool completely. Spread top of cooled cake with filling mixture. Serve topped with seafoam cream.

Yield: 16 servings

High Altitude—Above 3,500 feet: Bake at 350° F. for 30 to 35 minutes. Cool 7 minutes; remove from pans. Cool completely.

Nutrition Per Serving: Calories 440; Protein 6g; Carbohydrate 51g; Fat 25g; Sodium 300mg

Whole Wheat Walnut Crumb Cake

Audrey Arpin *Phoenix, Arizona*
Bake-Off® Contest 32, 1986

This lightly spiced whole wheat cake can be baked in cake layer pans or in a 13×9-inch pan. It's great for picnics.

STREUSEL
1 cup chopped walnuts or pecans
$^1/_3$ cup firmly packed brown sugar
1 teaspoon cinnamon

CAKE
2 cups whole wheat flour
1 cup sugar
3 teaspoons baking powder
$^1/_2$ teaspoon salt
1 cup milk
$^1/_3$ cup margarine or butter, softened
1 egg

GLAZE
$^3/_4$ cup powdered sugar
1 to 2 tablespoons water

Heat oven to 350° F. Grease and flour two 8- or 9-inch round cake pans.* In small bowl, mix all streusel ingredients until well blended; set aside.

In large bowl, combine all cake ingredients. Beat at low speed until moistened; beat 2 minutes at medium speed. Spread about $^3/_4$ cup of batter in each greased and floured pan; sprinkle $^1/_4$ of streusel mixture evenly over batter in each pan.

Carefully spread remaining batter over streusel in each pan; sprinkle with remaining streusel mixture.

Bake at 350° F. for 20 to 30 minutes or until toothpick inserted in center comes out clean. Cool slightly. In small bowl, combine powdered sugar and enough water for desired drizzling consistency; blend until smooth. Drizzle over warm cakes.

Yield: 16 servings

*Tip: Cake can be baked in 13×9-inch pan. Spread half of batter in greased and floured pan; sprinkle half of streusel mixture evenly over batter. Carefully spread remaining batter over streusel; sprinkle with remaining streusel mixture. Bake at 350° F. for 25 to 35 minutes or until toothpick inserted in center comes out clean.

Yield: 16 servings

High Altitude—Above 3,500 feet: Increase flour to $2^1/_4$ cups. Bake at 375° F. for 20 to 30 minutes.

Nutrition Per Serving: Calories 230; Protein 4g; Carbohydrate 36g; Fat 9g; Sodium 220mg

Chocolate Praline Layer Cake

Julie Konecne *Bemidji, Minnesota*
Bake-Off® Contest 33, 1988 Grand Prize Winner

Created by a university professor of music, this easy-to-prepare cake is spectacular to serve and marvelous to eat! It's best if made a few hours ahead and refrigerated before serving.

CAKE
$^1/_2$ cup butter or margarine
$^1/_4$ cup whipping cream
1 cup firmly packed brown sugar
$^3/_4$ cup coarsely chopped pecans
1 (1 lb. 2.25-oz.) pkg. pudding-included devil's food cake mix
$1^1/_4$ cups water
$^1/_3$ cup oil
3 eggs

TOPPING
$1^3/_4$ cups whipping cream
$^1/_4$ cup powdered sugar
$^1/_4$ teaspoon vanilla
12 to 16 whole pecans, if desired
12 to 16 chocolate curls, if desired

Heat oven to 325° F. In small heavy saucepan, combine butter, $^1/_4$ cup whipping cream and brown sugar. Cook over low heat just until butter is melted, stirring occasionally. Pour into two 9- or 8-inch round cake pans; sprinkle evenly with chopped pecans.

Chocolate Praline Layer Cake

In large bowl, combine cake mix, water, oil and eggs at low speed until moistened; beat 2 minutes at high speed. Carefully spoon batter over pecan mixture.

Bake at 325° F. for 35 to 45 minutes or until cake springs back when touched lightly in center. Cool 5 minutes. Remove from pans. Cool completely.

In small bowl, beat $1^3/_4$ cups whipping cream until soft peaks form. Blend in powdered sugar and vanilla; beat until stiff peaks form.

To assemble cake, place 1 layer on serving plate, praline side up. Spread with half of whipped cream. Top with second layer, praline side up; spread top with remaining whipped cream. Garnish with whole pecans and chocolate curls. Store in refrigerator.

Yield: 16 servings

Tip: Cake can be prepared in 13×9-inch pan. Bake at 325° F. for 50 to 60 minutes or until cake springs back when touched lightly in center. Cool 5 minutes; invert onto serving platter. Cool completely. Frost cake or pipe with whipped cream. Garnish with pecan halves and chocolate curls. Serve with any remaining whipped cream. Store in refrigerator.

Yield: 16 servings

High Altitude—Above 3,500 feet: Add $^1/_3$ cup flour to dry cake mix; increase water to $1^1/_3$ cups. Bake at 350° F. for 30 to 35 minutes. Immediately remove from pans.

Nutrition Per Serving: Calories 460; Protein 4g; Carbohydrate 43g; Fat 30g; Sodium 340mg

Fate

Many finalists have won a trip to the Bake-Off® Contest the very first time they entered—and many of these people have never entered any previous cooking contest of any kind. Is it any wonder that many contestants feel like fate was smiling down on them?

- One contestant's entry arrived badly burned around the edges, attached to a letter from the U. S. Post Office saying: "Our sincere apologies for the present condition of the enclosed mail. The damage resulted from an accident and fire while the mail was being transported by a commercial carrier." The charred entry made it all the way through the selection process, and saw its creator all the way to the Bake-Off® Contest.

- One baker's wife was shocked when she found herself a finalist. Her husband's professional status had led her to think that her own recipes were too plain, but her daughter had entered her recipe anyway. She went on to win a cash prize.

- Another contestant was stunned when she received the call from Pillsbury, because she had finished the entry blank, but forgot to mail it before the deadline. It turned out her young son had mailed it himself, since he wanted to accompany his mom to Disney World, where the contest was taking place that year.

Glazed Sweet Potato Mini-Cakes

Jean Olson *Wallingford, Iowa*
Bake-Off® Contest 36, 1994 Prize Winner

Maple, cinnamon, orange and sweet potatoes are combined in this recipe for individual glazed cakes that are a flavor sensation!

CAKE
1 (1 lb. 2.25-oz.) pkg. pudding-included yellow cake mix
1 tablespoon finely grated orange peel
2 teaspoons cinnamon
1 cup unsweetened applesauce (natural)
1/3 cup oil
1/4 cup water
1/2 teaspoon maple flavor
4 eggs
2 cups finely grated peeled dark-orange sweet potatoes
1 cup chopped pecans

GLAZE
2 tablespoons butter or margarine
1/4 cup firmly packed brown sugar
1/4 cup dairy sour cream
1/8 teaspoon maple flavor
3/4 to 1 cup powdered sugar

GARNISH
1/3 to 1/2 cup chopped pecans
2 to 3 teaspoons grated orange peel, if desired
1 orange, sliced, if desired

Heat oven to 350° F. Grease and flour 12 Bundt mini-muffin cups (six 1-cup fluted molds to a pan).* In large bowl, combine cake mix,

1 tablespoon orange peel, cinnamon, applesauce, oil, water, 1/2 teaspoon maple flavor and eggs. Beat at low speed until moistened; beat 2 minutes at high speed. Stir in sweet potatoes and 1 cup pecans. Fill greased Bundt cups 3/4 full. (If using only one pan, refrigerate remaining batter until ready to use.)

Bake at 350° F. for 20 to 30 minutes or until toothpick inserted in center comes out clean. Cool on wire rack 5 minutes; remove from pans. Melt butter in small saucepan over medium-low heat; stir in brown sugar. Add sour cream, stirring constantly until mixture is hot and brown sugar is dissolved. DO NOT BOIL. Stir in 1/8 teaspoon maple flavor and enough powdered sugar for desired drizzling consistency; beat until smooth. Drizzle over warm cakes; sprinkle with desired amount of pecans and orange peel. Garnish serving plate with orange slices.

Yield: 12 servings
(1 mini-cake per serving)

*Tip: Regular muffin pans can be substituted. Grease and flour 28 muffin cups. Prepare batter as directed above. Fill muffin cups to rim. Bake at 350° F. for 15 to 20 minutes.

High Altitude—Above 3,500 feet: Add 1/4 cup flour to dry cake mix. Bake as directed above.

Nutrition Per Serving: Calories 490; Protein 5g; Carbohydrate 63g; Fat 24g; Sodium 330mg

Tropical Fruit Fling Cake

Jo Anne Hagen *Bloomington, Minnesota*
Bake-Off® Contest 32, 1986

When broiling the topping on this fruit-filled cake, watch it carefully and remove the cake from the oven as soon as the topping begins to bubble.

CAKE
1 (1 lb. 2.25-oz.) pkg. pudding-included yellow cake mix
1 (20-oz.) can crushed pineapple in unsweetened juice, drained, reserving 1/2 cup liquid
1/3 cup oil
3 eggs

Cake Tips

- Don't fill cake pans more than 3/4 full of batter; the batter may spill over as it expands during baking.
- Make sure there are at least 2 inches between cake pans in the oven, so air can circulate and cakes will be evenly baked.
- What makes a cake fall? Sudden changes in temperature or movement of the cake. Try not to open the oven during the first 15 minutes of baking, and not much after that, either. Close the oven door gently, if you do open it.

TOPPING
$^1/_4$ **cup margarine or butter**
Reserved drained pineapple
$^3/_4$ **cup firmly packed brown**
sugar
$^3/_4$ **cup coconut**
$^1/_2$ **cup chopped nuts**
$^1/_4$ **cup chopped maraschino**
cherries

Heat oven to 350°F. Grease and flour 13×9-inch pan. In large bowl, combine cake mix, reserved $^1/_2$ cup pineapple liquid, oil and eggs at low speed until moistened; beat 2 minutes at high speed. Fold in $^1/_2$ cup of the pineapple, reserving remaining pineapple for topping. Pour batter into greased and floured pan. Bake at 350°F. for 35 to 45 minutes or until toothpick inserted in center comes out clean.

Meanwhile, melt margarine in medium saucepan. Stir in reserved pineapple and remaining topping ingredients. Carefully spread over hot cake, covering completely. Broil 3 to 5 inches from heat for 3 to 5 minutes or until topping is bubbly. Cool completely. Store in refrigerator.

Yield: 12 servings

High Altitude—Above 3,500 feet: Add $^1/_3$ cup flour to dry cake mix; add $^1/_3$ cup water to cake batter. Bake as directed above.

Nutrition Per Serving: Calories 420; Protein 4g; Carbohydrate 58g; Fat 19g; Sodium 360mg

Orange Kiss-Me Cake

Lily Wuebel *Redwood City, California*
Bake-Off® Contest 2, 1950 Grand
Prize Winner

Lily Wuebel described her cake as "a man's cake, not too sweet, just a simple cake." Her creation is as popular today as when it won top honors more than 40 years ago.

CAKE
1 orange
1 cup raisins
$^1/_3$ **cup walnuts**
2 cups all-purpose flour
1 cup sugar
1 teaspoon baking soda
1 teaspoon salt
1 cup milk
$^1/_2$ **cup margarine or butter,**
softened, or shortening
2 eggs

TOPPING
Reserved $^1/_3$ cup orange juice
$^1/_3$ **cup sugar**
1 teaspoon cinnamon
$^1/_4$ **cup finely chopped walnuts**

Heat oven to 350°F. Grease and flour 13×9-inch pan. Squeeze orange, reserving $^1/_3$ cup juice for topping; remove seeds. In blender container, food processor bowl with metal blade or food mill, grind together orange peel and pulp, raisins and $^1/_3$ cup walnuts; set aside.

In large bowl, combine flour and remaining cake ingredients at low speed until moistened; beat 3 minutes at medium speed. Stir in orange-raisin mixture. Pour batter into greased and floured pan.

Bake at 350°F. for 35 to 45 minutes or until toothpick inserted in center comes out clean. Drizzle reserved $^1/_3$ cup orange juice over warm cake in pan.

In small bowl, combine $^1/_3$ cup sugar and cinnamon; mix well. Stir in $^1/_4$ cup walnuts; sprinkle over cake. Cool completely.

Yield: 16 servings

High Altitude—Above 3,500 feet: Increase flour to 2 cups plus 2 tablespoons. Bake at 375°F. for 35 to 40 minutes.

Nutrition Per Serving: Calories 250; Protein 4g; Carbohydrate 40g; Fat 10g; Sodium 300mg

Lily Wuebel: Orange Kiss-Me Cake

Part of Pillsbury's reason for starting the Bake-Off® Contest was to celebrate the many unsung heroes of America's kitchens, who hadn't received public credit for the trays of cookies, the platters of cakes and the baskets of bread that issued from their kitchens.

Of course, for every Bake-Off® winner, there is still an unpublicized kitchen hero for whom the appreciation of her family is reward enough. Lily Wuebel was lucky enough to have both. When asked what he thought of his wife's $25,000 cake, Peter Wuebel said he'd always loved the cake, and "it's worth a million to me."

Golden Apricot Cake

Dale P. Grant *Corpus Christi, Texas*
Bake-Off® Contest 32, 1986 Prize Winner

Dale Grant is a retired naval lieutenant commander. Now that he has time to indulge in his hobby of baking, he creates winning desserts like this apricot-flavored layer cake with a rich cream cheese frosting.

CAKE
1 (1 lb. 2.25-oz.) pkg. pudding-included yellow cake mix
1 cup apricot nectar
1/3 cup oil
1/4 cup honey
3 eggs

FROSTING AND FILLING
1 (10-oz.) jar apricot preserves
1 (3-oz.) pkg. cream cheese, softened
1/4 cup margarine or butter, softened
2 1/2 cups powdered sugar
1/3 cup chopped pecans or walnuts

Heat oven to 350°F. Grease and flour two 8- or 9-inch round cake pans. In large bowl, combine all cake ingredients at low speed until moistened; beat 2 minutes at high speed. Pour batter into greased and floured pans. Bake at 350°F. for 25 to 35 minutes or until toothpick inserted in center comes out clean. Cool 10 minutes; remove from pans. Cool completely.

Reserve 2/3 cup of the preserves. In small saucepan, heat remaining preserves until melted, stirring occasionally; set aside.

In small bowl, beat cream cheese and margarine until smooth. Add powdered sugar; beat at low speed until well blended. Add enough warm preserves to cream cheese mixture for desired spreading consistency. Stir in pecans.

To assemble cake, place 1 layer, top side down, on serving plate; spread with reserved 2/3 cup preserves. Top with second layer, top side up. Frost sides and top of cake with frosting mixture. Refrigerate until frosting is firm; store in refrigerator.

Yield: 12 servings

Dale Grant: Golden Apricot Cake

Once I made a German chocolate cake using a yeast dough," Dale Grant reported when asked about any cooking mishaps he had had. "I split two layers horizontally to make four layers, to put filling between them. As I prepared the frosting, the cake fell apart—much like a huge mound of dirt collapsing. All that remained of the top three layers were crumbs." Who doesn't know what that feels like? Luckily, Dale didn't get discouraged and quit, he went on to create this easy, wonderful cake.

High Altitude—Above 3,500 feet: Add 5 tablespoons flour to dry cake mix. Decrease apricot nectar to 1/2 cup and honey to 1 tablespoon. Add 1/2 cup water. Bake at 375°F. for 30 to 40 minutes.

Nutrition Per Serving: Calories 540; Protein 4g; Carbohydrate 85g; Fat 20g; Sodium 380mg

Caramel Pear Upside-Down Cake

Margaret Faxon *Palmyra, Missouri*
Bake-Off® Contest 5, 1953

The unique upside-down layer cake is a yummy combination of pears and caramel. We've added new-fashioned ease to this old-fashioned cake by using a cake mix.

1 (29-oz.) can pear halves, drained, reserving 1/2 cup liquid
28 vanilla caramels, unwrapped
2 tablespoons margarine or butter
1 (1 lb. 2.25-oz.) pkg. pudding-included yellow cake mix
1 cup water
1/3 cup oil
3 eggs
1/4 cup chopped nuts
Whipped cream, if desired

Heat oven to 350°F. Generously grease 13×9-inch pan. Slice pear halves; arrange over bottom of greased pan. In small saucepan over medium heat, melt caramels in reserved pear liquid, stirring frequently until smooth. Stir in margarine; blend well. Pour mixture evenly over pears. In large bowl, combine cake mix, water, oil and eggs at low speed until moistened; beat 2 minutes at high speed. Spoon batter evenly over pear mixture.

Bake at 350° F. for 40 to 50 minutes or until toothpick inserted in center comes out clean. Cool 5 minutes; turn onto serving plate. Sprinkle with nuts. Serve warm or cool with whipped cream.

Yield: 12 servings

High Altitude—Above 3,500 feet: Add 3 tablespoons flour to dry cake mix. Bake at 375° F. for 35 to 45 minutes.

Nutrition Per Serving: Calories 470; Protein 5g; Carbohydrate 66g; Fat 21g; Sodium 370mg

Caramel Apple Cake

Josephine DeMarco *Chicago, Illinois*
Bake-Off® Contest 27, 1976 Prize Winner

In the 1970s, homespun desserts edged out earlier elaborate dessert entries. Caramel and apple was a popular flavor combination. This family favorite apple-nut sheet cake shows why.

CAKE
1³/₄ cups all-purpose flour
1¹/₂ cups firmly packed brown sugar
¹/₂ teaspoon salt
¹/₂ teaspoon baking powder
¹/₂ teaspoon baking soda

1¹/₂ teaspoons cinnamon
1 teaspoon vanilla
³/₄ cup margarine or butter, softened
3 eggs
1¹/₂ cups (2 to 3 medium) finely chopped peeled apples
¹/₂ to 1 cup chopped nuts
¹/₂ cup raisins, if desired

FROSTING
2 cups powdered sugar
¹/₄ teaspoon cinnamon
¹/₄ cup margarine or butter, melted
¹/₂ teaspoon vanilla
4 to 5 teaspoons milk

Heat oven to 350° F. Grease and flour 13×9-inch pan. In large bowl, combine flour, brown sugar, salt, baking powder, baking soda, 1¹/₂ teaspoons cinnamon, 1 teaspoon vanilla, ³/₄ cup margarine and eggs; beat 3 minutes at medium speed. Stir in apples, nuts and raisins. Pour batter into greased and floured pan.

Bake at 350° F. for 30 to 40 minutes or until toothpick inserted in center comes out clean. Cool completely.

In small bowl, blend all frosting ingredients, adding enough milk for desired spreading consistency. Spread over cooled cake.

Yield: 15 servings

High Altitude—Above 3,500 feet: Decrease brown sugar to 1 cup. Bake at 375° F. for 25 to 35 minutes.

Nutrition Per Serving: Calories 390; Protein 4g; Carbohydrate 56g; Fat 18g; Sodium 280mg

Double Lemon Streusel Cake

Betty Engles *Midland, Michigan*
Bake-Off® Contest 28, 1978 Prize Winner

Perfect for dessert or for a coffee break, this quick lemony cake has a luscious cream cheese topping.

CAKE
1 (1 lb. 2.25-oz.) pkg. pudding-included lemon cake mix*
¹/₃ cup margarine or butter, softened
¹/₂ cup milk
2 eggs

TOPPING
1 (8-oz.) pkg. cream cheese, softened
¹/₄ cup sugar
4 teaspoons lemon juice
¹/₂ teaspoon grated lemon peel
¹/₂ cup chopped nuts

Heat oven to 350° F. Generously grease and flour 13×9-inch pan. In large bowl, combine cake mix and margarine at low speed until crumbly. Reserve 1 cup of crumb mixture for topping. To remaining crumb mixture, add milk and eggs; beat 2 minutes at high speed. Pour batter into greased and floured pan.

In small bowl, combine all topping ingredients except nuts; beat until smooth.

Drop topping mixture by teaspoonfuls onto cake batter; carefully spread evenly to cover. In small bowl, combine reserved 1 cup crumb mixture and nuts.

Sprinkle over topping mixture. Bake at 350° F. for 30 to 40 minutes or until top springs back when touched lightly in center. Cool completely. Store in refrigerator.

Yield: 15 servings

*Tip: Yellow cake mix can be substituted for the lemon cake mix.

High Altitude—Above 3,500 feet: Add ¹/₄ cup flour to dry cake mix. Bake at 375° F. for 30 to 40 minutes.

Nutrition Per Serving: Calories 280; Protein 4g; Carbohydrate 32g; Fat 15g; Sodium 310mg

Peanut Butter Crunch Cake

Shirley Allen *Morgantown, West Virginia*
Bake-Off® Contest 32, 1986

No frosting is needed for this family-pleasing cake, which is also ideal to bring to a potluck or other gathering.

1 (1 lb. 2.25-oz.) pkg. pudding-included yellow cake mix
¹/₂ cup firmly packed brown sugar
1 cup chunky peanut butter
1 cup water
¹/₄ cup oil
3 eggs
¹/₂ cup semi-sweet chocolate chips
¹/₂ cup peanut butter chips*
¹/₂ cup chopped peanuts

Heat oven to 350° F. Grease and flour 13×9-inch pan. In large bowl, combine cake mix, brown sugar

and peanut butter at low speed until crumbly. Reserve ¹/₂ cup peanut butter mixture; set aside. To remaining peanut butter mixture add water, oil and eggs; blend at low speed until moistened. Beat 2 minutes at high speed. Stir ¹/₄ cup of the chocolate chips and ¹/₄ cup of the peanut butter chips into batter. Pour batter into greased and floured pan.

In small bowl, combine reserved ¹/₂ cup peanut butter mixture, remaining chocolate chips and peanuts; sprinkle evenly over batter.

Bake at 350° F. for 40 to 50 minutes or until toothpick inserted in center comes out clean. Immediately sprinkle with remaining peanut butter chips; gently press into top of cake. Cool completely.

Yield: 15 servings

*Tip: Semi-sweet chocolate chips can be substituted for the peanut butter chips.

High Altitude—Above 3,500 feet: Decrease brown sugar to ¹/₄ cup; increase water to 1¹/₄ cups. Add ¹/₄ cup flour with water, oil and eggs. Bake as directed above.

Nutrition Per Serving: Calories 420; Protein 9g; Carbohydrate 46g; Fat 22g; Sodium 380mg

Chocolate Fudge Snack Cake

Nancy Woodside *Sonora, California*
Bake-Off® Contest 34, 1990 Prize Winner

Hot fudge ice cream topping adds extra moistness to this snack cake. Serve it warm with vanilla ice cream for a special treat.

CAKE
¹/₂ cup margarine or butter
1 (11.75-oz.) jar hot fudge ice cream topping
1¹/₂ cups all-purpose flour
1¹/₂ cups sugar
1 cup mashed potato flakes
1 teaspoon baking soda
³/₄ cup buttermilk*
1 teaspoon vanilla
2 eggs
1 cup finely chopped walnuts
1 (6-oz.) pkg. (1 cup) semi-sweet chocolate chips

GLAZE
¹/₂ cup sugar
¹/₄ cup buttermilk**
¹/₄ cup margarine or butter
1¹/₂ teaspoons light corn syrup or water
¹/₄ teaspoon baking soda
¹/₂ teaspoon vanilla
2 tablespoons chopped walnuts

Heat oven to 350° F. Grease and flour 13×9-inch pan. In small saucepan over low heat, melt ¹/₂ cup margarine and fudge topping, stirring constantly until smooth. In large bowl, combine flour and remaining cake ingredients except 1 cup walnuts and chocolate chips; beat at low speed until well blended. Add fudge mixture; beat 2 minutes at medium speed. By hand, stir in 1 cup walnuts and chocolate chips. Pour batter into greased and floured pan.

Bake at 350°F. for 40 to 45 minutes or until toothpick inserted in center comes out clean.

In small saucepan, combine all glaze ingredients except vanilla and 2 tablespoons walnuts. Bring to a boil over medium heat. Reduce heat; simmer 5 minutes or until light golden brown, stirring constantly. Remove from heat; stir in vanilla. Pour warm glaze over warm cake, spreading to cover. Sprinkle with 2 tablespoons walnuts. Serve warm or cool.

Yield: 16 servings

*Tips: To substitute for buttermilk in cake, use 2¼ teaspoons vinegar or lemon juice plus milk to make ¾ cup.

**To substitute for buttermilk in glaze, use ¾ teaspoon vinegar or lemon juice plus milk to make ¼ cup.

High Altitude—Above 3,500 feet: Increase flour to 1¾ cups; decrease sugar in cake to 1 cup. Bake as directed above. Increase simmering time for glaze to 8 minutes.

Nutrition Per Serving: Calories 450; Protein 6g; Carbohydrate 57g; Fat 22g; Sodium 220mg

White Chocolate Fudge Cake

Cindy Henry Redman *Boyne City, Michigan Bake-Off® Contest 36, 1994*

The name says it all—this is indeed a taste creation few people will be able to resist!

FROSTING
1 (16-oz.) can vanilla frosting
3 oz. white baking bar or vanilla-flavored candy coating, melted
1 teaspoon vanilla
1 (8-oz.) container frozen whipped topping, thawed

CAKE
1 (1 lb. 2.25-oz.) pkg. pudding-included white cake mix
1¼ cups water
⅓ cup oil
1 teaspoon vanilla
2 eggs
3 oz. white baking bar or vanilla-flavored candy coating, melted

FUDGE FILLING
¼ cup powdered sugar
1 (6-oz.) pkg. (1 cup) semi-sweet chocolate chips
3 tablespoons margarine or butter
2 tablespoons light corn syrup

GARNISH
Chocolate curls, if desired

In large bowl, beat vanilla frosting at medium speed, gradually adding 3 oz. melted white baking bar. Beat at high speed 30 seconds or until smooth and well blended. Fold in vanilla and whipped topping. Refrigerate.

Heat oven to 350°F. Grease and flour 13×9-inch pan. In large bowl, combine all cake ingredients except white baking bar at low speed until moistened; beat 2 minutes at high speed. Gradually beat in 3 oz. melted white baking bar until well blended. Pour batter into greased and floured pan.

Bake at 350°F. for 25 to 35 minutes or until toothpick inserted in center comes out clean. Cool 10 minutes.

In small saucepan over low heat, heat all fudge filling ingredients until melted and well blended, stirring constantly. Spread fudge filling over warm cake. Cool completely.

Frost cake. Garnish with chocolate curls. Store in refrigerator. Let stand at room temperature 10 minutes before cutting.

Yield: 15 servings

High Altitude—Above 3,500 feet: Add ½ cup flour to dry cake mix. Bake as directed above.

Nutrition Per Serving: Calories 560; Protein 4g; Carbohydrate 72g; Fat 28g; Sodium 330mg

Starlight Double-Delight Cake

Helen Weston *La Jolla, California*
Bake-Off® Contest 3, 1951 Grand Prize Winner

In this unique cake, part of the frosting mixture is used in the cake for a peppermint and chocolate taste treat.

FROSTING
2 (3-oz.) pkg. cream cheese, softened
¹/₂ cup margarine or butter, softened
¹/₂ teaspoon vanilla
¹/₂ teaspoon peppermint extract
6 cups powdered sugar
¹/₄ cup hot water
4 oz. semi-sweet chocolate, melted

CAKE
¹/₄ cup margarine or butter, softened
3 eggs
2 cups all-purpose flour
1¹/₂ teaspoons baking soda
1 teaspoon salt
³/₄ cup milk

Heat oven to 350°F. Grease and flour two 9-inch round cake pans. In large bowl, combine cream cheese, ¹/₂ cup margarine, vanilla and peppermint extract; blend until smooth. Add powdered sugar alternately with hot water, beating until smooth. Blend in chocolate.

In another large bowl, combine 2 cups of the frosting mixture and ¹/₄ cup margarine; blend well. Beat in eggs 1 at a time, beating well after each addition. Add flour, baking soda, salt and milk; beat until smooth. Pour batter evenly into greased and floured pans.

Bake at 350°F. for 30 to 40 minutes or until toothpick inserted in center comes out clean. Cool 5 minutes; remove from pans. Cool completely.

To assemble cake place 1 layer top side down on serving plate; spread with about ¹/₄ of frosting. Top with second layer top side up. Spread sides and top of cake with remaining frosting. Store in refrigerator.

Yield: 12 servings

High Altitude—Above 3,500 feet: Increase flour to 2¹/₂ cups and use 1¹/₂ cups of frosting mixture in cake. Bake as directed above.

Nutrition Per Serving: Calories 530; Protein 6g; Carbohydrate 83g; Fat 21g; Sodium 540mg

Upside-Down German Chocolate Cake

Betty Nelson *Fridley, Minnesota*
Bake-Off® Contest 27, 1976

Next time you want a special cake-to-take, try this one. The cake and frosting bake all in one.

TOPPING
¹/₄ cup margarine or butter
³/₄ cup water
²/₃ cup firmly packed brown sugar
1 cup coconut
1¹/₂ cups miniature marshmallows
¹/₂ cup chopped nuts

CAKE
1 (1 lb. 2.25-oz.) pkg. pudding-included German chocolate cake mix
1 cup water
¹/₂ cup dairy sour cream
¹/₃ cup oil
3 eggs

Heat oven to 350°F. In small saucepan over low heat, melt margarine with ³/₄ cup water. Stir in brown sugar. Pour into ungreased 13×9-inch pan. Sprinkle coconut, marshmallows and nuts evenly over top.

In large bowl, combine all cake ingredients at low speed until moistened; beat 2 minutes at high speed. Spoon batter evenly over topping mixture in pan. Bake at 350°F. for 38 to 48 minutes or until toothpick inserted in center comes out clean. Cool slightly. To serve, cut into squares; transfer and invert onto individual plates. Serve warm or cool.

Yield: 16 servings

High Altitude—Above 3,500 feet: Add 2 tablespoons flour to dry cake mix. Bake at 375°F. for 40 to 50 minutes.

Nutrition Per Serving: Calories 330; Protein 3g; Carbohydrate 42g; Fat 17g; Sodium 270mg

"My Inspiration" Cake

Lois Kanago *Webster, South Dakota*
Bake-Off® Contest 5, 1953 Grand Prize Winner

This cake could inspire a party! Each layer has a ribbon of chocolate running through it and a toasted nut topping baked right in. The layers are attractively put together with buttery chocolate and white frostings. The bonus is that the recipe is even easier to make now, using a cake mix!

CAKE
1 cup chopped pecans
1 (1 lb. 2.25-oz.) pkg. pudding-included white cake mix

1¹/₄ cups water
¹/₄ cup oil
3 egg whites or 2 whole eggs
2 oz. semi-sweet chocolate, grated

FROSTING
¹/₂ cup sugar
2 oz. unsweetened chocolate
¹/₄ cup water
¹/₂ cup margarine or butter, softened
1 teaspoon vanilla
2¹/₄ cups powdered sugar
1 to 2 tablespoons water

Heat oven to 350° F. Grease and flour two 8- or 9-inch round cake pans. Sprinkle pecans evenly over bottom of both greased and floured pans. In large bowl, combine cake mix, 1¹/₄ cups water, oil and egg whites at low speed until moistened; beat 2 minutes at high speed. Carefully spoon ¹/₄ of batter into each nut-lined pan; sprinkle

with grated chocolate. Spoon remaining batter over grated chocolate; spread carefully.

Bake at 350° F. for 20 to 28 minutes or until golden brown and top springs back when touched lightly in center. Cool 15 minutes; remove from pans. Cool completely.

In small saucepan, combine sugar, unsweetened chocolate and ¹/₄ cup water; cook over low heat until melted, stirring constantly until smooth. Remove from heat; cool. In small bowl, combine margarine and vanilla. Gradually add 2 cups of the powdered sugar until well blended. Reserve ¹/₃ cup white frosting. To remaining frosting, add cooled chocolate mixture, remaining ¹/₄ cup powdered sugar and enough water for desired spreading consistency.

To assemble cake, place 1 cake layer, nut side up, on serving plate. Spread top with about ¹/₂ cup chocolate frosting. Top with remaining layer, nut side up. Frost sides and ¹/₂ inch around top edge of cake with remaining chocolate frosting. If necessary, thin reserved white frosting with enough water for desired piping consistency; pipe around edge of nuts on top of cake.

Yield: 16 servings

High Altitude—Above 3,500 feet: Add 3 tablespoons flour to dry cake mix; increase water in cake to 1¹/₃ cups. Bake as directed above.

Nutrition Per Serving: Calories 410; Protein 3g; Carbohydrate 54g; Fat 20g; Sodium 280mg

Tricks of Memory

Any finalist will tell you that nerves are a big part of the Bake-Off® Contest experience. Some contestants, however, are affected more than others.

• Pillsbury asks contestants for any biographical information they would like released, so that interviewers may ask questions that the contestants are comfortable with. At the thirty-second Bake-Off® Contest, one finalist told Pillsbury at length about her large collection of unusual candy jars, but when television host Gary Collins asked her about them she couldn't remember what she collected!

• Art Linkletter, the Bake-Off® Contest's emcee for many years, knew what to expect from America's most ambitious cooks. But no one was more surprised than he when he asked a prize winner what she had baked and she replied, "I forgot!"

• One finalist reported that on the way to the Bake-Off® Contest she handed her bank teller a grocery list to cash instead of a check.

KRISTINA VANNI

There are two kinds of cooks: those who master cooking as adults and those who learn the skill from the cradle, peeking out from their bassinets or playpens, wondering what smells so good and what all the excitement is about.

"I'm from a cooking family," says Kristina Vanni. "My great-grandma taught my grandma, my grandma taught my mom, my mom taught, well—it's just gone on and on. When I was little my mom would be cooking in the kitchen, and even before I was in school, I would just sit there and watch. So I think I absorbed a whole lot just by watching—I always liked to play with the flour; it was my little indoor sandbox."

This chain of cooks and cooking resulted in something truly extraordinary: Both Kristina and

her grandmother, Pat Bradley, won trips to the thirty-fifth Bake-Off® Contest. Kristina certainly proved herself a great up-and-coming cook that year, capturing a cash prize (just like grandma) for her Raspberry-Filled Apricot Cake—a crowd-pleasing, low-calorie dessert.

"Cooking is definitely a family thing," says Kristina. "If my grandma's over, it's bonding time. The kitchen is the center of the house, the place everyone passes through. It's where a lot of things go on—it's always a nice warm place." The warmth comes from both the cranked-up oven and burners, and the spirit of nurturing when it's occupied by families that support creativity, and each other, so well.

Raspberry-Filled Apricot Cake

Kristina Vanni *Libertyville, Illinois*
Bake-Off® Contest 35, 1992 Prize Winner

This prize-winning apricot-flavored cake looks like a dream, tastes wonderfully delicious and is ideal for calorie counters!

CAKE
1 (1 lb. 2.25-oz.) pkg. pudding-included yellow cake mix

1¹/₃ cups apricot nectar
2 eggs

FILLING
1 cup raspberry spreadable fruit or jam

FROSTING
1 (1-oz.) pkg. sugar-free instant vanilla pudding and pie filling mix
¹/₂ cup skim or low-fat milk
2 tablespoons apricot nectar
1 (8-oz.) container frozen light whipped topping, thawed
3 tablespoons coconut, toasted*

Heat oven to 350° F. Lightly grease and flour two 9- or 8-inch round cake pans. In large bowl, combine cake mix, 1¹/₃ cups apricot nectar and eggs at low speed until moistened; beat 2 minutes at high speed. Pour into greased and floured pans.

Bake at 350° F. for 25 to 35 minutes or until toothpick inserted in center comes out clean. Cool 15 minutes; remove from pans. Cool completely.

To assemble cake, slice each cake layer in half horizontally to make 4 layers. Place 1 cake layer cut side up on serving plate; spread with ¹/₃ cup spreadable fruit. Repeat with second and third cake layers and spreadable fruit. Top with remaining cake layer.

In small bowl, combine pudding mix, milk and 2 tablespoons apricot nectar; blend well. Add thawed whipped topping; beat at low speed for 2 minutes. Frost sides and top of cake. Sprinkle top with toasted coconut. Refrigerate at least 2 hours before serving. Store in refrigerator.

Yield: 16 servings

*Tip: To toast coconut, spread on cookie sheet; bake at 350° F. for 7 to 8 minutes or until light golden brown, stirring occasionally. Or spread in thin layer in microwave-safe pie pan. Microwave on LOW for 4¹/₂ to 8 minutes or until light golden brown, tossing with fork after each minute.

High Altitude—Above 3,500 feet: Add ¹/₃ cup flour to dry cake mix. Bake at 350° F. for 25 to 35 minutes. (Bake 8-inch pans 30 to 40 minutes.)

Nutrition Per Serving: Calories 250; Protein 2g; Carbohydrate 47g; Fat 6g; Sodium 310mg

Costa Rican Cream Cake

Janice Weinrick *La Mesa, California Bake-Off® Contest 34, 1990 Prize Winner*

This recipe is a version of a popular dessert from Central America. And because it's made as a sheet cake, it's easy to prepare and serve.

CAKE
1 (1 lb. 2.25-oz.) pkg. pudding-included yellow cake mix
1 cup water
¹/₃ cup oil
3 eggs

SAUCE
1 cup whipping cream
¹/₃ cup rum, or 1 teaspoon rum extract plus ¹/₃ cup water
1 (14-oz.) can sweetened condensed milk (not evaporated)
1 (12-oz.) can evaporated milk

TOPPING
1 cup whipping cream
¹/₃ cup coconut, toasted*
¹/₃ cup chopped macadamia nuts

Heat oven to 350° F. Grease 13×9-inch (3-quart) baking dish. In large bowl, combine all cake ingredients at low speed until moistened; beat 2 minutes at high speed. Pour into greased dish. Bake at 350° F. for 25 to 35 minutes or until toothpick inserted in center comes out clean.

While cake is baking, in large bowl, combine all sauce ingredients; blend well. Remove cake from oven; cool 5 minutes. Using long-tined fork, pierce hot cake in pan every 1 to 2 inches. Slowly pour sauce mixture over cake. Do not cover cake; refrigerate at least 3 hours to chill. (Cake will absorb most of sauce mixture.)

Before serving, in small bowl, beat 1 cup whipping cream until stiff peaks form. Spread over cold cake. Sprinkle with coconut and macadamia nuts. Store in refrigerator.

Yield: 15 servings

*Tip: To toast coconut, spread on cookie sheet; bake at 350° F. for 7 to 8 minutes or until light golden brown, stirring occasionally. Or spread in thin layer in microwave-safe pie pan. Microwave on LOW for 4¹/₂ to 8 minutes or until light golden brown, tossing with fork after each minute.

High Altitude—Above 3,500 feet: Add ¹/₃ cup flour to dry cake mix; increase water by 2 tablespoons. Bake as directed above.

Nutrition Per Serving: Calories 470; Protein 7g; Carbohydrate 47g; Fat 27g; Sodium 310mg

Janice Weinrick: Costa Rican Cream Cake

Bake-Off® winners' creativity is not confined to their cooking. Janice Weinrick was equally innovative when deciding what name to use after she was married. "In keeping with merger mania," Janice tells us, "we took half of my husband Michael's name (Weintraub) and half of mine (Myrick) and created the name 'Weinrick,' which became our legally married name." With her mind again on mergers, Janice adapted a traditional Costa Rican Cream Cake for the contemporary American kitchen, proving that doing things by half measures is sometimes a brilliant solution.

Heavenly Hawaiian Cake Roll

Judith Merritt *Syracuse, New York*
Bake-Off® Contest 33, 1988

It is important that the baking pan used in this recipe be at least 1 inch deep to prevent the batter from over-flowing. Some 15×10-inch pans are not as deep, so check yours before pouring in the batter.

FILLING
$1/3$ cup butter or margarine, melted
$1/2$ cup firmly packed brown sugar
1 cup coconut
2 tablespoons chopped maraschino cherries
1 (8-oz.) can crushed pineapple in unsweetened juice, well drained, reserving $1/2$ cup liquid

CAKE
Powdered sugar
3 eggs
1 cup sugar
Reserved $1/2$ cup pineapple liquid
1 cup all-purpose flour
1 teaspoon baking powder
$1/4$ teaspoon salt

TOPPING
$1/2$ cup whipping cream
2 tablespoons powdered sugar
$1/2$ teaspoon vanilla
$1/4$ cup chopped macadamia nuts, toasted*

Heat oven to 375°F. Line 15×10×1-inch baking pan with foil. Spread butter evenly in bottom of pan; sprinkle with brown sugar. Sprinkle coconut, maraschino cherries and pineapple evenly over brown sugar; lightly press down. Set aside.

Lightly sprinkle clean towel with powdered sugar; set aside. In small bowl, beat eggs at high speed until thick and lemon colored, about 5 minutes. Gradually add sugar; beat well. If necessary, add enough water to reserved pineapple liquid to measure $1/2$ cup. At low speed, add reserved pineapple liquid; blend well. Add flour, baking powder and salt; beat until smooth. Spread evenly over filling mixture in pan.

Bake at 375°F. for 13 to 18 minutes or until top springs back when touched lightly in center. Invert cake onto sugared side of towel. Gently lift sides of foil from cake; carefully remove foil. Starting with shorter end and using towel to guide cake, roll up. (Do not roll towel into cake.) Wrap towel around rolled cake; cool completely on wire rack.

In small bowl, combine whipping cream, powdered sugar and vanilla; beat until stiff peaks form. Place cake roll on serving plate, seam side down. Spread topping over sides and top of cake roll; sprinkle with nuts. Store in refrigerator.

Yield: 12 servings

*Tip: Chopped, toasted almonds or pecans can be substituted for maca-damia nuts. To toast macadamia nuts, spread nuts on a cookie sheet; bake at 350°F. for 5 to 10 minutes or until light golden brown, stirring occasionally. Or, spread nuts in a single layer on microwave-safe pan. Microwave on HIGH for 4 to 8 minutes or until light golden brown, stirring frequently.

High Altitude—Above 3,500 feet: No change.

Nutrition Per Serving: Calories 300; Protein 3g; Carbohydrate 41g; Fat 14g; Sodium 140mg

Chocolate 'Tato Cake

Rosalie Giuffre *Milwaukee, Wisconsin*
Bake-Off® Contest 13, 1961

When convenience products were still new, a quick tip in the original 1961 recipe was to use reconstituted mashed potato flakes for the cooked fresh potato. Now they are included in the recipe, where they help keep this chocolate-glazed tube cake moist and delicious.

CAKE
4 oz. sweet cooking chocolate
1 cup mashed potato flakes
1 cup boiling water
$1 1/2$ cups all-purpose flour
$1 1/4$ cups sugar
$1 1/4$ teaspoons baking soda
1 teaspoon salt
1 teaspoon vanilla
$1/2$ cup margarine, softened, or shortening
$1/2$ cup dairy sour cream
3 eggs
$1/2$ cup chopped pecans, if desired

GLAZE
2 oz. sweet cooking chocolate
1 tablespoon water
1 tablespoon margarine or butter
$1/2$ cup powdered sugar
$1/4$ teaspoon vanilla
Dash salt

Heat oven to 350° F. Generously grease 12-cup Bundt or 10-inch tube pan. Break 4 oz. chocolate into pieces; place in large bowl. Add potato flakes; pour boiling water over flakes and chocolate. Let stand 5 minutes or until potato flakes are softened and chocolate is melted; stir to combine. Add flour and remaining cake ingredients except pecans. Blend at low speed until moistened; beat 3 minutes at medium speed. Stir in pecans. Pour batter into greased pan.

Bake at 350° F. for 45 to 60 minutes or until toothpick inserted near center comes out clean. Cool upright in pan 30 minutes; invert onto serving plate. Cool completely.

In small saucepan over low heat, melt 2 oz. chocolate with water and margarine. Remove from heat; add powdered sugar, 1/4 teaspoon vanilla and dash salt, beating until smooth. Stir in additional water, a few drops at a time, if needed for desired glaze consistency.

Immediately spoon glaze over cooled cake, allowing some to run down sides.

Yield: 20 servings

High Altitude—Above 3,500 feet: Decrease sugar to 1 cup. Bake as directed above.

Nutrition Per Serving: Calories 240; Protein 3g; Carbohydrate 30g; Fat 12g; Sodium 260mg

***Top to bottom:* Chocolate 'Tato Cake, Upside-Down German Chocolate Cake, page 247**

Buttercream Pound Cake

Phyllis Lidert *Oak Lawn, Illinois*
Bake-Off® Contest 19, 1968 Grand Prize Winner

This lemon-poppy seed pound cake was so popular that Pillsbury developed a similar scratch recipe after a frosting mix, a key cake ingredient in the original recipe, no longer was available.

CAKE

1 lb. (2 cups) butter, softened (do not use margarine)
2¹/₂ cups powdered sugar
6 eggs
2 teaspoons grated lemon peel
3 tablespoons lemon juice
4 cups all-purpose flour
1 tablespoon baking powder
1 (12¹/₂-oz.) can poppy seed filling

GLAZE

1 cup powdered sugar
1 to 2 tablespoons lemon juice or milk

Heat oven to 350°F. In large bowl, beat butter until light and fluffy. Gradually add powdered sugar; mix well. At medium speed, add eggs 1 at a time, beating well after each addition. Beat in lemon peel and 3 tablespoons lemon juice. At low speed, gradually beat in flour and baking powder; blend well.

In medium bowl, combine 3 cups batter with poppy seed filling; blend well. Spread half of plain batter over bottom of ungreased 10-inch tube pan. Alternately add spoonfuls of poppy seed batter and remaining plain batter.

Bake at 350°F. for 1 hour and 15 minutes to 1 hour and 25 minutes or until toothpick inserted near ceter comes out clean. Cool 15 minutes; remove from pan. Cool completely.

In small bowl, combine glaze ingredients, adding enough lemon juice for desired drizzling consistency; blend until smooth. Drizzle over cake.

Yield: 16 servings

High Altitude—Above 3,500 feet: Increase flour in cake to 4¹/₂ cups. Bake as directed above.

Nutrition Per Serving: Calories 510; Protein 7g; Carbohydrate 62g; Fat 27g; Sodium 360mg

Almond Mocha Cake

Debbie Russell *Colorado Springs, Colorado*
Bake-Off® Contest 33, 1988

"It melts in your mouth" describes the texture of this brownielike chocolate cake. Coffee and amaretto enhance its deep dark chocolate flavor.

¹/₂ cup chopped almonds
1¹/₄ cups strong coffee*
¹/₂ cup margarine or butter
1 (12-oz.) pkg. (2 cups) semi-sweet chocolate chips
1 cup sugar
¹/₄ cup amaretto or 2 teaspoons almond extract*
2 cups all-purpose flour
1 teaspoon baking soda
1 teaspoon vanilla
2 eggs
Powdered sugar

Heat oven to 325°F. Generously grease 12-cup Bundt or 10-inch tube pan. Gently press almonds in bottom and half way up sides of greased pan. In medium saucepan over low heat, warm coffee. Add margarine and chocolate chips; cook until mixture is smooth, stirring constantly. Remove from heat; stir in sugar and amaretto. Place in large bowl; cool 5 minutes.

At low speed, gradually blend flour and baking soda into chocolate mixture until moistened. Add vanilla and eggs; beat at medium speed about 30 seconds or just until well blended. Pour into greased and nut-lined pan.

Bake at 325°F. for 60 to 75 minutes or until toothpick inserted in center comes out clean. Cool upright in pan 25 minutes; invert onto serving plate. Cool completely; sprinkle with powdered sugar.

Yield: 16 servings

Debbie Russell: Almond Mocha Cake

Setting out after new recipes takes a certain amount of bravery and self-confidence—the confidence that your ideas are good ones, and the bravery to accept failures without too much embarrassment. Both Bake-Off® finalist Debbie Russell and her husband certainly don't lack bravery. "I met him in a canoe, we became engaged in a hot air balloon and we spent our honeymoon sailing and scuba diving," Debbie recalls. "My husband and I are both adventurous, daring and eat anything. I enjoy experimenting with foods on him." When these experiments result in Almond Mocha Cake, it's a good guess that Debbie's husband enjoys her experiments.

*Tip: If using almond extract for amaretto, increase coffee to 1^1/$_2$ cups.

High Altitude—Above 3,500 feet: No change.

Nutrition Per Serving: Calories 320; Protein 4g; Carbohydrate 41g; Fat 16g; Sodium 150mg

Black Bottom Cups

Doris Geisert *Orange, California*
Bake-Off® Contest 13, 1961 Prize Winner

In this Bake-Off® Contest favorite, a delicate cream cheese filling is surrounded by moist and tender chocolate cake. For best results, bake these cupcakes in muffin cups lined with paper baking cups.

2 (3-oz.) pkg. cream cheese, softened
^{1}/$_3$ cup sugar
1 egg
1 (6-oz.) pkg. (1 cup) semisweet chocolate chips
1^1/$_2$ cups all-purpose flour
1 cup sugar
^{1}/$_4$ cup unsweetened cocoa
1 teaspoon baking soda
^{1}/$_2$ teaspoon salt
1 cup water
^{1}/$_3$ cup oil
1 tablespoon vinegar
1 teaspoon vanilla
^{1}/$_2$ cup chopped almonds, if desired
2 tablespoons sugar, if desired

Heat oven to 350°F. Line 18 muffin cups with paper baking cups. In small bowl, combine cream cheese, ^{1}/$_3$ cup sugar and egg; mix

well. Stir in chocolate chips; set aside. In large bowl, combine flour, 1 cup sugar, cocoa, baking soda and salt. Add water, oil, vinegar and vanilla; beat 2 minutes at medium speed. Fill paper-lined muffin cups ^{1}/$_2$ full. Top each with 1 tablespoon cream cheese mixture. Combine almonds and 2 tablespoons sugar; sprinkle evenly over cream cheese mixture.

Bake at 350°F. for 20 to 30 minutes or until cream cheese mixture is light golden brown. Cool 15 minutes; remove from pans. Cool completely. Store in refrigerator.

Yield: 18 servings
(1 cupcake per serving)

High Altitude—Above 3,500 feet: No change.

Nutrition Per Serving: Calories 250; Protein 3g; Carbohydrate 31g; Fat 13g; Sodium 160mg

Swiss Almond Apple Cake

Stephen Hill *Sacramento, California*
Bake-Off® Contest 33, 1988

Serve this European-style cake for dessert or anytime with coffee or tea. Sliced apples, a rippling of raspberry preserves and ground almonds make the cake an extra-special delicacy.

CAKE
^{2}/$_3$ cup sugar
^{1}/$_2$ cup butter or margarine, softened
2 eggs
2 tablespoons lemon juice
2 cups all-purpose flour
2 teaspoons baking powder

^{1}/$_4$ teaspoon salt
^{1}/$_4$ cup raspberry preserves
4 apples, peeled, thinly sliced (3^1/$_2$ cups)

TOPPING
1 cup ground almonds
^{1}/$_2$ cup sugar
^{1}/$_2$ cup dairy sour cream
2 eggs, beaten
2 tablespoons all-purpose flour
1 teaspoon grated lemon peel

GLAZE
^{1}/$_4$ cup powdered sugar
1 to 2 teaspoons lemon juice

Heat oven to 350°F. Grease and flour 9- or 10-inch springform pan. In large bowl, combine ^{2}/$_3$ cup sugar and butter; beat until light and fluffy. Add 2 eggs and 2 tablespoons lemon juice; beat until well blended. In small bowl, combine 2 cups flour, baking powder and salt; mix well. Add to egg mixture; beat at low speed until well blended. Spread in greased and floured pan. Spoon preserves over batter; carefully spread to cover. Top with apple slices; slightly press into batter. In medium bowl, combine all topping ingredients; blend well. Pour over apples.

Bake at 350°F. for 55 to 65 minutes or until apples are tender, edges are light golden brown and toothpick inserted in center comes out clean. Cool 10 minutes. Carefully remove sides of pan. In small bowl, blend all glaze ingredients until smooth; drizzle over cake. Serve warm or cool.

Yield: 16 servings

High Altitude—Above 3,500 feet: No change.

Nutrition Per Serving: Calories 280; Protein 5g; Carbohydrate 39g; Fat 12g; Sodium 150mg

Nutty Graham Picnic Cake

Esther Tomich *San Pedro, California Bake-Off® Contest 28, 1978 Grand Prize Winner*

The growing interest in whole grains and homespun foods in the 1970s was reflected in Bake-Off® entries. So it's not surprising that a great-tasting cake that included crushed graham crackers, orange juice and nuts would gain the approval of Bake-Off® judges.

CAKE
- 2 cups all-purpose flour
- 1 cup (14 squares) finely crushed graham crackers or graham cracker crumbs
- 1 cup firmly packed brown sugar
- 1/2 cup sugar
- 1 teaspoon baking powder
- 1 teaspoon baking soda
- 1 teaspoon salt
- 1/2 teaspoon cinnamon
- 1 cup margarine or butter, softened
- 1 cup orange juice
- 1 tablespoon grated orange peel
- 3 eggs
- 1 cup chopped nuts

GLAZE
- 2 tablespoons brown sugar
- 5 teaspoons milk
- 1 tablespoon margarine or butter
- 3/4 cup powdered sugar
- 1/4 cup chopped nuts

Heat oven to 350° F. Generously grease and flour 12-cup Bundt pan

Top to bottom: **Nutty Graham Picnic Cake, Streusel Spice Cake, page 263**

or 10-inch tube pan. In large bowl, combine all cake ingredients except nuts; beat 3 minutes at medium speed. By hand, stir in 1 cup nuts. Pour batter into greased and floured pan.

Bake at 350° F. for 40 to 60 minutes or until toothpick inserted in center comes out clean. Cool upright in pan 15 minutes; invert onto serving plate. Cool completely.

In small saucepan, combine 2 tablespoons brown sugar, milk and 1 tablespoon margarine; cook over low heat just until sugar is dissolved, stirring constantly. Remove from heat. Stir in powdered sugar; blend until smooth. Drizzle over cake; sprinkle with 1/4 cup nuts.

Yield: 16 servings

High Altitude—Above 3,500 feet: No change.

Nutrition Per Serving: Calories 370; Protein 5g; Carbohydrate 47g; Fat 20g; Sodium 440m

Spicy Raisin Brunch Cake

Shirley A. Domeier *New Ulm, Minnesota Bake-Off® Contest 32, 1986 Prize Winner*

This versatile raisin-nut Bundt cake is just right for snacks and family dessert, as well as a sweet finale when you entertain at brunch.

CAKE
- 2 cups all-purpose flour
- 1/2 cup raisins
- 1/2 cup chopped walnuts
- 1/2 teaspoon baking soda
- 1 1/2 teaspoons pumpkin pie spice

- 1/4 to 1/2 teaspoon cloves
- 1 cup firmly packed brown sugar
- 1/2 cup apricot preserves
- 1/2 cup margarine or butter, softened
- 2 tablespoons rum or 1/2 teaspoon rum extract
- 4 eggs
- 2/3 cup buttermilk*

GLAZE
- 1 cup powdered sugar
- 1 teaspoon margarine or butter, softened
- 1/2 teaspoon rum, if desired
- 5 to 6 teaspoons milk

Heat oven to 350° F. Grease and flour 12-cup Bundt pan. In medium bowl, combine flour, raisins, walnuts, baking soda, pumpkin pie spice and cloves; set aside. In large bowl, combine brown sugar, preserves, margarine, rum and eggs; beat well. Alternately add flour mixture and buttermilk to sugar mixture, beating well after each addition. Pour batter into greased and floured pan.

Bake at 350° F. for 40 to 50 minutes or until toothpick inserted in center comes out clean. Cool upright in pan for 45 minutes. Invert onto serving plate.

In small bowl, combine all glaze ingredients until smooth; drizzle over cake. Store frosted cake loosely covered.

Yield: 16 servings

*Tip: To substitute for buttermilk, use 2 teaspoons vinegar or lemon juice plus milk to make 2/3 cup.

High Altitude—Above 3,500 feet: No change.

Nutrition Per Serving: Calories 280; Protein 4g; Carbohydrate 44g; Fat 10g; Sodium 140mg

Kentucky Butter Cake

Nell Lewis *Platte City, Missouri*
Bake-Off® Contest 15, 1963

This was the year the contest became popularly known simply as "the Bake-Off®." Old family recipes were still eligible, if they had a new twist. Here the idea was the hot butter sauce poured slowly over the buttermilk pound cake as it came from the oven.

CAKE
3 cups all-purpose flour
2 cups sugar
1 teaspoon salt
1 teaspoon baking powder
1/2 teaspoon baking soda
1 cup buttermilk*
1 cup butter or margarine, softened
2 teaspoons vanilla or rum extract
4 eggs

BUTTER SAUCE
3/4 cup sugar
1/3 cup butter or margarine
3 tablespoons water
1 to 2 teaspoons vanilla or rum extract

GARNISH
2 to 3 teaspoons powdered sugar

Heat oven to 325°F. Generously grease and lightly flour 12-cup Bundt pan or 10-inch tube pan. In large bowl, combine all cake ingredients; blend at low speed until moistened. Beat 3 minutes at medium speed. Pour batter into greased and floured pan.

Bake at 325°F. for 55 to 70 minutes or until toothpick inserted in center comes out clean.

In small saucepan, combine all sauce ingredients; cook over low heat, stirring occasionally, until butter melts. DO NOT BOIL. Using long-tined fork, pierce cake 10 to 12 times. Slowly pour hot sauce over warm cake. Let stand 5 to 10 minutes or until sauce is absorbed. Invert cake onto serving plate. Just before serving, sprinkle with powdered sugar. Serve with whipped cream, if desired.

Yield: 12 servings

*Tip: To substitute for buttermilk, use 1 tablespoon vinegar or lemon juice plus milk to make 1 cup.

High Altitude—Above 3,500 feet: Decrease sugar in cake to 1³/4 cups; increase buttermilk to 1 cup plus 2 tablespoons. Bake at 350°F. for 60 to 70 minutes.

Nutrition Per Serving: Calories 510; Protein 6g; Carbohydrate 72g; Fat 23g; Sodium 520mg

Peppermint Swirl Fudge Nut Cake

Elsie Wigdahl *Ruthven, Iowa*
Bake-Off® Contest 28, 1978

Here's a chocolate cake that's made with white cake mix! The reason: with the addition of crème de menthe syrup, half the batter becomes the green peppermint swirl. The result: A picture-pretty cake that tastes as good as it looks.

CAKE
1 (1 lb. 2.25-oz.) pkg. pudding-included white cake mix
1 (3-oz.) pkg. cream cheese, softened
1/2 cup water
1/4 cup oil
3 eggs
1/4 cup crème de menthe syrup
1/2 teaspoon peppermint extract
4 oz. (4 squares) semi-sweet chocolate, melted
3 tablespoons water
1/4 cup finely chopped walnuts

GLAZE
1 oz. (1 square) semi-sweet chocolate
1 cup powdered sugar
2 to 3 tablespoons water

Heat oven to 350°F. Generously grease and flour 12-cup Bundt pan or 10-inch tube pan. In large bowl, combine cake mix, cream cheese, 1/2 cup water, oil and eggs at low speed until moistened; beat 2 minutes at high speed. Place 1¹/2 cups

batter in small bowl; stir in crème de menthe syrup and peppermint extract until well blended. Set aside. To remaining batter, add 4 oz. melted chocolate and 3 tablespoons water; blend well. Stir in walnuts. Spoon half of chocolate batter into greased and floured pan. Spoon peppermint batter randomly over chocolate batter; top with remaining chocolate batter. Pull knife through batter from top to bottom in a folding motion, turning pan while folding.

Bake at 350° F. for 40 to 50 minutes or until cake springs back when touched lightly near center. Cool upright in pan 30 minutes; turn out onto serving plate. Cool completely.

In small saucepan, melt 1 oz. chocolate; stir in powdered sugar and enough water for desired drizzling consistency. Spoon glaze over cake, allowing some to run down sides. Store in refrigerator.

Yield: 16 servings

High Altitude—Above 3,500 feet: Add ¹/₄ cup flour to dry cake mix. Bake as directed above.

Nutrition Per Serving: Calories 310; Protein 4g; Carbohydrate 43g; Fat 13g; Sodium 240mg

Peppermint Swirl Fudge Nut Cake

Delicate Pear Cake with Caramel Sauce

Jacqueline McComas *Frazer, Pennsylvania*
Bake-Off® Contest 34, 1990

This sensational cake dessert helped set the trend at the thirty-fourth contest for beautifully presented, indulgent desserts. Your guests will love it!

CAKE
1 (16-oz.) can pear halves in
    light syrup
1 (1 lb. 2.25-oz.) pkg.
    pudding-included white
    cake mix
1/3 cup oil
3 egg whites

FROSTING
1 cup whipping cream
2 tablespoons sugar
1 tablespoon pear brandy or
    1 teaspoon vanilla
1 (16-oz.) can pear halves in
    light syrup, drained
1/2 cup finely chopped
    hazelnuts or walnuts,
    toasted*

SAUCE
1 cup firmly packed brown
    sugar
1 cup whipping cream
1/2 cup butter or margarine

Heat oven to 350° F. Grease and flour 10-inch tube pan. Drain pear halves, reserving 1/3 cup liquid. Place pear halves in food processor bowl with metal blade or blender container; process until smooth.

In large bowl, combine cake mix, pureed pears, reserved 1/3 cup pear liquid, oil and egg whites at low speed until moistened; beat 2 minutes at high speed. Pour into greased and floured pan.

Bake at 350° F. for 40 to 45 minutes or until toothpick inserted in center comes out clean. Cool upright in pan 15 minutes; invert onto serving plate. Cool completely.

In small bowl, beat 1 cup whipping cream and sugar until stiff peaks form. Fold in pear brandy. Frost cooled cake with whipped cream. Cut drained pear halves lengthwise into about 32 slices. Arrange on top of cake, slightly overlapping slices. Press nuts into sides of cake. Refrigerate until serving time.

In medium saucepan, combine all sauce ingredients; mix well. Bring to a boil. Boil over medium heat 5 minutes, stirring occasionally. Remove from heat. Cool to room temperature. Drizzle 2 tablespoons sauce over pear slices.

To serve, spoon about 2 tablespoons sauce onto individual dessert plates. Place slice of cake on sauce. Store cake and sauce in refrigerator.

Yield: 16 servings

*Tip: To toast hazelnuts, spread on cookie sheet; bake at 350° F. for 8 to 10 minutes or until golden brown, stirring occasionally. Or spread in microwave-safe pie pan. Microwave on HIGH for 7 to 8 minutes or until golden brown, stirring frequently.

High Altitude—Above 3,500 feet: Add 1/4 cup flour to dry cake mix. Bake as directed above.

Nutrition Per Serving: Calories 460; Protein 3g; Carbohydrate 50g; Fat 27g; Sodium 290mg

Banana Crunch Cake

Bonnie Brooks *Salisbury, Maryland*
Bake-Off® Contest 24, 1973 Grand Prize Winner

Thrifty Bonnie Brooks wanted to use up two overripe bananas. Starting with a cake mix, she created a lovely tube cake, layered and topped with crunchy streusel. It's still worthy of a grand prize.

1/2 cup all-purpose flour
1 cup coconut
1 cup rolled oats
3/4 cup firmly packed brown
    sugar
1/2 cup chopped pecans
1/2 cup margarine or butter
1 1/2 cups (2 large) sliced *very ripe* bananas
1/2 cup dairy sour cream
4 eggs
1 (1 lb. 2.25-oz.) pkg.
    pudding-included yellow
    cake mix

Heat oven to 350° F. Grease and flour 10-inch tube pan. In medium bowl, combine flour, coconut, rolled oats, brown sugar and pecans; mix well. Using fork or pastry blender, cut in margarine until mixture is crumbly; set aside.

In large bowl, combine bananas, sour cream and eggs; blend until smooth. Add cake mix; beat 2 minutes at high speed. Spread 1/3 of batter in greased and floured pan; sprinkle with 1/3 of coconut mixture. Repeat layers 2 more times using remaining

Delicate Pear Cake with Caramel Sauce

batter and coconut mixture, ending with coconut mixture.

Bake at 350° F. for 50 to 60 minutes or until toothpick inserted near center comes out clean. Cool upright in pan 15 minutes; remove from pan. Place on serving plate, coconut side up. Cool completely.

Yield: 16 servings

High Altitude—Above 3,500 feet: Add 3 tablespoons flour to dry cake mix. Bake at 375° F. for 45 to 55 minutes.

Nutrition Per Serving: Calories 360; Protein 5g; Carbohydrate 49g; Fat 16g; Sodium 320mg

Ella Rita Helfrich: Tunnel of Fudge Cake

Did someone invent birthday candles? Christmas trees? Jack-o'-lanterns? If someone did, that someone deserves applause for introducing a whole lot of happiness into a whole bunch of lives.

And who came up with taffy apples? Chocolate truffles? Pecan pralines? No one knows, but we know for sure that someone did invent the Tunnel of Fudge Cake, and that someone was Ella Rita Helfrich. She spent days of "trial-and-error baking" to come up with the distinctive treat, and her cake has become an American classic, one which hundreds of thousands of people make for their special celebrations.

Tunnel of Fudge Cake

Ella Rita Helfrich *Houston, Texas*
Bake-Off® Contest 17, 1966 Prize Winner

The recipe arguably the most closely identified with the Bake-Off® Contest, this divine chocolate cake mysteriously develops a "tunnel of fudge" filling as it bakes. Don't scrimp on the nuts, or it won't work!

CAKE
1³/₄ cups sugar
1³/₄ cups margarine or butter, softened
6 eggs
2 cups powdered sugar
2¹/₄ cups all-purpose flour
³/₄ cup unsweetened cocoa
2 cups chopped walnuts*

GLAZE
³/₄ cup powdered sugar
¹/₄ cup unsweetened cocoa
4 to 6 teaspoons milk

Heat oven to 350° F. Grease and flour 12-cup Bundt pan or 10-inch tube pan. In large bowl, combine sugar and margarine; beat until light and fluffy. Add eggs 1 at a time, beating well after each addition. Gradually add 2 cups powdered sugar; blend well. By hand, stir in flour and remaining cake ingredients until well blended. Spoon batter into greased and floured pan; spread evenly.

Bake at 350° F. for 45 to 50 minutes or until top is set and edges are beginning to pull away from sides of pan.** Cool upright in pan on wire rack for 1½ hours. Invert onto serving plate; cool at least 2 hours.

In small bowl, combine all glaze ingredients, adding enough milk for desired drizzling consistency. Spoon over top of cake, allowing some to run down sides. Store tightly covered.

Yield: 16 servings

***Tips:** Nuts are essential for the success of this recipe.

****Since this cake has a soft filling, an ordinary doneness test cannot be used. Accurate oven temperature and baking times are essential.

High Altitude—Above 3,500 feet: Increase flour to 2¹/₄ cups plus 3 tablespoons. Bake as directed above.

Nutrition Per Serving: Calories 550; Protein 8g; Carbohydrate 58g; Fat 32g; Sodium 300mg

Brownie Soufflé Cake with Mint Cream

Edwina Gadsby *Great Falls, Montana*
Bake-Off® Contest 38, 1998 Prize Winner

Here's a dessert to exhilarate the senses. Topped by a luxuriously light white chocolate and mint cream, this decadent fudge brownie cake will be an unmistakable taste sensation.

MINT CREAM
²/₃ cup whipping cream
3 oz. white chocolate baking bar, finely chopped
¹/₄ to ¹/₂ teaspoon mint extract

CAKE
1 (1 lb. 3.5-oz.) pkg. fudge brownie mix
¹/₂ cup water

½ cup oil
½ to 1 teaspoon mint extract,
  if desired
4 eggs, separated
Powdered sugar
Mint sprigs, if desired

Heat oven to 375° F. Spray 9- or
10-inch springform pan with nonstick cooking spray. In medium
microwave-safe bowl, microwave
whipping cream on HIGH for 45 to
60 seconds or until warm. Add
white chocolate and ¼ to ½ teaspoon mint extract; stir until chocolate is melted. Refrigerate at least 1
hour or until well chilled.

Meanwhile, in large bowl, combine brownie mix, water, oil, ½ to 1
teaspoon mint extract and egg
yolks; beat 50 strokes with spoon.
In small bowl, beat egg whites until
soft peaks form. Gradually fold into
brownie mixture. Pour batter into
sprayed pan.

Bake at 375° F. for 32 to 38
minutes or until center is almost
set. Cool 30 minutes. (Center will
sink slightly.) Carefully remove
sides of pan. Sprinkle top of cake
with powdered sugar.

Just before serving, beat chilled
mint cream until soft peaks form.
Cut cake into wedges; top each
wedge with mint cream. Garnish
with mint sprigs. Refrigerate leftover mint cream.

Yield: 12 servings

High Altitude—Above 3,500 feet:
Add ½ cup flour to dry brownie
mix. Decrease water to ⅓ cup;
decrease oil to ⅓ cup. Bake at
375° F. for 31 to 36 minutes.

Nutrition Per Serving: Calories 390; Protein 5g;
Carbohydrate 43g; Fat 22g; Sodium 160mg

Streusel Spice Cake

Rose DeDominicis *Verona, Pennsylvania
Bake-Off® Contest 23, 1972 Grand
Prize Winner*

Streusel *is a German word for "sprinkle" or "strew." This spicy streusel filling is combined with chocolate for an
extra-special cake.*

CAKE
1 (1 lb. 2.25-oz.) pkg.
  pudding-included yellow cake
  mix
¾ cup milk
½ cup margarine or butter,
  softened
5 eggs
¼ cup coconut
¼ cup chopped nuts
1 oz. unsweetened chocolate,
  melted

FILLING
½ cup coconut
½ cup chopped nuts
½ cup firmly packed brown
  sugar
2 tablespoons all-purpose flour
2 teaspoons cinnamon

GLAZE
1 cup powdered sugar
1 tablespoon margarine or
  butter, softened
2 to 3 tablespoons milk

Heat oven to 350° F. Grease and
flour 10-inch tube or 12-cup Bundt
pan. In large bowl, combine cake
mix, ¾ cup milk, ½ cup margarine
and eggs at low speed until moistened; beat 2 minutes at high speed.
Stir in ¼ cup coconut and ¼ cup

nuts. With spoon, marble chocolate
through batter. Pour half of batter
(about 2 cups) into greased and
floured pan.

In small bowl, combine all filling ingredients; reserve ½ cup filling. Sprinkle remaining filling over
batter in pan. Cover with remaining
batter; sprinkle with ½ cup
reserved filling.

Bake at 350° F. for 55 to 70
minutes or until toothpick inserted
near center comes out clean. Cool
upright in pan 30 minutes. Remove
from pan. Cool completely.

In small bowl, blend all glaze
ingredients until smooth, adding
enough milk for desired drizzling
consistency. Drizzle over cake.

Yield: 16 servings

High Altitude—Above 3,500 feet:
Add ⅓ cup flour to dry cake
mix. Bake at 375° F. for 45 to
55 minutes.

Nutrition Per Serving: Calories 350; Protein 5g;
Carbohydrate 45g; Fat 17g; Sodium 330mg

Lemon Platinum Cake

Elizabeth Penney *San Diego, California*
Bake-Off® Contest 33, 1988

This fabulous cake deserves a special occasion! Layered with lemon cream filling and frosted with mounds of whipped cream, it guarantees a grand entrance.

CAKE
8 egg whites
1 teaspoon cream of tartar
1/2 teaspoon salt
1 cup sugar
7 egg yolks
1 cup all-purpose flour
1/3 cup lemon juice
2 teaspoons grated lemon peel

FILLING
1 cup sugar
1/4 cup cornstarch
Dash salt
1 1/4 cups water
2 egg yolks
3 tablespoons lemon juice
1 tablespoon margarine or
  butter
2 teaspoons grated lemon peel

TOPPING
2 cups whipping cream
3 to 4 drops yellow food
  color, if desired
2 kiwifruit, peeled, sliced, if
  desired

Heat oven to 325°F. In large bowl, beat egg whites until foamy. Add cream of tartar and 1/2 teaspoon salt; beat until soft peaks form. Gradu-

Lemon Platinum Cake

ally add 1/2 cup of the sugar, beating until stiff peaks form. Set aside.

In small bowl, beat 7 egg yolks until lemon colored, about 2 minutes. Gradually add remaining 1/2 cup sugar, beating until thick and light lemon colored. Add flour, 1/3 cup lemon juice and 2 teaspoons lemon peel to egg yolk mixture; beat at low speed for 1 minute. By hand, gently fold egg yolk mixture into egg white mixture. Pour batter into ungreased 10-inch tube pan.

Bake at 325°F. for 40 to 55 minutes or until top springs back when touched lightly in center. Immediately invert cake onto funnel or soft drink bottle; let hang until completely cool. Remove from pan.

In small saucepan, combine 1 cup sugar, cornstarch and dash salt; mix well. Gradually stir in water. Cook over medium heat until mixture thickens and boils, stirring constantly; remove from heat. In small bowl, beat 2 egg yolks; gradually blend small amount of hot mixture into egg yolks. Return egg yolk mixture to saucepan; cook over low heat 2 to 3 minutes or until thickened, stirring constantly. Remove from heat; stir in 3 tablespoons lemon juice, margarine and 2 teaspoons lemon peel. Cool. Reserve 1/2 cup filling mixture for topping.

In small bowl, beat whipping cream until slightly thickened. Add reserved 1/2 cup filling mixture and food color; beat until thickened, about 30 seconds. DO NOT OVERBEAT.

To assemble cake, slice cake horizontally to make 3 layers. Place bottom layer on serving plate; spread with half (about 1/2 cup) of filling mixture. Place middle layer on top; spread with

remaining filling. Top with third layer. Spread sides, center and top of cake with topping. Refrigerate at least 1 hour before serving. Just before serving, cut kiwifruit slices in half and arrange on cake or garnish as desired. Store in refrigerator.

Yield: 16 servings

High Altitude—Above 3,500 feet: No change.

Nutrition Per Serving: Calories 290; Protein 5g; Carbohydrate 36g; Fat 15g; Sodium 130mg

Baking Power!

There's electricity in the air at all the Bake-Off® Contests— but at the first event that simply wasn't enough. Mere hours before Pillsbury's first Bake-Off® Contest in 1949, known then as the Grand National Recipe and Baking Contest, organizers were dismayed to find that baking in the world's largest kitchen would be impossible! The 100 brand-new electric ranges that had been carefully set up in the ballroom of the Waldorf-Astoria Hotel needed alternating current to run, but the generator that supplied the hotel provided only direct current. In the quiet of the night, Pillsbury had electricians break a hole in the wall and drop a cable down into the city's subway system, to tap into the alternating current cable there. (A more colorful version of this tale holds that the power was tapped from the subway's third rail. Although this isn't true, it's a great story to impress young electricians with.)

Chocolate Mousse Fantasy Torte

Christine Vidra *Maumee, Ohio*
Bake-Off® Contest 34, 1990 Prize Winner

Create a memory that lingers—an unforgettably fudgy, rich brownie topped with a luscious creamy chocolate mousse layer.

BASE
1 (1 lb. 3.5-oz.) pkg. fudge brownie mix
2 teaspoons instant coffee granules or crystals
1/2 cup butter or margarine, softened
2 tablespoons water
2 eggs

TOPPING
1 1/2 cups semi-sweet chocolate chips
1 oz. unsweetened chocolate
1 teaspoon instant coffee granules or crystals
1/4 cup water
2 tablespoons butter or margarine
1 cup whipping cream
1/2 oz. unsweetened chocolate, melted

Heat oven to 350°F. Grease 9- or 10-inch springform pan. In large bowl, combine all base ingredients; beat at medium speed 1 minute. Spread batter in greased pan. Bake at 350°F. for 36 to 42 minutes or until set. Cool in pan on wire rack for 1 hour. Remove sides of pan; cool completely.

In small saucepan, combine chocolate chips, 1 oz. unsweetened chocolate, 1 teaspoon coffee granules, 1/4 cup water and 2 tablespoons butter. Cook over low heat until mixture is smooth, stirring constantly. Remove from heat. Cool 15 minutes, stirring occasionally.

In small bowl, beat whipping cream until soft peaks form. Fold warm chocolate mixture into whipped cream. Using pastry tube fitted with decorative tip, pipe topping mixture evenly over cooled base. Or spread topping over base.

Drizzle 1/2 oz. melted unsweetened chocolate over topping. Refrigerate at least 1 hour or until topping is set. Let stand at room temperature about 30 minutes before serving. Store in refrigerator.

Yield: 16 servings

High Altitude—Above 3,500 feet: Decrease butter to 1/3 cup. Bake as directed above.

Nutrition Per Serving: Calories 380; Protein 4g; Carbohydrate 40g; Fat 23g; Sodium 180mg

Ring-of-Coconut Fudge Cake

Rita Glomb *Whitehall, Pennsylvania*
Bake-Off® Contest 22, 1971 Prize Winner

This chocolate cake, with its macaroonlike tunnel of cream cheese, coconut and chocolate chips, has certainly made its mark. Its popularity encouraged Pillsbury to add pudding-filled flavors to its line of Bundt-style cake mixes.

FILLING
1 (8-oz.) pkg. cream cheese, softened
1/4 cup sugar
1 teaspoon vanilla
1 egg
1/2 cup flaked coconut
1 (6-oz.) pkg. (1 cup) semi-sweet or milk chocolate chips

CAKE
2 cups sugar
1 cup oil
2 eggs
3 cups all-purpose flour
3/4 cup unsweetened cocoa
2 teaspoons baking soda
2 teaspoons baking powder
1 1/2 teaspoons salt
1 cup hot coffee or water
1 cup buttermilk*
1 teaspoon vanilla

Christine Vidra: Chocolate Mousse Fantasy Torte

Who says too many cooks spoil the soup? "My son Bobby gets a lot of the credit for my Bake-Off® Contest winner Chocolate Mousse Fantasy Torte," Christine Vidra says. "When he was seven, I made him chocolate mousse all the time, with melted chocolate and whipped cream, and he said for his birthday he wanted me to make him a cake, using that mousse. Even as a three-year-old he loved to taste my coffee whenever he could. He thinks that coffee enhances the flavor of chocolate, so every time he makes something with chocolate, he wants to add coffee to it—so that's what we did." Sometimes, an extra cook is just the perfect extra ingredient.

$^1/_2$ cup chopped nuts

GLAZE

1 cup powdered sugar

3 tablespoons unsweetened
   cocoa

2 tablespoons margarine or
   butter

2 teaspoons vanilla

1 to 3 tablespoons hot water

Heat oven to 350° F. Generously grease and lightly flour 10-inch tube or 12-cup Bundt pan. In medium bowl, combine all filling ingredients; blend well. Set aside.

In large bowl, combine 2 cups sugar, oil and eggs; beat 1 minute at high speed. Add remaining cake ingredients except nuts; beat 3 minutes at medium speed, scraping bowl occasionally. Stir in nuts. Pour $^1/_2$ of the batter into greased and floured pan. Carefully spoon filling over batter; top with remaining batter.

Bake at 350° F. for 70 to 75 minutes until top springs back when touched lightly in center. Cool upright in pan 15 minutes; remove from pan. Cool completely.

In medium bowl, combine all glaze ingredients, adding enough hot water for desired glazing consistency. Spoon over cake, allowing some to run down sides. Store in refrigerator.

Yield: 16 servings

*Tip: To substitute for buttermilk, use 1 tablespoon vinegar or lemon juice plus milk to make 1 cup.

High Altitude—Above 3,500 feet: No change.

Nutrition Per Serving: Calories 510; Protein 7g; Carbohydrate 57g; Fat 28g; Sodium 480mg

Fudgy Orange Cappuccino Torte

Sharla Jack *Springfield, Oregon*
Bake-Off® Contest 35, 1992 Prize Winner

This rich indulgent torte is simple to make with brownie mix and is finished off with an orangy-chocolate filling and topping. It's a real showstopper!

BROWNIE

1 (1 lb. 3.5-oz.) pkg. fudge
   brownie mix

$^1/_2$ cup oil

$^1/_4$ cup water

$^1/_4$ cup orange-flavored liqueur
   or orange juice

2 eggs

1 teaspoon grated orange peel

4 oz. sweet dark chocolate or
   semi-sweet baking chocolate,
   coarsely chopped

FILLING

1 cup sweetened condensed
   milk (not evaporated)

6 oz. sweet dark chocolate or
   semi-sweet baking chocolate,
   chopped

2 egg yolks, slightly beaten

2 tablespoons orange-flavored
   liqueur or orange juice

$^3/_4$ cup finely chopped nuts

TOPPING

1$^1/_2$ cups whipping cream

$^3/_4$ cup powdered sugar

$^1/_3$ cup unsweetened cocoa

2 tablespoons orange-flavored
   liqueur or orange juice

1 teaspoon grated orange peel

$^1/_8$ teaspoon salt

GARNISH, IF DESIRED

Orange slices, twisted

Orange leaves

Heat oven to 350° F. Grease bottom of 9- or 10-inch springform pan. In large bowl, combine all brownie ingredients except 4 oz. chocolate; beat 50 strokes by hand. Stir in chocolate. Spread in greased pan. Bake at 350° F. for 40 to 45 minutes or until center is set. Cool completely.

In medium saucepan, combine condensed milk and 6 oz. chocolate. Cook over low heat, stirring constantly, until chocolate is melted and mixture is smooth. Remove from heat. Stir 2 tablespoons hot mixture into egg yolks. Gradually stir yolk mixture into hot mixture in saucepan. Cook over medium heat 3 minutes, stirring constantly. Remove from heat. Stir in 2 tablespoons liqueur and nuts. Refrigerate until just cool, about 25 minutes. Spread filling mixture over top of cooled brownies. Refrigerate at least 1 hour or until filling is set.

Run knife around sides of pan to loosen; remove sides of pan. To serve, place brownie on serving plate. In large bowl, beat all topping ingredients until stiff peaks form. Pipe or spoon topping mixture evenly over chilled filling. Garnish with orange slices and leaves. Store in refrigerator.

Yield: 16 servings

High Altitude—Above 3,500 feet: Add $^1/_2$ cup flour to dry brownie mix. Bake at 375° F. for 35 to 45 minutes.

Nutrition Per Serving: Calories 540; Protein 6g; Carbohydrate 60g; Fat 30g; Sodium 160mg

Mocha Cream Chocolate Torte

Natalie C. Glomb *Whitehall, Pennsylvania*
Bake-Off® Contest 32, 1986

While studying art in Belgium, Natalie Glomb enjoyed a pastry shop chocolate torte that she was determined to duplicate. Her much easier version turns a chocolate sheet cake into a four-layer torte, frosted with a not-too-sweet cooked mocha cream.

CAKE
1 (1 lb. 2.25-oz.) pkg. pudding-included German chocolate cake mix
1¹/₄ cups water
¹/₃ cup oil
3 eggs

FROSTING
¹/₂ cup sugar
¹/₄ cup cornstarch
2 tablespoons instant coffee granules or crystals
1¹/₄ cups milk
1 cup margarine or butter, softened
¹/₄ cup powdered sugar

GARNISH, IF DESIRED
Chocolate sprinkles
Whole blanched almonds

Heat oven to 350°F. Grease and flour 13×9-inch pan. In large bowl, combine all cake ingredients at low speed until moistened; beat 2 minutes at high speed. Pour batter into greased and floured pan. Bake at 350°F. for 30 to 40 minutes or until toothpick inserted in center comes out clean. Cool 15 minutes; remove from pan. Cool completely.

Meanwhile, in medium saucepan, combine sugar, cornstarch and instant coffee; blend well. Gradually stir in milk. Cook over medium heat until mixture thickens and boils, stirring constantly. Remove from heat; cover with plastic wrap. Refrigerate 30 minutes or until cool. (Mixture will be very thick.) In large bowl, beat margarine and powdered sugar until well blended. Gradually add cooled coffee mixture; beat until light and fluffy.

To assemble torte, cut cooled cake in half lengthwise. Slice each half in half horizontally to make 4 layers. Place 1 layer on serving tray. Spread top with about ¹/₃ cup frosting. Repeat with remaining layers and frosting. Frost sides and top of cake. Sprinkle top of torte with chocolate sprinkles; garnish with almonds. Store in refrigerator.

Yield: 12 servings

High Altitude—Above 3,500 feet: See package for directions.

Nutrition Per Serving: Calories 480; Protein 5g; Carbohydrate 51g; Fat 28g; Sodium 470mg

Key Lime Cream Torte

Joan Wittan *North Potomac, Maryland*
Bake-Off® Contest 35, 1992

The flavors of Key lime pie are combined in an impressive yet quick and easy torte that was developed by the contestant when visiting Key West.

CAKE
1 (1 lb. 2.25-oz.) pkg. pudding-included butter flavor cake mix
2 tablespoons lime juice plus water to equal 1 cup
¹/₂ cup butter or margarine, softened
3 eggs

FILLING
1 (14-oz.) can sweetened condensed milk (not evaporated)
¹/₂ cup lime juice
2 cups whipping cream

GARNISH
Lime slices, if desired

Heat oven to 350°F. Grease and flour two 9- or 8-inch round cake pans. In large bowl, combine all cake ingredients at low speed until moistened; beat 2 minutes at high speed. Pour batter into greased and floured pans.

Bake at 350°F. Bake 9-inch pans 30 to 40 minutes, bake 8-inch pans 35 to 45 minutes, or until toothpick inserted in center

comes out clean. Cool 15 minutes; remove from pans. Cool completely.

In small bowl, combine sweetened condensed milk and $1/2$ cup lime juice; mix well. In large bowl, beat whipping cream until stiff peaks form. Reserve 1 cup of whipped cream. Fold condensed milk mixture into remaining whipped cream just until blended.

To assemble cake, slice each cake layer in half horizontally to make 4 layers. Place 1 cake layer cut side up on serving plate; spread with $1/3$ of whipped cream filling. Repeat with second and third cake layers. Top with remaining cake layer. Pipe in decorative pattern or spread reserved whipped cream over top of torte. Refrigerate 2 to 3 hours before serving. Garnish with lime slices. Store in refrigerator.

Yield: 12 servings

High Altitude—Above 3,500 feet: Add $1/3$ cup flour to dry cake mix. Bake at 350° F. for 25 to 35 minutes.

Nutrition Per Serving: Calories 510; Protein 7g; Carbohydrate 56g; Fat 29g; Sodium 430mg

Key Lime Cream Torte

PROFILE

KURT WAIT

Single parents have their work cut out for them: cooking, cleaning, working, balancing family time and private time, and all without the benefit of an extra pair of hands. Million-dollar Bake-Off® Contest winner Kurt Wait tackled these challenges.

Kurt Wait couldn't help but notice that his eight-year-old son Cy stuck closer to home when Kurt baked desserts. "He loves the end product, and he loves to lick the bowl and spoons." Soon Kurt noticed his son's neighborhood pals were sticking closer to their house, too: "All the kids in the neighborhood always get chunks of whatever I'm cooking if they're in the right place at the right time, and they usually seem to be on weekends."

Kurt had been a devoted fan of the Bake-Off® Contest for years. "I never cooked at home when I was a kid, but I watched my mom, who's English and was really good at cakes, pies and cookies. But I didn't start cooking until I was in college, when I was on my own. I started making the Bake-Off® Contest winners in col-

lege, and I've made most of the winning recipes since. I bought my first spring-form pan when the Almond Cookie Cake won, and I bought my first Bundt pan after the Tunnel of Fudge Cake won." Like many home cooks who followed the Bake-Off® Contest from afar, Kurt was soon inspired to enter it. He found a ready partner in his son: "Cy's the best tester there is, because he's brutally honest about what he likes. His little buddies in the neighborhood are the same way; they're real honest and they'll tell you if they like it or not."

Kurt, who works in marketing, credits his marketing instincts and his son for his dessert's success. He picked chocolate for its popularity, macadamia nuts for their beauty, and then young Cy encouraged him with his Macadamia Fudge Torte because of its tasty chocolate sauce. Kurt and Cy's teamwork paid off big, and Kurt has stashed most of his prize money for his son's education. Kurt and Cy Wait have proved once and for all that bonding over chocolate certainly can be sweet.

Macadamia Fudge Torte

Kurt Wait *Redwood City, California*
Bake-Off® Contest 37, 1996 Grand Prize Winner

Kurt Wait is the first man in the forty-seven-year history of the Bake-Off® Contest to win the grand prize. His streusel-topped chocolate-pear torte brought him a million dollars, the largest prize ever in a cooking contest.

FILLING
1/3 cup low-fat sweetened condensed milk (not evaporated)
1/2 cup semi-sweet chocolate chips

CAKE
1 (1 lb. 2.25-oz.) pkg. pudding-included devil's food cake mix
1 1/2 teaspoons cinnamon
1/3 cup oil

1 (15-oz.) can sliced pears in light syrup, drained
3 eggs
1/3 cup chopped macadamia nuts or pecans
2 teaspoons water

SAUCE
1 (17-oz.) jar butterscotch caramel fudge ice cream topping
1/3 cup milk

Macadamia Fudge Torte

Heat oven to 350°F. Spray 9- or 10-inch springform pan with non-stick cooking spray. In small saucepan, combine filling ingredients. Cook over medium-low heat until chocolate is melted, stirring occasionally.

In large bowl, combine cake mix, cinnamon and oil; blend at low speed for 30 seconds or until crumbly. (Mixture will be dry.) Place pears in blender container or food processor bowl with metal blade; cover and blend until smooth.

In large bowl, combine 2¹/₂ cups of the cake mix mixture, pureed pears and eggs; beat at low speed until moistened. Beat 2 minutes at medium speed. Spread batter evenly in spray-coated pan. Drop filling by spoonfuls over batter. Stir nuts and water into remaining cake mix mixture. Sprinkle over filling.

Bake at 350°F. for 45 to 50 minutes or until top springs back when touched lightly in center. Cool 10 minutes. Remove sides of pan. Cool 1¹/₂ hours or until completely cooled.

In small saucepan, combine sauce ingredients. Cook over medium-low heat for 3 to 4 minutes or until well blended, stirring occasionally. To serve, spoon 2 tablespoons warm sauce onto each serving plate; top with wedge of torte. If desired, serve with vanilla ice cream or frozen yogurt and garnish with chocolate curls.

Yield: 12 servings

High Altitude—Above 3,500 feet: Add ¹/₃ cup flour to dry cake mix. Bake as directed above.

Nutrition Per Serving: Calories 460; Protein 6g; Carbohydrate 73g; Fat 16g; Sodium 500mg

Dark Chocolate Sacher Torte

Phyllis Trier *Grand View, New York*
Bake-Off® Contest 31, 1984

This extremely rich Viennese classic is made with layers of chocolate cake filled with apricot jam and covered with a creamy chocolate glaze. Serve it with billows of whipped cream.

CAKE
¹/₂ **cup finely chopped dried apricots**
¹/₂ **cup rum***
1 **(1 lb. 2.25-oz.) pkg. pudding-included devil's food or dark chocolate cake mix**
³/₄ **cup water**
¹/₃ **cup oil**
3 **eggs**

GLAZE
2 **(10-oz.) jars apricot preserves**
2 **tablespoons rum****

FROSTING
1 **(6-oz.) pkg. (1 cup) semi-sweet chocolate chips**
³/₄ **cup margarine or butter**
¹/₂ **to 1 cup sliced almonds**

Heat oven to 350°F. Grease and flour two 9- or 8-inch round cake pans. In small bowl, combine apricots and ¹/₂ cup rum; let stand 10 minutes. In large bowl, combine apricot-rum mixture and remaining cake ingredients at low speed until moistened; beat 2 minutes at high speed. Pour into greased and floured pans.

Bake at 350°F. Bake 9-inch pans 25 to 35 minutes, 8-inch pans 35 to 45 minutes, or until toothpick inserted in center comes out clean.

Cool 15 minutes; remove from pans. Cool completely.

In small saucepan over low heat, melt glaze ingredients; strain to remove large apricot pieces. To assemble torte, carefully slice each layer in half horizontally to make 4 layers. Place 1 layer on serving plate; spread with ¹/₄ cup glaze. Repeat with remaining layers and glaze, ending with cake layer. Spread remaining ¹/₄ cup glaze over top of torte, allowing some to run down sides. Refrigerate 1 hour or until glaze is set.

In small saucepan over low heat, melt chocolate chips and margarine, stirring constantly until smooth. Refrigerate 30 minutes or until slightly thickened, stirring occasionally. Spread frosting over sides and top of cake. Arrange almond slices on sides of cake. Refrigerate at least 1 hour before serving. Garnish as desired. Store in refrigerator.

Yield: 16 servings

***Tips:** To substitute for ¹/₂ cup rum in cake, use 2 teaspoons rum extract plus water to make ¹/₂ cup.

****To substitute for 2 tablespoons rum in glaze, use 1 teaspoon rum extract plus water to make 2 tablespoons.

High Altitude—Above 3,500 feet: Add 3 tablespoons flour to dry cake mix. Bake at 375°F. for 30 to 40 minutes.

Nutrition Per Serving: Calories 470; Protein 5g; Carbohydrate 58g; Fat 23g; Sodium 380mg

Dark Chocolate Sacher Torte

Tiramisù Toffee Torte

Christie Henson *Conway, Arkansas*
Bake-Off® Contest 35, 1992 Prize Winner

Tiramisù is Italy's wonderful answer to the English trifle. This version of tiramisù is actually a layered "torte" that's filled and frosted with a delectable creamy coffee and chocolate combination.

CAKE
1 (1 lb. 2.25-oz.) pkg. pudding-included white cake mix
1 cup strong coffee, room temperature
4 egg whites
4 (1.4-oz.) toffee candy bars, very finely chopped

FROSTING
²/₃ cup sugar
¹/₃ cup chocolate syrup
¹/₂ (8-oz.) pkg. (4 oz.) cream cheese, softened
2 cups whipping cream
2 teaspoons vanilla

1 cup strong coffee, room temperature

GARNISH
Chopped toffee candy bars or chocolate curls, if desired

Heat oven to 350° F. Grease and flour two 9- or 8-inch round cake pans. In large bowl, combine cake mix, 1 cup coffee and egg whites at low speed until moistened; beat 2 minutes at high speed. Fold in chopped toffee bars. Spread batter in greased and floured pans.

Tiramisù Toffee Torte

Bake at 350°F. Bake 9-inch pans 20 to 30 minutes, bake 8-inch pans 30 to 40 minutes, or until toothpick inserted in center comes out clean. Cool 10 minutes; remove from pans. Cool completely.

In medium bowl, combine sugar, chocolate syrup and cream cheese; beat until smooth. Add whipping cream and vanilla; beat until light and fluffy. Refrigerate until ready to use.

To assemble cake, slice each layer in half horizontally to make 4 layers. Drizzle each cut side with 1/4 cup coffee. Place 1 layer coffee side up on serving plate; spread with 3/4 cup frosting. Repeat with second and third cake layers. Top with remaining cake layer. Frost sides and top of cake with remaining frosting. Garnish with chopped toffee bars. Store in refrigerator.

Yield: 12 servings

High Altitude—Above 3,500 feet: Add 1/4 cup flour to dry cake mix. Bake at 350°F. for 30 to 35 minutes.

Nutrition Per Serving: Calories 540; Protein 6g; Carbohydrate 63g; Fat 29g; Sodium 400mg

Christie Henson: Tiramisù Toffee Torte

If at first you don't succeed, try, try, again . . .

Christie Henson volunteered an early disaster story: "One time I made cream pie and added the eggs too late. I ended up with scrambled eggs in my chocolate pie." Christie never gave up, thanks to the unwavering support of her family. "My poor father ate whatever I made, no matter how it turned out." Christie ultimately mastered the tricky arts of éclair making and converting European classics for busy American cooks—and then she captured a cash prize at Bake-Off® Contest 35 for her efforts.

Praline Torte with Chocolate Truffle Filling

Merrie Wimmer *Flower Mound, Texas Bake-Off® Contest 35, 1992 Prize Winner*

This incredible cake features a praline whipped cream frosting and fudgy truffle filling. It's perfect for a party and can be made ahead of time.

TORTE
1 2/3 cups all-purpose flour
2 teaspoons baking powder
1/4 teaspoon salt
4 egg whites
1 1/2 cups sugar
1 1/2 cups butter or margarine, softened
4 egg yolks
3/4 cup milk

CHOCOLATE TRUFFLE CREAM FILLING
6 oz. dark chocolate candy bar or semi-sweet baking chocolate, chopped
1 tablespoon butter or margarine
1/3 cup whipping cream

MOCHA PRALINE CREAM
1/2 cup sliced almonds
1/4 cup sugar
1 1/2 cups whipping cream
1 tablespoon sugar
1 teaspoon instant coffee granules or crystals
1/4 teaspoon almond extract

Heat oven to 375°F. Grease and flour three 8- or 9-inch round cake pans.* In medium bowl, combine flour, baking powder and salt; set aside. In small bowl, beat egg whites until soft peaks form; set aside.

In large bowl, combine 1 1/2 cups sugar, 1 1/2 cups butter and egg yolks; beat until light and fluffy. Add flour mixture alternately with milk, beating well after each addition. Fold in beaten egg whites. Pour batter into greased and floured pans.

Bake at 375°F. for 15 to 20 minutes or until toothpick inserted in center comes out clean. Cool 5 minutes; remove from pans. Cool completely.

In small heavy saucepan over very low heat, melt chocolate, stirring constantly until smooth. Remove from heat; stir in 1 tablespoon butter and 1/3 cup whipping cream. If necessary, refrigerate until thickened and of desired spreading consistency, 15 to 30 minutes.

Line cookie sheet with foil. In small skillet over low heat, cook almonds and 1/4 cup sugar, stirring constantly, until sugar is melted and almonds are coated. Place on foil-lined cookie sheet; cool. Place coated almonds in plastic bag; coarsely crush with wooden mallet or rolling pin. Set aside.

Assemble torte 2 to 3 hours before serving. Place 1 cake layer on serving plate; spread with half of filling. Repeat with second cake layer and remaining filling. Top with remaining cake layer.

In small bowl, combine 1¹/₂ cups whipping cream, 1 tablespoon sugar, instant coffee granules and almond extract; beat just until stiff peaks form. DO NOT OVERBEAT. Reserve 2 tablespoons crushed almonds for garnish; fold in remaining crushed almonds. Frost top and sides of cake. Before serving, garnish with reserved crushed almonds. Cover; store in refrigerator.

Yield: 12 servings

*Tip: Layers can be baked 1 at a time if 3 pans are not available.

High Altitude—Above 3,500 feet: Increase flour to 2 cups; decrease sugar in torte to 1¹/₄ cups. Bake as directed above.

Nutrition Per Serving: Calories 640; Protein 7g; Carbohydrate 53g; Fat 47g; Sodium 380mg

White Chocolate Raspberry Torte

Cindy Kohlhoff *Houston, Texas*
Bake-Off® Contest 35, 1992 Prize Winner

White baking bar chocolate is a high-quality bar form of white chocolate. In most recipes as in this one, white vanilla chips can be substituted for the white baking bar.

TORTE
16 oz. coarsely chopped white baking bars or 2¹/₂ cups white vanilla chips
¹/₂ cup butter or margarine
4 eggs

³/₄ cup sugar
1¹/₂ cups all-purpose flour
¹/₈ teaspoon salt
¹/₄ teaspoon almond extract
1 cup fresh raspberries or frozen raspberries without syrup, thawed, drained on paper towels
²/₃ cup coarsely chopped sliced almonds

GLAZE
¹/₂ cup semi-sweet chocolate chips
1 teaspoon powdered sugar, if desired

Heat oven to 350° F. Lightly grease and flour bottom and sides of 9- or 10-inch springform pan. In medium saucepan over very low heat, melt 8 oz. of the white baking bars and butter, stirring constantly until smooth. Cool slightly.

In large bowl, beat eggs on high speed until light lemon colored, about 3 minutes. Gradually add sugar, beating until thickened and very light yellow. By hand, fold in flour, salt, almond extract, melted white chocolate and remaining 8 oz. of chopped white baking bars. Fold in raspberries. Spread in greased and floured pan. Sprinkle with almonds; press lightly.

Bake at 350° F. for 55 to 65 minutes or until top is golden brown and springs back when touched lightly in center. Cool 30 minutes. Remove sides of pan; cool completely.

Melt chocolate chips in small saucepan over low heat, stirring constantly, until smooth. Using wire whisk, beat in powdered sugar until smooth. Drizzle glaze over top of torte; allow to set. Serve at room temperature. Store in refrigerator.

Yield: 16 servings

High Altitude—Above 3,500 feet: Decrease sugar to ¹/₂ cup; increase flour to 1³/₄ cups. Bake as directed above.

Nutrition Per Serving: Calories 360; Protein 6g; Carbohydrate 41g; Fat 20g; Sodium 125mg

Tuxedo Brownie Torte

Patricia Lapiezo *LaMesa, California.*
Bake-Off® Contest 35, 1992.

The combination of a dark chocolate base, raspberry filling and creamy white chocolate topping looks and tastes like it came from the pastry cart in a fine restaurant.

BROWNIE
1 (1 lb. 3.5-oz.) pkg. fudge brownie mix
¹/₂ cup oil
¹/₄ cup water
2 eggs

FILLING
1 (10-oz.) pkg. frozen raspberries in syrup, thawed
1 tablespoon sugar
1 tablespoon cornstarch
1 cup fresh raspberries or frozen whole raspberries without syrup, thawed, drained on paper towel, reserving 3 for garnish

TOPPING
1 (8-oz.) pkg. cream cheese, softened
¹/₃ cup powdered sugar
2 tablespoons white crème de cacao, if desired
1 cup white vanilla chips, melted

1 cup whipping cream, whipped

GARNISH
1 tablespoon grated semi-sweet chocolate
3 whole fresh or frozen raspberries, if desired
3 mint leaves, if desired

Heat oven to 350° F. Grease bottom and sides of 9- or 10-inch spring-form pan. In large bowl, combine all brownie ingredients. Beat 50 strokes by hand. Spread batter in greased pan.

Bake at 350° F. for 40 to 45 minutes or until center is set. Cool 30 minutes. Run knife around sides of pan to loosen; remove sides of pan. Cool completely.

Place thawed raspberries in syrup in blender container or food processor bowl with metal blade. Cover; blend or process until pureed. Strain to remove seeds. In small saucepan, combine sugar and cornstarch. Gradually add raspberry puree; mix well. Bring to a boil; cook until mixture is clear, stirring constantly. Cool 5 minutes. Spread over brownie layer to within ¹/₂ inch of edges. Arrange 1 cup fresh raspberries evenly over raspberry mixture; refrigerate.

In medium bowl, combine cream cheese, powdered sugar and crème de cacao; beat until smooth. Add melted vanilla chips; beat until smooth. Fold in whipped cream. Cover; refrigerate 45 minutes.

Stir topping mixture until smooth. Spread 1¹/₂ cups of the topping over raspberries. Pipe or spoon on remaining topping. Refrigerate at least 1 hour or until firm. Sprinkle grated chocolate in 1 inch border around outside edge of torte. Garnish center with 3 whole raspberries and 3 mint leaves. Store in refrigerator.

Yield: 16 servings

High Altitude—Above 3,500 feet: Add ¹/₃ cup flour to dry brownie mix; increase water to ¹/₃ cup. Bake as directed above.

Nutrition Per Serving: Calories 420; Protein 4g; Carbohydrate 46g; Fat 24g; Sodium 160mg

Tuxedo Brownie Torte

Chapter 8

Pies and Tarts

The old saw runs that nothing is as American as apple pie—but pecan pie, pumpkin pie, peach pie, shoofly pie, sweet potato pie, French silk pie and Key lime pie are all runners-up. The variety of pie and tart recipes available to the contemporary baker is almost infinite. There are summer pies and winter pies, Southern pies and New England pies, cream pies and meringue pies, fruit pies and nut pies, fancy pies and plain pies—and, the same is true for tarts. Pies and tarts allow for a great deal of creativity, since their fillings are such a matter of imagination and personal taste.

Pies have been a favorite throughout the Bake-Off® Contest, and many from the early days of the contest are still popular, like 1949's Company's Coming Cashew Pie, 1951's French Silk Chocolate Pie and 1952's Caramel Candy Pie. Women didn't have the easy access to supermarkets that we have today, so most of these early recipes could be made out of ordinary pantry ingredients. The pies of the 1960s tended to be fluffy, pretty creations, like 1960's Chocolate Dream Pie or 1964's Strawberry Devonshire Pie. The 1970s for the most part were not an innovative time for pies, but saw the rise of "squares," pielike bar cookies. The most recent pies have shown a complex exploration and adaption of U.S. regional flavors, such as 1992's Pennsylvania Dutch Cake and Custard Pie, or 1994's Buttered Rum Banana Pecan Pie, which is a version of a New Orleans specialty.

No matter what goes into dessert pies or tarts, smiles and delight are sure to result because, for all their complex variation, they are always the surefire crowd-pleasing combination of a crispy crust, something sweet and the cook's own creativity.

Cream Cheese Brownie Pie, page 318

Buttered Rum Banana Pecan Pie

Barbara Morgan *Concord, California*
Bake-Off® Contest 36, 1994

Bananas Foster is a dessert created in New Orleans in the 1950s that consists of bananas sautéed in rum, brown sugar and liquor. This heavenly pie will remind you of the famous dessert.

1 refrigerated pie crust (from 15-oz. pkg.)

FILLING
2 tablespoons butter or margarine
1 cup chopped pecans
2 ripe medium bananas, sliced
20 caramels, unwrapped
3 tablespoons butter or margarine
3 tablespoons whipping cream
2 tablespoons dark rum*
1¼ cups powdered sugar

TOPPING
1 cup whipping cream
2 tablespoons powdered sugar
1 teaspoon vanilla

Heat oven to 450° F. Prepare pie crust according to package directions for *one-crust baked shell* using 9-inch pie pan. Bake at 450° F. for 9 to 11 minutes or until lightly browned. Cool completely.

Melt 2 tablespoons butter in large skillet. Add pecans; cook over medium heat until golden brown, 3 to 4 minutes, stirring constantly. Spoon pecans evenly over cooled baked shell. Layer banana slices over pecans. In small heavy saucepan, combine caramels,

3 tablespoons butter and 3 tablespoons whipping cream. Cook over low heat until caramels are melted and mixture is smooth, stirring occasionally. Remove from heat. Add rum; blend well. Beat in 1¼ cups powdered sugar until well blended. Immediately spread over banana slices. Cool at room temperature 1½ hours to allow caramel to settle.

In small bowl, beat all topping ingredients until stiff peaks form. Spread over cooled filling. Refrigerate at least 2 hours before serving. Store in refrigerator.

Yield: 8 servings

*Tip: To substitute for rum, use 1½ teaspoon rum extract plus water to make 2 tablespoons.

Nutrition Per Serving: Calories 600; Protein 4g; Carbohydrate 59g; Fat 39g; Sodium 270mg

Caramel Candy Pie

Florence E. Ries *Sleepy Eye, Minnesota*
Bake-Off® Contest 4, 1952 Prize Winner

This winning recipe from the fourth Bake-Off® Contest is simplified with refrigerated pie crusts. Caramel candies are melted into a smooth and luscious filling and caramelized almonds add the finishing touch.

1 refrigerated pie crust (from 15-oz. pkg.)

FILLING
1 envelope unflavored gelatin
¼ cup cold water
1 (14-oz.) pkg. vanilla caramels, unwrapped

1 cup milk
1½ cups whipping cream, whipped

TOPPING
2 tablespoons sugar
¼ cup slivered almonds

Heat oven to 450° F. Prepare pie crust according to package directions for *one-crust baked shell* using 9-inch pie pan. Bake at 450° F. for 9 to 11 minutes or until light golden brown. Cool completely.

In small bowl, sprinkle gelatin over water; let stand to soften. In medium saucepan, combine caramels and milk. Cook over low heat until caramels are melted and mixture is smooth, stirring occasionally. Stir in softened gelatin. Refrigerate 45 to 60 minutes or until slightly thickened. Fold thickened caramel mixture into whipped cream. Spoon into cooled baked shell. Refrigerate 2 hours or until set.

Line cookie sheet with foil. In small skillet, combine sugar and almonds. Cook over low heat until sugar is melted and almonds are golden brown, stirring constantly. Immediately spread on foil-lined cookie sheet. Cool completely; break apart. Just before serving, garnish pie with caramelized almonds. Store in refrigerator.

Yield: 8 servings

Nutrition Per Serving: Calories 530; Protein 6g; Carbohydrate 55g; Fat 32g; Sodium 280mg

Lemon Cloud Pie

Shirley Ordiway *Jamesville, New York*
Bake-Off® Contest 11, 1959 Prize Winner

This contestant was persistent enough to send her lemon pie recipe as an entry for two years in a row. She must have known it was a winner!

1 refrigerated pie crust (from 15-oz. pkg.)

FILLING
1 cup sugar
3 tablespoons cornstarch
1 cup water
1/3 cup lemon juice
2 egg yolks, slightly beaten
1/2 (8-oz.) pkg. (4 oz.) cream cheese, cubed, softened
1 to 2 teaspoons grated lemon peel
1/2 cup whipping cream

TOPPING
1/2 cup whipping cream, whipped

Heat oven to 450° F. Prepare pie crust according to package directions for *one-crust baked shell* using 9-inch pie pan. Bake at 450° F. for 9 to 11 minutes or until light golden brown. Cool completely.

In medium saucepan, combine sugar and cornstarch; mix well. Stir in water, lemon juice and egg yolks. Cook over medium heat until mixture thickens and boils, stirring constantly. Boil 1 minute. Add cream cheese and lemon peel, stirring until cream cheese is melted and mixture is smooth. Cool to room temperature.

In large bowl, beat 1/2 cup whipping cream until soft peaks form; fold into lemon mixture. Spoon filling mixture evenly into cooled baked shell. Cover surface with plastic wrap; refrigerate for 6 to 8 hours or overnight. Spoon or pipe whipped cream over filling. Garnish as desired. Store in refrigerator.

Yield: 8 servings

Nutrition Per Serving: Calories 400; Protein 3g; Carbohydrate 42g; Fat 25g; Sodium 190mg

Mystery Pecan Pie

Mary McClain *North Little Rock, Arkansas*
Bake-Off® Contest 16, 1964 Prize Winner

Solve the mystery when you taste the smooth cream cheese filling hiding under the rich pecan topping in this extra-special pie.

1 refrigerated pie crust (from 15-oz. pkg.)

FILLING
1 (8-oz.) pkg. cream cheese, softened
1 egg
1 teaspoon vanilla
1/3 cup sugar
1/4 teaspoon salt
3 eggs
1/4 cup sugar
1 cup corn syrup
1 teaspoon vanilla
1 1/4 cups chopped pecans

Prepare pie crust according to package directions for *one-crust filled pie* using 9-inch pie pan.

Heat oven to 375° F. In small bowl, combine cream cheese, 1 egg, 1 teaspoon vanilla, 1/3 cup sugar and salt; beat at low speed until smooth and well blended. Set aside. In another small bowl, beat 3 eggs. Stir in 1/4 cup sugar, corn syrup and 1 teaspoon vanilla; blend well. Spread cream cheese mixture in bottom of crust-lined pan. Sprinkle with pecans. Gently pour corn syrup mixture over pecans.

Bake at 375° F. for 35 to 45 minutes or until center is set. Cover edge of pie crust with strips of foil after 15 to 20 minutes of baking to prevent excessive browning. Cool completely. Store in refrigerator.

Yield: 8 servings

Nutrition Per Serving: Calories 550; Protein 8g; Carbohydrate 61g; Fat 32g; Sodium 340mg

Mary McClain: Mystery Pecan Pie

One of the delights of cooking is the almost magical transformation food goes through—from raw flour to rich mellow bread, from ordinary eggs to a soaring soufflé. Mary McClain marvels at the mysteries of the pecan pie she adapted to win a cash prize in the sixteenth Bake-Off® Contest. "What happens to the extra 'sweet' of the pecan pie in its old form, and the fact that the cream cheese and pecans seem to change places—only the oven knows, I guess."

Apricot Coconut Cream Pie

Harriet Warkentin *San Jacinto, California*
Bake-Off® Contest 33, 1988

Since Harriet Warkentin's children are grown and she no longer has to cook for a family of eight, she has time for more indulgent recipes like this apricot cream pie. Both filling and finished pie need to be refrigerated, so start it well in advance of serving.

1 refrigerated pie crust (from 15-oz. pkg.)

FILLING
1 envelope unflavored gelatin
1 cup apricot nectar
2 (16-oz.) cans apricot halves, drained
1/2 cup sugar
1/4 cup cornstarch
1/4 teaspoon salt
1 3/4 cups milk
4 egg yolks, beaten
1 tablespoon margarine or butter
1/2 teaspoon vanilla
1/2 cup coconut, toasted*

TOPPING
1 cup whipping cream
1 tablespoon sugar
1/4 teaspoon vanilla
2 to 3 tablespoons apricot preserves, melted
1/2 cup coconut, toasted*

Heat oven to 450°F. Prepare pie crust according to package directions for *one-crust baked shell* using 9-inch pie pan. Bake at 450°F. for 9 to 11 minutes or until light golden brown. Cool completely.

In small bowl, sprinkle gelatin over 1/4 cup of the apricot nectar; let stand to soften. Set aside. In another small bowl, cut 1 can of the apricot halves into small pieces. Set aside. In blender container or food processor bowl with metal blade, combine remaining 3/4 cup apricot nectar and remaining can apricot halves. Cover; blend until smooth.

In medium saucepan, combine 1/2 cup sugar, cornstarch and salt; mix well. Stir in milk and apricot mixture. (Mixture will look curdled.) Cook over medium heat until mixture thickens and boils, stirring constantly. Boil 2 minutes, stirring constantly. Remove from heat. Blend a small amount of hot mixture into egg yolks. Gradually stir yolk mixture into hot mixture in saucepan. Cook over medium heat until mixture comes to a boil, stirring constantly. Cook 2 minutes, stirring constantly. Remove from heat; stir in margarine, 1/2 teaspoon vanilla and softened gelatin. Fold in 1/2 cup toasted coconut. Refrigerate about 30 minutes or until slightly thickened. Fold in apricot pieces. Spoon into cooled baked shell. Refrigerate about 45 minutes or until filling is partially set.

In large bowl, beat whipping cream until soft peaks form. Add 1 tablespoon sugar and 1/4 teaspoon vanilla; beat until stiff peaks form. Gently fold in apricot preserves. Pipe or spoon whipped topping mixture over cooled filling.

Garnish with 1/2 cup toasted coconut. Refrigerate 3 to 4 hours or until set. Store in refrigerator.

Yield: 8 servings

*Tip: To toast coconut, spread on cookie sheet; bake at 350°F. for 7 to 8 minutes or until light golden brown, stirring occasionally. Or spread in a thin layer in microwave-safe pie pan. Microwave on LOW for 4 1/2 to 8 minutes or until light golden brown, tossing with fork after each minute.

Nutrition Per Serving: Calories 480; Protein 7g; Carbohydrate 51g; Fat 27g; Sodium 270mg

Harriet Warkentin: Apricot Coconut Cream Pie

For some of us, learning to cook is a gradual process, something we pick up slowly; for others, it is a trial by fire. "When I married my husband in 1958," Harriet Warkentin told Pillsbury, "I not only married him but took over a family of five children ranging in age from fifteen months to eleven years. I went from cooking for myself to cooking and caring for a large family." Tasty desserts like Harriet's Apricot Coconut Cream Pie smoothed that transition, and "a year and a half later we had a beautiful baby girl." Thank heavens for refrigerated pie crusts!

Apricot Coconut Cream Pie

Almond Macaroon Cherry Pie

Rose Anne LeMon *Sierra Vista, Arizona*
Bake-Off® Contest 32, 1986

A delectable mixture of coconut and almonds makes a crunchy top crust for this cherry pie.

1 refrigerated pie crust
(from 15-oz. pkg.)

FILLING
1 (21-oz.) can cherry fruit pie
filling
1/4 to 1/2 teaspoon cinnamon
1/8 teaspoon salt, if desired
1 teaspoon lemon juice

TOPPING
1 cup coconut
1/2 cup sliced almonds
1/4 cup sugar
1/8 teaspoon salt, if desired
1/4 cup milk
1 tablespoon margarine or
butter, melted
1/4 teaspoon almond extract
1 egg, beaten

Prepare pie crust according to package directions for *one-crust filled pie* using 9-inch pie pan.

Heat oven to 400°F. In large bowl, combine all filling ingredients; spoon into crust-lined pan. Bake at 400°F. for 20 minutes; remove from oven.

Meanwhile, in medium bowl, combine all topping ingredients; spread evenly over partially baked pie. Bake an additional 15 to 30 minutes or until crust and topping are golden brown. Cover pie with foil during last 5 to 10 minutes of baking if necessary to prevent excessive browning.

Yield: 8 servings

Nutrition Per Serving: Calories 380; Protein 4g; Carbohydrate 58g; Fat 16g; Sodium 200mg

Apple Date Pie

Susan Dunne *Summit, New Jersey*
Bake-Off® Contest 7, 1955

The contest was still called the Grand National in 1955. Most homemakers were still spending hours in the kitchen and pie was the favorite dessert. This spicy variation on apple pie still has lots of family appeal—but today you can save time with ready-prepared pie crust.

1 (15-oz.) pkg. refrigerated
pie crusts

FILLING
1/2 cup sugar
1 tablespoon all-purpose flour
1/2 teaspoon cinnamon
1/4 teaspoon ginger
1/4 teaspoon nutmeg
1/4 teaspoon salt
1 teaspoon grated lemon peel
5 cups thinly sliced peeled
apples (5 medium)
1/2 cup pitted dates, cut into
pieces
1 teaspoon lemon juice
1 tablespoon margarine or
butter

Prepare pie crust according to package directions for *two-crust pie* using 9-inch pie pan.

Heat oven to 425°F. In large bowl, combine sugar, flour, cinnamon, ginger, nutmeg, salt and lemon peel; mix well. Add apple slices and dates; mix well. Spoon into crust-lined pan. Sprinkle with lemon juice. Dot with margarine. Top with second crust; seal edges and flute. Cut slits in top crust.

Bake at 425°F. for 35 to 40 minutes or until apples are tender and crust is golden brown. Cover edge of crust with strips of foil after 15 to 20 minutes of baking to prevent excessive browning.

Yield: 8 servings

Nutrition Per Serving: Calories 370; Protein 2g; Carbohydrate 53g; Fat 16g; Sodium 350mg

Cherry-Berry Pie

Eva Carter *Elroy, Wisconsin*
Bake-Off® Contest 7, 1955

Be sure to use tart red pie cherries, not cherry pie filling, for this generously filled two-crust pie.

1 (15-oz.) pkg. refrigerated
pie crusts

FILLING
3/4 cup sugar
2 tablespoons quick-cooking
tapioca
2 tablespoons cornstarch
1/4 teaspoon salt
1 (16-oz.) can pitted tart red
cherries, drained, reserving
liquid
1 (10-oz.) pkg. frozen
strawberries with syrup,
thawed, drained, reserving
syrup
1 tablespoon lemon juice
2 teaspoons sugar

Prepare pie crust according to package directions for *two-crust pie* using 9-inch pie pan.

Heat oven to 400° F. In medium saucepan, combine ¾ cup sugar, tapioca, cornstarch and salt; mix well. Stir in reserved cherry and strawberry liquids. Cook over medium heat 5 to 10 minutes or until mixture thickens and boils, stirring constantly. Remove from heat. Stir in cherries, strawberries and lemon juice. Spoon fruit mixture into crust-lined pan. Top with second crust; seal edges and flute. Sprinkle with 2 teaspoons sugar. Cut slits in top crust.

Bake at 400° F. for 30 to 35 minutes or until golden brown. Cover edges of crust with strips of foil during last 10 to 15 minutes of baking to prevent excessive browning. Cool.

Yield: 8 servings

Nutrition Per Serving: Calories 400; Protein 2g; Carbohydrate 66g; Fat 15g; Sodium 340mg

Chocolate Caramel Satin Pie

Phelles Friedenauer *Rockford, Illinois*
Bake-Off® Contest 33, 1988

Let your hospitality show with this decadent, velvety-rich pie. A caramel nut filling is topped with dark sweet chocolate followed by white chocolate whipped cream. Serve it well chilled.

1 refrigerated pie crust (from 15-oz. pkg.)

FILLING
24 vanilla caramels, unwrapped
⅓ cup water
⅔ cup firmly packed brown sugar
⅔ cup dairy sour cream
2 eggs, beaten
1 teaspoon vanilla
½ cup chopped walnuts
½ oz. (⅓ cup) grated sweet cooking chocolate, reserving 2 tablespoons

TOPPING
1 cup white vanilla chips*
¼ cup milk
1 cup whipping cream

Heat oven to 450° F. Prepare pie crust according to package directions for *one-crust baked shell* using 9-inch pie pan. Bake at 450° F. for 8 to 9 minutes or until light golden brown. Cool slightly.

Meanwhile, in medium heavy saucepan, combine caramels and water. Cook over low heat until caramels are melted and mixture is smooth, stirring occasionally. Remove from heat. Stir in brown sugar, sour cream, eggs, vanilla and walnuts; blend well. Pour into baked shell. Reduce heat to 350° F. *Immediately* return to oven. Bake an additional 30 to 40 minutes or until edges of filling are set. Cool 15 minutes. Sprinkle chocolate over pie. Refrigerate until firm, about 2 hours.

In small heavy saucepan, combine white vanilla chips and milk. Cook over low heat until chips are melted, stirring constantly. Remove from heat; cool. In small bowl, beat whipping cream until stiff peaks form. Fold in melted chip mixture. Spread over cooled filling. Sprinkle with 2 tablespoons reserved chocolate. Refrigerate until serving time. Store in refrigerator.

Yield: 10 servings

*Tip: Do not substitute almond bark or vanilla-flavored candy coating.

Nutrition Per Serving: Calories 540; Protein 6g; Carbohydrate 57g; Fat 32g; Sodium 240mg

Phelles Friedenauer: Chocolate Caramel Satin Pie

Most families have special dishes for special occasions. "Christmas Eve wouldn't be complete without meatballs in wine sauce and Shrimp DeJonge after midnight mass, and every July Fourth we drag out the crank freezer and make homemade ice cream," says Phelles Friedenauer.

But nonholidays are important, too. "I knew very little about cooking when I got married," says Phelles, "but I soon learned how important it is to put good food on the table." Too often everyday dinners don't get the applause they should. Kids are tired, adults are frazzled, even pets seem impatient, clamoring for the attention they missed all day. However, a rich, chocolatey dessert like Phelles's Chocolate Caramel Satin Pie always gets a big hand.

Chocolate Dream Pie

Lirene Alexander *Tampa, Florida*
Bake-Off® Contest 12, 1960

This chocolate lovers' choice makes a great company dessert. It needs long refrigeration, so you can make it a day ahead. And it's so rich, it serves ten guests.

1 refrigerated pie crust (from 15-oz. pkg.)

FILLING
¹/₂ cup sugar
¹/₄ cup cornstarch
¹/₈ teaspoon salt
1 cup milk
1 (6-oz.) pkg. (1 cup) semi-sweet chocolate chips
2 egg yolks, slightly beaten
1 (3-oz.) pkg. cream cheese, cubed, softened
1¹/₂ cups whipping cream
1 teaspoon vanilla

Heat oven to 450°F. Prepare pie crust according to package directions for *one-crust baked shell* using 9-inch pie pan. Bake at 450°F. for 9 to 11 minutes or until light golden brown. Cool completely.

In medium saucepan, combine sugar, cornstarch and salt; mix well. Gradually stir in milk. Add chocolate chips and egg yolks. Cook over medium heat until mixture is thickened, stirring constantly. Remove from heat; stir in cream cheese, beating until smooth. Cover surface with plastic wrap. Refrigerate until just cool, about 1 hour.

In large bowl, beat whipping cream and vanilla until soft peaks form. Reserve 1 cup whipped cream for topping. Fold remaining whipped cream into cooled chocolate mixture. Spoon evenly into cooled baked shell. Spoon or pipe reserved whipped cream over filling. Refrigerate 6 to 8 hours or overnight. Store in refrigerator.

Yield: 10 servings

Nutrition Per Serving: Calories 400; Protein 4g; Carbohydrate 34g; Fat 29g; Sodium 190mg

Luscious Almond Caramel Pie

Bettie Sechrist *Montgomery, Alabama*
Bake-Off® Contest 34, 1990

This indulgent pie has a memorable almond filling topped with caramel and whipped cream.

1 refrigerated pie crust (from 15-oz. pkg.)

FILLING
¹/₄ cup unsalted butter, butter or margarine, softened
2 teaspoons all-purpose flour
1 (7-oz.) pkg. almond paste, cut into small pieces
2 eggs
1 (12.5-oz.) jar (1 cup) caramel ice cream topping
3 tablespoons all-purpose flour
1 cup sliced almonds

TOPPING
1 to 2 cups whipping cream
2 to 3 tablespoons powdered sugar

Prepare pie crust according to package directions for *one-crust filled pie* using 9-inch pie pan.

Heat oven to 400°F. In small bowl, combine butter, 2 teaspoons flour, almond paste and eggs at medium speed until well blended. (Mixture will not be smooth.) Spoon mixture evenly into crust-lined pan. Bake at 400°F. for 17 to 20 minutes or until filling is set and light golden brown. Remove from oven.

Reserve ¹/₃ cup of the caramel topping. In small bowl using wire whisk, blend remaining caramel topping and 3 tablespoons flour. Stir in almonds. Carefully spoon over filling in pie pan. Return to oven; bake an additional 9 to 12 minutes or until golden brown. Cool on wire rack 30 minutes. Refrigerate 2 to 3 hours.

In large bowl, beat whipping cream and powdered sugar until stiff peaks form. Pipe or spoon whipped cream around edge of chilled pie, leaving 4-inch circle in center. Just before serving, drizzle about 2 teaspoons of the reserved caramel topping over each piece. Store in refrigerator.

Yield: 10 servings

Nutrition Per Serving: Calories 590; Protein 10g; Carbohydrate 49g; Fat 40g; Sodium 220mg

Chocolate Dream Pie

Open Sesame Pie

Dorothy Koteen *Washington, D.C.*
Bake-Off® Contest 6, 1954 Grand Prize Winner

This recipe created a profitable rush to the country's supermarkets. It wasn't the date chiffon filling, but the sesame seed crust that caused such commotion. Within hours after this pie was announced as the winning recipe, a virtual "out of stock" was declared on sesame seed. And from that time on, it has been a regularly stocked item on most supermarket shelves.

**1 refrigerated pie crust
   (from 15-oz. pkg.)**
**2 tablespoons sesame seed,
   toasted***

FILLING
**1 envelope unflavored
   gelatin**
$^1/_4$ cup cold water
**1 (8-oz.) pkg. (1$^3/_4$ cups)
   chopped dates**
$^1/_4$ cup sugar
$^1/_4$ teaspoon salt
1 cup milk
2 egg yolks
1 teaspoon vanilla
1$^1/_2$ cups whipping cream
2 tablespoons sugar
$^1/_8$ to $^1/_4$ teaspoon nutmeg

Heat oven to 450° F. Prepare pie crust according to package directions for *one-crust baked shell* using 9-inch pie pan. Press toasted seeds into bottom of crust-lined pan. Bake at 450° F. for 9 to 11 minutes or until lightly browned. Cool completely.

In small bowl, sprinkle gelatin over $^1/_4$ cup cold water; set aside to soften. In medium saucepan, combine dates, $^1/_4$ cup sugar, salt, milk and egg yolks. Cook over medium heat 10 to 12 minutes or until mixture is slightly thickened, stirring constantly. Remove from heat. Add softened gelatin and vanilla; stir until gelatin is dissolved. Refrigerate until date mixture is thickened and partially set, stirring occasionally.

In small bowl, combine whipping cream and 2 tablespoons sugar; beat until stiff peaks form. Fold into date mixture. Spoon filling into cooled baked pie shell; sprinkle with nutmeg. Refrigerate at least 2 hours before serving. Store in refrigerator.

Yield: 8 servings

*Tip: To toast sesame seed, spread on cookie sheet; bake at 375° F. for 3 to 5 minutes or until light golden brown, stirring occasionally. Or spread in small skillet; stir over medium heat for about 5 minutes or until light golden brown.

Nutrition Per Serving: Calories 430; Protein 5g; Carbohydrate 45g; Fat 27g; Sodium 240mg

Frost-on-the-Pumpkin Pie

Kathleen S. Johnson *Columbus, Ohio*
Bake-Off® Contest 29, 1980

Enjoy this delicate pumpkin pie with a no-bake filling any time of the year.

CRUST
**1$^1/_4$ cups (18 squares) graham
   cracker crumbs**
3 tablespoons sugar
$^1/_2$ teaspoon cinnamon
$^1/_4$ teaspoon nutmeg
$^1/_8$ teaspoon cloves
**$^1/_3$ cup margarine or butter,
   melted**

FILLING
1 (16-oz.) can vanilla frosting
1 cup dairy sour cream
1 cup canned pumpkin
1 teaspoon cinnamon
$^1/_2$ teaspoon ginger
$^1/_4$ teaspoon cloves
**1 (8-oz.) container (4 cups)
   frozen whipped topping,
   thawed**

Heat oven to 350° F. In small bowl, combine all crust ingredients; stir until blended. Reserve 2 tablespoons of crust mixture for topping. Press remaining crust mixture in bottom and up sides of 9- or 10-inch pie pan. Bake at 350° F. for 6 minutes. Cool.

In large bowl, combine all filling ingredients except whipped topping; beat 2 minutes at medium speed. Fold in 1 cup of the whipped topping; pour into prepared crust. Refrigerate until set. Spread remaining whipped topping over filling; sprinkle with reserved crust mixture. Refrigerate at least 4 hours or until serving time.*

Yield: 8 servings

*Tip: If substituting other nonfrozen whipped toppings or whipped cream, refrigerate 6 hours or overnight before serving.

Nutrition Per Serving: Calories 560; Protein 3g; Carbohydrate 64g; Fat 32g; Sodium 320mg

LEONARD (LEN) THOMPSON

Challenges are as certain in life as love and taxes. "I like challenges," says Leonard Thompson. Len remembers childhood baking, using a temperamental gasoline stove. "You would have to tiptoe across the floor so the cake wouldn't fall." Len didn't get a chance to perfect his baking back then—the intervening years were dominated by the adventures of raising four children and navigating a successful career. But he always met the demands of making special time for family. "On weekends, usually on Sunday morning, it would be my pancake breakfast day, eggs, bacon, everything . . . the whole family uses my pancake recipe now.

"Since I retired I've gotten back into baking," Len says. The challenges had waited for him. For Thanksgiving he started a pecan pie, "but I made one little mistake, using a pan with holes in the bottom. Every-

thing turned out fine—except there was a black cloud of smoke pouring out of the oven. Half the filling leaked out. And we were supposed to go to Thanksgiving dinner that day! My wife suggested I put chocolate pudding in there, so I did, topped it off with a little whipped cream, and named it 'Disaster Pie.' People really liked it, so I improved it . . . My wife suggested that I enter it in the Bake-Off® Contest. I only sent in one entry, and lo and behold . . ." Chocolate Silk Pecan Pie was on its way to becoming a Pillsbury classic.

Len considers his journey to the Bake-Off® Contest to have been as rewarding as the outcome. "Getting to the Bake-Off® Contest is a challenge, and if you like challenges, it's a tremendous one, and I do like challenges."

Chocolate Silk Pecan Pie

Leonard (Len) Thompson *San Jose, California*
Bake-Off® Contest 32, 1986 Prize Winner

In this luscious pie, smooth-as-silk chocolate crowns a rich-flavored pecan pie. It is one of our favorites! For best results, be sure to measure ingredients accurately.

1 refrigerated pie crust
   (from 15-oz. pkg.)

PECAN FILLING
$^1/_3$ cup sugar
$^1/_2$ cup dark corn syrup
3 tablespoons margarine or
   butter, melted
$^1/_8$ teaspoon salt, if desired
2 eggs
$^1/_2$ cup chopped pecans

FILLING
1 cup hot milk
$^1/_4$ teaspoon vanilla
1$^1/_3$ cups semi-sweet
   chocolate chips

TOPPING
1 cup whipping cream
2 tablespoons powdered
   sugar
$^1/_4$ teaspoon vanilla

Chocolate curls, if desired

Prepare pie crust according to package directions for *one-crust filled pie* using 9-inch pie pan. Heat oven to 350°F. In small bowl, combine sugar, corn syrup, margarine, salt and eggs; beat 1 minute at medium speed. Stir in pecans. Pour into crust-lined pan. Bake at 350°F. for 40 to 55 minutes or until center of pie is puffed and golden brown. Cool 1 hour.

While filled crust is cooling, in blender container or food processor bowl with metal blade, combine all filling ingredients; blend 1 minute or until smooth. Refrigerate about 1 1/2 hours or until mixture is slightly thickened but not set. Gently stir; pour into cooled filled crust. Refrigerate until firm, about 1 hour.

In small bowl, beat topping ingredients until stiff peaks form. Spoon or pipe over filling. Garnish with chocolate curls. Store in refrigerator.

Yield: 10 servings

Nutrition Per Serving: Calories 490; Protein 5g; Carbohydrate 46g; Fat 32g; Sodium 240mg

Pennsylvania Dutch Cake and Custard Pie

Gladys Fulton *Summerville, South Carolina Bake-Off® Contest 35, 1992 Grand Prize Winner*

Applesauce, sour cream and molasses combine for a luscious custardlike filling in this take-off of a shoofly pie.

1 refrigerated pie crust (from 15-oz. pkg.)

FILLING
1/3 cup sugar
2 tablespoons all-purpose flour
1 teaspoon apple pie spice*
1 cup applesauce
2/3 cup dairy sour cream
1/3 cup molasses
1 egg, beaten

CAKE
1/2 cup sugar
1/4 cup margarine or butter, softened
1/2 cup sour milk**
1 egg
1 teaspoon vanilla
1 1/4 cups all-purpose flour
1 teaspoon baking powder
1/2 teaspoon salt
1/4 teaspoon baking soda

GLAZE
1/2 to 3/4 cup powdered sugar
2 tablespoons coffee

Prepare pie crust according to package directions for *one-crust filled pie* using 9-inch pie pan or 9-inch deep-dish pie pan.

Heat oven to 350°F. In medium bowl, combine 1/3 cup sugar, 2 tablespoons flour and apple pie spice; mix well. Stir in remaining filling ingredients; blend well. Set aside.

In small bowl, combine 1/2 cup sugar and margarine; beat until well blended. Beat in sour milk, 1 egg and vanilla. (Mixture will look curdled.) Add flour, baking powder, salt and baking soda; mix well. Spoon into crust-lined pan. Carefully pour filling mixture over batter.

Bake at 350°F. for 50 to 65 minutes or until center springs back when touched lightly and top is deep golden brown. Filling will sink to bottom during baking.

In small bowl, combine powdered sugar and coffee until of desired drizzling consistency; blend well. Drizzle over warm pie. Serve warm.

Yield: 10 servings

*Tips: A mixture of 1/2 teaspoon cinnamon, 1/4 teaspoon ginger, 1/8 teaspoon nutmeg and 1/8 teaspoon allspice can be substituted for the apple pie spice.

**To make sour milk, add 1 teaspoon lemon juice to 1/2 cup milk; let stand 5 minutes.

High Altitude—Above 3,500 feet: Increase flour in cake to 1 1/3 cups. Bake as directed above.

Nutrition Per Serving: Calories 400; Protein 5g; Carbohydrate 62g; Fat 15g; Sodium 380mg

Chocolate Silk Pecan Pie, page 289

Company's Coming Cashew Pie

Hazel Frost *Chicago, Illinois*
Bake-Off® Contest 1, 1949

In this recipe from the first Bake-Off® Contest, cashew nuts are used instead of pecans to make a rich, decadent pie. Garnish each slice of pie with whipped cream and a whole cashew nut.

1 refrigerated pie crust (from 15-oz. pkg.)

FILLING
³/₄ cup firmly packed brown sugar
3 tablespoons margarine or butter, softened
³/₄ cup light corn syrup
1 teaspoon vanilla
3 eggs
1 cup chopped cashews

Prepare pie crust according to package directions for *one-crust filled pie* using 9-inch pie pan.

Heat oven to 350°F. In large bowl, beat brown sugar and margarine at high speed until light and fluffy. Add corn syrup and vanilla; beat at medium speed until smooth. Beat in eggs 1 at a time, blending well after each addition. Stir in cashew nuts. Pour into crust-lined pan.

Bake at 350°F. for 45 to 50 minutes or until top of pie is deep golden brown. Cover edge of crust with strips of foil after 15 to 20 minutes of baking to prevent excessive browning.

Yield: 8 servings

Nutrition Per Serving: Calories 450; Protein 6g; Carbohydrate 60g; Fat 22g; Sodium 350mg

Raspberry Angel Cream Pie

Kay Bare *Terreton, Idaho*
Bake-Off® Contest 33, 1988

No need to heat up your kitchen on a warm spring day. This fluffy pie can be prepared using the microwave.

CRUST
1 refrigerated pie crust (from 15-oz. pkg.)
¹/₄ cup chopped walnuts or pecans

FILLING
25 large marshmallows
¹/₂ cup milk
1 cup whipping cream, whipped

TOPPING
¹/₃ cup sugar
2 tablespoons cornstarch
³/₄ cup water
1 teaspoon lemon juice
1 teaspoon orange-flavored liqueur, if desired
1 teaspoon red food color, if desired
2 cups fresh or frozen raspberries without syrup, thawed, drained

GARNISH
Whipped cream
Whole raspberries

Heat oven to 450°F. Prepare pie crust according to package directions for *one-crust baked shell* using 9-inch pie pan. Press walnuts into bottom of crust-lined pan. Generously prick crust with fork. Bake at 450°F. for 9 to 11 minutes or until light golden brown. Cool completely.

Microwave Directions: In 2-quart microwave-safe bowl, combine marshmallows and milk. Microwave on HIGH for 2 to 3 minutes or until marshmallows are puffed. With wire whisk, beat mixture until smooth and creamy. Cover; refrigerate until thickened but not set, 35 to 45 minutes. Fold in whipped cream. Spread over bottom of cooled baked shell. Refrigerate until thoroughly chilled, about 1 hour.

In medium microwave-safe bowl, combine sugar and cornstarch; mix well. Gradually stir in water, lemon juice, liqueur and food color. Stir in 1 cup of the raspberries. Microwave on HIGH for 2 minutes; mix well. Microwave on HIGH for an additional 2 to 5 minutes or until thickened and clear, stirring once halfway through cooking. Cover surface with plastic wrap. Refrigerate until just cool, about 1 hour. Fold in remaining 1 cup raspberries. Spoon evenly over cooled filling. Refrigerate until set, 1 to 2 hours. Garnish with whipped cream and whole raspberries. Store in refrigerator.

Yield: 8 servings

Nutrition Per Serving: Calories 400; Protein 3g; Carbohydrate 44g; Fat 24g; Sodium 160mg

Company's Coming Cashew Pie

French Silk Chocolate Pie

Mrs. Kendall E. Cooper *Silver Springs, Maryland*
Bake-Off® Contest 3, 1951 Prize Winner

The original recipe for this ultra-rich pie used raw eggs in the uncooked filling. It now calls for either pasteurized eggs or fat-free egg product. Pasteurized eggs are uncooked eggs that have been heat-treated to kill bacteria that can cause food poisoning. They can be found in the dairy case at large supermarkets.

1 refrigerated pie crust (from 15-oz. pkg.)

FILLING
3 oz. unsweetened chocolate, cut into pieces
1 cup butter, softened (do not use margarine)
1 cup sugar
1/2 teaspoon vanilla
4 pasteurized eggs or 1 cup refrigerated or frozen fat-free egg product, thawed

TOPPING
1/2 cup sweetened whipped cream
Chocolate curls, if desired

Heat oven to 450° F. Prepare pie crust according to package directions for *one-crust baked shell* using 9-inch pie pan. Bake at 450° F. for 9 to 11 minutes or until light golden brown. Cool completely.

Melt chocolate in small saucepan over low heat; cool. In small bowl, beat butter until fluffy.

Gradually add sugar, beating until light and fluffy. Blend in cooled chocolate and vanilla. Add eggs, 1 at a time, beating at high speed 2 minutes after each addition. Beat until mixture is smooth and fluffy. Pour into cooled baked shell. Refrigerate at least 2 hours before serving. Top with whipped cream and chocolate curls. Store in refrigerator.

Yield: 10 servings

Nutrition Per Serving: Calories 470; Protein 4g; Carbohydrate 34g; Fat 35g; Sodium 300mg

Chocolate Orange Layer Pie

Julia Walker *Jacksonville, Florida*
Bake-Off® Contest 5, 1953

In this recipe, smooth extra-rich chocolate filling is topped with a fluffy orange layer. For a lovely finishing touch, garnish each serving with a mandarin orange segment dipped in chocolate.

1 refrigerated pie crust (from 15-oz. pkg.)

CHOCOLATE FILLING
1/2 cup sugar
3 tablespoons cornstarch
1/4 teaspoon salt
2 tablespoons milk
2 oz. unsweetened chocolate
1 cup milk
2 egg yolks, slightly beaten
2 tablespoons margarine or butter
1/2 teaspoon vanilla

ORANGE FILLING
1 teaspoon unflavored gelatin
1/4 cup frozen orange juice concentrate, thawed
1 cup whipping cream
1/4 cup powdered sugar

Heat oven to 450° F. Prepare pie crust according to package directions for *one-crust baked shell* using 9-inch pie pan. Bake at 450° F. for 9 to 11 minutes or until light golden brown. Cool completely.

In small bowl, combine sugar, cornstarch and salt; mix well. Stir in 2 tablespoons milk. Set aside. In medium heavy saucepan over low heat, melt unsweetened chocolate with 1 cup milk, stirring constantly until smooth. Blend in cornstarch mixture. Cook over low heat until mixture is thickened and boils, stirring constantly. Boil 1 minute. Blend about 1/4 cup of hot mixture into egg yolks. Gradually stir yolk mixture into hot mixture in saucepan. Cook over low heat for 3 minutes, stirring constantly. Remove from heat; stir in margarine and vanilla. Cover surface with plastic wrap. Refrigerate until just cool, about 1 hour. Spoon chocolate filling evenly into cooled baked shell.

In small saucepan, combine gelatin and orange juice concentrate. Stir over low heat until gelatin dissolves. Cool slightly. In small bowl, combine whipping cream and powdered sugar; beat until soft peaks form. Fold orange juice mixture into whipped cream. Spread evenly over chocolate filling. Refrigerate 1 hour. Store in refrigerator.

Yield: 8 servings

Nutrition Per Serving: Calories 400; Protein 5g; Carbohydrate 37g; Fat 27g; Sodium 270mg

Chocolate Orange Layer Pie

Lemon Luscious Pie

Helen Gorsuch *Santa Ana, California*
Bake-Off® Contest 14, 1962 Prize Winner

The delicate tartness of sour cream complements the lemon in this pie filling. This pie can be made a day ahead of serving, making it a perfect party food.

1 refrigerated pie crust (from 15-oz. pkg.)

FILLING
1 cup sugar
3 tablespoons cornstarch
1 cup milk
¼ cup lemon juice
3 egg yolks, slightly beaten
¼ cup margarine or butter
1 tablespoon grated lemon peel
1 cup dairy sour cream

Heat oven to 450° F. Prepare pie crust according to package directions for *one-crust baked shell* using 9-inch pie pan. Bake at 450° F. for 9 to 11 minutes or until light golden brown; cool.

In medium saucepan, combine sugar and cornstarch; blend well. Stir in milk, lemon juice and egg yolks; cook over medium heat until thick, stirring constantly. Remove from heat; stir in margarine and lemon peel. Cool slightly. Fold in sour cream. Spoon into cooled baked shell. Refrigerate at least 2 hours or until set. Garnish as desired. Store in refrigerator.

Yield: 8 servings

Nutrition Per Serving: Calories 430; Protein 4g; Carbohydrate 44g; Fat 27g; Sodium 270mg

Pineapple Crunch Pie

June L. McVey *Lincoln, Nebraska*
Bake-Off® Contest 3, 1951

In the 1950s, when pie often was served as an everyday dessert, homemakers welcomed new recipes that would impress family or friends. This two-layer pineapple pie topped with a brown sugar-pecan layer still makes a big hit.

1 (15-oz.) pkg. refrigerated pie crusts

FILLING
2 tablespoons cornstarch
2 tablespoons sugar
Dash salt
1 (20-oz.) can crushed pineapple in heavy syrup, undrained*
1 tablespoon lemon juice
1 tablespoon margarine or butter

TOPPING
¼ cup firmly packed brown sugar
2 tablespoons margarine or butter
1 tablespoon corn syrup
½ cup chopped pecans

Prepare pie crust according to package directions for *two-crust pie* using 9-inch pie pan.

Heat oven to 425° F. In medium saucepan, combine cornstarch, sugar and salt; mix well. Stir in pineapple. Cook over medium heat until mixture thickens and boils, stirring constantly. Boil 1 minute. Remove from heat; stir in lemon juice and 1 tablespoon margarine. Pour into crust-lined pan. Top with

second crust; seal edges and flute. Cut slits in top crust. Bake at 425° F. for 15 to 20 minutes or until light golden brown.

Meanwhile, in small heavy saucepan, combine all topping ingredients. Cook over low heat until sugar is dissolved, stirring constantly. Remove pie from oven.

Spoon and spread warm topping mixture evenly over top of pie. Cover edge of crust with strips of foil to prevent excessive browning. Bake at 425° F. for an additional 10 to 15 minutes or until crust is deep golden brown.

Yield: 8 servings

*Tip: One (20-oz.) can crushed pineapple in unsweetened juice, undrained, can be substituted for crushed pineapple in heavy syrup.

Nutrition Per Serving: Calories 430; Protein 3g; Carbohydrate 52g; Fat 24g; Sodium 340mg

Grandmother's Raisin Cream Pie

Naomi Ware *Anchorage, Alaska*
Bake-Off® Contest 5, 1953

Rich, sweet raisin pies are an old-time favorite. They are easy to make and call for ingredients one usually has on hand. This Bake-Off® Contest favorite is topped with a delicate meringue.

1 refrigerated pie crust (from 15-oz. pkg.)

FILLING
¾ cup sugar
3 tablespoons all-purpose flour
1 teaspoon cinnamon

¹/₄ teaspoon cloves
1¹/₂ cups dairy sour cream
3 egg yolks, slightly beaten
1 cup raisins
¹/₂ cup chopped walnuts

MERINGUE
3 egg whites
¹/₄ teaspoon cream of tartar
Dash salt
6 tablespoons sugar

Heat oven to 450° F. Prepare pie crust according to package directions for *one-crust baked shell* using 9-inch pie pan. Bake at 450° F. for 9 to 11 minutes or until light golden brown. Cool completely.

In medium heavy saucepan, combine ³/₄ cup sugar, flour, cinnamon and cloves; mix well. Stir in sour cream and egg yolks until smooth. Cook over medium heat until filling is thickened, stirring constantly. Remove from heat; stir in raisins and walnuts. Cover surface with plastic wrap. Refrigerate 1 hour. Pour into cooled baked shell.

Heat oven to 350° F. In small bowl, beat egg whites, cream of tartar and salt at medium speed until soft peaks form, about 1 minute.

Beating at high speed, gradually add 6 tablespoons sugar 1 tablespoon at a time, until stiff peaks form and sugar is dissolved. Spoon meringue over filling. Seal to edge of crust. Bake at 350° F. for 10 to 15 minutes or until lightly browned. Cool completely. Store in refrigerator.

Yield: 10 servings

Nutrition Per Serving: Calories 370; Protein 5g; Carbohydrate 47g; Fat 19g; Sodium 160mg

Grandmother's Raisin Cream Pie

Caribbean Truffle Pie

Julie DeMatteo *Clementon, New Jersey*
Bake-Off® Contest 37, 1996 Prize Winner

Julie DeMatteo works in her husband's entertainment production business, so she knows the importance of dramatic presentation. Her creamy lemon-lime pie topped with coconut streusel and garnished with whipped cream and lime slices gets star billing as a special occasion dessert.

CRUST
1 refrigerated pie crust
  (from 15-oz. pkg.)
2 tablespoons coconut

STREUSEL
1/4 cup all-purpose flour
1/4 cup sugar
4 teaspoons margarine or
  butter
1/4 cup coconut

FILLING
1 (2.9-oz.) pkg. lemon
  pudding and pie filling mix
  (not instant)
1/2 cup sugar
3 tablespoons lime juice
2 egg yolks
2 cups water
1 teaspoon grated lime peel
1 cup white vanilla chips or
  chopped white baking bar
1 (8-oz.) pkg. cream cheese,
  softened
6 tablespoons dairy sour
  cream

TOPPING AND GARNISH
1/2 cup whipping cream
Lime slices, cut into fourths

Heat oven to 450° F. Allow crust pouch to stand at room temperature for 15 to 20 minutes. Remove pie crust from pouch. Unfold crust. Sprinkle with 2 tablespoons coconut; press in lightly. Carefully place crust, coconut side up, in 9-inch pie pan; press in bottom and up sides of pan. Flute edge; prick crust generously with fork. Bake at 450° F. for 9 to 11 minutes or until golden brown. Cool crust while preparing streusel and filling. Reduce oven temperature to 425° F.

In small bowl, combine flour and 1/4 cup sugar. With pastry blender or fork, cut in margarine until mixture resembles coarse crumbs. Stir in 1/4 cup coconut. Spread mixture in ungreased shallow baking pan. Bake at 425° F. for 4 to 8 minutes or until light golden brown, stirring every minute. Set aside.

In medium saucepan, combine pudding mix, 1/2 cup sugar, lime juice and egg yolks; mix well. Stir in 2 cups water. Cook and stir over medium heat until mixture comes to a full boil. Remove from heat; stir in lime peel. In small bowl, combine vanilla chips and 1/2 cup of the hot pudding mixture; stir until chips are melted.

In small bowl, beat cream cheese until light and fluffy. Add vanilla chip mixture; beat until smooth. Spoon and spread in baked crust. Stir sour cream into remaining pie filling mixture; blend well. Spoon and spread over cream cheese layer. Refrigerate 2 hours or until chilled.

In small bowl, beat whipping cream until stiff peaks form. Pipe or spoon around edge of pie; gar-nish with lime slices. Sprinkle streusel in center of pie. Store in refrigerator.

Yield: 8 servings

Nutrition Per Serving: Calories 590; Protein 6g; Carbohydrate 61g; Fat 36g; Sodium 340mg

Winter Fruit Pie

Joan Verdeal *Arvada, Colorado*
Bake-Off® Contest 35, 1992

This unique pie features a cranberry and raisin filling laced with sweet spices and fragrant orange peel—it's wonderful!

1 (15-oz.) pkg. refrigerated
  pie crusts

FILLING
1 cup fresh or frozen
  cranberries
1 cup raisins
3/4 cup water
1/3 cup orange juice
2 tablespoons margarine or
  butter
1 1/2 to 3 teaspoons grated
  orange peel
1 cup sugar
1 cup chopped walnuts
1/2 teaspoon cinnamon
1/2 teaspoon nutmeg
1/8 teaspoon allspice
1 egg, well beaten
1/4 cup finely crushed saltine
  crackers
1 tablespoon margarine or
  butter, melted
1 tablespoon sugar
Vanilla ice cream, if desired

Prepare pie crust according to package directions for *two-crust pie* using 9-inch pie pan. Place 1 prepared crust in pan; press in bottom and up sides of pan, leaving 1/2 inch of bottom crust extending beyond edge of pan.

Heat oven to 425°F. In large saucepan, combine cranberries, raisins and water. Cook over medium-high heat until mixture boils, stirring constantly. Reduce heat; simmer about 10 minutes or until cranberries pop open. Remove from heat. Stir in orange juice, 2 tablespoons margarine, orange peel, 1 cup sugar, walnuts, cinnamon, nutmeg and allspice; mix well. Add egg and cracker crumbs; beat well. Pour into crust-lined pan. Top with second crust; seal and flute edges. Cut slits in top crust in spoke fashion; brush with 1 tablespoon melted margarine. Sprinkle with 1 tablespoon sugar.

Bake at 425°F. for 10 minutes. Reduce oven temperature to 375°F. Bake an additional 20 to 30 minutes or until golden brown. Serve warm or cool with ice cream.

Yield: 10 servings

Nutrition Per Serving: Calories 500; Protein 5g; Carbohydrate 64g; Fat 26g; Sodium 250mg

Taffy Apple Cheesecake Pie

Mary Ann Sasso *Franklin Park, Illinois. Bake-Off® Contest 36, 1994.*

It's both cheesecake and caramel apples, a culinary inspiration!

FILLING
2 tablespoons butter or margarine
1/2 cup firmly packed brown sugar
4 medium apples, peeled, cored and thinly sliced (about 5 cups)
21 caramels, unwrapped
1/4 cup half-and-half
1 (8-oz.) pkg. cream cheese, softened
1/2 cup firmly packed brown sugar
1/2 teaspoon pumpkin pie spice
1 1/2 teaspoons vanilla
1 egg

CRUST
1 refrigerated pie crust (from 15-oz. pkg.)

TOPPING
1/2 cup milk chocolate chips, finely chopped
3/4 cup pecans, finely chopped

GARNISH
1 teaspoon pumpkin pie spice
1 (8-oz.) container frozen whipped topping, thawed

In large skillet over medium-high heat, melt butter and 1/2 cup brown sugar, stirring constantly. Add apples; cook and stir 12 to 15 minutes or until apples are caramel in color and tender. Set aside.

In top of double boiler or in medium heavy saucepan over low heat, melt caramels with half-and-half until mixture is smooth, stirring frequently.* Keep warm.

In small bowl, beat cream cheese and 1/2 cup brown sugar until light and fluffy. Add 1/2 teaspoon pumpkin pie spice, vanilla and egg; beat until blended.

Prepare pie crust according to package directions for *one-crust filled pie* using 10-inch deep-dish pie pan or 9-inch springform pan.

Heat oven to 375°F. Fold half of caramel mixture into cream cheese mixture. Add apple mixture to remaining caramel mixture; mix well. Spoon apple caramel mixture into crust-lined pan. In small bowl, combine topping ingredients; reserve 2 tablespoons mixture. Sprinkle remaining topping over apple mixture. Top with caramel cream cheese mixture.

Bake at 375°F. for 35 to 45 minutes or until deep golden brown and filling is set. Cool completely. Refrigerate 30 minutes or until cold. Fold 1 teaspoon pumpkin pie spice into whipped topping. Pipe or spoon mixture onto pie; sprinkle

Marion L. Maire: Toffee Dream Pie

What's a peacock without a tail, a train without a caboose, a fairy tale without a "happily-ever-after"? That's how Marion Maire feels about desserts: "They are pretty to look at," she says, "delicious to eat and, I've always felt, 'completed' a meal." Ending with a Toffee Dream Pie is indeed a "happily-ever-after" of the first order.

with 2 tablespoons reserved topping. Store in refrigerator.

Yield: 10 servings

*Tip: To prepare caramel filling in microwave, in small microwave-safe bowl combine caramels and half-and-half. Microwave on HIGH for 1¹/₂ to 2 minutes, stirring once halfway through cooking. Stir until smooth.

Nutrition Per Serving: Calories 560; Protein 6g; Carbohydrate 64g; Fat 33g; Sodium 260mg

Toffee Dream Pie

Marion L. Maire *Avon Lake, Ohio*
Bake-Off® Contest 16, 1964

A dollop of whipped cream and a drizzle of chocolate sauce are perfect garnishes for this quick-and-easy pie.

1 refrigerated pie crust (from 15-oz. pkg.)

FILLING
32 large marshmallows
¹/₃ cup milk
3 (1.4-oz.) toffee candy bars, very finely chopped
1 cup whipping cream
2 tablespoons finely chopped toasted almonds, if desired*

Heat oven to 450° F. Prepare pie crust according to package directions for *one-crust baked shell* using 9-inch pie pan. Bake at 450° F. for 9 to 11 minutes or until light golden brown. Cool completely.

In heavy medium saucepan, combine marshmallows and milk. Cook over low heat until marshmallows are melted, stirring constantly. Remove from heat. Add chopped

toffee bars; stir until partially melted. Refrigerate 15 to 25 minutes or until thickened but not set.

In small bowl, beat whipping cream until soft peaks form. Fold whipped cream into marshmallow mixture. Spoon into cooled baked shell. Refrigerate 3 hours or until firm. Garnish with toasted almonds. Store in refrigerator.

Yield: 10 servings

*Tip: To toast almonds, spread on cookie sheet; bake at 350° F. for 5 to 10 minutes or until golden brown, stirring occasionally. Or spread in thin layer in microwave-safe pie pan. Microwave on HIGH for 4 to 7 minutes or until golden brown, stirring frequently.

Nutrition Per Serving: Calories 400; Protein 4g; Carbohydrate 38g; Fat 26g; Sodium 150mg

Strawberry Devonshire Pie

Grayce Berggren *State College, Pennsylvania*
Bake-Off® Contest 16, 1964

Devonshire cream is a rich, thickened cream from England, traditionally served with scones and tea. In this pie, the contestant has combined the flavor of this cream with strawberries to create a one-of-a-kind dessert!

1 refrigerated pie crust (from 15-oz. pkg.)

FILLING
1 envelope unflavored gelatin
¹/₄ cup water
¹/₃ cup sugar
¹/₈ teaspoon salt
1 cup dairy sour cream

2 tablespoons milk
2 egg yolks, slightly beaten
1 cup whipping cream, whipped

TOPPING
2 tablespoons sugar
1 tablespoon cornstarch
1 (10-oz.) pkg. frozen strawberries in unsweetened juice, thawed, drained, reserving liquid

Heat oven to 450° F. Prepare pie crust according to package directions for *one-crust baked shell* using 9-inch pie pan. Bake at 450° F. for 9 to 11 minutes or until light golden brown. Cool completely.

In small bowl, sprinkle gelatin over water; let stand to soften. In medium saucepan, combine ¹/₃ cup sugar, salt, sour cream, milk and egg yolks; mix well. Cook over medium heat 10 to 15 minutes or until very hot, stirring constantly. DO NOT BOIL. Stir in softened gelatin. Cover surface with plastic wrap; refrigerate 45 to 60 minutes until slightly thickened. Fold in whipped cream. Spoon into cooled baked shell. Refrigerate until set, about 2 hours.

In small saucepan, combine 2 tablespoons sugar and cornstarch; mix well. Gradually stir in reserved strawberry liquid. Cook over medium heat until mixture thickens and boils, stirring constantly. Boil 1 minute. Stir in strawberries. Cool to room temperature. Spoon strawberry mixture evenly over filling. Refrigerate until set, about 2 hours. Store in refrigerator.

Yield: 8 servings

Nutrition Per Serving: Calories 380; Protein 4g; Carbohydrate 33g; Fat 26g; Sodium 200mg

Orange Kist Coconut Cream Pie

Eugenia Ward *Amherst, Wisconsin*
Bake-Off® Contest 34, 1990 Prize Winner

This contestant developed her recipe as an updated coconut pie. But it will remind you of eating an orange-flavored ice cream treat.

1 refrigerated pie crust (from 15-oz. pkg.)

FILLING
1 cup sugar
3 tablespoons cornstarch
1 cup water
¹/₄ cup orange juice
¹/₄ cup margarine or butter
1 tablespoon grated orange peel
3 egg yolks
¹/₂ cup coconut, toasted*
¹/₂ cup dairy sour cream
¹/₂ cup whipping cream, whipped

TOPPING
¹/₂ cup whipping cream
2 tablespoons powdered sugar
¹/₄ cup coconut, toasted*
2 tablespoons sliced almonds, toasted**

Heat oven to 450° F. Prepare pie crust according to package directions for *one-crust baked shell* using 9-inch pie pan. Bake at 450° F. for 9 to 11 minutes or until light golden brown. Cool completely.

In medium saucepan, combine sugar and cornstarch; mix well. Stir in water, orange juice, margarine, orange peel and egg yolks. Cook over medium heat about 5 minutes

or until mixture thickens and boils, stirring constantly. Cover surface with plastic wrap. Refrigerate until just cool, about 1 hour. Stir in ¹/₂ cup toasted coconut and sour cream. Fold in whipped cream. Spoon into cooled baked shell.

In small bowl, beat ¹/₂ cup whipping cream and powdered sugar until stiff peaks form. Spread over filling. Garnish with ¹/₄ cup toasted coconut and almonds. Refrigerate 1 to 2 hours. Store in refrigerator.

Yield: 8 servings

*Tips: To toast coconut, spread on cookie sheet; bake at 375° F. for about 5 minutes or until light golden brown, stirring occasionally. Or spread in thin layer in microwave-safe pie pan. Microwave on MEDIUM for 5 to 8 minutes or until light golden brown, tossing with fork after each minute.

**To toast almonds, spread on cookie sheet; bake at 350° F. for 5 to 10 minutes or until light golden brown, stirring occasionally. Or spread in thin layer in microwave-safe pie pan. Microwave on HIGH for 5 to 7 minutes or until light golden brown, stirring frequently.

Nutrition Per Serving: Calories 490; Protein 4g; Carbohydrate 46g; Fat 32g; Sodium 220mg

Peacheesy Pie

Janis Boykin *Melbourne, Florida*
Bake-Off® Contest 16, 1964 Grand Prize Winner

This contestant created this recipe for a home economics assignment and became the first teenager to win the Bake-Off® Contest's Grand Prize. Now the pie is easier to make using refrigerated pie crust.

1 (15-oz.) pkg. refrigerated pie crusts

FILLING
¹/₂ cup sugar
2 tablespoons cornstarch
1 to 2 teaspoons pumpkin pie spice
2 tablespoons light corn syrup
2 teaspoons vanilla
1 (28-oz.) can peach slices, drained, reserving 3 tablespoons liquid

TOPPING
¹/₃ cup sugar
1 tablespoon lemon juice
2 eggs, slightly beaten
¹/₂ cup dairy sour cream
1 (3-oz.) pkg. cream cheese, softened
2 tablespoons margarine or butter

Allow crust pouches to stand at room temperature for 15 to 20 minutes.

Meanwhile, in medium bowl, combine ¹/₂ cup sugar, cornstarch, pumpkin pie spice, corn syrup, vanilla and peach slices; mix well. Set aside.

In small saucepan, combine 2 tablespoons of the reserved peach liquid, ¹/₃ cup sugar, lemon juice and eggs; mix well. Cook over medium heat until mixture thick-

ens and boils, stirring constantly. Boil 1 minute. Remove from heat. In small bowl, beat sour cream and cream cheese until smooth. Gradually beat in hot egg mixture until well blended. Set aside.

Heat oven to 425°F. Prepare pie crust according to package directions for *one-crust filled pie* using 9-inch pie pan. Spoon filling into crust-lined pan. Dot with margarine. Spoon topping mixture evenly over filling. Unfold second pie crust. Using floured 3-inch round cutter, cut out 8 circles from crust. Brush tops of circles with remaining 1 tablespoon reserved peach liquid. Arrange pie crust circles over topping.

Bake at 425°F. for 10 minutes. Reduce oven temperature to 350°F; bake an additional 35 to 40 minutes or until crust is golden brown. Cover edge of pie crust with strips of foil after 15 to 20 minutes of baking to prevent excessive browning. Cool. Store in refrigerator.

Yield: 8 servings

Nutrition Per Serving: Calories 510; Protein 5g; Carbohydrate 68g; Fat 26g; Sodium 370mg

Peacheesy Pie

White Chocolate Pecan Mousse Pie

Jeannette Allman *Mesa, Arizona*
Bake-Off® Contest 34, 1990

This light and fluffy mousse pie, flavored with buttered pecans, will melt in your mouth! It's best served well chilled.

1 refrigerated pie crust (from 15-oz. pkg.)

FILLING
2 tablespoons butter
2 cups chopped pecans
6 oz. (1 cup) vanilla milk chips or chopped white baking bar
1/4 cup milk
2 cups whipping cream
1/3 cup sugar
1 teaspoon vanilla

GARNISH
1 tablespoon grated chocolate or 1/4 cup chocolate-flavored syrup, if desired

Heat oven to 450°F. Prepare pie crust according to package directions for *one-crust baked shell* using 10-inch springform pan or 9-inch pie pan. Place prepared crust in pan; press in bottom and up sides of pan. With fork dipped in flour, press top edge of crust to sides of pan. Generously prick crust with fork. Bake at 450°F. for 9 to 11 minutes or until light golden brown. Cool completely.

Melt butter in 10-inch skillet over medium heat. Stir in pecans. Cook until pecans are golden brown, about 6 minutes, stirring constantly. Cool at room temperature 1 hour.

In small saucepan over low heat, melt white vanilla chips with milk, stirring constantly with wire whisk. Cool at room temperature 1 hour.

In large bowl, beat whipping cream until stiff peaks form. Fold in sugar, vanilla, pecans and melted white vanilla chips. Spoon into cooled baked shell. Refrigerate 4 hours before serving. Just before serving, garnish with grated chocolate or chocolate syrup. Store in refrigerator.*

Yield: 12 servings

*Tip: Pie can be frozen. Let stand at room temperature 30 to 45 minutes before serving.

Nutrition Per Serving: Calories 470; Protein 4g; Carbohydrate 27g; Fat 39g; Sodium 140mg

Peanut Butter Luster Pie

Helen Macinkowicz *Sterling Heights, Michigan*
Bake-Off® Contest 34, 1990

Helen Macinkowicz considers herself an expert pie baker. When she bakes for company, she likes to pull out all the stops with new combinations like this peanut butter chiffon filling between thin layers of semi-sweet chocolate.

1 refrigerated pie crust (from 15-oz. pkg.)

CHOCOLATE LAYER
1/2 cup semi-sweet chocolate chips
1 tablespoon margarine or butter
2 to 3 teaspoons water
1/4 cup powdered sugar

FILLING
1 cup margarine or butter
1 cup firmly packed brown sugar
1 cup peanut butter
1 (12-oz.) container frozen whipped topping, thawed

TOPPING
1/2 cup semi-sweet chocolate chips
1 tablespoon margarine or butter
2 to 3 teaspoons milk
1 1/2 teaspoons corn syrup

GARNISH
1 cup frozen whipped topping, thawed
2 tablespoons chopped peanuts

Heat oven to 450°F. Prepare pie crust according to package directions for *one-crust baked shell* using 9-inch pie pan. Bake at 450°F. for 9 to 11 minutes or until light golden brown. Cool completely.

In small saucepan over low heat, melt 1/2 cup chocolate chips and 1 tablespoon margarine with 2 teaspoons water, stirring constantly until smooth. Blend in powdered sugar until smooth. Add additional water if necessary for desired spreading consistency. Spread mixture over bottom and up sides of cooled baked shell. Refrigerate.

In medium saucepan, combine 1 cup margarine and brown sugar. Cook over medium heat until margarine is melted and mixture is smooth, stirring frequently. Refrig-

Peanut Butter Luster Pie

erate 10 minutes. In large bowl, beat peanut butter and brown sugar mixture at low speed until blended. Beat 1 minute at medium-high speed. Add 12 oz. whipped topping; beat 1 additional minute at low speed or until mixture is smooth and creamy. Pour over chocolate layer. Refrigerate.

In small saucepan over low heat, melt $1/2$ cup chocolate chips and 1 tablespoon margarine with 2 teaspoons milk and corn syrup, stirring constantly until smooth. Add additional milk if necessary for desired spreading consistency. Spoon and gently spread topping mixture evenly over filling. Refrigerate at least 2 hours to set topping.* Garnish with whipped topping and peanuts. Store in refrigerator.

Yield: 12 servings

Tip: For ease in serving, use sharp knife to score chocolate topping into serving pieces before topping is completely set. To serve, use sharp knife dipped in warm water to cut through scored lines.

Nutrition Per Serving: Calories 630; Protein 8g; Carbohydrate 48g; Fat 47g; Sodium 420mg

Vienna Chocolate Pie

Dorothy Wagoner *Lufkin, Texas*
Bake-Off® Contest 11, 1959

As it bakes, the filling in this pie forms three distinct layers, each unique in flavor and color. Serve wedges of the pie with dollops of whipped cream.

Dorothy Wagoner: Vienna Chocolate Pie

Many of the recipes in this book are heirloom recipes, passed down from parent to child over many generations. However, many of us aren't lucky enough to have our own family recipes. Dorothy Wagoner had the idea of inventing her own heirloom recipe, describing the effort as "searching for a flavor to match a memory."

"My father came to this country [from Germany] when he was a young man, and I was never to meet any of his family," Dorothy said. "Dad had a vivid memory, and through the stories of his childhood I could picture Grandmother's kitchen, the many wonderful things she baked and the dark, luxurious pastries that were Dad's favorite." Dorothy tried different flavor combinations, and then decided to make her dessert a pie, combining her own memories of her mother's cooking—her mother died when Dorothy was twelve—with her father's memories of his mother's pastries. "My mother was a wonderful cook, and loved to bake. Saturday was baking day, and our big old kitchen would be filled with the fragrance of bread and sweet rolls, and always pie." Through long experimentation Dorothy came up with her Vienna Chocolate Pie—a true labor of love. Since the 1959 Bake-Off® Contest, Dorothy's pie has become an heirloom recipe for families nationwide.

1 refrigerated pie crust (from 15-oz. pkg.)

FILLING
$1^1/2$ cups sugar
3 tablespoons all-purpose flour
$3/4$ teaspoon instant coffee granules
$1/4$ teaspoon cinnamon
Dash salt
4 eggs
$1/2$ cup buttermilk*
$1^1/2$ teaspoons vanilla
$1/2$ cup margarine or butter, softened
2 oz. unsweetened chocolate, melted
$1/4$ cup slivered almonds

Prepare pie crust according to package directions for *one-crust filled pie* using 9-inch pie pan.

Heat oven to 400°F. In medium bowl, combine sugar, flour, instant coffee, cinnamon and salt; mix well. In large bowl, beat eggs at high speed until light in color. Beat in dry ingredients. Add buttermilk, vanilla, margarine and chocolate; mix well. (Filling may look curdled.) Pour into crust-lined pan. Sprinkle with slivered almonds.

Bake at 400°F. for 25 to 30 minutes or until center is set and crust is deep golden brown. Cover edge of crust with strips of foil after 15 to 20 minutes of baking to prevent excessive browning.

Yield: 8 servings

Tip: To substitute for buttermilk, use 1 teaspoon vinegar or lemon juice plus milk to make $1/2$ cup.

Nutrition Per Serving: Calories 480; Protein 7g; Carbohydrate 53g; Fat 27g; Sodium 330mg

Vienna Chocolate Pie

Topsy Turvy Apple Pie

Ronelva Gaard *Kensington, Minnesota*
Bake-Off® Contest 3, 1951

Just as good today as in 1951, this is a fun-to-serve upside-down pie. Traditional apple filling is baked between two flaky refrigerated pie crusts and topped off with a rich pecan glaze.

GLAZE AND CRUST
1/4 **cup firmly packed brown sugar**
1 **tablespoon margarine or butter, melted**
1 **tablespoon corn syrup**
1/4 **cup pecan halves**
1 **(15-oz.) pkg. refrigerated pie crusts**

FILLING
2/3 **cup sugar**
2 **tablespoons all-purpose flour**
1/2 **teaspoon cinnamon**
4 **cups sliced peeled apples (4 medium)**

Whipped cream, if desired

In 9-inch pie pan, combine brown sugar, margarine and corn syrup; spread evenly over bottom of pan. Arrange pecans over mixture in pan. Prepare pie crust according to package directions for *two-crust pie;* place bottom crust over mixture in pan. Heat oven to 425° F.

In small bowl, combine sugar, 2 tablespoons flour and cinnamon; mix well. Arrange half of apple slices in crust-lined pan; sprinkle with half of sugar mixture. Repeat with remaining apple slices and sugar mixture. Top with second crust; seal and flute. Cut slits in several places.

Bake at 425° F. for 8 minutes. Reduce oven temperature to 325° F. Bake an additional 25 to 35 minutes or until apples are tender and crust is golden brown. (Place pan on foil or cookie sheet during baking to catch any spills.)

Loosen edge of pie; carefully invert onto serving plate. Serve warm or cold with whipped cream.

Yield: 8 servings

Nutrition Per Serving: Calories 440; Protein 2g; Carbohydrate 59g; Fat 22g; Sodium 350mg

Melba Streusel Pie

Elaine Stoeckel *Minneapolis, Minnesota*
Bake-Off® Contest 15, 1963

Melba is a sauce containing strained raspberries, red currant jelly, sugar and cornstarch. This pie with the melba-flavored filling is delicious served warm with cream poured over the top.

1 **refrigerated pie crust (from 15-oz. pkg.)**

TOPPING
3/4 **cup all-purpose flour**
1/2 **cup firmly packed brown sugar**
1/4 **cup margarine or butter**

FILLING
1/3 **cup sugar**
2 **tablespoons cornstarch**
1/4 **teaspoon cinnamon**

1 **(16-oz.) pkg. frozen peaches, thawed, drained**
1 **(10-oz.) pkg. frozen raspberries in light syrup, thawed**
1 **tablespoon lemon juice**

Prepare pie crust according to package directions for *one-crust filled pie* using 9-inch pie pan.

Heat oven to 375° F. In small bowl, combine flour and brown sugar; mix well. With fork or pastry blender, cut in margarine until mixture is crumbly; set aside.

In large bowl, combine sugar, cornstarch and cinnamon; mix well. Stir in fruits. Sprinkle with lemon juice; mix well. Pour into crust-lined pan. Bake at 375° F. for 35 to 40 minutes or until filling is partially set in center. Sprinkle evenly with topping mixture. Cover edge of crust with strips of foil to prevent excessive browning. Bake at 375° F. for an additional 12 to 15 minutes or until topping is light golden brown.

Yield: 8 servings

Nutrition Per Serving: Calories 350; Protein 3g; Carbohydrate 55g; Fat 13g; Sodium 210mg

Chocolate-Laced Apricot Walnut Tart

Patricia Kiewiet *LaGrange, Illinois*
Bake-Off® Contest 36, 1994 Prize Winner

As a young child, Patricia Kiewiet created an unappreciated "apple" pie using sliced potatoes. Her prize-winning apricot-walnut tart obviously was much more successful. It's deliciously rich, so serve small pieces with whipped cream.

1 refrigerated pie crust (from 15-oz. pkg.)

FILLING
¹/₃ cup firmly packed brown sugar
1 cup apricot preserves
2 tablespoons butter or margarine, melted
3 eggs
1¹/₂ cups chopped walnuts

GLAZE
1 oz. semi-sweet chocolate, melted

GARNISH, IF DESIRED
¹/₂ cup whipping cream
1 tablespoon powdered sugar

Heat oven to 450°F. Prepare pie crust according to package directions for *one-crust filled pie* using 10-inch tart pan with removable bottom or 9-inch pie pan. Place crust in pan; press in bottom and up sides of pan. Trim edges if necessary. DO NOT PRICK CRUST. Bake at 450°F. for 9 to 11 minutes or until lightly browned. If crust puffs up during baking, gently press crust down with back of wooden spoon.

Reduce oven temperature to 350°F. In large bowl, combine brown sugar, preserves, butter and eggs; blend well. Stir in walnuts. Pour into baked crust.

Bake at 350°F. for 25 to 35 minutes or until filling is light golden brown and set. Cool 10 minutes. Place melted chocolate in small resealable plastic freezer bag. Snip off 1 corner of bag to make very small hole; drizzle chocolate over warm tart. Cool completely.

In small bowl, combine whipping cream and powdered sugar; beat until stiff peaks form. Serve tart with whipped cream. Store in refrigerator.

Yield: 10 servings

Nutrition Per Serving: Calories 420; Protein 6g; Carbohydrate 44g; Fat 26g; Sodium 160mg

Apple Nut Lattice Tart

Mary Lou Warren *Colorado Springs, Colorado*
Bake-Off® Contest 32, 1986 Grand Prize Winner

A distinctive lattice top, golden raisins and walnuts make this contemporary apple pie special enough to win the top prize.

1 (15-oz.) pkg. refrigerated pie crusts

FILLING
3 to 3¹/₂ cups thinly sliced peeled apples (3 to 4 medium)
¹/₂ cup sugar
3 tablespoons golden raisins
3 tablespoons chopped walnuts or pecans

¹/₂ teaspoon cinnamon
¹/₄ to ¹/₂ teaspoon grated lemon peel
2 teaspoons lemon juice

1 egg yolk, beaten
1 teaspoon water

GLAZE
¹/₄ cup powdered sugar
1 to 2 teaspoons lemon juice

Prepare pie crust according to package directions for *two-crust pie* using 10-inch tart pan with removable bottom or 9-inch pie pan. Place 1 prepared crust in pan; press in bottom and up sides of pan. Trim edges if necessary.

Heat oven to 400°F. Place cookie sheet in oven to preheat. In large bowl, combine apples, sugar, raisins, walnuts, cinnamon, lemon peel and 2 teaspoons lemon juice; toss lightly to coat. Spoon into crust-lined pan.

To make lattice top, cut second crust into ¹/₂-inch-wide strips. Arrange strips in lattice design over filling. Trim and seal edges. In small bowl, combine egg yolk and water; gently brush over lattice.

Place tart on preheated cookie sheet. Bake at 400°F. for 40 to 60 minutes or until apples are tender and crust is golden brown. Cover edge of crust with strips of foil after 15 to 20 minutes of baking to prevent excessive browning. Cool 1 hour.

In small bowl, combine glaze ingredients, adding enough lemon juice for desired drizzling consistency. Drizzle over slightly warm tart. Cool; remove sides of pan.

Yield: 8 servings

Nutrition Per Serving: Calories 360; Protein 3g; Carbohydrate 50g; Fat 17g; Sodium 270mg

Apricot Tea Tart

Betty Eder *Lytle Creek, California*
Bake-Off® Contest 35, 1992 Prize Winner

Pretty as a picture, this apricot tart is topped with an easy lattice crust. It's lovely to serve for tea or coffee or dessert any time of year!

1 (15-oz.) pkg. refrigerated pie crust

APRICOT FILLING
1¹/₂ cups chopped dried apricots
¹/₂ cup orange juice
2 eggs
¹/₂ cup sugar
2 tablespoons all-purpose flour
¹/₂ cup light corn syrup
2 tablespoons margarine or butter, melted
1 teaspoon vanilla

CREAM CHEESE FILLING
1 (3-oz.) pkg. cream cheese, softened
¹/₄ cup sugar
1 tablespoon all-purpose flour
¹/₃ cup dairy sour cream
1 egg

TOPPING
1 teaspoon orange juice
1 teaspoon sugar

Heat oven to 375°F. Prepare pie crust according to package directions for *two-crust pie* using 10-inch tart pan with removable bottom or 9-inch pie pan. Place 1 prepared crust in pan; press in bottom and up sides of pan. Trim edges if necessary.

In medium saucepan, combine apricots and ¹/₂ cup orange juice; bring to a boil. Reduce heat to low; simmer uncovered for 1 to 2 minutes. Cool slightly. Reserve 1 tablespoon apricot mixture for cream cheese filling.

Beat 2 eggs in small bowl; reserve 1 teaspoon for topping. Stir remaining beaten eggs, ¹/₂ cup sugar, 2 tablespoons flour, corn syrup, margarine and vanilla into apricot mixture in saucepan; mix well. Spoon into crust-lined pan.

In small bowl, combine all cream cheese filling ingredients and reserved 1 tablespoon apricot mixture; beat at medium speed until well blended. Spoon over apricot filling. Heat cookie sheet in oven for 10 minutes.

Meanwhile, to make lattice top, cut remaining crust into ¹/₂-inch-wide strips. Arrange strips in lattice design over filling. Trim and seal edges. In small bowl, combine 1 teaspoon orange juice and reserved 1 teaspoon beaten egg; blend well. Gently brush over lattice crust; sprinkle with 1 teaspoon sugar.

Place tart on preheated cookie sheet. Bake at 375°F. for 45 to 55 minutes or until crust is golden brown. Cover edge of crust with strips of foil after 15 to 20 minutes of baking to avoid excessive browning. Cool; remove sides of pan. Store in refrigerator.

Yield: 12 servings

Nutrition Per Serving: Calories 380; Protein 4g; Carbohydrate 53g; Fat 17g; Sodium 200mg

Coconut Fudge Crescent Tart

Debi Wolf *Salem, Oregon*
Bake-Off® Contest 34, 1990 Prize Winner

It's hard to believe that this elegant tart can be made so quickly with so few ingredients.

1 (8-oz.) can refrigerated crescent dinner rolls
¹/₂ cup apricot preserves

FILLING
1 (6-oz.) pkg. (1 cup) semi-sweet chocolate chips
1 tablespoon apricot brandy*
3 eggs
1 (15-oz.) can coconut pecan frosting

TOPPING
1 tablespoon powdered sugar
¹/₄ cup semi-sweet chocolate chips
1 tablespoon shortening

Heat oven to 350°F. Lightly grease 10-inch tart pan with removable bottom or 9-inch pie pan. Separate dough into 8 triangles. Place in greased pan; press in bottom and up sides to form crust. Seal perforations. Spread preserves evenly over bottom of crust. Cover edge of crust with strips of foil.

In food processor bowl with metal blade or blender container, process 1 cup chocolate chips until finely ground. Add brandy, eggs and frosting; process well. Pour into dough-lined pan. Bake at 350°F. for 35 to 45 minutes or until filling is puffy and center is almost set. Remove foil strips from crust; cool 15 minutes.

Sprinkle powdered sugar over top of tart. In small saucepan over low heat, melt ¼ cup chocolate chips with shortening, stirring constantly until smooth. Drizzle over top of tart. Refrigerate 4 hours or overnight. Store in refrigerator.

Yield: 16 servings

*Tip: To substitute for apricot brandy, use ½ teaspoon brandy extract plus water to make 1 tablespoon.

Nutrition Per Serving: Calories 290; Protein 3g; Carbohydrate 34g; Fat 16g; Sodium 170mg

Apple Nut Cookie Tart

Mary Lou Cook *Fallbrook, California*
Bake-Off® Contest 37, 1996 Prize Winner

Mary Lou Cook says her pretty nut-topped tart looks like more work than it is, making it an ideal dessert for entertaining. Refrigerated cookie dough forms the easy bottom and top crusts. The filling is spicy apple butter and walnuts.

½ cup finely chopped walnuts
3 tablespoons sugar
½ teaspoon cinnamon
½ teaspoon grated orange peel
1 (18-oz.) pkg. refrigerated sugar cookies, well chilled
⅓ cup purchased apple butter
1 teaspoon all-purpose flour
¼ teaspoon cinnamon
16 pecan halves
32 slivered almonds (1 tablespoon)
Sweetened whipped cream or vanilla ice cream, if desired

Heat oven to 325° F. Place cookie sheet in oven to preheat. Spray 9½-inch tart pan with removable bottom or 9-inch springform pan with nonstick cooking spray.

In medium bowl, combine walnuts, sugar, ½ teaspoon cinnamon and orange peel; mix well. Set aside.

Remove half of cookie dough from wrapper; refrigerate remaining half. With floured fingers, press dough into bottom of spray-coated pan. Spread apple butter over dough to within ½ inch of edge; top apple butter with walnut mixture.

Place remaining half of dough between 2 sheets of lightly floured waxed paper; roll to 9½-inch round. Peel off top sheet of waxed paper. Carefully invert dough over walnut mixture; remove waxed paper. Press edges to fit pan.

In small bowl, combine flour and ¼ teaspoon cinnamon. Dipping knife into flour mixture before each cut, score top of tart into 16 wedges. Press 1 pecan half in each wedge, centered 1 inch from edge of pan. Press 2 almonds in V-shape just below each pecan.

Place tart on heated cookie sheet. Bake at 325° F. for 45 to 55 minutes or until tart is light golden brown and center is set. Cool 15 minutes. Remove sides of pan; cool 1½ hours.

To serve, top with whipped cream. Store in refrigerator.

Yield: 16 servings

Nutrition Per Serving: Calories 240; Protein 2g; Carbohydrate 28g; Fat 13g; Sodium 120mg

Fudge Crostata with Raspberry Sauce

Paula Cassidy *Berkeley, California*
Bake-Off® Contest 34, 1990 Prize Winner

A beautiful lattice crust bakes into the chocolate fudge filling. The raspberry sauce adds a dazzling finishing touch.

1 (15-oz.) pkg. refrigerated pie crusts

FILLING
1 (6-oz.) pkg. (1 cup) semi-sweet chocolate chips
½ cup butter or margarine, softened
⅔ cup sugar
1 cup ground almonds
1 egg
1 egg yolk

SAUCE
1 (12-oz.) pkg. frozen raspberries without syrup, thawed
¾ cup sugar
1 teaspoon lemon juice

GARNISH, IF DESIRED
Sweetened whipped cream
Chocolate curls
Whole raspberries

Prepare pie crust according to package directions for *two-crust pie* using 10-inch tart pan with removable bottom or 9-inch pie pan. Place 1 prepared crust in pan; press in bottom and up sides of pan. Trim edges if necessary.

Place cookie sheet in oven to preheat. Heat oven to 375° F. In

Apple Nut Cookie Tart

small saucepan, melt chocolate chips and 2 tablespoons of the butter over low heat, stirring constantly until smooth. In medium bowl, combine remaining 6 tablespoons butter and ⅔ cup sugar; beat until light and fluffy. Add almonds, egg, egg yolk and melted chocolate; blend well. Spread mixture evenly in bottom of crust-lined pan.

To make lattice top, cut second crust into ½-inch-wide strips. Arrange strips in lattice design over chocolate mixture. Trim and seal edges.

Place tart on preheated cookie sheet. Bake at 375°F. for 45 to 50 minutes or until crust is golden brown. If necessary, cover edge of crust with strips of foil during last 10 to 15 minutes of baking to prevent excessive browning. Cool completely.

Meanwhile, in blender container or food processor bowl with metal blade, blend raspberries at high speed until smooth. Place strainer over small saucepan; pour berries into strainer. Press berries with back of spoon through strainer to remove seeds; discard seeds. Add ¾ cup sugar and lemon juice; blend well. Bring mixture to a boil, stirring constantly. Reduce heat to medium-low; boil 3 minutes, stirring constantly. Cool; refrigerate until serving time.

Garnish crostata with whipped cream, chocolate curls and whole raspberries. Serve with raspberry sauce. Store in refrigerator.

Yield: 12 servings

Nutrition Per Serving: Calories 500; Protein 4g; Carbohydrate 57g; Fat 28g; Sodium 230mg

Coffee Crunch Chocolate Tart

Vesta Frizzel *Independence, Missouri*
Bake-Off® Contest 32, 1986

Deliciously rich and dense, this is a real treat for anyone who enjoys the taste of mocha.

1 refrigerated pie crust (from 15-oz. pkg.)

CRUMB LAYER
½ cup crisp coconut cookie crumbs (3 to 4 cookies)
2 tablespoons all-purpose flour
2 tablespoons brown sugar
1 to 2 teaspoons instant coffee granules or crystals
1 tablespoon margarine or butter

FILLING
1 cup powdered sugar
1 (3-oz.) pkg. cream cheese, softened
1½ teaspoons vanilla
2 oz. unsweetened chocolate, melted
2 cups whipping cream
6 to 8 dark roasted or chocolate-coated candied coffee beans or crushed coconut cookies, if desired

Heat oven to 450°F. Prepare pie crust according to package directions for *one-crust baked shell* using 10-inch tart pan with removable bottom or 9-inch pie pan. Place prepared crust in pan; press in bottom and up sides of pan. Trim edges if necessary. Generously prick crust with fork.

In small bowl, combine cookie crumbs, flour, brown sugar and instant coffee. Using fork or pastry

blender, cut in margarine until mixture is crumbly. Sprinkle over bottom of crust-lined pan. Bake at 450°F. for 12 to 16 minutes or until light golden brown. Cool completely.

In large bowl, beat powdered sugar, cream cheese and vanilla until well blended. Add chocolate; beat until smooth. Gradually add whipping cream, beating until firm peaks form. Spread filling into cooled baked shell. Refrigerate 2 to 3 hours. Remove sides of pan; garnish with coffee beans or crushed coconut cookies. Store in refrigerator.

Yield: 12 servings

Nutrition Per Serving: Calories 350; Protein 3g; Carbohydrate 27g; Fat 27g; Sodium 150mg

Vesta Frizzel: Coffee Crunch Chocolate Tart

So many people trust Pillsbury to provide them with good cooking ideas that finalists returning from the Bake-Off® Contest frequently find that their winning recipes have preceded them, and are featured in family dinners, on restaurant menus and even in cafeterias. Vesta Frizzel, a three-time finalist, found one of her winners was a favorite in a senior citizens' home. "Winning was a pleasurable experience," she says, "but learning that the dish is a special treat for others touches my heart!"

Cranberry Cheesecake Tart

James Sloboden *Puyallup, Washington*
Bake-Off® Contest 34, 1990 Prize Winner

Because this recipe uses canned cranberry sauce, you can make this irresistible two-layer cheesecake any time of year.

1 refrigerated pie crust (from 15-oz. pkg.)

FILLING
1 (16-oz.) can whole berry cranberry sauce
¹/₂ cup chopped pecans
1 cup sugar, reserving 2 tablespoons for topping
1 tablespoon cornstarch
1¹/₂ (8-oz.) pkg. (12 oz.) cream cheese, softened
2 eggs
1 tablespoon milk

TOPPING
1 cup dairy sour cream
¹/₂ teaspoon vanilla

Heat oven to 450°F. Prepare pie crust according to package directions for *one-crust baked shell* using 10-inch tart pan with removable bottom or 9-inch pie pan. Place prepared crust in pan; press in bottom and up sides of pan. Trim edges if necessary. Generously prick crust with fork. Bake at 450°F. for 9 to 11 minutes. Cool completely. Reduce heat to 375°F.

In medium bowl, combine cranberry sauce, pecans, 6 tablespoons of the sugar and cornstarch; spread into cooled baked shell.

In medium bowl, beat cream cheese, eggs, remaining ¹/₂ cup sugar and milk at medium speed until smooth. Spoon evenly over cranberry mixture. Bake at 375°F. for 25 to 30 minutes or until set.

In small bowl, combine sour cream, reserved 2 tablespoons sugar and vanilla; mix well. Spoon evenly over filling. Bake at 375°F. for an additional 5 minutes. Cool slightly. Refrigerate 3 to 4 hours or until set. Store in refrigerator.

Yield: 10 servings

Nutrition Per Serving: Calories 480; Protein 6g; Carbohydrate 51g; Fat 28g; Sodium 220mg

Pineapple Blueberry Cream Tart

Carole Holt *St. Paul, Minnesota*
Bake-Off® Contest 36, 1994

This refreshing fruit and cream tart is perfect to serve for any occasion. The pie can be made ahead of time, but be sure to spoon the topping on just before serving.

1 refrigerated pie crust (from 15-oz. pkg.)

FILLING
1 (2.9-oz.) pkg. lemon pudding and pie filling mix (not instant)
¹/₂ cup sugar
¹/₄ cup water
2 egg yolks
²/₃ cup canned crushed pineapple with juice
1¹/₃ cups water
1 teaspoon grated lemon peel
2 cups fresh or frozen blueberries, thawed, drained on paper towels

¹/₂ cup blueberry preserves, warmed

TOPPING
1¹/₂ cups whipping cream
¹/₃ cup powdered sugar
¹/₂ teaspoon vanilla
1¹/₂ teaspoons grated lemon peel

Heat oven to 450°F. Prepare pie crust according to package directions for *one-crust baked shell* using 10-inch tart pan with removable bottom or 9-inch pie pan. Place prepared crust in pan; press in bottom and up sides of pan. Trim edges if necessary. DO NOT PRICK CRUST. Bake at 450°F. for 9 to 11 minutes or until lightly browned. If crust puffs up during baking, gently press crust down with back of wooden spoon. Cool.

In medium saucepan, combine pudding mix, sugar, ¹/₄ cup water and egg yolks; mix until smooth. Add pineapple, 1¹/₃ cups water and 1 teaspoon lemon peel; cook and stir over medium heat until mixture comes to a boil. Remove from heat; cool slightly.

In small bowl, combine blueberries and preserves. Spread over cooled baked shell. Spoon pudding mixture over blueberry mixture. Refrigerate 30 minutes or until cold.

In small bowl, combine whipping cream, powdered sugar and vanilla; beat until stiff peaks form. Spoon or spread over pudding mixture; sprinkle with 1¹/₂ teaspoons lemon peel. Serve immediately. Store in refrigerator.

Yield: 8 servings

Nutrition Per Serving: Calories 480; Protein 3g; Carbohydrate 61g; Fat 25g; Sodium 210mg

Chocolate Swirl Coconut Almond Tart

Beverley Ann Crummey *Brooksville, Florida*
Bake-Off® Contest 37, 1996 Prize Winner

Single crust tarts with rich fillings were much in evidence among the special occasion dessert entries in the 37th Bake-Off® Contest. World traveler Beverley Ann Crummey usually focuses on healthy eating but occasionally indulges in treats, like her elegant chocolate almond tart.

1 refrigerated pie crust
(from 15-oz. pkg.)

FILLING
2 eggs
1 cup coconut
$^1/_2$ cup chopped almonds,
   toasted*
1 (14-oz.) can sweetened
   condensed milk (not
   evaporated)
1 tablespoon vanilla
$^1/_4$ teaspoon coconut extract
1$^1/_2$ oz. bittersweet chocolate,
   finely chopped ($^1/_4$ cup)

TOPPING
2 oz. bittersweet chocolate,
   melted

$^1/_4$ cup sliced almonds,
   toasted*
Whipped cream or topping
Fresh mint sprig, if desired

Heat oven to 400° F. Prepare pie crust according to package directions for *one-crust filled pie* using 10-inch tart pan with removable bottom or 9-inch pie pan. Place prepared crust in pan; press in bottom and up sides of pan. Trim edges if necessary. DO NOT PRICK CRUST. Bake at 400° F. for 10 to 12 minutes or until light

Chocolate Swirl Coconut Almond Tart

golden brown. If crust puffs up, gently press back to bottom and sides of pan with wooden spoon.

Meanwhile, in large bowl, beat eggs slightly. Add coconut, chopped almonds, condensed milk, vanilla and coconut extract; blend well. Fold in finely chopped chocolate. Pour into baked crust. Reduce oven temperature to 350°F.; bake 20 to 25 minutes or until filling is set. Cool 30 minutes.

Drizzle tart with melted chocolate; sprinkle with sliced almonds. Refrigerate 30 minutes. Serve topped with whipped cream; garnish with mint sprig. Store in refrigerator.

Yield: 10 servings

*Tip: To toast almonds, spread on cookie sheet. Bake at 350°F. for 5 to 10 minutes or until light golden brown, stirring occasionally. Or spread in thin layer in microwave-safe pie pan. Microwave on HIGH for 5 to 7 minutes or until light golden brown, stirring frequently.

Nutrition Per Serving: Calories 400; Protein 7g; Carbohydrate 43g; Fat 22g; Sodium 200mg

Taste o' Lemon Cream Tart

Betty Eder *Cucamonga, California Bake-Off® Contest 32, 1986*

There's no need for meringue on this lemon pie. Luscious layers of tangy lemon cream bake inside a flaky crust and a sprinkling of sugar and nutmeg is all that's needed on top!

1 (15-oz.) pkg. refrigerated pie crusts

CREAM CHEESE FILLING
1 (8-oz.) pkg. cream cheese, softened
1/3 cup sugar
1 teaspoon lemon juice
1 egg

LEMON FILLING
1/4 cup sugar
2 tablespoons all-purpose flour
3/4 cup light corn syrup
1/3 cup lemon juice
2 tablespoons margarine or butter, softened
1 teaspoon grated lemon peel

2 eggs, beaten, reserving 1 teaspoon for topping

TOPPING
1 teaspoon sugar
1/4 teaspoon nutmeg

Prepare pie crust according to package directions for *two-crust pie* using 10-inch tart pan with removable bottom or 9-inch pie pan. Place 1 prepared crust in pan; press in bottom and up sides of pan. Trim edges if necessary.

Heat oven to 375°F. In small bowl, combine all cream cheese filling ingredients at medium speed until well blended. Spoon into crust-lined pan. In same bowl, combine all lemon filling ingredients at low speed. Carefully pour over cream cheese filling. Top with second crust; trim edges if necessary.* Cut slits in top crust. Brush with 1 teaspoon reserved egg. Combine 1 teaspoon sugar and nutmeg; sprinkle over crust.

Bake at 375°F. for 45 to 55 minutes or until filling is set and crust is golden brown. Cool completely; remove sides of pan. Store in refrigerator.

Yield: 10 servings

*Tip: If using 9-inch pie pan, top with second crust; seal edges and flute. Cut slits in top crust. Continue as directed above.

Nutrition Per Serving: Calories 440; Protein 5g; Carbohydrate 52g; Fat 23g; Sodium 340mg

Mishaps with the Press

The presence of reporters and photographers certainly adds a novel dimension to the Bake-Off® Contest. One finalist accidentally dropped her finished cake as she was setting it on the cart for judging. A photographer slapped his forehead, wishing he had caught it on film, so the obliging contestant gathered up the crumbs and dropped them again—before going to work on another entry. One contestant was so unnerved by all the hubbub around her that she sat on the finished pie she had set down to cool! Sometimes, however, the press is in for surprises, too—like the *Life* photographer who wanted to take a picture of the 100 winning dishes, but found that someone couldn't resist, and had eaten one. *Life* had to be content with a picture of the remaining 99.

Tangy Crescent Nut Tart

Debi Wolf *Salem, Oregon*
Bake-Off® Contest 32, 1986 Prize Winner

Refrigerated crescent roll dough forms the easy flaky crust for this tart. Coconut and hazelnuts give texture and subtle flavor to the lemony filling.

1 (8-oz.) can refrigerated
  crescent dinner rolls
1 cup sugar
1/4 cup all-purpose flour
2 to 3 teaspoons grated lemon
  peel
3 to 4 tablespoons lemon juice
1 teaspoon vanilla
4 eggs
1 cup coconut
1 cup finely chopped hazelnuts
  (filberts) or walnuts
1 to 2 tablespoons powdered
  sugar

Heat oven to 350°F. Lightly grease 10-inch tart pan with removable bottom.* Separate dough into 8 triangles. Place in greased pan; press in bottom and up sides to form crust. Seal perforations. Bake at 350°F. for 5 minutes. Cool 5 minutes; gently press sides of warm crust to top of pan.

In large bowl, combine sugar, flour, lemon peel, lemon juice, vanilla and eggs; beat 3 minutes at medium speed. Stir in coconut and hazelnuts. Pour filling into partially baked crust.

Bake at 350°F. for an additional 25 to 30 minutes or until filling is set and crust is golden brown. Cool completely. Sprinkle with powdered sugar. Store in refrigerator.

Yield: 12 servings

*Tip: A 10-inch round pizza pan can be substituted for the tart pan. Bake crust at 350°F. for 5 minutes; bake filled crust an additional 20 to 25 minutes.

Nutrition Per Serving: Calories 230; Protein 5g; Carbohydrate 23g; Fat 14g; Sodium 180mg

Pecan Caramel Tart

Kathy Specht *Carlsbad, California*
Bake-Off® Contest 33, 1988

Wow! You'll love this "confection in a crust." So unbelievably easy—so irresistibly delicious.

1 refrigerated pie crust (from
  15-oz. pkg.)

FILLING
36 vanilla caramels,
  unwrapped
1/2 cup whipping cream
3 1/2 cups pecan halves

TOPPING
1/4 cup semi-sweet chocolate
  chips
1 teaspoon margarine or
  butter
1 tablespoon whipping cream

Heat oven to 450°F. Prepare pie crust according to package directions for *one-crust baked shell* using 10-inch tart pan with removable bottom or 9-inch pie pan. Place prepared crust in pan; press in bottom and up sides of pan. Trim edges if necessary. Generously prick crust with fork. Bake at 450°F. for 9 to 11 minutes or until light golden brown. Cool completely.

In medium heavy saucepan, combine caramels and 1/2 cup whipping cream; cook over low heat until caramels are melted and mixture is smooth, stirring occasionally. Remove from heat. Add pecans; stir well to coat. Spread evenly over cooled baked shell.

In small saucepan over low heat, melt chocolate chips with margarine, stirring constantly. Add 1 tablespoon whipping cream; stir until well blended. Drizzle over pecan filling. Refrigerate 1 hour or until filling is firm. Garnish with sweetened whipped cream, if desired. Store in refrigerator.

Yield: 12 servings

Nutrition Per Serving: Calories 440; Protein 4g; Carbohydrate 34g; Fat 33g; Sodium 150mg

Cream Cheese Brownie Pie

Bobbie Sonefeld *Hopkins, South Carolina*
Bake-Off® Contest 39, 2000 Grand Prize Winner

The best dessert flavors are baked into this cream cheese-filled brownie pie. The combination is bound to bring rave reviews from any crowd.

1 refrigerated pie crust (from
  15-oz. pkg.)
1 (8-oz.) pkg. cream cheese,
  softened
3 tablespoons sugar
1 teaspoon vanilla
3 eggs
1 (15.1-oz.) pkg. fudge
  brownie mix with hot fudge
  swirl
1/4 cup oil
2 tablespoons water
1/2 cup chopped pecans

BOBBIE SONEFELD

Most people hear about Roberta (Bobbie) Sonefeld's Bake-Off® 2000 Contest win and immediately zero in on the $1 million Grand Prize she was awarded for her decadently rich Cream Cheese Brownie Pie. But Bobbie says the richest part of the experience was the Bake-Off® weekend itself, a dazzling trip she and her husband, Steve, have christened their "second honeymoon."

The 2000 Bake-Off® Contest took place in the San Francisco Marriott, an opulent hotel in downtown San Francisco. "Neither of us had ever been to the West Coast," recalled Bobbie. "The way Pillsbury treated us was just great: Three gourmet meals a day plus all kinds of tours and sightseeing." An added benefit, said Bobbie, was that "all the activity had a calming effect." When the day of the cooking contest rolled around, "I was used to the idea." Didn't she get nervous? "Well, yes," she admits, "But I didn't get the butterflies bad until the night before. The next morning—once I was done baking and there wasn't anything I could do about it—I was fine. Then I thought, 'Wow, I already feel like a winner, it doesn't matter what happens next.'"

What happened next is part of history: Bobbie's Cream Cheese Brownie Pie, entered in the Fast & Fabulous Desserts & Treats category, won the Grand Prize. The Sonefelds' second honeymoon became even more extravagant, as they jetted to New York City for a whirlwind round of television and radio appearances. They also went to Philadelphia to appear on QVC. Bobbie remembers New York as another great restaurant town where she had meals she never even dreamed of two weeks before.

After an amazing week traveling the country together, Bobbie and Steve returned home to Hopkins, South Carolina, their full-time jobs and their family. And that's when the trip stopped being a honeymoon, and turned into a homecoming, as Bobbie and Steve returned to the loving arms of their very excited sons.

Heat oven to 350° F. Place pie crust in 9-inch pie pan according to package directions for *one-crust filled* pie.

In medium bowl, combine cream cheese, sugar, vanilla and 1 of the eggs; beat until smooth. Set aside.

Reserve hot fudge packet from brownie mix for topping. In large bowl, combine brownie mix, oil, 1 tablespoon of the water and remaining 2 eggs; beat 50 strokes with spoon. Spread ½ cup brownie mixture in bottom of crust-lined pan. Spoon and carefully spread cream cheese mixture over brownie layer. Top with remaining brownie mixture; spread evenly. Sprinkle with pecans.

Bake at 350° F. for 40 to 50 minutes or until center is puffed and crust is golden brown. If necessary, cover edge of crust with strips of foil after 15 to 20 minutes of baking to prevent excessive browning. (Pie may have cracks on surface.)

Place hot fudge from packet in small microwave-safe bowl. Microwave on HIGH for 30 seconds. Stir in remaining tablespoon water. Drizzle fudge over top of pie. Cool 3 hours or until completely cooled. Store in refrigerator.

Yield: 8 servings

High Altitude—Above 3,500 feet: Add 3 tablespoons flour to dry brownie mix. Bake as directed above.

Nutrition Per Serving: Calories 600; Protein 8g; Carbohydrate 60g; Fat 36g; Sodium 370mg

Chapter 9

Other Desserts

Imagination is the basic ingredient for all desserts. The same eggs, flour, butter, cream, chocolate and sugar can be used to make hundreds of kinds of cookies, candies or cake—or something no one has ever dreamed of. Cheesecakes, pies and cakes have been around since ancient times, but "squares," "parfaits" and crescent cups are all newcomers to the dessert table, inspired both by innovations in technology and by imagination.

It's hard to conceive of a kitchen without a refrigerator and freezer, but not long ago refrigeration was a new technology. Ruby Razz Crunch, a 1956 Bake-Off® recipe, was inspired in part by the new refrigerators in middle-class homes, and it combines the then newly available frozen fruits with the idea of freezing whipped cream for a topping. It's also hard to remember a time without boxed mixes or refrigerated dough, but 1968's Cookie Cheesecake Squares depends on those once-new products. Peaches and Cream Crescent Dessert, from the 1978 contest, would have taken a whole day with rolling pins and pastry boards before refrigerated crescent dinner rolls became available. In 1990, Praline Pecan Cheesecake was inspired in part by the explosion in availability and variety of products such as candy bars and ice cream topping, which contribute to a decadent cake fit for a king.

Who knows what the desserts of the future will be like, influenced by new inventions and combinations of ingredients? We have yet to imagine. Whatever evolves, these desserts will depend on the inspiration of creative cooks, for technology is all but useless without imagination to put it to work.

Peach Elizabeth, page 331

Apple Pie '63

Julia Smogor *South Bend, Indiana*
Bake-Off® Contest 14, 1962 Grand
Prize Winner

As more women entered the work force
in the 1960s, Bake-Off® rules
changed. A recipe still had to include
at least ¹/₂ cup of flour, but conve-
nience products now could be used as
ingredients. This apple, cream cheese
and caramel dessert probably was the
first contest recipe to use candy
caramels to make caramel sauce.

CARAMEL SAUCE
28 caramels, unwrapped
¹/₂ cup half-and-half or
   evaporated milk

CRUST
2¹/₂ cups all-purpose flour
¹/₄ cup sugar
1¹/₂ teaspoons salt
¹/₂ cup margarine or butter
¹/₄ cup oil
¹/₄ cup water
1 egg, beaten

APPLE FILLING
6 cups sliced peeled apples
   (about 6 medium)
1 cup sugar
¹/₃ cup all-purpose flour
1 to 2 teaspoons grated
   lemon peel
2 tablespoons lemon juice

TOPPING
1 (8-oz.) pkg. cream cheese,
   softened
¹/₃ cup sugar
1 egg
¹/₃ cup chopped nuts

Heat oven to 375° F. In small
saucepan, combine caramels and
half-and-half; cook over low heat,
stirring occasionally, until caramels

are melted. Keep warm.

In large bowl, combine
2¹/₂ cups flour, ¹/₄ cup sugar and
salt. Using pastry blender or fork,
cut in margarine until mixture
resembles coarse crumbs. Add oil,
water and egg; mix well. Press
crust mixture evenly in bottom and
up sides of ungreased 15×10×1-
inch baking pan.

In large bowl, combine all apple
filling ingredients; toss lightly.
Spoon into crust-lined pan. Drizzle
warm caramel sauce over apples.

In small bowl, combine all topping ingredients except nuts; beat
until smooth. Spoon over apples,
spreading slightly. Sprinkle with
nuts.

Bake at 375° F. for 35 to 45
minutes or until light golden brown.
Cool. Cut into squares. Store in
refrigerator.

Yield: 18 servings

High Altitude—Above 3,500 feet: No
change.

Nutrition Per Serving: Calories 360; Protein 5g;
Carbohydrate 49g; Fat 17g; Sodium 320mg

Almond Brickle Dessert

Louise Bork *Garfield Heights, Ohio*
Bake-Off® Contest 18, 1967 Prize Winner

Small squares of this rich, almond-
flavored cake dessert will satisfy your
sweet tooth. The buttery brickle top-
ping adds the flavor of a premium ice
cream.

¹/₂ cup slivered almonds
¹/₃ cup sugar
¹/₂ cup margarine or butter
¹/₄ cup honey
1 tablespoon milk
1³/₄ cups all-purpose flour
²/₃ cup sugar
2 teaspoons baking powder
¹/₂ cup margarine or butter,
   softened
¹/₃ cup milk
1 teaspoon almond extract
2 eggs

Heat oven to 350° F. Grease 9-inch
square pan. In small saucepan,
combine almonds, ¹/₃ cup sugar,
¹/₂ cup margarine, honey and
1 tablespoon milk. Cook over
medium heat until mixture boils,
about 9 to 11 minutes, stirring constantly; boil an additional 2 minutes. Remove from heat; set aside.

In large bowl, combine 1 cup
flour, ²/₃ cup sugar, baking powder,
¹/₂ cup margarine, ¹/₃ cup milk,
almond extract and eggs. Blend at
low speed until moistened; beat
3 minutes at medium speed. By
hand, stir in remaining ³/₄ cup
flour; mix well. Spread batter in
greased pan. Spoon almond mixture
over batter; spread evenly to cover.
Bake at 350° F. for 25 to 35 minutes or until toothpick inserted in
center comes out clean.

Yield: 9 servings

High Altitude—Above 3,500 feet: No
change.

Nutrition Per Serving: Calories 450; Protein 6g;
Carbohydrate 49g; Fat 26g; Sodium 310mg

Almond-Filled Cookie Cake

Almond-Filled Cookie Cake

Elizabeth Meijer *Danbury, Connecticut Bake-Off® Contest 30, 1982 Grand Prize Winner*

This buttery almond dessert recipe is adapted from a Dutch pastry. Thinly slice this tempting dessert to serve.

CRUST

2²/₃ cups all-purpose flour
1¹/₃ cups sugar
1¹/₃ cups butter, softened (do not use margarine)
¹/₂ teaspoon salt
1 egg

FILLING

1 cup finely chopped almonds
¹/₂ cup sugar
1 teaspoon grated lemon peel
1 egg, slightly beaten
4 whole blanched almonds

Heat oven to 325°F. Place cookie sheet in oven to preheat. Grease 10- or 9-inch springform pan. In large bowl, blend all crust ingredients at low speed until dough forms. If desired, refrigerate for easier handling. Divide dough in half; spread half in bottom of greased pan to form crust.

In small bowl, combine all filling ingredients except whole almonds; blend well. Spread over crust to within ¹/₂ inch of sides of pan. Between 2 sheets of waxed paper, press remaining dough to 10- or 9-inch circle. Remove top sheet of waxed paper; place dough over filling. Remove waxed paper; press dough into place. Top with whole almonds.

Place cake on preheated cookie sheet. Bake at 325°F. for 65 to 75 minutes or until top is light golden brown. Cool 15 minutes; remove sides of pan. Cool completely.

Yield: 24 servings

Nutrition Per Serving: Calories 240; Protein 3g; Carbohydrate 27g; Fat 14g; Sodium 50mg

Cherry Cream Crunch

Joyce Herr *Rogers, Arkansas*
Bake-Off® Contest 14, 1962

A buttery crunchy crust and topping of coconut, oats and nuts add a contrast to the creamy lemon and fruit layers.

BASE
1 cup all-purpose flour
¹/₂ cup firmly packed brown
  sugar
¹/₂ teaspoon cinnamon
Dash salt
¹/₂ cup margarine or butter,
  softened
1 teaspoon vanilla
1 cup coconut
¹/₂ cup rolled oats
¹/₂ cup chopped walnuts

FILLING
1 (14-oz.) can sweetened
  condensed milk
  (not evaporated)
1 tablespoon grated lemon
  peel
¹/₄ cup lemon juice
Dash salt
2 eggs, slightly beaten
1 (21-oz.) can cherry or
  blueberry fruit pie filling

Heat oven to 375° F. In large bowl, combine flour, brown sugar, cinnamon, dash salt, margarine and vanilla; mix at low speed until crumbly. Stir in coconut, oats and walnuts.

Press 2¹/₂ cups crumb mixture into bottom of ungreased 12×8-inch (2-quart) baking dish or 13×9-inch pan; reserve remaining crumb mixture for topping. Bake at 375° F. for 12 minutes or until light golden brown.

In medium bowl, combine all filling ingredients except fruit pie filling. Stir until mixture thickens. Spread evenly over crust. Carefully spoon fruit pie filling evenly over lemon filling mixture. Sprinkle reserved crumb mixture over filling. Bake at 375° F. for an additional 15 to 18 minutes or until golden brown. Cool; refrigerate 2 to 3 hours before serving. Store in refrigerator.

Yield: 12 servings

Nutrition Per Serving: Calories 420; Protein 7g; Carbohydrate 62g; Fat 17g; Sodium 170mg

Apricot Dessert Bars

Gregory Patent *San Francisco, California*
Bake-Off® Contest 10, 1958 Prize Winner

This prize-winning recipe was developed by a second-year pre-med student at the City College of San Francisco. He says he learned to cook by watching television! If you love apricots, don't miss this one.

FILLING
2 (6-oz.) pkg. dried apricots,
  finely cut up (2¹/₂ cups)
1¹/₂ cups water
³/₄ cup sugar

BASE
1³/₄ cups all-purpose flour
1 cup sugar
¹/₂ teaspoon salt
¹/₂ teaspoon baking soda
³/₄ cup margarine or butter
1 cup coconut
¹/₂ cup chopped walnuts

In medium saucepan, combine apricots and water. Cook over medium heat 10 to 15 minutes or until apricots are very soft, stirring occasionally. Stir in ³/₄ cup sugar.

Heat oven to 400° F. Grease bottom only of 13×9-inch baking pan. In large bowl, combine flour, 1 cup sugar, salt and baking soda. Using fork or pastry blender, cut in margarine until mixture is crumbly. Add coconut and walnuts. Press 3 cups of crumb mixture in bottom of greased pan. Bake at 400° F. for 10 minutes. Remove from oven.

Spread apricot filling evenly over crust. Sprinkle with remaining crumb mixture. Bake at 400° F. for an additional 15 to 20 minutes until golden brown. Cool. Cut into bars.

Yield: 15 servings

High Altitude—Above 3,500 feet: No change.

Nutrition Per Serving: Calories 330; Protein 3g; Carbohydrate 48g; Fat 14g; Sodium 220mg

Top to bottom: **Cherry Cream Crunch, Apricot Dessert Bars**

Peaches and Cream Crescent Dessert

Marilyn Blankschien *Clintonville, Wisconsin*
Bake-Off® Contest 28, 1978

Some of the favorite Bake-Off® winners are the simplest, like these layered peach and cream cheese squares. This easy recipe turns everyday ingredients into a creative dessert for family or guests.

1 (8-oz.) can refrigerated
   crescent dinner rolls
1 (8-oz.) pkg. cream cheese,
   softened
1/2 cup sugar
1/4 to 1/2 teaspoon almond
   extract
1 (21-oz.) can peach fruit pie
   filling*
1/2 cup all-purpose flour
1/4 cup firmly packed brown
   sugar
3 tablespoons margarine or
   butter, softened
1/2 cup sliced almonds or
   chopped nuts

Heat oven to 375°F. Separate dough into 2 long rectangles. Place in ungreased 13×9-inch pan; press in bottom to form crust. Seal perforations. Bake at 375°F. for 5 minutes.

In small bowl, combine cream cheese, sugar and almond extract; blend until smooth. Spread over partially baked crust. Spoon fruit filling evenly over cream cheese mixture. In medium bowl, combine flour and brown sugar. Using fork or pastry blender, cut in margarine until mixture is crumbly. Stir in almonds; sprinkle crumb mixture over fruit filling.

Bake at 375°F. for an additional 25 to 30 minutes or until golden brown. Cool completely. Store in refrigerator. Cut into squares.

Yield: 12 servings

*Tip: Cherry or apple fruit pie filling can be substituted for peach fruit filling.

Nutrition Per Serving: Calories 300; Protein 4g; Carbohydrate 38g; Fat 15g; Sodium 260mg

Crescent Macadamia Truffle Cups

Gloria Pleasants *Williamsburg, Virginia*
Bake-Off® Contest 34, 1990 Prize Winner

Make this indulgent, winning recipe for those times when a small bite of sweet is all you need.

FILLING
1 (4-oz.) bar sweet cooking
   chocolate, chopped
1/4 cup unsalted butter, butter
   or margarine
1/4 cup firmly packed brown
   sugar
2 tablespoons all-purpose
   flour
2 tablespoons coffee-flavored
   liqueur or cold coffee
1 egg
1 (8-oz.) can refrigerated
   crescent dinner rolls
24 whole macadamia nuts

TOPPING
3 oz. (3 squares) white baking
   bar, chopped
1/3 cup soft cream cheese
1/2 cup whipping cream
2 tablespoons powdered
   sugar
1 teaspoon vanilla

Heat oven to 350°F. In small saucepan over low heat, melt sweet chocolate and 1/4 cup butter, stirring constantly until smooth. Remove from heat. Stir in brown sugar, flour, liqueur and egg; set aside.

Unroll dough into 2 long rectangles; firmly press perforations to seal. Cut each rectangle in half lengthwise. Cut each half crosswise into six 2-inch squares. Press or roll out each square to 2³/₄-inch square. Place 1 square in each of 24 ungreased miniature muffin cups. Firmly press in bottom and up sides, leaving corners of dough extended over edges of each cup. Place 1 macadamia nut in each dough-lined cup. Spoon about 2 teaspoons filling mixture over nut in each cup.

Bake at 350°F. for 12 to 15 minutes or until filling is set and corners of dough are golden brown. Cool 5 minutes; remove from pan. Place on wire racks; cool completely. Refrigerate 1 hour or until thoroughly chilled.

In small saucepan over low heat, melt white baking bar and cream cheese, stirring constantly until smooth. Cover with plastic wrap; refrigerate until thoroughly chilled, about 1 hour, stirring occasionally.

In small bowl, beat whipping cream, powdered sugar and vanilla just until soft peaks form. Add chilled white baking bar mixture; mix at low speed just until well blended. Pipe or spoon topping over top of chilled cups. Refrigerate to set topping. Store in refrigerator.

Yield: 24 servings

Nutrition Per Serving: Calories 160; Protein 2g; Carbohydrate 13g; Fat 11g; Sodium 95mg

Praline Crescent Dessert

Marjorie Hooper *Lakeland, Florida*
Bake-Off® Contest 30, 1982 Prize Winner

Baked in muffin cups and topped with whipped cream, this simple dessert has everyone's favorite flavors.

¹/₃ **cup margarine or butter**
¹/₂ **cup firmly packed brown sugar**
3 **tablespoons dairy sour cream**
1 **cup crisp rice cereal**
¹/₂ **cup chopped pecans or nuts**
¹/₂ **cup coconut**
1 **(8-oz.) can refrigerated crescent dinner rolls**
1 **(3-oz.) pkg. cream cheese, softened**
2 **tablespoons powdered sugar**
Whipping cream, whipped, if desired

Heat oven to 375°F. Melt margarine in medium saucepan over low heat. Add brown sugar; cook 2 minutes, stirring constantly. Add sour cream; cook 4 minutes, stirring occasionally. Remove from heat. Add cereal, nuts and coconut; stir until evenly coated. Separate dough into 8 triangles. Place each triangle in ungreased muffin cup;

press dough to cover bottom and sides. Combine cream cheese and powdered sugar. Spoon rounded teaspoonful into each cup; spread over bottom. Divide brown sugar mixture evenly into cups.

Bake at 375°F. for 11 to 16 minutes or until deep golden brown. Serve warm or cool topped with whipped cream. Store in refrigerator.

Yield: 8 servings

Tip: To make ahead, prepare, cover and refrigerate up to 2 hours; bake as directed.

Nutrition Per Serving: Calories 390; Protein 4g; Carbohydrate 33g; Fat 27g; Sodium 400mg

Cookie Crust Pecan Pie

Louise Schlinkert *China City, California*
Bake-Off® Contest 20, 1969 Prize Winner

Ever-popular pecan pie is baked in a 13×9-inch pan for a new shape, and refrigerated cookie dough makes an unusual quick-to-prepare crust.

1 **(18-oz.) pkg. refrigerated sugar cookies**
1 **(3.4-oz.) pkg. instant butterscotch pudding and pie filling mix**
Dash salt
³/₄ **cup dark corn syrup**
²/₃ **cup milk**
¹/₂ **teaspoon vanilla, if desired**
1 **egg**
1¹/₂ **cups pecan halves or pieces**
1 **cup whipped cream or 1 pint ice cream, if desired**

Heat oven to 350°F. Slice cookie dough into ¹/₄-inch slices.* Press slices in bottom and 1 inch up sides of ungreased 13×9-inch pan to form crust. (Press dough as thin as possible on sides.) In medium bowl, combine pudding mix, salt, corn syrup, milk, vanilla and egg; blend well. Fold in pecans. Pour into crust-lined pan.

Bake at 350°F. for 25 to 35 minutes or until edges are deep golden brown and filling is set. Cool completely; cut into squares. Serve with whipped cream or ice cream.

Yield: 12 servings

*Tip: For easier slicing of cookie dough, place in freezer 10 minutes before slicing.

Nutrition Per Serving: Calories 410; Protein 4g; Carbohydrate 53g; Fat 20g; Sodium 320mg

Country French Apple Crescent Casserole

Sharon Richardson *Dallas, Texas*
Bake-Off® Contest 34, 1990 Prize Winner

This recipe for apple dumplings in custard earns a place on the brunch buffet as well as the dessert table.

DUMPLINGS
2 tablespoons sugar
¹/₂ to 1 teaspoon cinnamon
1 (8-oz.) can refrigerated
 crescent dinner rolls
1 large apple, peeled, cut into
 8 slices

SAUCE
¹/₂ cup sugar
¹/₂ cup whipping cream
1 tablespoon almond extract
 or amaretto
1 egg

TOPPING
¹/₂ cup sliced almonds
Cinnamon

Heat oven to 375° F. In small bowl, combine 2 tablespoons sugar and ¹/₂ teaspoon cinnamon; blend well. Separate dough into 8 triangles; sprinkle sugar mixture evenly over each. Gently press sugar mixture into each triangle, flattening each slightly. Place apple slice on wide end of each triangle; tuck in edges around apple slice. Roll up, starting at wide end; roll to opposite point. Seal all seams. Place tip side down in ungreased 9-inch round baking dish or pie pan, placing long side of 7 filled crescents around outside edge of dish and 1 in center. Bake at 375° F. for 15 to 20 minutes or until golden brown.

In small bowl using wire whisk, combine ¹/₂ cup sugar, whipping cream, almond extract and egg until well blended. Spoon sauce mixture evenly over partially baked rolls. Sprinkle with almonds and cinnamon. Bake at 375° F. for an additional 13 to 18 minutes or until deep golden brown. Cover top of pan with foil during last 5 minutes of baking time if necessary to prevent excessive browning. Serve warm. Store in refrigerator.

Yield: 8 servings

Nutrition Per Serving: Calories 270; Protein 4g; Carbohydrate 31g; Fat 15g; Sodium 250mg

Ruby Razz Crunch

Achsa Myers *Fort Collins, Colorado*
Bake-Off® Contest 8, 1956 Prize Winner

Keep frozen rhubarb and raspberries on hand to make this terrific dessert, garnished with a frozen whipped cream topping.

FILLING
1 (10-oz.) pkg. frozen raspberries with syrup, thawed, drained, reserving liquid

Country French Apple Crescent Casserole

1 (16-oz.) pkg. frozen rhubarb, thawed, drained, reserving liquid
¹/₂ cup sugar
3 tablespoons cornstarch

TOPPING*
¹/₂ cup whipping cream, whipped
2 tablespoons sugar
1 to 3 drops red food color, if desired

CRUST
1 ¹/₄ cups all-purpose flour
1 cup firmly packed brown sugar
1 cup quick-cooking rolled oats
1 teaspoon cinnamon
¹/₂ cup margarine or butter, melted

Heat oven to 325° F. Reserve 2 tablespoons raspberries for topping. In measuring cup, combine reserved raspberry and rhubarb liquids. If necessary, add water to make 1 cup. In medium saucepan, combine ¹/₂ cup sugar and cornstarch; stir in reserved liquids. Cook over medium heat until thickened, stirring constantly; remove from heat. Stir remaining raspberries and rhubarb into cornstarch mixture. Set aside.

Line cookie sheet with waxed paper. In small bowl, combine whipped cream, 2 tablespoons sugar, reserved raspberries and food color. Drop in 9 mounds onto waxed paper-lined cookie sheet; freeze until firm.

In large bowl, combine flour, brown sugar, rolled oats and cinnamon. Stir in margarine until crumbly. Press ²/₃ of crust mixture in bottom of ungreased 9-inch square pan. Spoon filling mixture

over crust, spreading evenly. Sprinkle with remaining crust mixture.

Bake at 325° F. for 45 to 55 minutes or until crust is golden brown and filling bubbles around edges. Cool slightly. To serve, cut into squares; top each serving with mound of frozen topping.

Yield: 9 servings

Microwave Directions: In 4-cup microwave-safe measuring cup, combine ¹/₂ cup sugar and cornstarch; mix well. Measure reserved liquids as directed above; stir into cornstarch mixture. Microwave on HIGH for 4 to 4¹/₂ minutes or until thick and bubbly, stirring once halfway through cooking. Stir in remaining raspberries and rhubarb; set aside.

Prepare topping as directed above. Place margarine in medium microwave-safe bowl. Microwave on HIGH for 45 to 60 seconds or until melted. Add remaining crust ingredients; mix until crumbly. Press ²/₃ of crust mixture in bottom of 8-inch square (1¹/₂-quart) microwave-safe dish. Spoon filling mixture over crust, spreading evenly. Sprinkle with remaining crust mixture. Microwave on MEDIUM for 10 minutes, turning dish ¹/₄ turn halfway through cooking. Turn ¹/₄ turn; microwave on HIGH for 4 to 5 minutes or until filling bubbles around edges. Cool at least 20 minutes before serving. To serve, cut into squares; top each serving with mound of frozen topping.

**Tip: If desired, topping can be prepared and served without freezing.

Nutrition Per Serving: Calories 440; Protein 4g; Carbohydrate 70g; Fat 16g; Sodium 220mg

Italian Crescent Crostata

Ann S. Mehl *Minneapolis, Minnesota*
Bake-Off® Contest 31, 1984 Prize Winner

Italian-born Ann Mehl's simple crostata (tart) includes the typical fruit preserve filling, baked in a crust and topped with thin strips of dough arranged in a crisscross diamond-shaped pattern.

2 (8-oz.) cans refrigerated crescent dinner rolls
1¹/₂ cups red raspberry preserves
³/₄ cup chopped walnuts or pecans
¹/₂ cup raisins or dried currants
1 egg, beaten, if desired
2 to 3 teaspoons powdered sugar

Heat oven to 350°F. Separate dough into 8 rectangles; separate 5 of the rectangles into 10 triangles. Reserve remaining 3 rectangles for lattice top. Place the 10 triangles in ungreased 12-inch pizza pan or 13×9-inch pan; press over bottom and ¹/₂ inch up sides to form crust. Press perforations to seal. Bake at 350°F. for 12 to 15 minutes or until light golden brown.

In medium bowl, combine preserves, walnuts and raisins. Spread over partially baked crust. To make lattice top, seal perforations of remaining 3 rectangles; cut each lengthwise into 5 strips to make 15 strips of dough. Arrange dough strips in lattice design over preserve mixture, pinching strips together where necessary. Gently brush beaten egg over lattice. Return to oven; bake an additional 17 to 22 minutes or until golden brown. Cool; sprinkle with powdered sugar.

Yield: 12 servings

Nutrition Per Serving: Calories 250; Protein 3g; Carbohydrate 41g; Fat 9g; Sodium 170mg

Chocolate Almond Frozen Mousse

Adelaide B. Shaw *Scarsdale, New Jersey*
Bake-Off® Contest 29, 1980

This is an ideal frozen dessert to have on hand for busy weekends!

CRUST
1 cup all-purpose flour
¹/₂ cup firmly packed brown sugar
¹/₂ cup ground almonds
¹/₂ cup margarine or butter, melted

FILLING
4 eggs, separated
¹/₄ cup milk
¹/₂ to 1 teaspoon almond extract
1 (16-oz.) can chocolate fudge frosting
1 cup whipping cream, whipped

Heat oven to 350°F. In medium bowl, combine all crust ingredients; mix until crumbly. Spread in bottom of ungreased 13×9-inch pan. Bake at 350°F. for 10 to 15 minutes or until light golden brown, stirring once; cool. Press 2 cups of the crumb mixture in bottom of ungreased 9- or 10-inch springform pan or 9-inch square pan. Reserve remaining crumbs.

In small saucepan, slightly beat egg yolks; add milk. Cook over medium heat until thickened, stirring constantly. Remove from heat; stir in almond extract. In large bowl, fold egg yolk mixture into frosting. In small bowl, beat egg whites until stiff peaks form. Fold egg whites and whipped cream into frosting mixture; pour over crumbs in pan. Freeze 1 hour; sprinkle with reserved crumbs. Return to freezer; freeze 3 to 4 hours or until firm. If desired, serve with additional whipped cream.

Yield: 12 servings

Nutrition Per Serving: Calories 410; Protein 5g; Carbohydrate 42g; Fat 25g; Sodium 210mg

Current Events

Some Bake-Off® recipes have been inspired by trends and news events. Witness the Split Levels and Steady Daters (both cookies) from the 1950s; and Jam Session Coffee Cake, Cheese-Niks (inspired by *Sputnik*) and Meat Balls a-Go-Go from the 1960s. Edelweiss Fudge Pie followed on the heels of the movie *The Sound of Music,* and Cheesy Moon Bread and Hawaiian Moon Drops celebrated the achievement of *Apollo 13.* However, the prize for "reading your news and eating it too" goes to a contestant from the thirteenth contest, who said her entree was inspired by the meeting between President John F. Kennedy and Soviet Premier Nikita Khrushchev. The dish? Russian Stroganoff with Irish Potatoes.

ROSEMARY SPORT

A pink stove might seem like an odd lucky charm, but it worked wonders for 1955 Bake-Off® Finalist Rosemary Sport. "At the time, we were living in a housing project. When I won, what I actually won was the trip and the range, but nobody made me an offer to buy the range at a fair price. So I kept that pink range in the living room in a crate."

The prize range "was the pivotal point in our lives," she says today. "We had wanted to buy a house anyway, but the motivation hadn't shown up—and the baby had." Motivation arrived after Rosemary's Bake-Off® trip, in the form of the pink electric range and the prestige of having been a Bake-Off® Contest finalist. "I went to work as a chef in a restaurant in Newton-Highlands. I said 'I am a Bake-Off® finalist,' and that made everybody think I could do anything. That's how I got the job in the restaurant. I worked

nights and my husband worked days—and we saved my money to buy a house to put the range in!" Two years later Rosemary and her family were the proud owners of a house in Abbington, Massachusetts. What happened to the pink electric range? "I bought a pink refrigerator and painted my kitchen in pink tones."

Rosemary raised her family in that house with a pink kitchen, cooking up quite a few batches of her tasty, Bake-Off® prize-winning Peach Elizabeth for dessert. A few years later Rosemary returned to school and won a prestigious Fulbright scholarship. Rosemary credits her Pillsbury recognition with starting her on "an uphill spiral," which, when paired with her hard work, created great success. When the spark of inspiration comes—even in the form of a pink electric range—anything is possible.

Peach Elizabeth

Rosemary H. Sport *Roxbury, Massachusetts*
Bake-Off® Contest 7, 1955

A sunny peach filling is nestled between two spicy butter-crunch layers— a dressed-up version of a fruit crisp.

¹/₂ **cup butter or margarine, softened**
¹/₂ **cup firmly packed brown sugar**
1 **teaspoon grated lemon peel**
1 **teaspoon lemon juice**
1 **cup all-purpose flour**
¹/₂ **teaspoon baking soda**
¹/₂ **teaspoon salt**
¹/₂ **teaspoon cinnamon**
¹/₄ **teaspoon nutmeg**
¹/₂ **cup crushed corn flakes or other flake cereal**
9 **fresh peach halves***

Heat oven to 350°F. Generously grease 8-inch square pan. In large bowl, beat butter, brown sugar, lemon peel and lemon juice until light and fluffy.

Add flour, baking soda, salt, cinnamon and nutmeg to butter mixture; beat until well blended. Stir in cereal until mixture resembles coarse crumbs. Press half of mixture in bottom of greased pan. Arrange peach halves, cut side down, over crust. Sprinkle with remaining crumb mixture.

Bake at 350°F. for 45 to 50 minutes or until golden brown. Serve warm or cold with cream or whipped cream. *Yield: 9 servings*

***Tip:** Canned peach halves can be substituted for fresh peaches.

High Altitude—Above 3,500 feet: No change.

Nutrition Per Serving: Calories 220; Protein 2g; Carbohydrate 31g; Fat 10g; Sodium 350mg

Lemon Meringue Dessert Squares

Tina Principato *West Roxbury, Massachusetts*
Bake-Off® Contest 23, 1972

For perfect slices of meringue desserts, dip the knife in water before cutting. Wipe the knife clean and dip it into the water again between each slice.

CRUST
1 (1 lb. 2.25-oz.) pkg. pudding-included yellow cake mix
¹/₂ cup margarine or butter
1 egg

FILLING
1¹/₃ cups sugar
¹/₂ cup cornstarch
Dash salt
1³/₄ cups water
4 egg yolks, slightly beaten
2 tablespoons margarine or butter
2 tablespoons grated lemon peel
¹/₂ cup lemon juice

MERINGUE
4 egg whites
¹/₄ teaspoon cream of tartar
¹/₂ cup sugar

Heat oven to 350°F. Grease 13×9-inch pan. In large bowl, combine cake mix, ¹/₂ cup margarine and egg; mix at low speed until crumbly. Press mixture in bottom of greased pan.

In medium saucepan, combine 1¹/₃ cups sugar, cornstarch and salt. Gradually stir in water; blend until smooth. Cook over medium heat until mixture boils, stirring constantly. Remove from heat. Stir about ¹/₂ cup of hot mixture into egg yolks; return egg mixture to saucepan. Cook until mixture is bubbly. (Mixture will be very thick.) Remove from heat; stir in 2 tablespoons margarine, lemon peel and lemon juice. Pour filling over crust.

In small bowl, beat egg whites and cream of tartar at medium speed until soft peaks form, about 1 minute. Add ¹/₂ cup sugar 1 tablespoon at a time, beating at high speed until stiff peaks form and

Lemon Meringue Dessert Squares

sugar is dissolved. Spread meringue over hot filling. Bake at 350°F. for 25 to 30 minutes or until meringue is golden brown. Cool 1 hour. Refrigerate at least 1 hour before serving. Cut into squares.

Yield: 12 servings

Nutrition Per Serving: Calories 440; Protein 4g; Carbohydrate 72g; Fat 15g; Sodium 440mg

Swedish Apple Mini-Dumplings

Stella Riley Bender *Colorado Springs, Colorado*
Bake-Off® Contest 36, 1994

This version easily made with refrigerated pie crust makes several small-sized dumplings.

1 **refrigerated pie crust (from 15-oz. pkg.)**
$^1/_2$ **cup firmly packed brown sugar**
$^1/_2$ **teaspoon cinnamon**
$^1/_4$ **teaspoon cardamom**
2 **teaspoons vanilla**
1 **tablespoon butter or margarine, softened**
1 **small Granny Smith apple, peeled, cored and cut into 8 slices**
$^1/_4$ **cup raisins**
$1^1/_2$ **cups apple juice**
3 **tablespoons sugar**
2 **tablespoons red cinnamon candies**
$^1/_4$ **cup half-and-half**

Allow crust pouch to stand at room temperature for 15 to 20 minutes.
Heat oven to 375°F. Spray 8-inch square (1$^1/_2$-quart) baking dish or pan with nonstick cooking spray. In small bowl, combine brown sugar, cinnamon, cardamom and vanilla; mix well. Set aside.

Remove crust from pouch; unfold. Spread crust with butter; sprinkle with brown sugar mixture. Cut into 8 wedges; place apple slice crosswise in center of each wedge. Starting with pointed end, fold over apple; fold corners of wide end of wedge over apple, forming dumpling and sealing completely. Place seam side down in spray-coated dish with sides touching. Sprinkle with raisins.

In small saucepan, combine apple juice, sugar and cinnamon candies. Bring to a boil over medium heat; cook and stir 1 minute or until cinnamon candies are melted. Carefully pour over dumplings.

Bake at 375°F. for 30 to 40 minutes or until crust is light golden brown, apples are tender and sauce thickens. Let stand 10 minutes. To serve, spoon dumplings into 4 individual serving dishes. Spoon sauce over dumplings; serve warm with half-and-half.

Yield: 4 servings

Nutrition Per Serving: Calories 530; Protein 3g; Carbohydrate 88g; Fat 20g; Sodium 330mg

Sour Cream Apple Squares

Luella Maki *Ely, Minnesota*
Bake-Off® Contest 26, 1975 Grand Prize Winner

This is one of those simple recipes that makes such good eating everyone asks for the recipe. It combines a crunchy crumb-nut base with a moist, lightly spiced apple cake layer. A scoop of ice cream or whipped cream simply gilds the lily.

2 **cups all-purpose flour**
2 **cups firmly packed brown sugar**
$^1/_2$ **cup margarine or butter, softened**
1 **cup chopped nuts**
1 to 2 **teaspoons cinnamon**
1 **teaspoon baking soda**
$^1/_2$ **teaspoon salt**
1 **cup dairy sour cream**
1 **teaspoon vanilla**
1 **egg**
2 **cups finely chopped peeled apples (2 medium)**

Heat oven to 350°F. In large bowl, combine flour, brown sugar and margarine; beat at low speed until

Stella Riley Bender: Swedish Apple Mini-Dumplings

In many families, cooking is an activity shared by mothers and daughters—and sometimes mothers-in-law. Stella Riley Bender credits the mothers in her life as inspiration for her wonderful dumplings: "A long time ago my Swedish-born mother-in-law taught me how to make her apple dumplings," Stella says. "I adapted her recipe to smaller portions, or 'mini-dumplings,' and I can thank my own mother for the idea of adding cinnamon candy—she always spices up her applesauce with a handful."

crumbly. Stir in nuts. Press 2¾ cups of crumb mixture in bottom of ungreased 13×9-inch pan. To remaining mixture, add cinnamon, baking soda, salt, sour cream, vanilla and egg; mix well. Stir in apples. Spoon evenly over base.

Bake at 350°F. for 30 to 40 minutes or until toothpick inserted in center comes out clean. Cut into squares. Serve with whipped cream or ice cream, if desired.

Yield: 12 servings

High Altitude—Above 3,500 feet: Bake at 375°F. for 25 to 35 minutes.

Nutrition Per Serving: Calories 410; Protein 5g; Carbohydrate 58g; Fat 19g; Sodium 310mg

Spicy Apple Twists

Dorothy DeVault *Delaware, Ohio*
Bake-Off® Contest 10, 1958 Grand Prize Winner

Serve these miniature apple dumplings warm or cool—either way, seconds will be in demand!

2 large baking apples, peeled, cored
1½ cups all-purpose flour
½ teaspoon salt
½ cup shortening
4 to 6 tablespoons cold water
1 tablespoon margarine or butter, softened

TOPPING
¼ cup margarine or butter, melted
½ cup sugar
1 teaspoon cinnamon
1 cup water

Heat oven to 425°F. Cut each apple into 8 wedges. In medium bowl, blend flour and salt. Using pastry blender or fork, cut in shortening until mixture resembles coarse crumbs. Sprinkle flour mixture with water 1 tablespoon at a time, mixing lightly with fork until dough is just moist enough to hold together. Shape dough into ball.

On floured surface, roll dough lightly from center to edge into 12-inch square. Spread with 1 tablespoon softened margarine. Fold 2 sides to center. Roll to 16×10-inch rectangle. Cut crosswise into sixteen 10-inch strips. Wrap 1 strip around each apple wedge. Place ½ inch apart in ungreased 13×9-inch pan. Brush each wrapped apple wedge with melted margarine. In small bowl, blend sugar and cinnamon; sprinkle over wrapped apples.

Bake at 425°F. for 20 minutes. Pour water into pan. Bake an additional 12 to 17 minutes or until golden brown. Spoon sauce in pan over twists. Serve warm or cool, plain or with whipped cream.

Yield: 16 servings

Nutrition Per Serving: Calories 170; Protein 1g; Carbohydrate 18g; Fat 10g; Sodium 110mg

Southern Pecan Pie Cappuccino Squares

Donna Hilgendorf *Waunakee, Wisconsin*
Bake-Off® Contest 36, 1994 Prize Winner

An elegant mocha pecan pie brownie— what could be more delicious?

FILLING
¼ cup butter or margarine
2 tablespoons all-purpose flour
¾ cup firmly packed brown sugar
2 eggs, lightly beaten
1 teaspoon instant coffee granules or crystals
1 teaspoon hot water
2 teaspoons bourbon
1 teaspoon vanilla
2 cups chopped pecans

BROWNIE
1 (1 lb. 3.5-oz.) pkg. fudge brownie mix
½ cup cold strong brewed coffee
⅓ cup oil
1 egg
½ cup semi-sweet chocolate chips

Dorothy DeVault: Spicy Apple Twists

Early Bake-Off® Contest winners had quite a lot to deal with when they returned to their hometowns—their new celebrity took all sorts of shapes. When pregnant Dorothy DeVault won the Grand Prize for her Spicy Apple Twists in the tenth Bake-Off® Contest, she used her prize money to build a new family home. "Our long-desired girl arrived early the morning of May 12," Dorothy wrote to Pillsbury, "and of course we think she is quite a doll. People say we should name her 'Apple Twist,' but we used Melinda Joanne instead. I did have to promise Apple Twists for the nurses as soon as I got back home, though."

GLAZE
**2 teaspoons butter or
  margarine**
**¹/₂ cup semi-sweet chocolate
  chips**
1 tablespoon whipping cream

TOPPING
1 cup whipping cream
¹/₄ cup powdered sugar
2 teaspoons bourbon

Heat oven to 350°F. Grease bottom only of 13×9-inch pan. In medium saucepan, melt ¹/₄ cup butter; stir in flour until smooth. Add brown sugar and 2 eggs; mix well. Cook over medium-low heat 5 minutes or until thickened, stirring constantly. Remove from heat. Dissolve instant coffee in hot water; stir into filling. Add 2 teaspoons bourbon, vanilla and pecans; mix well. Set aside.

In large bowl combine brownie mix, coffee, oil and 1 egg; beat 50 strokes by hand. Stir in ¹/₂ cup chocolate chips. Spread in greased pan. Spoon and spread filling evenly over top.

Bake at 350°F. for 30 to 40 minutes or until set and deep golden brown. DO NOT OVERBAKE.

In small saucepan over very low heat, melt glaze ingredients, stirring constantly. Immediately drizzle over warm brownies. Cool completely.

To serve, beat topping ingredients until stiff peaks form. Top each dessert square with whipped cream. Garnish with chocolate-dipped pecans, if desired. Store in refrigerator.

Yield: 15 servings

High Altitude—Above 3,500 feet: Add ¹/₄ cup flour to dry brownie mix. Bake as directed above.

Nutrition Per Serving: Calories 530; Protein 5g; Carbohydrate 55g; Fat 32g; Sodium 160mg

Spicy Apple Twists

Royal Marble Cheesecake

Dora Feinstein *Atlantic City, New Jersey*
Bake-Off® Contest 16, 1964

Ribbons of dark chocolate are swirled throughout to produce this delectable creation. Placing a shallow pan half full of water on the bottom oven rack will help keep the surface of the cheesecake moist and prevent cracks.

CRUST
³/₄ cup all-purpose flour
2 tablespoons sugar
Dash salt
¹/₄ cup margarine or butter
1 (6-oz.) pkg. (1 cup) semi-sweet chocolate chips, melted

FILLING
3 (8-oz.) pkg. cream cheese, softened
1 cup sugar
¹/₄ cup all-purpose flour
2 teaspoons vanilla
6 eggs
1 cup dairy sour cream

Heat oven to 400°F. In small bowl, combine ³/₄ cup flour, 2 tablespoons sugar and salt. Using pastry blender or fork, cut in margarine until mixture resembles coarse crumbs. Stir in 2 tablespoons of the melted chocolate. Reserve remaining chocolate for filling. Press in bottom of ungreased 9-inch springform pan. Bake at 400°F. for 10 minutes or until very light brown. Remove from oven. Reduce oven temperature to 325°F.

In large bowl, beat cream cheese and 1 cup sugar until light and fluffy. Add ¹/₄ cup flour and vanilla; blend well. At low speed, add eggs 1 at a time, beating just until blended. Add sour cream; mix well. Place 1³/₄ cups filling mixture in medium bowl; stir in reserved melted chocolate. Pour half of plain filling over crust. Top with spoonfuls of half of the chocolate filling. Cover with remaining plain filling, then with spoonfuls of remaining chocolate filling. Using table knife, swirl chocolate filling through plain filling.

Bake at 325°F. for 60 to 75 minutes or until center is almost set. Cool 10 minutes; remove sides of pan. Cool 2 to 3 hours. Refrigerate 8 hours or overnight before serving. Store in refrigerator.

Yield: 16 servings

Nutrition Per Serving: Calories 370; Protein 7g; Carbohydrate 28g; Fat 26g; Sodium 200mg

Praline Pecan Cheesecake

Sue Zappa *St. Paul, Minnesota*
Bake-Off® Contest 34, 1990

Calling all cheesecake lovers! This heavenly dessert combines an easy cake mix crust with a creamy candy filling and caramel topping—it's an incredible version of cheesecake!

CRUST
1 (1 lb. 2.25-oz.) pkg. pudding-included butter flavor cake mix
¹/₂ cup butter or margarine, softened

FILLING
3 (8-oz.) pkg. cream cheese, softened
¹/₃ cup sugar
3 tablespoons all-purpose flour
1 to 1¹/₂ teaspoons rum extract
3 eggs
4 (1.4-oz.) toffee candy bars, coarsely crushed

TOPPING
¹/₂ cup firmly packed brown sugar
1 cup chopped pecans
¹/₃ cup caramel ice cream topping

Heat oven to 325°F. In large bowl, combine cake mix and butter at low speed until crumbly. Reserve 1 cup of crumb mixture for topping. With floured fingers, press remaining mixture in bottom and 1¹/₂ inches up sides of ungreased 10- or 9-inch springform pan.

In same large bowl, combine cream cheese, sugar, flour and rum extract; beat until smooth. Add eggs; mix well. Stir in crushed candy bars. Pour into crust-lined pan. In small bowl, combine reserved crumb mixture, brown sugar and pecans; mix well. Sprinkle evenly over filling.

Bake at 325°F. for 70 to 85 minutes or until center is set and topping is golden brown. Remove from oven; drizzle caramel topping over top. Bake an additional 8 to 10 minutes to set topping. Cool 30 minutes. Run knife around sides of pan to loosen. Cool completely. Remove sides of pan. Refrigerate 4 to 5 hours or overnight before serving. Store in refrigerator.

Yield: 16 servings

High Altitude—Above 3,500 feet: No change.

Nutrition Per Serving: Calories 500; Protein 7g; Carbohydrate 50g; Fat 31g; Sodium 430mg

Royal Marble Cheesecake

Easy Lemon Cheesecake

Amelia Villers *Lee's Summit, Missouri*
Bake-Off® Contest 36, 1994

This easy cheesecake can be made ahead and is perfect to serve to a crowd.

CRUST
1 (1 lb. 2.25-oz.) pkg. pudding-included lemon cake mix*
1/2 cup butter or margarine, softened

FILLING
2 (8-oz.) pkg. cream cheese, softened
3 eggs
1 (8-oz.) container lemon yogurt
1 (16-oz.) can lemon creme frosting

Heat oven to 325°F. Lightly grease bottom only of 10- or 9-inch springform pan. In large bowl, combine cake mix and butter at low speed until crumbly. Reserve 1 cup of crumb mixture for topping. With floured fingers, press remaining mixture in bottom and 1 1/2 inches up sides of greased pan.

In same bowl, combine all filling ingredients; beat at medium speed until smooth. Pour into crust-lined pan. Sprinkle reserved crumb mixture evenly over filling.

Bake at 325°F. for 1 to 1 1/2 hours or until center is just set and edges are golden brown. Cool 30 minutes. Run knife around sides of pan to loosen. Remove sides of pan. Refrigerate 2 hours before serving. Store in refrigerator.

Yield: 16 servings

*Tip: Yellow cake mix can be substituted for the lemon cake mix.

Nutrition Per Serving: Calories 430; Protein 5g; Carbohydrate 49g; Fat 24g; Sodium 420mg

Cake 'n Cheese Cake

Imogene Noar *Paramount, California*
Bake-Off® Contest 14, 1962 Prize Winner

Imogene Noar liked cheesecake, but wanted a substitute for the usual graham cracker crust. So she cleverly used the recipe for a cake batter as a "crust" and the results were fabulous! To add a colorful touch to this winning make-ahead dessert, garnish it with fresh raspberries.

FILLING
1 (8-oz.) pkg. cream cheese, softened
2/3 cup sugar
1/2 cup dairy sour cream
1 teaspoon vanilla
2 eggs

CAKE
1 cup all-purpose flour
1 teaspoon baking powder
Dash salt
1/2 cup margarine or butter, softened
2/3 cup sugar
2 eggs
1 tablespoon milk
1 teaspoon vanilla

TOPPING
1 cup dairy sour cream
2 tablespoons sugar
1 teaspoon vanilla

Heat oven to 325°F. Grease and flour bottom only of 10-inch deep dish pie pan or 9-inch square pan. In small bowl, beat cream cheese and 2/3 cup sugar until light and fluffy. Add 1/2 cup sour cream and 1 teaspoon vanilla; blend well. Add eggs 1 at a time, beating at low speed. Set aside.

In medium bowl, combine flour, baking powder and salt. In large bowl, beat margarine and 2/3 cup sugar until light and fluffy. Add eggs 1 at a time, beating well after each addition. Stir in milk and 1 teaspoon vanilla. Add dry ingredients at low speed until moistened. Beat 1 minute at medium speed. Spread batter in bottom and up sides of greased and floured pie pan, spreading thinner on sides. Pour cream cheese mixture over batter.

Bake at 325°F. for 40 to 45 minutes or until cheesecake is almost set in center and cake is golden brown.

Meanwhile, in small bowl, combine all topping ingredients. Remove cake from oven; spread evenly with topping. Bake an additional 5 minutes. Cool; refrigerate 3 to 4 hours before serving. Store in refrigerator.

Yield: 10 servings

High Altitude—Above 3,500 feet: Decrease sugar in filling to 1/2 cup; decrease sugar in cake to 1/2 cup. Bake as directed above.

Nutrition Per Serving: Calories 430; Protein 7g; Carbohydrate 41g; Fat 27g; Sodium 260mg

Cookie Cheesecake Squares

Grace M. Wold *Phoenix, Arizona*
Bake-Off® Contest 19, 1968

Garnishing with fresh strawberries and a dollop of whipped cream will add a refreshing springtime touch to this quick and easy dessert.

Cake 'n Cheese Cake

1 (18-oz.) pkg. refrigerated sugar cookies
³/₄ cup strawberry preserves
1 (8-oz.) pkg. cream cheese, softened
¹/₄ cup sugar
1 (8-oz.) container dairy sour cream
¹/₂ teaspoon vanilla
1 egg

Heat oven to 375° F. Slice dough into ¹/₄-inch slices.* Press slices in bottom of ungreased 13×9-inch pan to form crust. Bake at 375° F. for 10 to 15 minutes or until light golden brown. (Cookie dough will appear puffy when removed from oven.)

Gently spread evenly with preserves.

In large bowl, combine cream cheese and sugar; beat at medium speed until fluffy. Add remaining ingredients; mix well. Pour mixture over preserves, spreading to edges. Bake at 375° F. for an additional 28 to 33 minutes or until knife inserted in cheese layer comes out clean. Cool. Store in refrigerator.

Yield: 12 servings

*Tip: For easier slicing of cookie dough, place in freezer 10 minutes, then slice.

Nutrition Per Serving: Calories 350; Protein 4g; Carbohydrate 44g; Fat 18g; Sodium 230mg

Cheesecake

Cheesecake is one of the oldest cakes around. In *The Deiphosophists*, a fifteen-volume anthology set down by the Greek scholar Athenaeus around A.D. 250, a large section was devoted to cheesecake and provided recipes. Apparently the first cheesecake was baked in the Aegean Islands, on Samos. Cooks forced cheese through a bronze sieve and mixed it with flour and honey, then baked it. Now we know why they call the Mediterranean the cradle of civilization!

Peanut Butter Chocolate Creme Cheesecake

Melissa Henninger *Northport, Alabama*
Bake-Off® Contest 36, 1994

Pure ecstasy is the only way to describe this heavenly no-bake dessert. Each bite brings a new delight in favorite flavors, blended perfectly.

CRUST
1½ cups finely crushed creme-filled chocolate sandwich cookies (about 18)
6 tablespoons sugar
3 tablespoons unsweetened cocoa
¼ cup butter or margarine, melted

FILLING
3 (8-oz.) pkg. cream cheese, softened
1 cup creamy peanut butter
1 (16-oz.) can vanilla frosting
1½ cups coarsely chopped creme-filled chocolate sandwich cookies (about 16)

TOPPING
4 (1.6-oz.) pkg. or 8 (0.6-oz.) chocolate-covered peanut butter cups, unwrapped, broken into pieces
¼ cup milk
1½ cups frozen whipped topping, thawed
3 tablespoons unsweetened cocoa
2 tablespoons sugar

GARNISH, IF DESIRED
1 chocolate-covered peanut butter cup, cut into 6 wedges
1 creme-filled chocolate sandwich cookie, cut into 6 wedges

In blender container, food processor bowl with metal blade or large bowl, combine all crust ingredients; mix well. Press in bottom of ungreased 9- or 10-inch springform pan; set aside.

In large bowl, beat cream cheese until smooth and creamy. Add peanut butter; beat until light and fluffy. Fold in frosting. Pour half of batter over crust; sprinkle evenly with 1½ cups chopped cookies. Cover with remaining batter. Refrigerate 2 hours or until set.

In small microwave-safe bowl, combine peanut butter cups and milk. Microwave on HIGH for 1½ to 3 minutes, stirring once halfway through cooking; stir until smooth.* Pour over top of cheesecake; refrigerate 1 hour or until set. Remove sides of pan.

In large bowl, combine whipped topping, 3 tablespoons cocoa and 2 tablespoons sugar; fold to blend well. Pipe or spoon 12 circular mounds around edge of cheesecake; top with candy and cookie wedges. Store in refrigerator.

Yield: 16 servings

*Tip: To melt peanut butter cups on stove top, in small saucepan, combine peanut butter cups and milk. Cook and stir over low heat for 2 to 3 minutes or until melted and smooth.

Nutrition Per Serving: Calories 620; Protein 10g; Carbohydrate 54g; Fat 41g; Sodium 440mg

Tropical Citrus Pastry Stack-Up

Doris Phillips *Fayetteville, Arkansas*
Bake-Off® Contest 36, 1994

This cream-filled dessert features three layers of flaky pastry and a yummy coconut meringue topping.

FILLING
6 tablespoons all-purpose flour
⅓ cup sugar
1 (8¼-oz.) can crushed pineapple in heavy syrup, drained, reserving syrup
½ cup orange juice
1 tablespoon lemon juice
3 egg yolks, slightly beaten

2 tablespoons butter or
    margarine
3/4 cup flaked coconut

PASTRIES
3 refrigerated pie crusts (from
    two 15-oz. pkg.)

MERINGUE
3 egg whites
1/4 cup sugar
3 tablespoons flaked coconut

In medium saucepan, combine flour and 1/3 cup sugar; mix well. Add water to reserved pineapple syrup to make 1/2 cup; add to saucepan. Stir in orange juice and lemon juice; blend until smooth. Cook over medium heat for 3 minutes or until mixture thickens, stirring constantly. Reduce heat to low; cover and cook an additional 2 minutes. Remove from heat. Stir about 1/2 cup of hot mixture into egg yolks; add egg mixture to saucepan. Cook over medium heat for 2 to 3 minutes or until thick, stirring constantly. Remove from heat. Stir in butter, 3/4 cup coconut and pineapple. Refrigerate 1 hour or until cold.

Heat oven to 400° F. Allow crust pouches to stand at room temperature for 15 to 20 minutes. Remove 1 crust from pouch; unfold. Press out fold lines. Place 1 crust on ungreased cookie sheet. Generously prick crust with fork. Bake at 400° F. for 9 to 12 minutes or until light golden brown. Repeat with remaining crusts. Cool.

In small bowl, beat egg whites at medium speed until soft peaks form. Gradually add 1/4 cup sugar 1 tablespoon at a time, beating at high speed until stiff glossy peaks form and sugar is dissolved.

To assemble, place 1 pastry round on ungreased cookie sheet; spread with half of filling. Top with second pastry round; spread with remaining filling. Top with remaining pastry round. Spread top and sides with meringue. Sprinkle top with 3 tablespoons coconut.

Bake at 400° F. for 6 to 10 minutes or until meringue is deep golden brown. Cool. Cut into wedges. Store in refrigerator.

Yield: 14 servings

Nutrition Per Serving: Calories 320; Protein 4g; Carbohydrate 38g; Fat 17g; Sodium 260mg

Peanut Chocolate Parfait Dessert

Karen Everly *Portland, Oregon*
Bake-Off® Contest 32, 1986 Prize Winner

A chocolaty cake crust with a rich, fluffy peanut cream filling makes a heavenly dessert. Serve it either refrigerated or frozen.

CRUST
1 (1 lb. 2.25-oz.) pkg.
    pudding-included devil's
    food cake mix
1/2 cup margarine or butter,
    melted
1/4 cup milk
1 egg
3/4 cup peanuts

FILLING
3/4 cup peanut butter
1 1/2 cups powdered sugar
1 (8-oz.) pkg. cream cheese,
    softened

2 1/2 cups milk
1 (8-oz.) container (3 1/2 cups)
    frozen whipped topping,
    thawed
1 (5.1-oz.) pkg. instant vanilla
    pudding and pie filling mix
    (6-serving size)

TOPPING
1/2 cup peanuts
1 (1.55-oz.) bar milk
    chocolate, chilled, grated

Heat oven to 350° F. Grease and flour bottom only of 13×9-inch pan. In large bowl, combine all crust ingredients at medium speed until well blended. Spread evenly in greased and floured pan. Bake at 350° F. for 20 to 25 minutes. DO NOT OVERBAKE. Cool.

In small bowl, combine peanut butter and powdered sugar at low speed until crumbly; set aside. In large bowl, beat cream cheese until smooth. Add milk, whipped topping and pudding mix; beat at low speed 2 minutes until well blended. Pour half of cream cheese mixture over cooled, baked crust. Sprinkle with half of peanut butter mixture. Repeat with remaining cream cheese and peanut butter mixtures. Sprinkle with 1/2 cup peanuts; gently press into filling. Sprinkle with grated chocolate. Cover; refrigerate or freeze until serving time. If frozen, let stand at room temperature for 15 minutes before serving. Store in refrigerator or freezer.

Yield: 16 servings

High Altitude—Above 3,500 feet: No change.

Nutrition Per Serving: Calories 550; Protein 11g; Carbohydrate 56g; Fat 31g; Sodium 630mg

Chapter 10

2002 Bake-Off® Winners: Quick & Easy Main Meals

The 2002 Bake-Off® Contest entries were vastly different from those in earlier contests, when recipes were made from scratch, ingredient lists and directions were lengthy, and breads and desserts were the bulk of the entries. Many of the 2002 recipes were about getting a healthful, delicious meal on the table fast. With the number of two-working-parent households on the rise, these inventive entries addressed a growing need for nutritious and easily prepared meals for families.

The taste-winning recipes met the challenges of our fast-paced lifestyle in new, often surprising ways. Ingredient lists included everyday pantry items such as purchased Alfredo sauce, peanut butter and dried pasta. Feeding hungry families fast was the main motivation behind many of the finalists' creative recipes, and using up leftovers in unique ways also provided inspiration. Parmesan Chicken with Pasta Rags was created as a way to use up half-filled boxes of lasagna noodles, and Fiesta Spaghetti was born when a finalist used leftover taco-seasoned meat to make spaghetti sauce. Pairing different ethnic flavors also continued as a popular trend. Chicken Manicotti Olé and Tex-Mex Pasta both crossed cooking borders by mixing the highly popular cuisines of Mexico and Italy.

Although the entries varied widely in terms of cooking techniques and tastes, they all shared a common thread: convenience. Chances are the question of what to make for dinner will continue for decades; fortunately, each new Bake-Off® provides dozens of wonderful, great-tasting answers.

Top to bottom: **Chicken Manicotti Olé, page 346, Tex-Mex Pasta, page 355**

Chicken and Black Bean Bake

Janet Mercer *Winter Park, Florida*
Bake-Off® Contest 40, 2002

Hot pork sausage adds a lot of zing to this easy chicken and black bean dish. If you prefer a milder flavor, use regular pork sausage instead.

1 (12-oz.) pkg. bulk hot pork
 sausage
¾ cup self-rising flour*
12 oz. (3 cups) shredded
 Cheddar cheese
3 cups diced cooked chicken
 or turkey
1½ cups chunky-style salsa
1 (15-oz.) can black beans,
 drained, rinsed
2 eggs
2 (4.5-oz.) cans chopped
 green chiles
Chunky-style salsa
Dairy sour cream
Fresh cilantro sprigs

Heat oven to 350°F. Cook sausage in medium skillet over medium-high heat until thoroughly cooked, stirring frequently. Drain.

In large bowl, combine flour, cooked sausage and 1 cup of the cheese; mix well. Spread in ungreased 13×9-inch (3-quart) glass baking dish. Sprinkle with chicken. Top with 1½ cups salsa and beans.

In medium bowl, combine eggs and chiles; beat well. Stir in 1 cup of the cheese. Pour over mixture in baking dish. Sprinkle with remaining 1 cup cheese.

Bake at 350°F. for 25 to 35 minutes or until set and edges are golden brown. Cool 5 minutes. Spoon onto individual serving plates. Garnish each serving with additional salsa, sour cream and cilantro.

Yield: 8 servings

*Tip: All-purpose flour can be substituted for the self-rising flour. Add 1¼ teaspoons baking powder and ⅛ teaspoon salt to flour.

Nutrition Per Serving: Calories 510; Protein 37g; Carbohydrate 24g; Fat 29g; Sodium 1280mg

Chicken Cheese Enchiladas

Barbie Lee *Tavernier, Florida*
Bake-Off® Contest 40, 2002
Prize Winner

If you have time, plan to refrigerate the chicken pieces with the taco seasoning mix for several hours. This allows the spices of the seasoning mix to flavor the chicken.

1 (1.25-oz.) pkg. taco
 seasoning mix
1 tablespoon olive oil
½ cup water
1 lb. boneless skinless chicken
 breasts, cut into bite-sized
 pieces or strips
12 oz. (3 cups) shredded
 Monterey Jack cheese
⅓ cup chopped fresh cilantro
½ teaspoon salt
1 (15-oz.) container ricotta
 cheese
1 (4.5-oz.) can chopped green
 chiles
1 egg
1 (16-oz.) jar chunky-style
 salsa
1 (10.5-oz.) pkg. (12 tortillas)
 flour tortillas for soft tacos
 and fajitas

Heat oven to 350°F. In resealable food storage plastic bag, combine taco seasoning mix, oil and ¼ cup of the water; seal bag and mix well. Add chicken pieces; reseal and turn bag to mix. Refrigerate 5 minutes or up to 12 hours to marinate.

In medium bowl, combine 2½ cups of the Monterey Jack cheese, cilantro, salt, ricotta cheese, chiles and egg; mix well. Heat large nonstick skillet over medium-high heat until hot. Add chicken with marinade; cook 5 to 10 minutes or until chicken is no longer pink in center, stirring frequently.

In ungreased 13×9-inch (3-quart) glass baking dish, combine ½ cup of the salsa and remaining ¼ cup water; mix well. Spread evenly in bottom of baking dish. Spoon ⅓ cup cheese mixture down center of a tortilla. Top with chicken; roll up. Place filled tortilla, seam side down, over salsa mixture in baking dish. Repeat with remaining tortillas. Drizzle enchiladas with remaining salsa. Sprinkle with remaining ½ cup Monterey Jack cheese.

Bake at 350°F. for 20 to 25 minutes or until cheese is melted.

Yield: 6 servings

Nutrition Per Serving: Calories 630; Protein 44g; Carbohydrate 40g; Fat 33g; Sodium 2160mg

Speedy Layered Chicken Enchilada Pie

Karen Hall *Minneapolis, Minnesota*
Bake-Off® Contest 40, 2002

This easy-to-prepare layered pie is fabulous. That's because it uses high-flavor, low-fat ingredients such as black beans, chicken and enchilada sauce.

1 (11.5-oz.) pkg. (8 tortillas) flour tortillas for burritos
2 cups cubed cooked chicken
½ cup uncooked instant white rice
8 oz. (2 cups) shredded reduced-fat Monterey Jack cheese
1 (15-oz.) can black beans, drained, rinsed
1 (19-oz.) can red enchilada sauce
1 cup frozen shoepeg white corn (from 1-lb. pkg.), thawed
1 cup chunky-style salsa
2 tablespoons thinly sliced green onions
Reduced-fat dairy sour cream, if desired
Additional chopped green onions, if desired

Heat oven to 350°F. Spray 9-inch round (2-quart) glass baking dish or casserole with nonstick cooking spray. Cut 5 of the tortillas in half. Cut remaining tortillas into 2½-inch-wide strips. In large bowl, combine chicken, rice, 1 cup of the cheese, beans and 1 cup of the enchilada sauce; mix well.

Layer 4 tortilla halves in bottom of sprayed baking dish. Top with ¼ cup enchilada sauce and half of the chicken mixture. Top with 2 tortilla halves; fill in empty spaces with 3 tortilla strips. Spoon corn over tortillas. Spread salsa over corn. Layer with 2 tortilla halves and 3 strips. Top with remaining half of chicken mixture. Continue layering with remaining 2 tortilla halves and strips, enchilada sauce, cheese and 2 tablespoons green onions.

Bake at 350°F. for 35 to 45 minutes or until mixture is thoroughly heated and cheese is melted. Cool 5 minutes. Top with sour cream and green onions.

Yield: 6 servings

Nutrition Per Serving: Calories 540; Protein 35g; Carbohydrate 57g; Fat 19g; Sodium 1410mg

Enchilada Pasta Soup

Barbara Catlin Craven *Kerrville, Texas*
Bake-Off® Contest 40, 2002

Here's the perfect recipe and it takes only 20 minutes from start to finish! All the ingredients can be on your pantry shelf ready and waiting, so you don't even have to make a special trip to the grocery store. Add some shredded cheese and chopped onion, if you like, but it's just as delicious if you don't have them on hand.

SOUP
3 (14½-oz.) cans ready-to-serve chicken broth
2 (14.75-oz.) cans cream-style corn
2 (10-oz.) cans red enchilada sauce
1 (4.5-oz.) can chopped green chiles
1 (10-oz.) can chunk white and dark chicken in water, undrained
1 (5-oz.) pkg. uncooked vermicelli, broken into pieces
1½ teaspoons cumin
½ teaspoon salt
½ teaspoon onion powder
½ teaspoon dried oregano leaves, crushed

GARNISH, IF DESIRED
1 medium onion, chopped
12 oz. (3 cups) shredded Colby-Monterey Jack cheese blend

In Dutch oven or large saucepan, combine broth, corn, enchilada sauce and chiles; mix well. Bring to a boil over medium-high heat. Add all remaining soup ingredients; mix well.

Reduce heat to low; simmer 8 minutes or until vermicelli is tender, stirring occasionally. Ladle soup into individual bowls. Garnish each serving with onion and cheese.

Yield: 6 servings

Nutrition Per Serving: Calories 560; Protein 34g; Carbohydrate 52g; Fat 24g; Sodium 2250mg

Chicken Manicotti Olé

Reneé McWilliams *Lincoln, Nebraska*
Bake-Off® Contest 40, 2002

An innovative twist has changed this manicotti, a traditional Italian dish, into a Mexican feast. Chunky salsa replaces the Italian tomato sauce, and adding black beans makes this a hearty dish. Your family will say Olé! every time you serve it!

10 uncooked manicotti
1 lb. ground chicken or ground turkey breast
1 (16-oz.) jar chunky-style salsa
1 (15-oz.) can black beans, drained, rinsed
¼ teaspoon garlic powder
¼ teaspoon pepper
4 oz. (1 cup) shredded Colby-Monterey Jack cheese blend

Heat oven to 350°F. Spray 13×9-inch (3-quart) glass baking dish with nonstick cooking spray. Cook manicotti to desired doneness as directed on package. Drain; rinse with cold water.

In large bowl, combine ground chicken, ¾ cup of the salsa, ¾ cup of the beans, garlic powder and pepper; mix well. In small bowl, combine remaining salsa and beans; mix well. Cover; reserve for topping.

Stuff manicotti with chicken mixture. Arrange in sprayed baking dish. Cover with foil.

Bake at 350°F. for 30 minutes. Uncover baking dish; top with reserved salsa mixture and cheese. Bake, uncovered, an additional 15 to 20 minutes or until chicken is thoroughly cooked and cheese is melted.

Yield: 5 servings

Nutrition Per Serving: Calories 440; Protein 30g; Carbohydrate 43g; Fat 16g; Sodium 1010mg

Parmesan Chicken with Pasta Rags

Mary Capone *Long Beach, California*
Bake-Off® Contest 40, 2002

Broken lasagna noodles are used to make the pasta "rags" in this chicken dish. What a delicious way to use those pasta odds and ends!

CHICKEN
3 garlic cloves, minced
½ teaspoon seasoned salt
3 tablespoons olive oil
1 tablespoon butter
½ cup garlic-herb dry bread crumbs
2 oz. (½ cup) grated fresh Parmesan cheese
1½ lb. boneless skinless chicken breast halves or thighs

PASTA
8 oz. uncooked lasagna noodles, broken into random 2-inch pieces
¼ cup olive oil
1 garlic clove, minced
1 (9-oz.) pkg. frozen spinach in a pouch, thawed, drained
½ teaspoon seasoned salt
1 cup cherry tomatoes, halved
2 tablespoons chopped fresh basil

GARNISH, IF DESIRED
Fresh basil sprigs
Shaved Parmesan cheese

Heat oven to 475°F. In shallow microwave-safe bowl, combine 3 garlic cloves, ½ teaspoon seasoned salt, 3 tablespoons oil and the butter. Microwave on HIGH for 1 minute or until butter is melted; stir to mix.

In another shallow bowl, combine bread crumbs and grated cheese; mix well. Coat chicken breast halves with garlic mixture; coat with crumb mixture. Place in ungreased 15×10×1-inch baking pan. Bake at 475°F. for 20 minutes or until chicken is fork-tender and juices run clear.

Meanwhile, cook broken lasagna noodles to desired doneness as directed on package. Drain; cover to keep warm. Heat ¼ cup oil in large skillet over medium-high heat until hot. Add 1 garlic clove; cook and stir 1 minute or until tender. Add spinach and ½ teaspoon seasoned salt; mix well. Cook 2 to 3 minutes or until spinach is cooked, stirring frequently.

Add cooked noodles, tomatoes and chopped basil to spinach mixture; cook 1 to 2 minutes or until thoroughly heated, stirring occasionally. Serve pasta mixture with chicken. Garnish with basil sprigs and shaved Parmesan cheese.

Yield: 4 servings

Nutrition Per Serving: Calories 800; Protein 54g; Carbohydrate 60g; Fat 38g; Sodium 1100mg

Parmesan Chicken with Pasta Rags

Bow-Thai Chicken

Mille Meehan *Richmond, Virginia*
Bake-Off® Contest 40, 2002
Prize Winner

Mille Meehan combined her favorite Thai flavors with two popular Italian ingredients, Alfredo sauce and bow tie pasta, to create this prize-winning recipe. You will enjoy this tasty main dish as much as the clever name!

7½ oz. (3 cups) uncooked bow tie pasta (farfalle)
⅛ teaspoon curry powder
2 teaspoons soy sauce
½ to ¾ lb. chicken breast strips for stir-frying, cut in half crosswise
1 tablespoon oil
1 (1-lb.) pkg. frozen stir-fry vegetables and zesty Szechuan sauce meal starter
2 teaspoons lime juice
1 teaspoon peanut butter
¾ cup purchased Alfredo sauce
3 tablespoons coconut
3 green onions, sliced
Lime wedges, if desired

Cook pasta in large saucepan to desired doneness as directed on package. Drain; return to saucepan. Cover to keep warm.

Meanwhile, in medium bowl, combine curry powder and soy sauce. Add chicken strips; toss to coat. Heat oil in large skillet or wok over medium-high heat until hot. Add chicken; cook and stir 4 to 5 minutes or until no longer pink in center.

Add frozen sauce and vegetables from meal starter. Bring to a boil. Reduce heat; cover and cook 6 to 9 minutes or until vegetables are crisp-tender, stirring frequently. Stir in lime juice and peanut butter.

Add Alfredo sauce to cooked pasta; toss to coat. Spoon vegetable mixture over pasta mixture; stir well. Spoon onto individual serving plates. Sprinkle with coconut, onions and peanuts from packet. Garnish each serving with lime wedge.

Yield: 4 servings

Nutrition Per Serving: Calories 560; Protein 33g; Carbohydrate 64g; Fat 19g; Sodium 1540mg

Maria Baldwin: Spicy Asian Lettuce Wraps

As a child, Maria Baldwin says she dreamed not of being Miss America but of being a finalist in the Pillsbury Bake-Off® Contest. Inspired by a dish she'd tasted at a local restaurant, Maria's version of Spicy Asian Lettuce Wraps "is very appealing visually, tastes divine and is quick and delicious." Pounding the meat and stir-frying the vegetables speed up the preparation time, making this recipe perfect for a fast weeknight meal. In the end, Maria's dream came with an added bonus: Her entry earned special recognition as the "most innovative" recipe.

Spicy Asian Lettuce Wraps

Maria Baldwin *Mesa, Arizona*
Bake-Off® Contest 40, 2002

This is a great, light meal for casual get-togethers. Place the lettuce-lined platter of the cooked vegetables, noodles and chicken, along with the bowl of peanut sauce, on the table. Everyone can make his or her own Asian wraps.

1 lb. boneless skinless chicken breast halves
1 (1-lb.) pkg. frozen lo mein noodles, stir-fry vegetables and flavorful stir-fry sauce meal starter
2 tablespoons purchased chili-garlic sauce
2 tablespoons soy sauce
3 tablespoons oil
2 garlic cloves, minced
1 tablespoon sugar
2 tablespoons peanut butter
2 tablespoons water
8 large leaves Bibb lettuce
1½ cups grated carrots
⅓ cup chopped peanuts
¼ cup finely chopped green onion
2 tablespoons finely chopped fresh cilantro, if desired

To flatten each chicken breast half, place, boned side up, between 2 pieces of plastic wrap or waxed paper. Working from center, gently pound chicken with flat side of meat mallet or rolling pin until about ¼ inch thick; remove wrap.

In small bowl, combine frozen sauce from meal starter, chili-garlic sauce and soy sauce; mix well. In medium bowl, combine chicken, ¼ cup soy sauce mixture and 2 tablespoons of the oil. Heat 12-inch nonstick skillet over medium-high heat until hot. Add chicken; cook 5 to 6 minutes or until no longer pink in center, stirring occasionally. Remove chicken from skillet; cut into 1-inch pieces. Cover to keep warm.

Heat remaining 1 tablespoon oil in same nonstick skillet over medium-high heat until hot. Add 3 tablespoons soy sauce mixture, garlic, and frozen noodles and vegetables from meal starter; cook 6 to 8 minutes or until vegetables are crisp-tender, stirring frequently. To remaining soy sauce mixture in small bowl, add sugar, peanut butter and water; mix well.

Arrange lettuce on part of large serving platter. Spoon carrots on platter next to lettuce. Arrange cooked vegetables and noodles on platter. Place chicken over vegetables and noodles. Sprinkle chicken with peanuts, onions and cilantro.

To serve, spread peanut sauce in center of each lettuce leaf. Top with chicken-noodle-vegetable mixture and carrots. Wrap lettuce around filling.

Yield: 8 servings

Nutrition Per Serving: Calories 250; Protein 18g; Carbohydrate 18g; Fat 12g; Sodium 790mg

Mexican Fried Rice

Katie Cook *Stafford, Virginia*
Bake-Off® Contest 40, 2002

This Mexican take on Chinese fried rice is a tasty and easy dish. If garlic-flavored olive oil isn't available, you may want to add ¼ teaspoon of garlic powder. Boneless, skinless chicken breasts can be used for the tenders; just cut each breast lengthwise into 1-inch strips.

1 cup uncooked jasmine rice
1½ cups water
1 egg
1 tablespoon garlic-flavored olive oil or olive oil
1 lb. fresh chicken tenders
½ cup chopped onion
2 garlic cloves, minced
1 (15-oz.) can black beans, drained
1 (11-oz.) can vacuum-packed whole kernel corn with red and green peppers
1 (7-oz.) jar sliced roasted red bell peppers, drained
1 (8-oz.) jar taco sauce
¼ cup chopped green onion
¼ cup chopped fresh cilantro

Cook rice in water as directed on package. Meanwhile, spray 12-inch skillet with nonstick cooking spray. Heat over medium heat until hot. Beat egg in small bowl. Add egg to skillet; cook 1 minute or until firm but still moist, stirring frequently. Remove from pan; cover to keep warm.

Heat oil in same skillet over medium heat until hot. Add chicken, onion and garlic; cook 4 to 6 minutes or until chicken is no longer pink in center, stirring frequently. Add beans, corn and roasted peppers; mix well. Cook 1 minute or until thoroughly heated, stirring constantly and breaking up chicken and roasted peppers as mixture cooks.

Add cooked egg and rice; cook and stir 1 minute. Stir in taco sauce; cook 2 minutes or until thoroughly heated, stirring occasionally. Stir in green onions. Spoon mixture onto serving platter. Garnish with cilantro.

Yield: 4 (2-cup) servings

Nutrition Per Serving: Calories 550; Protein 38g; Carbohydrate 76g; Fat 10g; Sodium 1080mg

Baja Chicken Salad with Taco Vinaigrette

Pat Harmon *Baden, Pennsylvania*
Bake-Off® Contest 40, 2002

This colorful salad will be the center of attention at any meal. It combines many of the wonderful flavors and colors of Mexican cooking. Grape tomatoes are baby Roma tomatoes and are slightly sweeter than cherry tomatoes, but cherry tomatoes can easily be used instead in this tasty salad.

1 (1.25-oz.) pkg. taco seasoning mix
1 tablespoon brown sugar
½ cup oil
½ cup cider vinegar
4 boneless skinless chicken breast halves, cut into 1-inch pieces

1 to 2 tablespoons oil
1 (10-oz.) pkg. mixed salad greens or baby greens
1 cup grape tomatoes, halved
½ cup sliced red onion
2⅔ oz. (⅔ cup) shredded Cheddar-Monterey Jack cheese blend
⅓ cup dairy sour cream
1 avocado, pitted, peeled and sliced
3 tablespoons sliced ripe olives
Blue tortilla chips

Pat Harmon:
Baja Chicken Salad with Taco Vinaigrette

Using packaged precut greens and boneless skinless chicken breasts makes Pat Harmon's Baja Chicken Salad with Taco Vinaigrette quick and easy. She believes the Southwest/Mexican flavor in the salad dressing is what gives the recipe its distinctive quality. "I was on vacation and visiting my daughter in Scottsdale, Arizona," Pat says, "and I wanted to use taco seasoning in a new way."

In medium bowl, combine taco seasoning mix, brown sugar, ½ cup oil and vinegar; mix well. Place chicken in shallow medium bowl. Pour ½ cup seasoning mixture over chicken. Reserve remaining mixture for dressing.

Heat 1 to 2 tablespoons oil in medium nonstick skillet over medium-high heat until hot. With slotted spoon, remove chicken from seasoning mixture; add to skillet. Cook 5 minutes or until no longer pink in center, stirring frequently. Discard remaining used seasoning mixture.

In large bowl, combine mixed greens, tomatoes and onion. Add reserved seasoning mixture; toss to coat. Arrange salad mixture on serving platter. Top with chicken, cheese, sour cream, avocado and olives. Arrange tortilla chips around salad.

Yield: 6 servings

Nutrition Per Serving: Calories 460; Protein 23g; Carbohydrate 15g; Fat 34g; Sodium 740mg

Baja Chicken Salad with Taco Vinaigrette

Chicken Cordon Bleu Stromboli

Dee Dee Glick *Clinton, Montana*
Bake-Off® Contest 40, 2002

Cordon bleu is a French term for a dish made with chicken or veal that is stuffed with ham and cheese, breaded and sautéed to a golden brown. This stromboli wraps refrigerated French loaf dough around chicken, ham and cheese, and bakes to a golden brown for a warm crusty sandwich oozing with melted cheese.

1 (11-oz.) can refrigerated French loaf
½ cup grated Parmesan cheese
4 oz. thinly sliced cooked ham
6 oz. thinly sliced cooked chicken
1 (6-oz.) jar sliced mushrooms, drained
1 large green bell pepper, thinly sliced
4 oz. (1 cup) shredded mozzarella cheese
6 oz. (1½ cups) shredded Swiss cheese
¼ cup purchased honey-Dijon salad dressing

Heat oven to 375°F. Spray cookie sheet with butter-flavored nonstick cooking spray. Unroll dough onto sprayed cookie sheet. Press to form 14×12-inch rectangle.

Reserve 2 tablespoons of the Parmesan cheese. Sprinkle remaining Parmesan cheese lengthwise in 4-inch-wide strip down center of dough to within ¼ inch of each end. Top with ham, chicken, mushrooms, bell pepper, cheeses and salad dressing.

Bring one long side of dough up and over filling, completely covering filling. Repeat with remaining long side, overlapping dough. Press edge to seal. Fold ends under. With sharp knife, cut 5 slits in top of dough to allow steam to escape. Sprinkle with reserved 2 tablespoons Parmesan cheese.

Bake at 375°F. for 18 to 24 minutes or until golden brown. Cool 5 minutes. Cut into slices.

Yield: 5 servings

Nutrition Per Serving: Calories 520; Protein 38g; Carbohydrate 34g; Fat 25g; Sodium 1470mg

Santa Fe Chicken Bread Bowls

Maureen Gill *Garfield Heights, Ohio*
Bake-Off® Contest 40, 2002

Bread bowls are easy when you start with refrigerated crusty French loaf dough. Just cut, shape and bake. While the bowls are baking, you can make the chicken stew—everything is ready in just 30 minutes. Others will think you spent hours in the kitchen making this impressive dish!

2 (11-oz.) cans refrigerated
  French loaf
1 tablespoon olive or
  vegetable oil
2 boneless skinless chicken
  breast halves, cut into
  ½-inch pieces
1 red bell pepper, chopped
¼ cup chopped red onion
1 (16-oz.) can chili beans,
  drained
1 (11-oz.) can vacuum-packed
  super sweet yellow and white
  corn, drained
1 (10-oz.) can red enchilada
  sauce
¾ cup dairy sour cream
½ cup ketchup
1 (1.25-oz.) pkg. taco
  seasoning mix
1 tablespoon dried parsley
  flakes
1 teaspoon dried basil leaves
2 oz. (½ cup) shredded
  Cheddar cheese, if desired

Heat oven to 350°F. Spray cookie sheet with nonstick cooking spray. Remove dough from cans. Cut each loaf into 3 pieces; shape each into ball, placing seam at bottom so dough is smooth on top. Place dough balls, seam side down, on sprayed cookie sheet. Bake at 350°F. for 22 to 26 minutes or until golden brown.

Meanwhile, heat oil in large saucepan over medium-high heat until hot. Add chicken, bell pepper and onion; cook 5 to 7 minutes or until chicken is no longer pink in center, stirring occasionally. Add all remaining ingredients except cheese; mix well. Bring to a boil. Reduce heat to medium-low; simmer 7 minutes or until thoroughly heated, stirring occasionally.

With sharp knife, cut small portion off top of each loaf. Lightly press center of bread down to form bowls. Place each bread bowl on individual serving plate. Spoon about 1 cup chicken mixture into each. Sprinkle evenly with cheese. Place top of each bread bowl next to filled bread bowl.

Yield: 6 servings

Nutrition Per Serving: Calories 590; Protein 26g; Carbohydrate 78g; Fat 18g; Sodium 1960mg

Chicken Florentine Panini

Denise JoAnne Yennie *Nashville, Tennessee*
Bake-Off® Contest 40, 2002
Grand Prize Winner

Panini is Italian for "small bread," referring to a sandwich that is sometimes grilled. Making this sandwich is easy because you start with a large bread made from refrigerated pizza dough and cut it into "small breads."

To save time, the onion is cooked with sugar and vinegar to give that great caramelized flavor without the long cooking time.

1 (10-oz.) can refrigerated
  pizza crust
1 (9-oz.) pkg. frozen spinach
  in a pouch
¼ cup light mayonnaise
2 garlic cloves, minced
1 tablespoon olive oil
1 cup chopped red onion
1 tablespoon sugar
1 tablespoon vinegar (cider,
  red wine or balsamic)
2 boneless skinless chicken
  breast halves
½ teaspoon dried Italian
  seasoning
4 (4-inch) slices provolone
  cheese

Heat oven to 375°F. Unroll dough; place in ungreased 15×10×1-inch baking pan. Starting at center, press out dough to edges of pan. Bake at 375°F. for 10 minutes. Cool 15 minutes or until completely cooled.

Meanwhile, cook spinach as directed on package. Drain well; squeeze dry with paper towels. In small bowl, combine mayonnaise and 1 of the minced garlic cloves; mix well. Refrigerate.

Heat oil in small saucepan over medium-high heat until hot. Add onion; cook and stir 2 to 3 minutes or until crisp-tender. Add sugar and vinegar. Reduce heat to low; simmer 3 to 5 minutes or until most of liquid has evaporated, stirring occasionally.

To flatten each chicken breast half, place boned side up between 2 pieces of plastic wrap or waxed paper. Working from center, gently pound chicken with flat side of

DENISE JOANNE YENNIE

Denise JoAnne Yennie says her cooking experiences got off to a rocky start. When she was nine, she made a tossed salad for her family. As she brought it to the table, she tripped and literally "tossed" the salad. To this day, Denise's mother also recalls a "Hawaiian" ham dish, lovingly prepared from a children's cookbook recipe, that 10-year-old Denise made in celebration of Mother's Day.

Denise confesses a lifelong passion for food, inspired by her mother, her aunts and her German grandmother, all good cooks. Still, to most of her acquaintances, Denise is known as a business consultant. Her consulting firm challenges clients' conventional wisdom in doing business, and Denise carries a bit of that renegade spirit into her cooking.

"Everything I do has to be quick and easy," the Nashville mother of two says. "My mom and grandmother used to cook things slowly, all day. Not me. I turn on the heat and crank it up." For the contest, "I wanted to create something special enough to get recognized," she says. And her recipe for Chicken Florentine Panini (see opposite) did just that. The Italian sandwich made with refrigerated pizza crust, garlic-flavored mayonnaise, sautéed chicken breasts, spinach and caramelized onions won the $1 million Grand Prize in the 2002 Pillsbury Bake-Off® Contest. The recipe's simple, convenient ingredients paired with sophisticated cooking techniques made it a standout.

Denise herself was described as a standout at the Bake-Off® Contest. Amid the soft whir of blenders, she turned heads as she used a mallet to noisily pound chicken breasts and an electric knife to cut her sandwiches into precise squares. "I pounded so much chicken that I have 'chicken-pounding elbow,'" she joked.

After her Bake-Off® victory, Denise made several television appearances. "I had to practice getting the preparation of the sandwich done in five minutes for the *Oprah* show and in two minutes for the *Today* show," she says. "The publicity came in a whirlwind and left just as quickly as it happened," she says. "The best part has been the impact and effect on all the people who know me—how they go and tell their friends. They get to live this joy with me."

meat mallet or rolling pin until about ¼ inch thick; remove wrap. Sprinkle chicken with Italian seasoning and remaining minced garlic clove.

Spray large skillet with nonstick cooking spray. Heat over medium-high heat until hot. Add chicken; cook 8 minutes or until browned, fork-tender and juices run clear, turning once.

Cut cooled pizza crust into 4 rectangles. Remove rectangles from pan; spread each with 1 tablespoon mayonnaise mixture. Top 2 rectangles with chicken, spinach, onion mixture, cheese and remaining crust rectangles, mayonnaise side down.

Heat large skillet or cast-iron skillet over medium heat until hot. Place sandwiches in skillet. Place smaller skillet on sandwiches to flatten slightly. Cook 1 to 2 minutes or until crisp and heated, turning once. Cut each warm sandwich into quarters.

Yield: 4 servings

Nutrition Per Serving: Calories 500; Protein 40g; Carbohydrate 44g; Fat 18g; Sodium 940mg

Chicken-Chile Stromboli

Debra Kelly *Wheeling, Illinois*
Bake-Off® Contest 40, 2002

A stromboli is an enclosed meat-and-cheese sandwich. This one is not only quick and easy but also uses lower-fat cream cheese and canned chicken packed in water to help trim a few calories. With strips of roasted red peppers and parsley on a golden brown crust, it looks as great as it tastes.

1 (10-oz.) can chunk white
   and dark chicken in water,
   drained
1 (4.5-oz.) can chopped green
   chiles

4 oz. ⅓-less-fat cream cheese
   (Neufchâtel), softened
¼ cup chopped roasted red
   bell peppers (from a jar)
1 tablespoon honey
Dash salt
Dash pepper
1 (11-oz.) can refrigerated
   French loaf
1 egg
1 teaspoon water
Dash dried parsley flakes
6 thin strips roasted red bell
   peppers (from a jar)
1 tablespoon butter, melted
Dash garlic powder

Heat oven to 350°F. Grease cookie sheet. In medium bowl, combine chicken, chiles, cream cheese, ¼ cup roasted peppers, honey, salt and pepper; mix well.

Remove dough from can; place on lightly floured surface. Carefully unroll dough. Spread chicken mixture evenly over dough to within 1 inch of edges. With lightly floured hands, carefully but firmly reroll dough. Gently press edges to seal; fold ends under. Place loaf on greased cookie sheet.

In small bowl, combine egg and water; beat well. Brush over top of loaf; sprinkle with parsley. Arrange roasted pepper strips about 2 inches apart on top of loaf. With sharp knife, cut 5 or 6 diagonal slices, ½ inch deep, on top of loaf.

Chicken-Chile Stromboli

Bake at 350°F. for 25 to 30 minutes or until edges are deep golden brown. In small bowl, combine butter and garlic powder. Brush over warm loaf. Cut into slices.

Yield: 6 servings

Nutrition Per Serving: Calories 290; Protein 17g; Carbohydrate 28g; Fat 11g; Sodium 710mg

Spicy Picnic Chicken

Yvonne Del Biaggio *Sacramento, California*
Bake-Off® Contest 40, 2002

This chicken is named for the very first time Yvonne Del Biaggio served it at a Fourth of July picnic. Family and friends love the spicy flavor, which comes from taco seasoning mix. It tastes like all-American fried chicken but is easier because it's "fried" in the oven.

1 cup buttermilk
1 (1.25-oz.) pkg. taco seasoning mix
1 cup Parmesan dry bread crumbs
¼ cup all-purpose flour
1 to 2 teaspoons salt
½ teaspoon pepper
8 pieces bone-in chicken, skin removed if desired
3 tablespoons butter, melted

Heat oven to 400°F. Spray broiler pan with nonstick cooking spray. In shallow bowl, combine buttermilk and 1 tablespoon of the taco seasoning mix; mix well. In another shallow bowl, combine remaining taco seasoning mix, bread crumbs, flour, salt and pepper; mix well.

Dip chicken pieces in buttermilk mixture; coat with bread crumb mixture. Place on sprayed broiler pan. Let stand 10 minutes. Discard any remaining buttermilk and coating mixture.

Drizzle chicken with butter. Bake at 400°F. for 45 to 55 minutes or until chicken is fork-tender and juices run clear.

Yield: 4 servings

Nutrition Per Serving: Calories 430; Protein 37g; Carbohydrate 31g; Fat 18g; Sodium 2990mg

Tex-Mex Pasta

Karen Wetch *Santa Rosa, California*
Bake-Off® Contest 40, 2002
Prize Winner

Karen Wetch's grandmother and aunt taught her to cook. "I wanted so much to be part of this wonderful grown-up thing that brought families and friends together," Karen remembers. This one-pan dish that combines the flavors of Tex-Mex with pasta will be a winner with your family and friends.

8 oz. uncooked penne (tube-shaped pasta)
1 lb. bulk Italian turkey sausage
1 medium onion, chopped
1 medium red bell pepper, chopped
1 small zucchini, chopped
2 cups frozen whole kernel corn (from 1-lb. pkg.)
1 cup chunky-style salsa
1 (14.5-oz.) can diced tomatoes, undrained
¾ teaspoon dried oregano leaves
6 oz. (1½ cups) reduced-fat shredded Cheddar cheese
½ cup fresh cilantro, chopped

Cook penne to desired doneness as directed on package. Drain; cover to keep warm.

Meanwhile, spray nonstick wok or large skillet with nonstick cooking spray. Heat over medium-high heat until hot. Add sausage; cook 5 minutes or until no longer pink and thoroughly cooked, stirring frequently. Drain. Add onion, bell pepper, zucchini, corn, salsa, tomatoes and oregano; mix well. Bring to a boil. Cook 5 minutes, stirring occasionally.

Reserve ½ cup cheese and 2 tablespoons cilantro. Add remaining 1 cup cheese and cilantro to mixture in skillet; mix well. Add cooked penne; toss to mix. Spoon mixture onto serving platter. Garnish with reserved cheese and cilantro.

Yield: 6 servings

Nutrition Per Serving: Calories 440; Protein 28g; Carbohydrate 49g; Fat 15g; Sodium 1140mg

Smoked Turkey Quesadillas

Dean Philipp *Portland, Oregon*
Bake-Off® Contest 40, 2002

A quesadilla is a flour tortilla folded in half over a savory filling and fried to a golden brown. This version is hearty enough to be served as a quick weeknight meal, as well as a snack or "game-day" treat when everyone is gathered around the TV watching his or her favorite sports event.

1 ripe avocado, pitted, peeled
4 oz. cream cheese or
   ⅓-less-fat cream cheese
   (Neufchâtel), softened
½ teaspoon cumin
¼ teaspoon garlic powder
¼ teaspoon salt
⅛ teaspoon pepper
½ cup julienne-cut oil-packed
   sun-dried tomatoes, drained
1 (4.5-oz.) can chopped green
   chiles, drained
4 oz. (1 cup) shredded hot
   pepper Monterey Jack or
   Monterey Jack cheese
1 (11.5-oz.) pkg. (8 tortillas)
   flour tortillas for burritos
8 (1½-oz.) slices smoked
   turkey breast
4 oz. (1 cup) shredded
   Cheddar cheese
2 tablespoons butter or
   margarine
4 ripe olive slices, if desired

Mash avocado in medium bowl. Add cream cheese, cumin, garlic powder, salt and pepper; blend well. Stir in tomatoes and chiles.

Sprinkle ¾ cup of the Monterey Jack cheese on 4 of the tortillas. Top each with turkey slice. Spread avocado mixture over turkey. Top with remaining turkey slices. Sprinkle with ¾ cup of the Cheddar cheese. Top with remaining tortillas.

Melt ½ tablespoon of the butter in 12-inch skillet over medium heat. Add 1 quesadilla; cook 2 to 4 minutes or until golden brown, turning once. Repeat with remaining butter and quesadillas. Garnish with remaining Monterey Jack and Cheddar cheese. Top each quesadilla with olive slice.

Yield: 4 servings

Nutrition Per Serving: Calories 825; Protein 40g; Carbohydrate 57g; Fat 51g; Sodium 2190mg

Fiesta Spaghetti

Michele C. Santos *Austin, Texas*
Bake-Off® Contest 40, 2002

Adding taco seasoning mix to tomato sauce brings a new flavor twist to spaghetti! Pop a can of refrigerated breadsticks in the oven, prepare a colorful fruit salad and you'll have dinner on the table in no time—and your family will love it!

16 oz. uncooked spaghetti
2 tablespoons olive oil
½ cup chopped onion
1 medium red bell pepper,
   chopped

1 lb. lean ground beef
⅓ cup sugar
1 (1.25-oz.) pkg. taco
   seasoning mix
1 (28-oz.) can crushed
   tomatoes, undrained
1 (8-oz.) can tomato sauce
1 (11-oz.) can vacuum-packed
   whole kernel corn with red
   and green peppers, drained
1 (4.5-oz.) jar sliced
   mushrooms, drained
Grated Parmesan cheese, if
   desired

Cook spaghetti to desired doneness as directed on package. Drain; cover to keep warm.

Meanwhile, heat oil in 12-inch nonstick skillet over medium heat until hot. Add onion and bell pepper; cook 3 to 4 minutes or until tender, stirring occasionally. Remove from skillet. Add ground beef to same skillet; cook until thoroughly cooked, stirring frequently. Drain.

Add onion and bell pepper to ground beef; mix well. Add sugar, taco seasoning mix, tomatoes, tomato sauce, corn and mushrooms; mix well. Bring to a boil. Reduce heat to low; simmer 5 minutes, stirring occasionally. Serve over spaghetti. Sprinkle with cheese.

Yield: 8 servings

Nutrition Per Serving: Calories 490; Protein 22g; Carbohydrate 72g; Fat 13g; Sodium 1050mg

Top to bottom: **Baked Steak Burritos, page 362, Smokey Turkey Quesadillas**

Stuffed Poblano Chile Peppers

Paula Blevins-Russell *Alabaster, Alabama*
Bake-Off® Contest 40, 2002

Poblano chiles are dark, sometimes almost black, green chiles with a rich flavor. The darker the color, the richer the flavor, which can vary from mild to snappy. Using lean ground turkey saves calories and fat, but lean ground beef is also tasty. Or for a spicier flavor, try seasoned ground pork sausage.

6 poblano chiles
1 lb. lean ground turkey
1 (1.25-oz.) pkg. taco seasoning mix
1 (15-oz.) can black beans, drained, rinsed
1 (11-oz.) can vacuum-packed whole kernel corn with red and green peppers, drained
8 oz. (2 cups) shredded light Mexican cheese blend
1 (14.5-oz.) can stewed tomatoes, undrained, chopped
1 (4.5-oz.) can chopped green chiles

Stuffed Poblano Chile Peppers

Heat oven to 350°F. Spray 13×9-inch (3-quart) glass baking dish with nonstick cooking spray. Cut opening in one side of each chile. Carefully remove seeds and membranes, leaving top stem intact; rinse and drain well.

Spray large skillet with nonstick cooking spray. Add ground turkey; cook over medium-high heat for 7 minutes or until no longer pink and thoroughly cooked, stirring frequently. Add taco seasoning mix; mix well. Add beans, corn and 1 cup of the cheese; mix well.

With small spoon, stuff chiles with turkey mixture. Place in sprayed baking dish. Lightly spray tops of chiles with cooking spray. In small bowl, combine tomatoes and green chiles; mix well. Pour over stuffed chiles in baking dish.

Bake at 350°F. for 30 to 40 minutes or until chiles are tender. Sprinkle with remaining 1 cup cheese. Bake an additional 3 minutes or until cheese is melted.

Yield: 6 servings

Nutrition Per Serving: Calories 400; Protein 32g; Carbohydrate 33g; Fat 15g; Sodium 1390mg

Spicy Jamaican Meat Pies with Island Salsa

Diane Joyce Phillips *Chesapeake, Virginia*
Bake-Off® Contest 40, 2002

Meat pies are popular fare in the Caribbean islands. Enjoying Jamaican meat pies at home is easy when you use refrigerated crescent rolls and start with purchased salsa to make the fruit salsa.

MEAT PIES
1 lb. lean ground beef
½ cup chopped onion
1 jalapeño chile, minced
2 garlic cloves, minced
4 teaspoons curry powder
½ teaspoon dried thyme leaves
½ teaspoon turmeric
¼ teaspoon freshly ground black pepper
⅛ teaspoon ground red pepper (cayenne)
Salt to taste
¼ cup unseasoned dry bread crumbs
¼ cup water
2 (8-oz.) cans refrigerated crescent dinner rolls

SALSA
1 cup chunky-style salsa
1 (15.25-oz.) can tropical mixed fruit, coarsely chopped, drained and reserving 1 tablespoon liquid
¼ teaspoon nutmeg

Heat oven to 375°F. In large skillet, combine ground beef, onion, chile and garlic; cook over medium-high heat until beef is thoroughly cooked, stirring frequently. Drain. Add curry powder, thyme, turmeric, pepper, ground red pepper and salt; mix well. Add bread crumbs and water; stir until thickened.

Separate dough into 8 rectangles; firmly press perforations to seal. Place 2 heaping tablespoons meat mixture on long half of each rectangle. Fold dough over filling; press edges to seal. Place on ungreased cookie sheet.

Bake at 375°F. for 15 to 20 minutes or until golden brown. Meanwhile, in medium bowl, combine all salsa ingredients; mix well. Serve with meat pies.

Yield: 4 servings

Nutrition Per Serving: Calories 760; Protein 30g; Carbohydrate 75g; Fat 38g; Sodium 1580mg

Paula Blevins-Russell: Stuffed Poblano Chile Peppers

When it came to fine-tuning her recipe for Stuffed Poblano Chile Peppers, Paula Blevins-Russell let her oven do the work. "Our family loves Mexican, and I love poblanos. Many recipes call for roasting poblano peppers first. To save time, I left out that step, and they taste great anyway. When they are in the oven, they 'roast' on their own." Paula said she came up with the recipe simply by "pulling things out of the cupboard." She advises, "Cooking is easy. Just be creative and think about what would taste good together."

Chuck Wagon Cheeseburger Skillet

Rosemary Warmuth *Wheeling, West Virginia*
Bake-Off® Contest 40, 2002

This hearty meat-and-potato dish is definitely a family pleaser. It's a one-pan meal with meat, vegetables, cheese and biscuits all baked in a large ovenproof skillet. To save time, you can use 1 tablespoon bacon flavor bits instead of cooking the bacon.

4 slices bacon
1 lb. lean ground beef
3 tablespoons chopped onion
3 tablespoons oil
2½ cups frozen hash-brown potatoes, thawed
1 (11-oz.) can vacuum-packed whole kernel corn with red and green peppers, drained
1 (4.5-oz.) can chopped green chiles, drained
½ cup barbecue sauce
8 oz. (2 cups) shredded Cheddar cheese
¼ teaspoon salt, if desired
¼ teaspoon pepper, if desired
1 (16.3-oz.) can large refrigerated buttermilk biscuits or reduced-fat buttermilk biscuits

Heat oven to 400°F. Cook bacon until crisp. Drain on paper towel; crumble. Set aside. In 12-inch cast-iron or ovenproof skillet, cook ground beef and onion over medium heat until beef is thoroughly cooked, stirring frequently. Drain. Place beef mixture in medium bowl; cover to keep warm.

Add oil to same skillet. Heat over medium-high heat until hot. Add potatoes; cook 3 to 5 minutes or until browned, stirring constantly. Add cooked ground beef, corn, chiles, barbecue sauce, cheese, salt and pepper; mix well. Cook until thoroughly heated, stirring occasionally. Sprinkle with bacon.

Separate dough into 8 biscuits. Arrange biscuits over hot mixture. Bake at 400°F. for 16 to 24 minutes or until biscuits are deep golden brown and bottoms are no longer doughy.

Yield: 5 servings

Nutrition Per Serving: Calories 880; Protein 38g; Carbohydrate 62g; Fat 53g; Sodium 1950mg

Sloppy Joe Loaf

Helena Crutcher *Hazel Green, Alabama*
Bake-Off® Contest 40, 2002
Prize Winner

Here's a fun twist on the popular Sloppy Joes. The beef mixture is sprinkled with mozzarella cheese and baked between layers of refrigerated French loaf dough. The warm, stringy cheese and crusty golden brown bread make this comfort food extra special.

1 lb. extra-lean ground beef
1 small onion, chopped
1 (8-oz.) can tomato sauce
1 tablespoon all-purpose flour
¼ teaspoon dried basil leaves
¼ teaspoon dried oregano leaves
¼ teaspoon fennel seed
1 (11-oz.) can refrigerated French loaf
4 oz. (1 cup) shredded mozzarella cheese

Heat oven to 350°F. Spray cookie sheet and large skillet with nonstick cooking spray. In sprayed skillet, cook ground beef and onion over medium-high heat until beef is thoroughly cooked, stirring frequently. Drain. Add tomato sauce, flour, basil, oregano and fennel seed; mix well. Reduce heat to medium-low; simmer 5 minutes. Remove from heat.

Meanwhile, remove dough from can; place on lightly floured surface. Cut loaf in half lengthwise. Roll each half to form 16×4-inch rectangle. Place 1 dough rectangle on sprayed cookie sheet, being careful not to change shape.

Stir ½ cup of the cheese into ground beef mixture. Spoon and spread mixture over dough rectangle on cookie sheet. Sprinkle with remaining ½ cup cheese. Top with remaining dough rectangle.

Bake at 350°F. for 25 to 30 minutes or until golden brown. Cut into slices.

Yield: 6 servings

Nutrition Per Serving: Calories 340; Protein 25g; Carbohydrate 28g; Fat 14g; Sodium 680mg

5-Way Cincinnati Pizza

Melody Levault *Mulkeytown, Illinois*
Bake-Off® Contest 40, 2002

Pizza or chili for dinner? You can enjoy both when you top pizza crust with chili. Apple pie spice adds another flavor dimension to the chili mixture; or use ¼ teaspoon cinnamon and ⅛ teaspoon each of ginger and cloves instead.

5-Way Cincinnati Pizza

1 (10-oz.) can refrigerated
  pizza crust
½ lb. lean ground beef
½ cup barbecue sauce
1 to 2 teaspoons chili powder
½ teaspoon salt
½ teaspoon cumin
½ teaspoon apple pie spice
1 (15- or 15.5-oz.) can red
  kidney beans, drained,
  rinsed
½ cup chopped onion
8 oz. (2 cups) shredded
  Cheddar cheese

Heat oven to 425°F. Spray 12-inch pizza pan or 13×9-inch pan with nonstick cooking spray. Unroll dough; place in sprayed pan. Starting at center, press out dough to edge of pan. Bake at 425°F. for 7 to 10 minutes or until light golden brown.

Meanwhile, cook ground beef in large skillet over medium-high heat until thoroughly cooked, stirring frequently. Drain. Add barbecue sauce, chili powder, salt, cumin and apple pie spice; mix well. Cook 1 minute, stirring constantly.

Remove crust from oven. Spread ground beef mixture over partially baked crust. Top with beans, onion and cheese.

Return to oven; bake an additional 11 to 14 minutes or until crust is deep golden brown.

Yield: 6 servings

Nutrition Per Serving: Calories 420; Protein 24g; Carbohydrate 37g; Fat 20g; Sodium 1000mg

Baked Steak Burritos

Becky Fuller *Westmont, Illinois*
Bake-Off® Contest 40, 2002

Burritos are often made with beef that is roasted and then shredded with two forks into bite-size pieces. This quick and easy version uses strips of sirloin steak, which cook in just 6 minutes.

½ cup butter
1 (1.25-oz.) pkg. taco seasoning mix
1½ lb. boneless beef sirloin tip steak, cut into thin bite-sized strips
1 (16-oz.) can refried beans
1 (10.5-oz.) pkg. (12 tortillas) flour tortillas for soft tacos and fajitas
8 oz. (2 cups) shredded Cheddar cheese
3 green onions, thinly sliced
1 (10-oz.) can red enchilada sauce
4 oz. (1 cup) shredded Mexican cheese blend

Heat oven to 400°F. Melt butter in large skillet over medium heat. Stir in taco seasoning mix. Add beef strips; cook 5 to 6 minutes or until desired doneness, stirring frequently. Drain.

Meanwhile, place refried beans in microwave-safe dish. Microwave on HIGH for 2 minutes, stirring once or twice.

Spread each tortilla with refried beans to within ¼ inch of edge. Top each with beef, Cheddar cheese and onions. Fold opposite sides over filling; roll up. Place seam side down in ungreased 13×9-inch (3-quart) glass baking dish. Pour enchilada sauce over burritos. Sprinkle with Mexican cheese blend.

Bake at 400°F. for 7 to 12 minutes or until burritos are thoroughly heated and cheese is melted.

Yield: 6 servings

Nutrition Per Serving: Calories 750; Protein 42g; Carbohydrate 45g; Fat 45g; Sodium 1990mg

Saucy Pork Medallions with Spiced Couscous

Susan Runkle *Walton, Kentucky*
Bake-Off® Contest 40, 2002
Prize Winner

Susan Runkle created her saucy pork medallions "because of my love of pork, which lends itself so well to a range of taste combinations, particularly fruit and spices."

PORK
1 lb. pork tenderloins, cut into ½-inch-thick slices
1 teaspoon salt
½ teaspoon pepper
2 tablespoons butter
1 teaspoon minced gingerroot
1 teaspoon minced garlic
1 tablespoon cornstarch
1 cup apple juice
¼ cup water
2 tablespoons balsamic vinegar
2 (4.5-oz.) jars sliced mushrooms, undrained

COUSCOUS
2 cups water
½ teaspoon salt
1¼ cups uncooked couscous
1 cup frozen gold and white super sweet corn (from 1-lb. pkg.)
½ medium red bell pepper, chopped
3 green onions, chopped
½ teaspoon Chinese five-spice powder

To flatten each pork slice, place between 2 pieces of plastic wrap or waxed paper. Working from center, gently pound pork with flat side of meat mallet or rolling pin until about ¼ inch thick; remove wrap. Sprinkle pork with 1 teaspoon salt and pepper.

Melt butter in 12-inch skillet over medium-high heat. Add pork; cook 8 minutes or until browned on both sides, turning once. Remove pork from skillet. Add gingerroot and garlic to skillet; cook and stir 1 minute or until tender. Remove from heat.

In medium bowl, combine cornstarch, apple juice, ¼ cup water and vinegar; blend well. Add to mixture in skillet. Bring to a boil. Reduce heat to medium-low. Add mushrooms with liquid and pork; cook 10 minutes or until sauce is of desired consistency, stirring occasionally.

Meanwhile, in medium saucepan, combine 2 cups water and ½ teaspoon salt. Bring to a boil. Stir in couscous, corn, bell pepper, onions and five-spice powder; mix well. Remove from heat. Cover; let stand 5 minutes. Serve couscous with pork mixture.

Yield: 4 servings

Nutrition Per Serving: Calories 480; Protein 35g; Carbohydrate 65g; Fat 11g; Sodium 1260mg

Saucy Pork Medallions with Spiced Couscous

Spicy Pork Chops Caribbean

Susan Carroll *Rochester, New York*
Bake-Off® Contest 40, 2002

The colorful topping of ripe bananas with chiles, bell peppers and spices turns an ordinary meal of baked pork chops into an exotic one. Serve these pork chops on yellow rice and peas, and you'll think you're on a Caribbean island.

1 (8-oz.) pkg. uncooked yellow rice
2½ cups water
4 (½-inch-thick) boneless pork chops
1 (3-oz.) pkg. seasoned coating mix for pork
1¼ cups frozen small sweet peas (from 1-lb. pkg.)
2 tablespoons oil
1¼ cups frozen chopped onions
1 cup fresh cilantro leaves
2 firm ripe bananas, peeled, thinly sliced
2 (4.5-oz.) cans chopped green chiles
1 (7-oz.) jar roasted red bell peppers, drained, coarsely chopped
½ teaspoon curry powder
½ teaspoon pumpkin pie spice
¼ to 1 teaspoon crushed red pepper flakes
¼ teaspoon dried shredded orange peel or freshly grated orange peel
⅓ cup orange juice

Heat oven to 425°F. Line 15×10×1-inch baking pan with foil. Cook rice in water as directed on package. Cover to keep warm.

Meanwhile, coat pork chops with coating mix as directed on package. Place in foil-lined pan. Bake at 425°F. for 15 to 20 minutes or until pork is no longer pink in center.

Cook peas as directed on package. Drain; stir into rice.

Heat oil in large skillet over medium heat until hot. Add onions, cilantro and bananas; cook 3 minutes or until bananas are just tender, stirring frequently. Add all remaining ingredients; mix well. Bring to a boil. Reduce heat to low; cook 5 minutes or until thickened, stirring occasionally.

Spoon rice mixture onto individual serving plates. Top each with pork chop and banana mixture. If desired, garnish with avocado and additional cilantro.

Yield: 4 servings

Nutrition Per Serving: Calories 750; Protein 47g; Carbohydrate 93g; Fat 21g; Sodium 1000mg

Luau Pork Stir-Fry

Sally Sibthorpe *Rochester Hills, Michigan*
Bake-Off® Contest 40, 2002

The combination of Hawaiian and teriyaki flavors makes this a winning recipe. The crushed pineapple and lime juice complement the sweet flavor of the coconut milk. Using a package of frozen vegetables with teriyaki sauce saves time because all the vegetables are ready with no cutting or chopping.

1 tablespoon olive oil
½ lb. pork tenderloin, cut into thin bite-sized strips
½ cup coconut milk (from 14-oz. can)
¼ cup crushed pineapple
2 teaspoons lime juice
1 (1-lb.) pkg. frozen stir-fry vegetables and traditional teriyaki sauce meal starter
¼ cup chopped macadamia nuts
¼ cup coconut
4 cups hot cooked rice

Heat oil in large skillet or wok over medium-high heat until hot. Add pork strips; cook and stir 5 to 6 minutes or until browned.

Add coconut milk, pineapple and lime juice; mix well. Reduce heat to low; simmer 3 minutes, stirring occasionally.

Add frozen sauce and vegetables from meal starter; mix well. Cook 7 to 10 minutes or until vegetables are crisp-tender, stirring frequently. Stir in nuts and coconut. Serve over rice.

Yield: 4 servings

Nutrition Per Serving: Calories 540; Protein 22g; Carbohydrate 65g; Fat 21g; Sodium 680mg

Jamaican Ham and Bean Soup

Marilou Robinson *Portland, Oregon*
Bake-Off® Contest 40, 2002

Jerk seasoning hails from the Caribbean island of Jamaica. This ground dry mixture contains chiles, thyme, cinnamon, ginger, allspice, cloves, garlic and onions. Look for it in the spice section of the grocery store.

SOUP
1 tablespoon oil
⅓ cup frozen chopped onion
2 (16-oz.) cans vegetarian refried beans
1 (11-oz.) can vacuum-packed whole kernel corn with red and green peppers
1 (11-oz.) can vacuum-packed white shoepeg corn
1 (4.5-oz.) can chopped green chiles
½ cup chunky-style salsa
1 (14½-oz.) can ready-to-serve chicken broth
1 teaspoon Jamaican jerk seasoning
1 lb. lean cooked ham, cut into ½-inch pieces
1 (2¼-oz.) can sliced ripe olives, drained
⅓ cup lime juice

GARNISH
6 tablespoons dairy sour cream
6 lime slices

Heat oil in large saucepan over medium heat until hot. Add onion; cook 3 to 4 minutes or until tender, stirring frequently.

Add refried beans, both cans of corn, chiles, salsa, broth and jerk seasoning; mix well. Bring to a boil. Reduce heat to low; simmer 5 minutes, stirring occasionally.

Add ham, olives and lime juice; mix well. Cook 3 to 4 minutes or until thoroughly heated, stirring occasionally. Ladle soup into individual bowls. Top each serving with 1 tablespoon sour cream and lime slice.

Yield: 6 (1¾-cup) servings

Nutrition Per Serving: Calories 430; Protein 27g; Carbohydrate 50g; Fat 13g; Sodium 2750mg

Gnocchi Alfredo Casserole

Kelly Lynne Baxter *Olympia, Washington*
Bake-Off® Contest 40, 2002

Gnocchi are Italian dumplings often made of cooked mashed potatoes. Here they are baked in a rich Alfredo sauce, another Italian favorite. You will find gnocchi in the refrigerated section of the supermarket.

1 (16-oz.) pkg. potato gnocchi
¼ cup butter
1 garlic clove, minced
1 cup whipping cream
6 oz. (1½ cups) shredded Romano cheese
¼ lb. cooked ham, coarsely chopped (¾ cup)
1 (10-oz.) pkg. frozen cut broccoli in a cheese-flavored sauce in a pouch, thawed
2 (4.5-oz.) jars sliced mushrooms, drained
½ cup Parmesan dry bread crumbs

Heat oven to 400°F. Cook gnocchi as directed on package, omitting salt.

Meanwhile, melt butter in large nonstick skillet over medium heat. Add garlic; cook and stir 3 minutes. Add cream and mix well. Gradually add 1 cup of the cheese, stirring after each addition until melted.

Add ham, broccoli in sauce, mushrooms and cooked gnocchi; mix well. Spoon into ungreased 8- or 9-inch square (2-quart) glass baking dish. In small bowl, combine bread crumbs and remaining ½ cup cheese; mix well. Sprinkle over casserole.

Bake at 400°F. for 30 minutes or until golden brown. Cool 5 minutes before serving.

Yield: 6 servings

Nutrition Per Serving: Calories 550; Protein 20g; Carbohydrate 42g; Fat 33g; Sodium 1630mg

Cheesy Broccoli Loaf

Becky Yeoman *New Braunfels, Texas*
Bake-Off® Contest 40, 2002

It takes only five ingredients to make this cheesy, highly flavored sandwich loaf. Just layer the cooked pork sausage, broccoli and two cheeses on refrigerated French loaf dough, then fold and bake. Add a fresh fruit salad of sliced oranges and pink grapefruit sections drizzled with poppy seed dressing, and dinner is ready.

2 cups frozen cut broccoli (from 1-lb. pkg.)
1 (12-oz.) pkg. bulk sage-flavored pork sausage
1 (11-oz.) can refrigerated French loaf
4 oz. (1 cup) shredded mozzarella cheese
4 oz. (1 cup) shredded Cheddar cheese

Heat oven to 350°F. Cook broccoli as directed on package. Drain. Cook sausage in medium skillet over medium-high heat until thoroughly cooked, stirring frequently. Drain.

Unroll dough onto ungreased cookie sheet. Press to form 14×12-inch rectangle. Spoon sausage down center of dough. Top with broccoli and cheeses. Fold long sides of dough over filling, meeting in center; press edges and ends to seal.

Bake at 350°F. for 20 to 30 minutes or until golden brown. Cut into crosswise slices.

Yield: 4 servings

Nutrition Per Serving: Calories 540; Protein 30g; Carbohydrate 38g; Fat 29g; Sodium 1320mg

Sandy Bradley: Ham and Eggs Frittata Biscuits

"If a meal's not quick and easy, it's not made in my home," says Sandy Bradley. Sandy learned how to cook "by reading cookbooks and trial and error," she says. Her recipe for Ham and Eggs Frittata Biscuits was inspired by a restaurant dish she modified to reflect her own tastes. But hers wasn't the only palate pleased: "I served this to my husband and toddler for Father's Day. Wow!" Now she makes the recipe often after coming home from work or for Sunday breakfast. "It fits well with a busy lifestyle," she says.

Ham and Eggs Frittata Biscuits

Sandy Bradley *Bolingbrook, Illinois*

Bake-Off® Contest 40, 2002

A frittata is an Italian omelet that is cooked slowly, and it's round because it isn't folded. This one is baked on biscuits, which creates an impressive dish for breakfast, brunch or dinner.

1 (16.3-oz.) can large refrigerated buttermilk biscuits
3 eggs
1¼ to 1½ teaspoons dried Italian seasoning
½ cup diced cooked ham
4 oz. (1 cup) shredded 6-cheese Italian blend
¼ cup roasted red bell peppers (from a jar), drained, chopped
½ cup diced seeded Italian plum tomatoes
2 tablespoons thinly sliced fresh basil leaves
Fresh basil sprigs
Cherry tomatoes

Heat oven to 375°F. Spray large cookie sheet with nonstick cooking spray. Separate dough into 8 biscuits. Place 3 inches apart on sprayed cookie sheet. Press out each biscuit to form 4-inch round with ¼-inch-high rim around outside edge.

Beat 1 of the eggs in small bowl. Brush over tops and sides of biscuits. Sprinkle with 1 teaspoon of the Italian seasoning.

In another small bowl, combine remaining 2 eggs and remaining ¼ to ½ teaspoon Italian seasoning; beat well. Spoon evenly into indentations in each biscuit. Top with ham, ½ cup of the cheese, roasted peppers, tomatoes, sliced basil and remaining ½ cup cheese.

Bake at 375°F. for 15 to 20 minutes or until biscuits are golden brown and eggs are set. Garnish with basil sprigs and cherry tomatoes.

Yield: 8 servings

Nutrition Per Serving: Calories 290; Protein 12g; Carbohydrate 26g; Fat 15g; Sodium 870mg

Ham and Eggs Frittata Biscuits

Monte Cristo Folds

Kelly B. Everhart *Seffner, Florida*
Bake-Off® Contest 40, 2002

Monte Cristos are turkey, ham and cheese sandwiches that are dipped into beaten egg and sautéed in butter until golden brown. Often they are sprinkled with powdered sugar and served with jam. Refrigerated biscuits are used to make these sandwiches, and they are brushed with egg to omit the dipping step. Baking, rather than sautéing, makes this dish easy because you just put it in the oven and set the timer.

¼ lb. chopped cooked ham
¼ lb. chopped cooked turkey
4 oz. sliced Swiss cheese, chopped (1 cup)
1 (16.3-oz.) can large refrigerated buttermilk biscuits
1 egg
1 tablespoon milk
¼ teaspoon cinnamon
¼ teaspoon nutmeg
Powdered sugar
Raspberry jam

Heat oven to 375°F. In medium bowl, combine ham, turkey and cheese; mix well.

Separate dough into 8 biscuits. Press or roll each to form 6- to 7-inch round. Place scant ⅓ cup ham mixture on one side of each biscuit. Fold dough over filling; press edges to seal. Place on ungreased cookie sheet.

In small bowl, combine egg, milk, cinnamon and nutmeg; beat well. Brush over tops of filled biscuits.

Bake at 375°F. for 12 to 19 minutes or until golden brown. Sprinkle with powdered sugar. Serve with jam.

Yield: 4 servings

Nutrition Per Serving: Calories 550; Protein 21g; Carbohydrate 64g; Fat 23g; Sodium 1650mg

Spinach, Prosciutto and Roasted Pepper Calzone

Jen Riley *West Roxbury, Massachusetts*
Bake-Off® Contest 40, 2002
Prize Winner

Calzones are folded stuffed pizzas that originated in Naples. Here, the best of Italian ingredients—roasted red bell peppers, prosciutto, cheese, spinach and pesto—are wrapped in refrigerated crescent dough and baked until golden brown. Serving this with a warm marinara dipping sauce is a nice touch.

2 (8-oz.) cans refrigerated crescent dinner rolls
1 (9-oz.) pkg. frozen spinach in a pouch, thawed, squeezed to drain*
8 oz. thinly sliced provolone cheese
2 large red bell peppers, roasted, quartered, or 1 (12-oz.) jar roasted red bell peppers, drained, quartered
4 oz. thinly sliced prosciutto
2 tablespoons purchased pesto
1 egg yolk
1 tablespoon water

Heat oven to 350°F. Grease large cookie sheet. Unroll both cans of dough into 2 long rectangles. Place dough rectangles with long sides together on greased cookie sheet, forming 15×10-inch rectangle. Press edges and perforations to seal.

Place spinach lengthwise in 4-inch-wide strip down center of dough to within ½ inch of each end. Top with half of the cheese, the roasted peppers and prosciutto. Spread pesto over prosciutto. Top with remaining cheese. Bring long sides of dough up over filling, overlapping 1 inch; press edges and ends to seal.

In small bowl, combine egg yolk and water; beat well. Brush over top of dough. Bake at 350°F. for 25 to 35 minutes or until golden brown. Cut into crosswise slices.

Yield: 6 servings

*Tip: To quickly thaw spinach, cut small slit in center of pouch; microwave on HIGH for 2 to 3 minutes or until thawed. Remove spinach from pouch; squeeze dry with paper towels.

Nutrition Per Serving: Calories 520; Protein 20g; Carbohydrate 34g; Fat 34g; Sodium 1630mg

Citrus Gazpacho with Honey-Lime Cream

Ashley Shepardson *Chicago, Illinois*
Bake-Off® Contest 40, 2002

If you like regular gazpacho, you will love citrus gazpacho! A jar of citrus salad adds texture and a pleasant citrus flavor to this cold uncooked soup. With the chucks of cucumber and bell pepper, it's a meal in itself. To make the soup a little heartier, sprinkle each serving with purchased croutons.

1 (26-oz.) jar refrigerated citrus salad
1 (16-oz.) jar chunky-style salsa
1½ cups chopped green bell pepper
1½ cups chopped seeded cucumber
2 cups tomato juice
1 cup chicken broth
1 tablespoon olive oil
½ cup chopped fresh cilantro
2 limes
½ to 1 cup reduced-fat dairy sour cream
1 tablespoon honey

Place citrus salad in large non-metal bowl. With fork, break up fruit into small pieces. Add salsa, bell pepper, cucumber, tomato juice, broth and oil. Reserve 2 tablespoons cilantro. Add remaining cilantro to mixture in bowl; stir to mix.

Grate the peel from 1 lime; set aside. Squeeze juice from lime into small bowl. Add to fruit mixture in bowl; mix well. Refrigerate at least 2 hours to blend flavors.

In small bowl, combine sour cream, honey and grated lime peel; mix well. Refrigerate until serving time.

To serve, cut remaining lime into thin slices; quarter each slice. Ladle gazpacho into individual shallow bowls. Top each serving with sour cream mixture. Sprinkle with reserved cilantro. Garnish with quartered lime slices. Store in refrigerator.

Yield: 4 (1¾-cup) servings

Nutrition Per Serving: Calories 380; Protein 8g; Carbohydrate 61g; Fat 12g; Sodium 1570mg

Tofu Black Bean Enchiladas

Kathy Dorr *Fairport, New York*
Bake-Off® Contest 40, 2002

Tofu is no longer just for Asian dishes. Mildly flavored with a taste similar to that of a very mild cheese, it easily absorbs the flavors of the salsa, hot pepper sauce and enchilada sauce in this dish. Tofu is also a good low-fat source of protein, so when it's paired with reduced-fat cheese and sour cream, it makes a hearty main dish that is tasty yet low in fat and calories.

1 (15-oz.) can black beans, drained
1 (11-oz.) can vacuum-packed whole kernel corn with red and green peppers, drained
1 cup chunky-style salsa
5⅓ oz. firm tofu, drained, cut into ¼-inch cubes (¾ cup)
½ teaspoon salt
⅛ teaspoon hot pepper sauce

12 (6-inch) corn tortillas, heated
1 (10-oz.) can red enchilada sauce
8 oz. (2 cups) reduced-fat shredded Cheddar cheese
1 cup reduced-fat dairy sour cream, if desired

Heat oven to 350°F. Spray 13×9-inch (3-quart) glass baking dish with nonstick cooking spray. In medium bowl, combine beans, corn, salsa, tofu, salt and hot pepper sauce; toss to mix.

Spoon ⅓ cup tofu mixture down center of each warm tortilla; roll up. Place seam side down in sprayed baking dish. Pour enchilada sauce over enchiladas. Sprinkle cheese over top.

Bake at 350°F. for 20 to 30 minutes or until enchiladas are thoroughly heated and cheese is melted. Garnish with sour cream.

Yield: 6 servings

Nutrition Per Serving: Calories 470; Protein 23g; Carbohydrate 53g; Fat 18g; Sodium 1330mg

Fiesta Flounder Fillets

Denise Lapnow *Bridgewater, New Jersey*
Bake-Off® Contest 40, 2002

Denise Lapnow says, "I'm always looking for ways to get my family to eat more fish and less meat." Her recipe, she explains, is "healthy, easy to prepare and tastes great. Kids love the Mexican flavor."

4 oz. (1 cup) shredded Colby-Monterey Jack cheese blend or shredded Cheddar cheese
½ cup unseasoned dry bread crumbs
2 (6-oz.) cans crabmeat, drained, flaked
1 (4.5-oz.) can chopped green chiles
2 teaspoons taco seasoning mix (from 1.25-oz. pkg.)
2 eggs
2 lb. flounder fillets (6 pieces)
2 teaspoons lemon juice
1 (16-oz.) jar chunky-style salsa
¼ cup water
1 tablespoon unseasoned dry bread crumbs

Heat oven to 400°F. In large bowl, combine cheese, ½ cup bread crumbs, crabmeat, 3 tablespoons of the chiles, taco seasoning mix and eggs; mix well. Sprinkle each flounder fillet with lemon juice. Spread crabmeat mixture over each fillet. Roll up each. Place in ungreased 12x8-inch (2-quart) glass baking dish.

In small bowl, combine salsa and water; mix well. Spoon over rolled fish. Sprinkle with remaining chiles and 1 tablespoon bread crumbs. If desired, sprinkle with additional cheese.

Bake at 400°F. for 20 to 30 minutes or until fish flakes easily with fork.

Yield: 6 servings

Nutrition Per Serving: Calories 350; Protein 47g; Carbohydrate 16g; Fat 11g; Sodium 1220mg

Swiss Spinach Strudel

Devon P. Delaney *Princeton, New Jersey*
Bake-Off® Contest 40, 2002

"I love spinach soufflé. I love bread. And I love warm, stuffed sandwiches," says Devon Delaney. "So I came up with what I feel is the perfect combination." Spinach, Swiss cheese and nutmeg make the "soufflé," which is wrapped in refrigerated flaky crescent rolls.

1 egg
½ cup chive and onion light cream cheese spread (from 8-oz. container)
1 (9-oz.) pkg. frozen spinach in a pouch, thawed, squeezed to drain*
4 oz. (1 cup) shredded Swiss cheese
¼ teaspoon salt
¼ teaspoon pepper
⅛ to ¼ teaspoon nutmeg
⅛ teaspoon hot pepper sauce
1 (8-oz.) can refrigerated reduced-fat or regular crescent dinner rolls

¼ cup sliced almonds
Olive oil, nonstick cooking spray or regular cooking spray
2 tablespoons Italian-style dry bread crumbs

Heat oven to 400°F. Beat egg in large bowl. Add cream cheese spread; blend well. Add spinach, Swiss cheese, salt, pepper, nutmeg and hot pepper sauce; mix well.

Unroll dough onto ungreased cookie sheet. Press to form 12×8-inch rectangle; firmly press perforations to seal. Spoon and spread spinach mixture lengthwise on half of dough. Sprinkle with almonds. Fold untopped half of dough over filling; press edges and ends to seal. Spray top of dough with cooking spray. Sprinkle with bread crumbs.

Bake at 400°F. for 18 to 24 minutes or until deep golden brown. Cool 5 minutes. Cut into crosswise slices.

Yield: 5 servings

*Tip: To quickly thaw spinach, cut small slit in center of pouch; microwave on HIGH for 2 to 3 minutes or until thawed. Remove spinach from pouch; squeeze dry with paper towels.

Nutrition Per Serving: Calories 360; Protein 16g; Carbohydrate 27g; Fat 21g; Sodium 820mg

Top to bottom: Fiesta Flounder Fillets, Spicy Picnic Chicken, page 355

Crescent Samosas

Gina DeRoma *Los Angeles, California*
Bake-Off® Contest 40, 2002

Gina DeRoma's cooking philosophy is "keeping things simple and letting a few ingredients shine." Samosas, an East Indian street food of fried filled pastry, are easy to make when you use refrigerated crescent rolls for the flaky pastry and bake them in the oven. The potatoes and peas in the meatless filling are both popular Indian vegetables. The yogurt sauce adds just the right amount of tartness and "cool" flavor when served with the samosas.

SAMOSAS

2 tablespoons olive oil
1 garlic clove, minced
1 (4.5-oz.) can chopped green chiles
1 (14½-oz.) can whole new potatoes, drained, diced
½ teaspoon salt
1 (15-oz.) can small early peas, drained
1 teaspoon curry powder
1½ teaspoons lemon juice
Pepper to taste
2 (8-oz.) cans refrigerated reduced-fat crescent dinner rolls

SAUCE

1 cup plain yogurt
2 tablespoons chopped fresh cilantro
1 garlic clove, minced
½ teaspoon cumin
¼ teaspoon salt
Dash pepper

Gina DeRoma: Crescent Samosas

Gina DeRoma didn't have nutrition at the front of her mind when she created her recipe for Crescent Samosas. "This is a low-fat recipe, but it doesn't taste like I skimped on the ingredients," she says. "I think that is the secret. It was only after I invented the dish that I realized I had added only a little oil." Gina got the idea to pair peas and potatoes from a pastry she tried at an Indian restaurant. "I took the dish to a couple of parties, and it got rave reviews," she says.

Heat oven to 375°F. Heat oil in large skillet over medium heat until hot. Add 1 garlic clove and 4 tablespoons of the chiles; cook and stir 2 minutes. Add potatoes and ½ teaspoon salt; cook 8 minutes or until potatoes are light golden brown, stirring frequently. Add peas, curry powder, lemon juice and pepper; cook and stir, mashing slightly, until heated.

Separate dough into 16 triangles. Place 2 rounded tablespoons potato mixture on shortest side of each triangle. Roll up, starting at shortest side of triangle, gently wrapping dough around filling and rolling to opposite point. Pinch edges to seal. Place on ungreased large cookie sheet.

Bake at 375°F. for 15 to 20 minutes or until samosas are golden brown.

Meanwhile, in blender container, combine all sauce ingredients. Cover; blend until smooth. Refrigerate until serving time. Garnish samosas with remaining chiles. Serve warm with sauce.

Yield: 8 servings

Nutrition Per Serving: Calories 310; Protein 8g; Carbohydrate 39g; Fat 13g; Sodium 1030mg

Arborio Rice Cake with Mushroom and Olive Ragout

Linda Miranda *Wakefield, Rhode Island*
Bake-Off® Contest 40, 2002

Baked rice cakes are an adaptation of risotto, a creamy rice mixture made with Arborio rice. The crusty rice cake wedges are a nice texture contrast to the vegetable ragout spooned over the top. The ragout, a thick well-seasoned French stew, makes this a hearty main dish, and no one will miss the meat.

RICE CAKE

⅔ cup uncooked short-grain Arborio rice
1⅓ cups water
1 tablespoon butter
½ cup Parmesan dry bread crumbs
1 egg
1 egg white
2 oz. (½ cup) grated Asiago cheese
2 tablespoons finely chopped green onions

2 tablespoons chopped fresh Italian parsley

RAGOUT
2 tablespoons olive oil
1 medium sweet onion, sliced
2 garlic cloves, minced
2 (4.5-oz.) jars sliced mushrooms, drained
1 (14.5-oz.) can diced tomatoes with Italian seasonings, undrained
¼ cup sliced ripe olives
¼ cup sliced green olives
1 tablespoon capers, rinsed, if desired
⅛ teaspoon pepper

Arborio Rice Cake with Mushroom and Olive Ragout

Heat oven to 350°F. Cook rice in water as directed on package. Stir in butter. Cool 5 minutes.

Spray 8- or 9-inch round cake or pie pan with olive oil nonstick cooking spray. Sprinkle pan with ¼ cup of the bread crumbs. Set aside.

In medium bowl, combine egg and egg white; beat until blended. Add cooked rice, cheese, green onions and 1 tablespoon of the parsley; mix well. Press into crumb-lined pan. Sprinkle remaining ¼ cup bread crumbs evenly over top. Bake at 350°F. for 18 to 20 minutes or until center is set.

Meanwhile, heat oil in large nonstick skillet over medium heat until hot. Add onion; cook 4 minutes or until golden brown and caramelized, stirring occasionally. Add garlic; cook 1 minute, stirring constantly. Add all remaining ragout ingredients; mix well. Bring to a boil. Reduce heat to low; simmer 5 minutes.

To serve, cut rice cake into wedges. Place wedges on individual serving plates. Top each serving with ragout. Sprinkle with remaining tablespoon parsley. If desired, garnish with shaved Asiago cheese.

Yield: 6 servings

Nutrition Per Serving: Calories 260; Protein 9g; Carbohydrate 28g; Fat 12g; Sodium 950mg

Index

Titles by The Pillsbury Editors

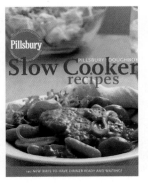

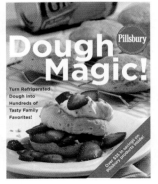

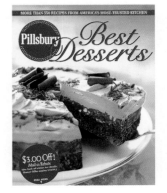

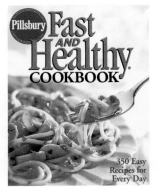

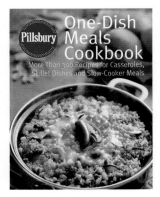